Cas
Sport Marketing

Cases in Sport Marketing

Mark A. McDonald, Ph.D.

Assistant Professor
University of Massachusetts
Amherst, Massachusetts

George R. Milne, Ph.D.

Associate Professor
University of Massachusetts
Amherst, Massachusetts

JONES AND BARTLETT PUBLISHERS

Sudbury, Massachusetts

BOSTON   TORONTO   LONDON   SINGAPORE

World Headquarters
Jones and Bartlett Publishers
40 Tall Pine Drive
Sudbury, MA 01776
978-443-5000
info@jbpub.com
www.jbpub.com

Jones and Bartlett Publishers Canada
P.O. Box 19020
Toronto, ON M5S 1X1
CANADA

Jones and Bartlett Publishers International
Barb House, Barb Mews
London W6 7PA
UK

Acquisitions Editor: Paul Shepardson
Production Editor: Lianne B. Ames
Manufacturing Buyer: Therese Bräuer
Design: Modern Graphics
Editorial Production Service: Modern Graphics
Typesetting: Modern Graphics
Cover Design: Dick Hannus
Printing and Binding: Courier
Cover Printing: Courier

Library of Congress Cataloging-in-Publication Data

McDonald, Mark A.
    Cases in sport marketing / by Mark A. McDonald and George R. Milne.
        p.   cm.
    Includes bibliographical references and index.
    ISBN 0-7637-0863-1
    1. Sports—United States—Marketing—Case studies.   2. Sports—Economic Aspects—United States—Case studies.   3. Case method.
I. Milne, George R.   II. Title.
GV716.M39   1998
796'.06'98—dc21   98-42614
                                                                            CIP

    Printed in the United States
02 01 00 99 98   10 9 8 7 6 5 4 3 2 1

Contents

Sport Marketing Theory   **339**

Acknowledgments

The two authors would like to acknowledge the following people and organizations that have provided information and assistance, which was essential in the completion of this book. First, we are very grateful for the contributions made by all the case authors. We also thank Susan Milne, Allyssa Bates, Kelli Bartlett, Bill Kackley, Mike Musante, and Andrew Rohm for their assistance on different aspects of this book. Additionally, we thank the three reviewers for their helpful suggestions on ways to improve the manuscript.

Brenda G. Pitts, Ph.D.
Associate Professor of Physical Education
Florida State University
Tallahassee, FL

Matthew J. Robinson, Ph.D.
Assistant Professor of Sport Management
Allentown College of St. Francis de Sales
Center Valley, PA

Terese Stratta, Ph.D.
Assistant Professor of Kinesiology and Health
Georgia State University
Atlanta, GA

A casebook cannot be written without the willingness of organizations to provide open access to their operations and personnel. Our book was certainly no exception to this rule. We would like to thank the following individuals and organizations for working extensively with our case authors and us: David Grandin and Fady Lamaa of Avid Sports, Reebok, William P. Stritzler of Smugglers' Notch Resort, Courtney Enterprises, Inc., Wade Martin and Advantage International, Joelle Dold and the Ladies Professional Golf Association (LPGA), Xerox, the administration and athletic department at Miami University, SGRnet, Haigis Hoopla, and Minutemen Marketing.

As with all major undertakings, many people were crucial to the successful publishing of this book. Without naming all who have provided assistance, we would like to say thank you.

To our families,
for your support and encouragement along the way.

Mark McDonald   **George Milne**

Preface

While the case study method is very popular in business schools, we have found a surprising lack of cases focusing on sport marketing issues. This book consists of 15 new sport marketing cases that can be used by instructors to supplement their marketing, sport marketing, sport enterprise, sport policy or sport management classes. Case studies not only provide an opportunity for students to apply materials that they have learned in class, but also enhance understanding of the relevance of those materials.

With the case study method, students gain an appreciation of the process involved in decision making. By working through the cases in this book, the reader is provided the opportunity to examine an array of sport management/marketing situations and gain experience grappling with actual problems faced by managers. Each case presents the critical issues at hand, possible alternatives for consideration and the criterion necessary to make an informed decision.

Our goal in writing this book was to expose future managers to a variety for challenging situations that sport marketers face. We have put together a wide range of cases that allow students of sport marketing to analyze the marketing problem and practice making the "big decisions." Because decision making can never be completely taught, experience is the best method of improving decision making skills. It is our hope that these cases can serve to simulate real life scenarios for sport marketers much the same way that the preseason is a simulator for sports teams. As is the case with sports teams, it is better to provide students a "exhibition game" in which they can make mistakes rather than have those mistakes take place during the real game.

In addition to educating students entering the world of sport marketing, this book will be of benefit to executives and sport marketing decision makers. Reviewing these cases will help them become familiar with the issues and types of decisions that must be made by leaders in the field. These cases allow the reader to practice the decision making process and consider other possible alternatives and directions that could have been implemented.

The book consists of three parts. In Part I, during the first three chapters, we introduce the case study method and various tools to use in the case analysis to sport marketing students and managers. Part

II, begins with a practice case and an example of a student analysis. Since the case method may be considered a significant departure from other learning approaches where memorization and lecture formats may be the dominant emphasis, we feel that it is essential that students read these first chapters. The case study method emphasizes and develops analytical skills, logic and reasoning and encourages application of the instructional materials to the situation at hand. Most importantly, it also illustrates that there are numerous possible alternatives to consider before making the final decision. This is a fundamental element of managerial decision making that cannot be communicated effectively without benefit of a case study approach.

The next fifteen chapters are the sport marketing cases, covering numerous sport marketing issues. We have written some of the cases. In other chapters, we have incorporated and edited cases submitted by other expert contributors—many of whom are either practicing sport managers or are academics teaching sport marketing courses. In Part III, we review sport marketing theory for those students not as familiar with the sport industry.

About the Authors

Mark A. McDonald, Ph.D.

Mark A. McDonald holds a Ph.D. in Sport Management from the University of Massachusetts-Amherst, an MBA from Tulane University, and a B.S. from Warren Wilson College. Dr. McDonald is currently an Assistant Professor in the Sport Management Program at the University of Massachusetts, Amherst. He has published numerous articles in such journals as the *Journal of Sport Management, Sport Marketing Quarterly*, and the *Journal of Sports Marketing and Sponsorship*. He recently served as a coeditor for a special *Sport Marketing Quarterly* issue on "Relationship Marketing in Sport." He has given over twenty-five presentations in the United States and abroad.

Over the past five years Dr. McDonald has consulted with sport organizations throughout the United States, such as the NBA, NHL, Orlando Magic, Cleveland Cavaliers, and Hoop-It-Up. Most notably, he has worked with the International Health, Racquet and Sportsclub Association (IHRSA) for the past seven years to produce the annual industry report "Profiles of Success." He has recently coauthored the book *Sport Marketing: Managing the Exchange Process*.

George R. Milne, Ph.D.

George R. Milne is Associate Professor of Marketing at the University of Massachusetts-Amherst. He earned a Ph.D. in marketing from the University of North Carolina (1990) and an M.A. and B.S. in economics from the University of Utah (1982, 1984). Since joining the School of Management in 1992, Dr. Milne has taught marketing management, database marketing, and applied multivariate statistics. Dr. Milne writes and consults in the areas of sport marketing, marketing management, strategy, and research methods. He has written over twenty-five articles on marketing issues and has made numerous presentations in the United States and internationally.

Dr. Milne's research in sport marketing has appeared in the *Journal of Sport Management, Sport Marketing Quarterly*, and *Journal of Sports Marketing and Sponsorship*. He has served as coeditor of a special issue of *Sport Marketing Quarterly*. He has served on editorial review boards of *Sport Marketing Quarterly, Journal of Sport Management,* and *Journal of Sports Marketing and Sponsorship*. He has recently coauthored the book *Sport Marketing: Managing the Exchange Process*. George is also an active sport participant, specializing in skiing/snowboarding, running, tennis, and golf.

Case Authors

Tom Boyd, Ph.D.

Dr. Thomas C. Boyd is an assistant professor of marketing at Miami University in Ohio. His research interests include how consumers evaluate products and services, consumer innovativeness, and consumption of sport. He actively consults, specializing in marketing strategy development, sports marketing, and assessing and improving customer service. Before returning to academics, he spent five years in product and marketing management at Motorola, Inc., in the communications division, where he was a product planning manager. He has taught executive training programs for several corporations and at University-sponsored programs. Tom earned his Ph.D. from the University of North Carolina at Chapel Hill.

T. Bettina Cornwell, Ph.D.

Dr. Cornwell received her B.A. (Marketing, 1981) from The Florida State University and her MBA (International Business Emphasis, 1983) and Ph.D. (Marketing with a minor area in Cognitive Psychology, 1988) from the University of Texas in Austin. Dr. Cornwell's teaching interests are in consumer behavior, international marketing and advertising, and her research interests are in the areas of international marketing; sponsorship of sports, arts, and cultural events; public policy; and consumer behavior.

Regarding activities related to sport and sponsorship, she edited a special issue of *International Marketing Review* on Sponsorship-linked marketing in 1997 and is an editorial board member for the new *Journal of Sports Marketing and Sponsorship*. Her research on sponsorship has recently appeared in *Journal of Consumer Affairs,* the *Asia-Australia Marketing Journal* and in *The Journal of Advertising*. She is also a board member of the Mason YMCA and regular sports participant.

Ronald P. Courtney

Ronald P. Courtney graduated from the University of New Hampshire in 1957 with a B.A. in economics. His first job was selling flashbulbs to retail and distributor accounts. In 1964, he won the Outstanding Salesmanship Award from Sylvania Electric Corporation. Determined to be in business for himself, he worked in the selling profession observing the retail field and building up a financial base. His first business was Photo Drive-Up Booths. The next venture, with his brother, was owning photo finishing stores combined with greeting cards and gifts. From there, he went to open twenty-one T shirt stores in most of the major malls in northern California. After selling the mall stores in 1990, he concentrated on festival marketplaces in tourist areas. Now, he has stores with over fourteen different concepts in the tourist areas of San Francisco, Hawaii, Las Vegas, San Diego, Orlando, and Mall of America in Minnesota.

Dan Covell, M.S.

Dan Covell received his B.A. in studio art from Bowdoin College in 1986, where he was also a two-time varsity football letter winner. He worked for eight years

as a high school teacher, coach, and athletic administrator before earning his
M.S. in sport studies from the University of Massachusetts at Amherst in 1995.
He has also worked as the compliance and special-events intern in the Harvard
University athletic department and is currently teaching and pursuing his
doctorate in sport studies at UMass. He has worked on research projects for
Advantage International, Major League Baseball, the National Association of
Collegiate Marketing Administrators, the NCAA, and the New England Bliz-
zard of the American Basketball League and has published several articles
and book chapters pertaining to legal aspects of sport and sport marketing. A
native of Waterville, Maine, Covell now lives in Northfield, Massachusetts with
his wife, Pam Safford, their two standard poodles, Lucy and Rey, and his
collection of over a hundred baseball caps.

Cindy L. Davis

Cindy Davis is the president and Chief Executive Officer of the Arnold Palmer
Golf Company. This company has been introducing advanced technology to the
industry since it was established in 1931. In addition to overseeing the Palmer
and Hot-Z bags franchise properties, Davis continues to lead the development
of NancyLopez Golf, a newly launched business division of the company. Prior
to joining the Arnold Palmer Golf, Davis was vice president of the Ladies
Professional Golf Association (LPGA). In that capacity, and during an important
period of the LPGA's growth, Davis led the development and implementation
of the LPGA's first fully integrated marketing and communications business
plan.

She currently is a member of the board of directors for the National Golf
Foundation (NGF), the advisory board of Women's Sports Wire, and is an
editorial advisor for *Sport Marketing Quarterly*. A native of the Washington,
D.C. area, Davis graduated from Furman University in 1984 with a B.A. in
economics and went on to receive her MBA with a concentration in marketing
and finance from the University of Maryland.

James M. Gladden, Ph.D.

James M. Gladden is an Assistant Professor of Sport Management at the
University of Massachusetts, Amherst. Dr. Gladden holds a B.A. from DePauw
University, an M.A. in sport administration from The Ohio State University, and
a Ph.D. in sport management from the University of Massachusetts, Amherst.

Dr. Gladden's research interests lie in the areas of sport marketing, event
management, and international sport management. Specifically, Dr. Gladden
has published research examining brand equity in the sport setting. Prior to
arriving at the University of Massachusetts, Gladden was a project manager
for Del Wilber & Associates, where he conducted market research and wrote
marketing plans for a variety of sport and event clients, including the Los
Angeles Dodgers, Iowa State University, Anheuser-Busch, and the Ladies Professional Golf Association.

Suzanne Lainson

Suzanne Lainson, president of SportsTrust, publishes two sports-related newsletters on the Internet and does marketing consulting for companies such as

Sports & Fitness Publishing, North American Roller Hockey, and Coors. In addition she freelanced for a number of magazines (including *Glamour, Mademoiselle, Cosmopolitan, Ms., Self, Savvy, The Olympian, American Skating World, MediaWeek,* and *Inline Retailer & Industry News*). She is the author of *Crash Course: The Instant MBA* (a Fortune Book Club Alternate Selection) and a contributor to several textbooks.

Susan Milne

Susan Milne graduated from the University of Utah in 1985 with a B.A. in finance. She is currently enrolled at the University of Massachusetts at Amherst as a graduate student. Before attending graduate school, Susan worked for six years as a systems analyst for GTE in Durham, North Carolina, and for two years as an accountant for Montgomery Securities in San Francisco, California. In the past two years she has written a number of computer programs used to gather on-site surveys for marketing analysis of sponsorship recognition at professional and amateur sporting events. Susan lives with her supportive husband and two active children in Amherst, Massachusetts.

Andrew Rohm

Currently pursuing his doctorate in marketing at the University of Massachusetts-Amherst, Andrew Rohm was most recently director of marketing for the Running, Tennis, and Adventure Sports categories at Reebok International Ltd. Altogether, he has been involved in the athletic footwear industry for ten years in marketing and sales, initially with Brooks Sports.

Having graduated from the University of Michigan with a B.S. in aerospace engineering, he has been an analytical engineer with Pratt & Whitney and worked in new business development for Electronic Data Systems (EDS) prior to joining Brooks Sports. He also worked on a sheep ranch in Australia. He now lives in the sleepy coastal town of Scituate, Massachusetts with his wife, two golden labs, and two black-and-white cats.

Dave Rosenthal, Ph.D.

Dr. David W. Rosenthal received his doctorate from the Darden School at the University of Virginia. Since 1980, he has been at Miami University, where he teaches marketing strategy and sales management. He has been an active case researcher and writer for over twenty years. He is a past president of the North American Case Research Association, member of the board of directors of the Society for Case Research, and reviewer for *The Case Research Journal* and *Annual Advances in Case Research.*

Donald Roy

Donald P. Roy is a Ph.D. Candidate, Fogelman College of Business and Economics, University of Memphis. His research interests include marketing strategy, brand equity, and event marketing. Prior to entering the Ph.D. program, he held industry positions in field sales and retail management.

David Shani, Ph.D.

David Shani is Professor of Marketing and coordinator of the marketing program at Kean University. Dr. Shani received his Ph.D. in Marketing from

Columbia University in New York in 1987. David has published extensively in the areas of Ambush Marketing, Sponsorship, Relationship Marketing, and Global Branding. His articles have appeared in *International Journal of Advertising, International Marketing Review, Journal of Advertising Research, Psychology and Marketing, Sport Marketing Quarterly, Journal of Consumer Marketing,* among others. Dr. Shani is the co-founder and current leader of the American Marketing Association's Sports and Special Event Marketing Special Interest Group. He serves on the editorial boards of the *Journal of Business, Industrial Marketing,* and *Journal of Sports Marketing and Sponsorship.* Dr. Shani consults in the area of sport and services marketing.

David K. Stotlar, Ed.D.

David K. Stotlar serves as the director of the School of Kinesiology and Physical Education at the University of Northern Colorado. He has published more than forty articles in professional journals and has written several textbooks and book chapters on sport, fitness, and physical education. He was selected by the USOC as a delegate to the International Olympic Academy in Greece and the World University Games Forum in Italy. He has conducted international seminars in sport management for the Hong Kong Olympic Committee, the National Sports Council of Malaysia, Mauritius National Sports Council, the National Council of Zimbabwe, the Singapore Sports Council, the Chinese Taipei University Sport Federation, the Bahrain Sport Institute, the government of Saudi Arabia, the South African National Sports Congress, and the Association of Sport Sciences in South Africa.

William A. Sutton, Ed.D.

William A. Sutton is an Associate Professor in the Sport Management Program at the University of Massachusetts, Amherst. Prior to assuming his present position, Dr. Sutton served as vice president for information services for Del Wilber & Associates, a sport and lifestyle marketing agency; served as coordinator of the sport management program at Ohio State University; and was a faculty member at Robert Morris College. A past president of NASSM and coeditor of *Sport Marketing Quarterly,* Dr. Sutton is also a principal in the consulting firm Audience Analysts and has worked for such clients as the LPGA, Hoop-It-Up, IBM, Mazda, the Cleveland Cavaliers, the Pittsburgh Pirates, the Indiana Pacers, and the Philadelphia 76ers. Dr. Sutton, a coauthor of *Sport Marketing,* is widely published in the field of sport marketing and has made over fifty national and international presentations.

Rod Warnick, Ph.D.

Rodney B. Warnick is a Professor of Recreation Resource Management in the Department of Hotel, Restaurant and Travel Administration at the University of Massachusetts-Amherst. Dr. Warnick has published over forty research and proceedings articles dealing with recreational activity trends, volume segmentation, recreation satisfaction, market share analysis, consumer behavior in recreation settings, and tourism marketing studies. He is currently consulting with Professional Golfers Association of America (PGA) to teach golf professionals marketing applications and the Ladies Professional Golf Association (LPGA) on consumer trends, and developing market surveys for major resort complexes such as Smugglers' Notch Resort in Vermont. Warnick holds a doctorate in recreation and parks from Penn State University (1983) with concentrations in marketing and sociology; a master's in regional planning with a concentration in recreation and tourism planning (1983); a master's in recreation management from the University of Montana (1976) with a concentration in business management; and B.S. in HPER from Frostburg State University in Maryland (1975) with concentrations in business/accounting and recreation management.

Glenn M. Wong, J.D.

Glenn M. Wong is a Professor of Sport Management at the University of Massachusetts-Amherst, where he teaches sports law. A lawyer, he is the author of *Essentials of Amateur Sports Law*. He has coauthored *Law and Business of Sport Industries*, Volumes I and II, and *The Sport Lawyer's Guide to Legal Periodicals*. He has also written several book chapters and articles. Professor Wong writes a monthly column entitled the "Sports Law Report" for *Athletic Business Magazine*. He is a member of the Arbitration Panel of the International Council of Arbitration for Sport and has served as a salary arbitrator for Major League Baseball. Professor Wong serves as the faculty athletics representative for the National Collegiate Athletic Association (NCAA) and served as interim director of athletics for the University of Massachusetts. He has also served as the acting dean of the School of Physical Education. Professor Wong received his B.S. in economics from Brandeis University and a J.D. from Boston College Law School.

The Case Method: Theory and Practice

1

An Introduction to the Case Method

Introduction

Sport marketing offers unique challenges to the marketing manager. The "product" being promoted is intangible and rapidly changing, and the sport marketer has little control over the core product (team performance) to be sold. To be successful at marketing such an ambiguous product, it is useful to first practice applying marketing theory within the safety of a classroom, where mistakes are not costly (at least in terms of money or professional standing), and where you can gradually develop your own style of problem solving.

One of the best ways to become proficient at marketing sport products and services is to use marketing concepts to solve a real business problem in the context of a case. A case is simply a narrative summary of the issues impacting a business at a given time. The case method is an exceptional tool for learning sport marketing because it allows you to practice applying marketing techniques to an actual business problem. The case method promotes independent thinking and confident problem solving in realistic business situations where information important for decision making is either not accessible or too costly in terms of time and/or money to gather. As in many business situations, there can be many ways to approach a solution to a case. Merging the case method with the discipline of sport marketing, therefore, creates a superior learning experience that simulates many management functions—analysis, planning, and strategy.

Definition of the Case Method

In the 1920s the Harvard Graduate School of Business Administration developed the case method of learning. Graduates of their master's degree program were having trouble applying the theories and methods taught in the classroom to the competitive and volatile business world, where they found that they were largely unprepared to use the knowledge gained through textbook study. Only after a period of apprenticeship spent learning from costly mistakes, or from the firm guidance of a business mentor, was the graduate ready to make good business decisions independently.

The case method was created to bridge the gap between the theory taught in the business school and the skills needed to perform effectively as a manager for companies in industries of various types and sizes. Using cases speeds up the learning curve by transforming students who traditionally tend to expect a formula for finding the right answer into decision-makers. In the case method, there is no one "formula" for finding the "right" solution, but there are certainly approaches that are more complete than others. It has been such a successful learning tool that the use of the case method is now prevalent in most business schools throughout the world.

Once again, a case is a written description of a real or simulated business situation. You are given facts, historical information, opinions of executives, and an indication of the missing but needed data. Using this information, you are asked to analyze the situation, to address the uncertainties presented. Using both quantitative and qualitative tools for the analysis, you create a few possible scenarios to resolve the problem. Then, you make a decision regarding which solution is most viable and support the decision with data from the case plus some relevant assumptions. Finally, you present and defend your position both orally in the classroom and in writing. The problem scenarios described are most often ambiguous and lend themselves to a variety of solutions, none of which can be considered the "right" answer, but many of which represent thoughtful business judgment.

Not only do you act as a business manager with a problem to solve but you also have a large role in creating and sustaining a dynamic learning environment in the classroom by participating in a case discussion. In case-based learning, the instructor acts as a facilitator for a debate among the students to determine, as a class, the best answer or answers to the case.

Attributes of the Case Method

Learning through case study helps build skills in problem solving. You gain confidence by practicing applying abstract marketing concepts to difficult and often unstable business situations. Cases are a reflection of the real business world. Sport marketers are often expected to provide solutions to problems where there is not perfect information (perhaps the data is old or too expensive to collect), and there is pressure to make a timely decision.

In order to become a good problem-solver, you must learn by doing, not just by memorizing facts or formulas. In the traditional classroom, the instructor lectures and the students take notes. This creates a flow of information *from* the instructor *to* the students. Students are expected to accept the instructor's information as fact, learn the theory being taught, and be able to restate or recognize this information later during an exam. However, it is very difficult to use the insights and knowledge of another person unless you have been able to take this knowledge and apply it yourself. This is exactly what cases aim to do.

Cases provide a type of experiential learning: learning from experiencing problem solving in a semi-structured environment. In addition, experiential learning helps students retain information, such as the methodology learned in basic sport marketing courses. This is due, in part, to the way in which people learn. Learning is a personal experience, and the best way to become enmeshed in a new subject is to apply your theoretical knowledge to real business problems.

Cases truly provide a personalized learning experience because each student must determine not only the best solution for the problem but also define the fundamental, or core, problems facing the firm. The core problems can be difficult to find because often the symptoms of a problem are the only stated parts of the case. Because there is no right answer to a case, different students will come up with different core problems. Since each student has a different interpretation of the problems and solutions for the company or industry in the case, the learning process is personalized and therefore quite effective.

Unlike a lecture format, the classroom structure used with cases creates an environment of dynamic cooperation. The instructor's role is to encourage debate among the students regarding the best way to approach the case and the most appropriate resolution. You become your own teacher, learning from the way the class as a whole takes a problem from beginning to end. The direction of learning comes from the students' experiences, not the instructor's.

Classmates contribute greatly to learning with cases by providing insight from personal work experience. Someone who has worked in a fitness club, for example, will be able to offer a unique perspective about the industry. Sharing experiences about how a 2-for-1 membership campaign was created to increase membership in the club will greatly enhance both the enjoyment of the discussion and the understanding of the decision process of an actual company.

The cases presented in this book expose you to a variety of sport marketing situations. The process you go through to develop an analysis and conclusion helps develop an internal guide for problem solving. You will learn to see patterns in various situations. From the patterns, you will then draw out general principles of marketing and begin to apply them to real problems.

Skills Needed by the Sport Marketing Manager

Sport marketing is a unique service because the marketer cannot control the core product (team performance). For instance, in professional sports, players can be injured or traded midseason, leading to unpredictable team performance. Another unique feature is that the sport product is intangible. When selling tickets for a baseball game, you don't focus on the outcome of the game as the major selling feature. You are selling more esoteric aspects of the game such as the camaraderie with other fans, competition between the teams, stadium food, the chance to watch a popular sports figure, or the occasion of a family outing. This type of selling is very different from selling traditional products like toothpaste or T-shirts. Creating solutions in the sport industry where the marketer has very little control over the quality of the core product demands a professional with wide-ranging marketing skills.

Relationship Building

One important skill needed is the ability to build relationships from facts. Suppose you are the marketing director of a football team where 75% of the fans are between the ages of 15 and 40. You read in the newspaper that the baby boom generation is aging and in the next decade the population of the United States is going to shift so that the largest segment will become the over-50 age group. What might you conclude about your fan base in the next ten years? A long-range marketing plan might focus on how to attract more fans in the 50 and older segment.

Customer Empathy

Another skill needed by sport marketers is the ability to make good judgments with incomplete information, by understanding intuitively both a fan's and a manager's perspective. In 1994, baseball owners and players had a major dispute over players' salaries, benefits, and mobility, halting the start of the baseball season. Midway through the season, the players and owners agreed to begin play. The result of delaying, and therefore shortening, the baseball season was unprecedented anger and/or apathy displayed by professional baseball fans. Baseball enthusiasts were so incensed by the perceived selfishness of both the players and the owners that many boycotted baseball—some temporarily, and some permanently. As of 1996, baseball was still suffering from the impact of the player strike, which impacted what we call fan equity (what fans feel they deserve for their loyalty). If you were advising a team owner during this period, would you have been able to anticipate or perceive the mood of the fans and provide well-informed and insightful counsel?

Communication

Finally, to be successful implementing your ideas, you need to be able to communicate well. These ideas may be technical or abstract in nature, and your audience may have little or no knowledge of marketing concepts. Your arguments need to be persuasive enough to sell yourself and your ideas. For example, you may be trying to sell athletic department administrators on an $8,000 marketing campaign to promote your Division I basketball program. If you are not persuasive, you may be allocated a reduced amount ($2,500), resulting in an unsuccessful campaign. Analyzing cases will hone your communication skills by providing a forum for you to express your ideas and allowing you to see what is most important to decision makers. Your measure of success will be in persuading your fellow students of the validity of your approach.

Advantages of Case-Based Learning

As with any teaching method, there are unique aspects to the case-based method of learning—advantages as well as disadvantages. One of the greatest benefits is that cases promote independent, creative thinking. There is no answer book to consult or specific rules to follow when analyzing a case. This forces you to come up with your own unique solutions.

Because there is no right answer, students tend to be more assertive about expressing and defending their opinions. Students exchange ideas with other students and the instructor. In fact, the students and the instructor have a unique equality in that everyone is provided with the same information—no more, no less. Since the playing field is level, the participants become competitors in a game of reason until someone's ideas and arguments win over class opinion. The instructor can be persuaded by a new perspective from the student and vice-versa. This can create a lively and exciting learning experience that is new to most students.

With cases, students are taken out of the passive role and become partners in learning. You are expected to think during a case discussion, both in defending your own position and in changing your stance because of new ideas presented by fellow students or the teacher. It is exciting to actively participate in class discussion when you have put a lot of time and energy into a case analysis. With a personal point of view at stake, it is easy to become embroiled in enthusiastic debate.

In addition to the thinking and communication skills developed during lively class discussions, the realistic conditions of cases makes learning more enjoyable. No one likes to sit through a lecture where slide after slide reveals new vocabulary words to memorize. Not only is boredom likely but the day after being tested on this type of material, much of it will be forgotten.

Consider, however, a situation where you are asked to calculate the break-even point for producing a new product, SharkBite Tennis Balls. Then you are asked to determine the optimal sales price, placing your tennis balls in competition with Wilson and Penn tennis balls. Later, you are able to compare and defend your answer to that of other bright, enthusiastic students. What a difference it makes in terms of enjoyment of learning (and the probability of retaining) a difficult concept like break-even analysis when you are able to use it to solve a concrete problem!

Challenges of Case-Based Learning

While the case method is an exceptional way to learn sport marketing, it does pose challenges for students. One challenge is that it can be hard to accept your new role as an equal in the classroom. Typically, students depend on instructors to provide all of the input and energy in the classroom. The student is the passive recipient of accepted theory. In this new role, you are expected to take responsibility for your own learning. The amount of effort put into preparing for class will directly impact the amount you learn during class discussion.

Students faced with cases for the first time can be frustrated with the process. At first, most students feel anxious and confused during the case analysis. It is normal to be frustrated because you have not thought of all aspects of the problem brought up by the students and teacher during class discussion. You may feel burdened by the responsibility of holding up your ideas to criticism. However, adjusting to this new way of learning, which is difficult at first, will pay off with the result of learning through your own efforts.

Those who are unwilling to risk the exposure of making a mistake will not gain the conviction of their own ideas or have the satisfaction of contributing ideas to create the best answer. Participation is the key to success using the case approach. It is better to be vociferous and reveal a weakness in your argument than to not participate at all—especially since you will need to be assertive in real business situations.

A second major challenge is realizing that the case method is not a perfect replica of the real world. Not only is the hypothetical situation less complex than what one might expect to see in a true-life situation but there are no serious repercussions for bad strategies. Although you might receive a poor mark for a sloppy or inaccurate analysis, this is not as serious as what might happen from a true gross error in judgment. The classroom sport marketing manager will not be fired, the company will not lose millions of dollars, and the organization will not be sued.

Finally, realize that as with most things that are worth achieving, hard work is required to come up with a successful case analysis. It takes a lot of preparation to be fully versed in the facts of the case and to do a thorough analysis. The analysis may include using a host of financial tools for contrast and comparison, developing three or four different solutions in order to choose the best case scenario, and producing a detailed case write-up.

Summary

We believe the unique advantages of the case method are worth the challenges. In order to be successful as a sport marketer, you must develop an internal guide to solving problems. Instead of taking years to gain experience in business (and making many mistakes along the way), we hope to speed up the learning curve by enabling you to practice integrating the theory of marketing by using cases. Business is not an exact science, and there are no right answers. The skills you develop by gaining an intimate knowledge of sport marketing theory through case-based learning will be used throughout your career.

Without a framework to work from to practice analyzing marketing issues, it would be difficult for a sport marketer to be successful. A good case analysis parallels the marketing process. In the next chapter, we will present a framework for preparing a good case analysis. This guide takes you from the initial review of the business situation to the final stage of determining how to measure the success of your chosen solutions.

A Framework for Case Analysis

Introduction

To become an effective sport marketer, each person must develop his or her own style of problem solving. By providing a framework for case analysis, we give you both a basic outline for structuring your analysis as well as specific guidelines that will help lead you toward a more thorough solution. There is no one way to analyze a case; likewise, there is no best way to create solutions in the sport business world. The following framework, however, provides a good foundation for organizing your thoughts and creating solutions for difficult cases and actual sport marketing situations. Figure 2.1 provides a flowchart for case analysis.

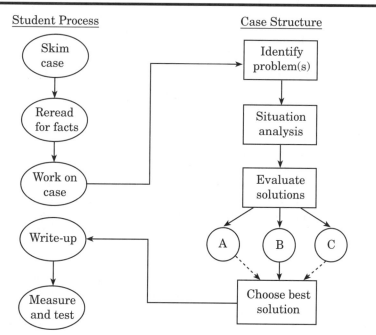

Figure 2.1 Framework for case analysis

The Case Analysis Framework

The flowchart in Figure 2.1 is divided into two columns. The first column is entitled "Student Process." The student follows a five-step process to perform a case analysis. The order in which a student works on a case is as follows:

Step 1: Skim the case for an overview;

Step 2: Reread the case carefully for specific detail;

Step 3: Work on the case to determine the core problem and best solution;

Step 4: Write a report that includes a case analysis and a solution; and,

Step 5: Test the solution both with specific measurements of effectiveness and during class discussion.

The second column provides details for the structure of the case analysis. When evaluating a case, you will begin by identifying the problem or problems that face the organization in question. Next, you will perform a thorough situation analysis and develop two or three viable solutions. Through this analysis, a "best choice" solution should become evident. Each step taken during the case structure process will provide material to be used when writing the case analysis report.

Next, we will explore the elements of the case analysis framework in more detail.

• *Step 1: Skim the Case.* Read the case quickly to get an overview of the problem. Do not get bogged down in the details. Briefly review the tables provided. This will be helpful during the next step as you will be able to refer to relevant tables when reading for details. Keep in mind the big picture, such as the subject of the case and the similarity of this case to others you have studied in class.

• *Step 2: Reread the Case for Details.* Read the case carefully, this time paying close attention to detail. Learn the key facts and relevant points. During this stage you must separate the facts of the case from the opinions of the manager whose problem you are trying to solve. Consider reading the case a third time in another sequence. While reading a long case it is easy to become fatigued while taking notes and referring to tables. If you reread the case from the end back to the beginning, your attention will be sharper for the pages read first (here, the end of the case, where you may have been less diligent the first time).

It is important during this initial phase of case analysis that you refrain from drawing any conclusions regarding the best answer. If you are tempted to solve your problem too early, the rest of the analysis will be slanted to support your premature conclusions. You may inadvertently miss important elements that would lead you to develop a different, more-informed solution.

• *Step 3: Work on the Case.* During this phase, follow the structure outlined in Figure 2.1. You will identify the core problem(s) facing the organization, create a situation analysis, develop one or more solutions to the problem, and choose the solution that best fits the goals of the organization. This section provides details for each component of the case structure. To complete a comprehensive case analysis, you should perform the following steps:

(a) *Identify the problem(s)*

Distinguishing a problem from a symptom is not as easy as it may seem. A 10% reduction in sales of tennis racquets may seem like the problem that needs to be tackled. You may want to do more advertising to increase sales. However, the core problem may be a poor distribution method that is causing stores to regularly run out of tennis racquets. Increased advertising will not help sales. It may, in fact, just irritate customers who want to buy the product and cannot find it on the shelves.

Given a complicated scenario with a lot of data and facts, it is sometimes helpful to divide a problem into small components. This will help organize your thoughts and provide a good structure for writing up a case analysis report.

(b) *Analyze the situation*

The situation analysis is the heart and soul of the case-based method. In this step, you use numerical data both given in the case and created by you using logical assumptions to form opinions on the strength or weakness of the company. The financial tools presented in Chapter 3 will be useful in reviewing the past success or failure of a firm's sport marketing strategy. For example, you may want to look at an organization's financial strength using break-even analysis and liquidity ratios, or compare its market share to the competition's. Creating pro-forma statements such as profit and loss projections may also help you predict where the company is headed and what troubles may be lurking in the near future.

In addition to a quantitative review, you will also need to use qualitative reasoning for each case scenario. For instance, how might the current boom in Internet use affect your company's sales of NFL T-shirts? If customers can order their favorite player's jersey through the Internet, will they stop coming to your shop in the mall? Knowledge of current events, past experience, and common sense will be your best guides when looking at problems and determining how national and global events might influence your marketing strategy.

Generally, cases mimic one of the biggest challenges in problem solving in the real world—the need for data that is not readily available. It is necessary, therefore to make reasonable assumptions to create data where it is not supplied. Making assumptions is a required step in developing a good case analysis. It is important, however, that your assumptions are explicitly stated during the analysis and write-up of the case.

(c) *Develop and evaluate multiple solutions*

In order to select the best solution during a case analysis, you have to develop two or three different scenarios for solving your problem. This will help to strengthen the eventual best-choice decision by comparing it to less effective approaches. Additionally, it will broaden the scope of decision making to include not just your first knee-jerk response and will also push you to perhaps find a better solution.

(d) *Choose the best solution*

The best solution will be defensible and responsive to management objectives. It will be supported with both quantitative and qualitative data. In addition, an application and implementation plan should be included in the discussion of the best solution.

• *Step 4: Write the Analysis.* Once you have completed all of the previous steps, the write-up should flow easily. You will be able to outline in detail the core problem(s) of the case and the thought process you used to come up with the best solution. Most of your case report should focus on the situation analysis. Since there is no one right answer, documenting the analysis that led you to your final conclusion is more important than the chosen conclusion.

• *Step 5: Measure and Test.* The final step in a case analysis is two-fold. First, you should create a way to evaluate the effectiveness of your solution. This can be stated in terms of specific goals. For example, your plan will be successful if sales increase by 10% in six months. Second, the ultimate test is holding up your plan to the scrutiny of your classmates and instructor during class discussion. If you have given a thoughtful review of your situation and used this framework to develop the best solution, you will be able to confidently defend your position in the classroom.

Issues to Consider During the Situation Analysis

This section will present many areas to explore and questions to ask during the situation analysis. This will help to prompt thought and promote a complete review of your case.

In addition to the ideas already presented in this chapter, there are other helpful approaches to completing the analysis phase of case study. Chapter 20 reviews general marketing concepts and sport marketing applications to give you the tools you need to develop a marketing strategy for sport products and services. Applying these concepts, however, can seem overwhelming at first. Therefore, we created a framework to use in structuring and organizing your thinking while reviewing your case (Figure 2.1). Step 3b, analyzing the situation, is a crucial and often difficult part of a good case analysis. As a result, we are providing a supplement to the framework to give you additional points to consider during this step. It is organized into five broad categories: the organization, the product, the customer, the industry, and the environment. This should give you a good starting point to determine which areas are most relevant to your situation and, as a result, require further review and development.

The Organization

What are the objectives of the organization? How will the sport-marketing manager meet these objectives? For example, the goal of a team owner may not be to maximize profit. It may be sufficient for the owner to gain prestige and pride of ownership rather than build a championship team.

STRENGTHS AND WEAKNESSES

What is the best thing this firm does? How can we capitalize on these strengths? How can we improve on the weakest areas? Are the weaknesses real problems with the product or a matter of consumer perception?

One technique used for problem solving that can be very effective in case analysis is called SWOT. The initials stand for Strengths, Weaknesses, Opportunities, and Threats. If you organize your analysis based on the SWOT variables, you are less likely to miss any important points. Here are examples of general and specific questions prompted by the SWOT technique that could provide insight into your case.

Strengths.   What are the strengths of your firm versus other firms in your industry? What was the financial strength of your organization last year or three years ago? What is unique about your company or product? How will the skills of your employees improve your performance?

Weaknesses.   Is the technology base of your firm slipping compared to others in your field? Is the life cycle of your product heading toward maturity? Will not having a computerized scouting system impact your success in drafting the best players for your franchise?

Opportunities.   What product extensions might boost sales of your product? What changes in the marketing mix could increase your market share? Are you efficiently using cash resources for capital expansion or research and development? How can you leverage the popularity of youth soccer to increase attendance for your professional soccer club? How might you use the season-ticket-holder database to enhance auxiliary income and build stronger relationships with your fan base?

Threats.   Does the company have enough cash to repay a note about to come due? Which companies are your greatest competitors? Is there one customer or supplier on which the company is too dependent? Will drug use among professional athletes have a negative impact on fan participation? What might be the impact of reduced leisure time for working parents on sports entertainment in general? How will the current losing streak of your team affect fan loyalty?

For instance, your firm produces a truly superior tennis shoe. The marketing strategy has been to set low prices and provide intensive distribution. Customers think your shoes are fine (but nothing special), so sales are weak. Your company's strength is that you make the best shoe on the market. Perhaps you are using the wrong marketing mix of price and place and thereby selling to the wrong customers. If you want to capitalize on the strength of your product, consider changing your distribution and pricing to reflect the superior quality of your tennis shoes.

KNOWLEDGE BASE

What skills are needed to resolve the company's core problem? If the firm does not have employees possessing the right skill set, what steps are necessary to develop these skills? The company could hire consultants, contractors, or new employees or train current employees. How much will this cost? What is the time frame for training/hiring skilled people?

FINANCIAL CONDITION

How strong is the company financially? To determine the soundness of the organization, use the financial tools we will present in Chapter 3, such as break-even analysis, liquidity tests, and balance sheet projections. Compare some key ratios of this company to those in similar companies to determine relative financial health.

COMPANY CULTURE

What is the work ethic of the employees in the organization? How can the current culture be used to the organization's advantage? How much resistance might there be to new products and ideas? For example, snowboarding began as a counterculture alternative to skiing. Those involved in the sport are seen as retro and pushing the limits of the traditional ski culture. A firm manufacturing snowboards whose corporate culture embodies that of its product (trendy, nonconformist) can be quite profitable while the product is in its early growth stages. One can imagine a business environment where the motto is "Hang loose, dude" without much concern for deadlines or objectives. However, as the product life cycle (popularity) of snowboards peaks and sales growth slows (as is typical of most new products), the manufacturers may need to use more mainstream marketing tools to maintain profit margins.

ORGANIZATIONAL STRUCTURE

Is the structure of the organization harmful or helpful to the marketing strategy being implemented? How might the structure be changed to incorporate a new product line or brand extension? Often, an organization is set up in a way that makes change difficult. For example, a company's organizational chart and reporting structure may make it difficult for the marketing manager to involve the product line manager in proposed changes to a product. The result can be that a great idea is thwarted at the manufacturing level because those who are producing the product are not convinced of the need for change or are unwilling to commit the resources of one department.

The Product

A description of the overall product of a business is usually given in a one-sentence summary of what is sold, for how much, through what methods, and where. These facts are commonly referred to as the marketing mix, or the four Ps of marketing—product, price, promotion, and place.

THE MARKETING MIX

Product.   Review the current product(s). What are the goals for the product? How can they be reached? Are there potential new product lines and brand extensions that should be considered? Without a coherent and cohesive strategy for the product, marketing efforts and funds may be misdirected.

Price.   What are the current pricing strategies? How do these compare to substitute or competing products? What is the margin for markup? What implications for pricing strategies can be inferred from a break-even analysis?

Promotion.   Review current advertising, publicity, sales promotions, type of media used, etc. Is the advertising budget sufficient and effective? What measurements could be set up to determine effectiveness? What is the message you are trying to send with your promotions?

Is cohesive strategy used throughout your campaigns? Are you concentrating enough on satisfying the 20% of your customers who are responsible for 80% of your revenue (referred to as the 80–20 rule of marketing)?

Place (distribution).   How is the product being delivered to the consumer? How could distribution be changed to increase sales or exposure? Undertake a review of the sports facility. An exercise club with an upscale image needs to constantly redecorate. If equipment, floors, the juice bar, or even personnel begin to seem tired, the trend-conscious exercisers will begin to look elsewhere. Is the distribution intensity (exclusive, selective, or intensive) appropriate for the goals of the product? What supply channels are being used? How effective are these channels?

COMPETITIVE ADVANTAGE

What makes our product or service different from other similar products or services? Two ski resorts may reside in the same canyon. They receive the same type of snow and have similar terrain. Consumers may choose one resort over the other based on attributes like customer service, the amount of time they spend in lift lines, or the quality of the rental equipment. Any one of these attributes could be considered a ski resort's competitive advantage.

SUBSTITUTE PRODUCTS

Which products or services are similar to yours? What products are competing for the dollars a consumer might spend on your product? What types of promotional tools are being successfully used to sell the substitute product? Why should a baseball fan use his discretionary income to purchase game tickets for his family instead of going to the local amusement park?

PRODUCT LIFE CYCLE

Where is this product in terms of a product's life cycle—introduction, growth, maturity, or the decline phase? Is this product more of a fad or a long-term product? If it is in the introduction phase, how can the firm attract the most consumers as quickly as possible? If it is in the maturity phase, how can costs be prevented from rising as sales are declining? If this is a long-term product entering the maturity phase, how can the firm continue to satisfy existing customers?

MARKET SHARE

Estimate the size of the market. What is the market share of the firm's product? What goals does the firm have regarding future market share?

How does the market share affect the type of advertising? Think about the past size of the market. What projections can be made for market growth?

The Customer

CUSTOMER PROFILE

Who is the typical customer? Use demographic and psychographic variables such as age, sex, and lifestyle to create a customer profile. What does a customer like or dislike about the product or service? How can customer satisfaction be increased? Why is the customer buying the product or service?

MARKET SEGMENTATION

How can you logically group the customers of the product or service? What categories can be used for segmenting this market? What kinds of different advertising should be used for the different segments of the market? For instance, purchasers of golf clubs are typically aged 40–60, are in the upper-income bracket, and read magazines such as *Golf Digest*. On the other extreme, purchasers of roller blades tend to be aged 18–35, are in the middle-income bracket, and watch MTV (a music video channel). Dividing customers into specific segments will provide a more focused and, therefore, more cost-effective approach to advertising.

TARGET MARKET

What is the target market? What market segment is the focus of promotional efforts? Would it be prudent to consider a different target market? Can a different type of customer be persuaded to buy the product or service? For example, a health club might view its target market as young professionals aged 25–40. Its advertising promotes the benefits of exercising at lunch and after work to maintain the physical and psychological edge necessary to get ahead in today's competitive business world. As a result, the club is busy during the lunch hour and from 5–9 p.m. but is almost deserted during the morning and afternoon. The marketing staff is developing an advertising campaign to gain new membership by targeting the stay-at-home mother who will use the club when it is underutilized, from 9 a.m. to noon and from 2–5 p.m. Advertising will emphasize on-site childcare as well as the benefits of exercising to improve physical and mental health.

BRAND AWARENESS AND LOYALTY

Is the target market aware of the firm's product? How do customers learn about the product or service? How complete is their knowledge of the qualities of the product? How loyal is the customer to the brand being sold? What makes a consumer committed to the product? What is the general attitude toward the firm's brand compared to similar brands?

PURCHASE DECISION PROCESS
What does a customer do before buying the product or service? Is it an impulse purchase or one that is more deliberate and likely to be preceded by information gathering? Why does a customer buy one product instead of another? How easy is it to purchase the product?

The Industry

EXISTING COMPETITORS
What are the strengths and weaknesses of the existing competitors? How can the firm use those to its advantage? What marketing mix and strategies have the competitors used successfully? What are their target markets? What is the market share of the competition? Are any of the competitors planning for large growth or expansion in the near future?

POTENTIAL COMPETITORS
What companies are positioned to steal some of the firm's customers? Who has the ability to move into its area of expertise? What companies are likely to make changes in their target market or marketing mix that might affect the firm's target market? A large supplier is a primary example of a potential threat to an organization's market share. Many times it has the knowledge and contacts to enter the market with relative ease and quickly capture a large share of the existing market.

BARRIERS TO MARKET ENTRY
How expensive is it to enter the market? What types of equipment or facilities are needed? Starting a new professional football franchise, for example, has high barriers to entry because of the large amount of start-up capital required. A stadium often needs to be built, coaches and administrators hired, players drafted and compensated, and a fan base cultivated. In contrast, the barriers of entry are small for a vendor wishing to sell hot dogs at the football game. All one needs are a few machines for cooking, a small inventory of paper goods and product, and part-time workers to sell the product during the game.

BARGAINING POWER OF SUPPLIERS AND BUYERS
How many, what types, and how powerful are the suppliers and buyers of the product or service? If there is only one source of supply for an ingredient needed to produce a product, the firm will have little recourse

if that company increases prices or provides poor service. Similarly, if there is only one buyer, or one major buyer, for a service, the entire business will be in jeopardy if this buyer decides to do business with someone else. A situation where either one supplier or buyer is too important to the firm's livelihood can be dangerous. Similarly, a strong supplier or buyer may decide to expand horizontally or vertically and enter a company's market in direct competition.

The Business Environment

Many outside forces influence a customer's purchasing behavior and the operation of the company.

SOCIAL VALUES

In what social context do people purchase and use the product? How does this affect customers' and potential customers' perception of the product? What are the cultural norms of the purchasers of the product or service? For example, gambling, drinking, and violence are part of the enjoyment of professional football games for some fans. How does this affect the ticket sales to families living in the "Bible Belt" region of the South? How would a marketer try to attract more conservative fans without alienating the current, boisterous fans?

POLITICAL CLIMATE

Local and national politics affect the mood of the nation, which in turn can affect the spending patterns of individuals. In addition, a typical Republican, pro-business climate versus a typical Democratic pro-government climate can impact variables such as interest rates, cash availability for borrowing money, taxes, and business regulations.

ECONOMY

Is the economy in a growth and expansion phase or a reduction and belt-tightening phase? The state of the economy will affect inflation, costs (facility rental fees), product pricing, etc. Business cycles follow a pattern of growth and recession periods. When developing future sales strategies a company needs to guess which direction the economy is headed. Unfortunately, this is extremely difficult. Even the nation's most educated economists cannot predict the future and often make inaccurate predictions.

LEGAL ISSUES

What are the industry's pressing legal issues? Are there pending contract disputes with players or umpires? How will Title IX, the law requiring equal spending on male and female sports in federally-supported schools, affect the sport industry? How will fan interest in professional and collegiate sports or the purchase of sport products be affected by this legislation and its related court decisions?

ENVIRONMENTAL CONCERNS

What environmental issues are relevant to the firm's products or services? Environmental issues include pollution, safety issues, recycling-reducing-reusing trash, noise factors, etc.

TECHNOLOGY

How will technology affect the firm's products or services in the next 5 years? What about 10 or 20 years from now? What technological advances are predicted for the firm's products in the near future? The Internet is predicted to have a large effect on ticket sales of professional and college sports in the next 5 years by allowing fans to purchase tickets directly from the stadium. How else might the Internet affect sales of sport products? If a golfer wants to buy a new set of clubs, he will soon be able to do comparison shopping on the Internet. He will be able to compare price, quality, features, and even how the clubs look. After deciding which clubs are right for him, he may then make his purchase through an Internet reseller. What impact might the Internet have on retail stores selling golf clubs?

How to Write a Case Analysis Report

After completing the case analysis using the preceding framework, the student is often asked to write a formal case analysis report. Putting thoughts down on paper in an organized and persuasive manner takes practice. To give you the best chance of creating a successful paper, we will provide a few pieces of general advice, an outline for the paper, and some common mistakes to avoid when preparing a case write-up.

The first piece of advice is to budget your time wisely. Each additional hour spent analyzing a case creates more information and data to sort through when developing solutions. It is easy to get carried away doing the analysis and forget to budget your time to provide enough time for writing. Also, keep in mind the old saying, "There is no such thing as good writing; only good rewriting."

Try to make the paper easy to follow by presenting the main ideas first and then providing the supporting analysis. To help focus the paper, choose only one or two main ideas as the final conclusion to your analysis.

Report Format

SUMMARY

Begin your report with a brief summary of the case analysis and the final recommendation(s). This can be in the form of an executive summary or a letter to the president. It should contain the main argument(s) for how and why you came to your conclusion.

PROBLEM OVERVIEW

Next, give an overview of the situation presented in the case. This does not mean, however, restating the facts of the case. Use the information from the case to develop a "big-picture" scenario in an insightful way. An overview should comment on the effectiveness of the marketing strategy. Use the section of this chapter entitled, "Issues to Consider During the Situation Analysis" and the SWOT technique (Strengths, Weaknesses, Opportunities, Threats) we described earlier to develop an accurate picture of the organization, the product, the customer, the industry, and the environment.

DIAGNOSIS

In the next section of the paper, detail the issues you found. Decide what the core and secondary problems are and give evidence to support your claims. Remember to distinguish between problems and symptoms. Include the short-term and long-term impacts of the problems on the organization.

SOLUTION SCENARIOS

After explaining the core problem and its effects, explicitly state two to three different scenarios for resolving the problem(s). Create a cost-benefit analysis for each scenario using quantitative and qualitative analysis.

RECOMMENDATION

Next, clearly state your choice for the best alternative. Justify your choice with specific reasons from the cost-benefit analysis. Give an implementation strategy for your plan, including deliverables and measures of success.

APPENDIX

At the end of the report, include an appendix with tables you created during the financial analysis. Label the tables with a title and table number so they can be easily referred to during the case write-up. Include other technical tables, such as industry averages in the appendix, if applicable.

Common Mistakes to Avoid

In providing guidelines for writing the best case analysis possible, we would be remiss in not adding to this chapter a list of mistakes commonly made during a case write-up.

RESTATING FACTS

Probably the most common mistake is restating the facts of the case during the write-up. Although it is necessary to provide an overview of the situation, this should be done in the context of giving insight to the problem facing the organization, not just reiterating the facts of the case.

MISSING THE PROBLEM

Another mistake frequently made by students is defining the problem inadequately. If the core problem is not identified, the rest of the case analysis is meaningless. Sometimes it is easy to mistake a symptom for a problem. In other cases, the student makes the problem definition too narrow. Instead of looking at the big picture, the student gets hung up on important but not encompassing details of the situation. Defining the real problem is one of the most important parts of the case analysis.p

AVOIDING ASSUMPTIONS

Another area that you may find difficult at first is making assumptions about the product, industry, or organization—assumptions are expected. As it is often necessary, both in the simulated world of cases and in the real business world, to make a best guess in order to find a solution assumptions are expected and essential. Making reasonable assumptions will become easier to do after practice with a few cases.

PROPOSING UNREALISTIC SOLUTIONS

Determining an appropriate solution can also be problematic. A good solution is specific, not general. For instance, claiming "marketing will strive to increase sales" is not as effective as stating "marketing will strive to increase sales by 10% in the next six months." Solutions also need to be realistic. While it is nice to think that the recommendation provided will change the firm from a small start-up operation to a Fortune 500 company in 2 years, this type of unrealistic posturing is neither sound case analysis nor appropriate managerial practice.

NOT DECIDING

Be careful when recommending further market research as a solution. If you do, be very specific about the expected costs and benefits of the market research. Include a time frame for completion and suggestions for what should be done. For example, if you recommend a survey to determine levels of fan satisfaction for a professional soccer team, you could create the survey to be used and attach it to the report as an appendix.

DECIDING TOO SOON

As previously noted, it is dangerous to decide on a solution before completing the case analysis. While struggling to form two or three different strategies to resolve the situation, you may be surprised at which solution is actually the most cost effective or holds the most promise. If the decision is made too early in the case analysis, it is difficult to keep an open mind and avoid making the entire analysis a support of the predetermined solution.

FORGETTING GOALS AND OBJECTIVES

Finally, always keep in mind the objectives of the managers as presented in the case. It is counterproductive to develop a brilliant strategy to increase profits if the management of the organization has specifically stated they want goodwill to be the overriding goal of research and development rather than increased margins.

Summary

The goal of this chapter has been to provide the student of sport marketing with the tools necessary to perform a thorough case analysis. Although each person must develop his or her own method of approaching and solving cases, it is helpful to have a framework to use as a guide. By using this format, and the sections pertaining to case analysis, we hope you will be prompted to think of other relevant issues affecting your situation. In turn, this will help you to focus on the solution. Writing a good case report is not simple. In the final section of this chapter, we have provided some practical advice for creating a logical and well-written case analysis report.

In the next chapter we will focus on some financial tools used by the sport marketer that provide the basis for analyzing the strength of companies and their marketing strategies.

Analytical Tools for Case Analysis

Introduction

Assessing the current financial situation of a company and forecasting its future position is an essential part of case analysis. Even in the world of sport paying attention to the bottom line is crucial. As a part of a case, financial analysis is used to support the conclusions of your case analysis. Quantitative support is key to rational thinking and avoiding the pitfall of making judgments purely on hunches and intuition. The goals of management, in both case analysis and the business world, are often expressed in financial terms. Case analysis affords you the opportunity to practice applying analytical financial tools to a simulated business situation in order to better understand the business problems presented. Of course, a good case analysis will rely on both quantitative and qualitative measures to determine what is the best direction for the company. It is up to you to decide which area should be given the most weight in each case study.

The quantitative tools we will review are certainly not the only formulas for analysis. We have chosen these as the most-often used and generally accepted measures used by businesses. This chapter is divided into sections to help organize the different types of tools that can be used during the financial analysis phase of case analysis. These sections include cost and contributions, types of cost/revenue analysis, and financial ratio analysis. We will begin by describing the business situation of a hypothetical shoe manufacturer.

The Athletic Shoe Company

A pictorial representation of the business arrangements, including cash flow (both inflow and outflow), for Athletic Shoe Company appears in Figure 3.1. For the remainder of this section, we will refer to this figure to illustrate the various costs and revenues of this fictitious business.

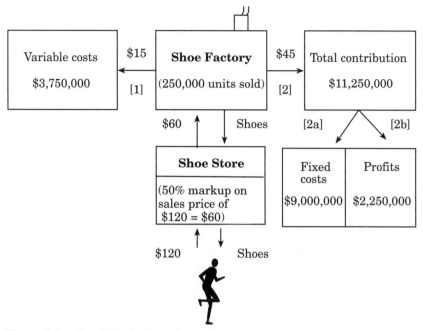

Figure 3.1   The Athletic Shoe Company

Costs and Contributions

Fixed and Variable Costs

We begin by defining two types of costs that are used as the basis for many calculations—fixed costs and variable costs. Fixed costs are those expenditures that do not change when there is a change in the number of units produced. For example, fixed costs include overhead such as equipment, management salaries, interest payments, advertising, and taxes. For the shoe manufacturer, its fixed costs will most likely include all of these expenses. In contrast, variable costs change with increases or decreases in production levels. Variable costs are items like the cost of raw materials used in producing a product, wages for hourly employees, packaging costs, and sales commissions.

Fixed costs are most often stated on a per-year basis. For our shoe factory, the fixed costs are $9,000,000 per year. Variable costs are most often calculated in per unit terms, such as variable costs = $15 per unit. Variable costs can also be stated as a percentage of the selling price. In the shoe factory example, variable costs are 25% of the selling price (25% × $60 = $15). To calculate the variable cost per year (or any other time period), you multiply the unit cost by volume of production or sales.

Formula 1: Variable Costs

Variable cost per year = Total units produced (or sold)
× Variable cost per unit

In our example (see Figure 3.1),

Total units produced   =   250,000
Variable cost per unit   × $15
Variable cost per year = $3,750,000

Total costs are the sum of fixed and variable costs and can be stated either in per unit value or as a total amount based on a certain production (or sales) volume.

Formula 2: Total Costs

Total costs = Fixed costs + Variable costs

The Athletic Shoe Company (see Figure 3.1) has total costs of $12,750,000.

Total costs = $9,000,000 + $3,750,000
= $12,750,000

Contribution to Fixed Costs and Profits

The contribution margin of a product is the amount of money that the sale of one unit will contribute to cover fixed costs and add to the profit of a company. Contribution margin is calculated two different ways: contribution margin per unit and total contribution margin. Contribution margin per unit is the difference between the price of a product and the variable cost of producing the product.

For example, our shoe manufacturer sells shoes for $60 a pair and has variable costs of $15 per pair. The calculation of contribution margin per unit is.

Formula 3: Contribution Margin per Unit

Contribution margin per unit = Sales price per unit
− Variable cost per unit

In Figure 3.1, the costs for the shoe company are given as follows:

Sales price per unit $60
Variable cost per unit   − $15
Contribution margin per unit = $45

Therefore each unit sold contributes $45 to cover fixed costs and profit.

Total contribution margin is the amount of contribution to fixed costs and profit based on the number of units sold. For example, if the company sold 250,000 pairs of athletic footwear (every pair it produced) and the contribution margin per unit was $45, the total contribution margin would be calculated using the following formula:

Formula 4: Total Contribution Margin

Total contribution margin = Contribution margin per unit
× Number of units sold

Contribution margin per unit	$45
Number of units sold	× 250,000
Total contribution margin =	$11,250,000

If relevant fixed costs in our example are $9,000,000, then the profit earned by this product is calculated as follows:

Formula 5: Gross Profit

Profit earned by product = Total contribution margin − Fixed costs

Total contribution margin	$11,250,000
Fixed costs	− 9,000,000
Gross profit earned by product =	$ 2,250,000

As the shoe factory generates sales, each pair of shoes sold adds $45 to the total contribution margin. This money must first pay off the fixed costs, which cannot be avoided. Essentially, fixed costs represent a bill of expenses to be paid. Once this bill is paid off, any additional contribution through sales goes right to gross profit. Thus, in the shoe manufacturer example, the first 200,000 units are used to pay off the fixed costs (200,000 x $45 = $9,000,000). The contribution margin from the next 50,000 units sold goes directly to profit (50,000 × $45 = $2,250,000).

Types of Cost/Revenue Analysis

Break-Even Analysis

Break-even analysis is used to determine the number of units that must be sold to cover total costs. *Break-even* means the company neither makes money nor loses money; it only covers costs. When revenue from sales is equal to total costs the company is at the break-even point. When sales volume exceeds the break-even point, the company begins to make a profit. (See Figure 3.2.) Up to this point, we have provided you with an intuitive examination of costs and profit. Now we will describe a more formal mathematical approach to calculating the break-even point.

To calculate the quantity that must be produced to break even, you need to know the fixed costs, the variable costs, and the sales price of the product.

Formula 6: Total Sales

$$\text{Total sales} = \text{Sales price} \times \text{Quantity (\# of units sold)}$$

The formula for the break-even point in units is

Formula 7: Break-even Point (in Units)

$$\text{Break-even point in units} = \frac{\text{Fixed costs}}{\text{Contribution margin per unit}}$$

Now let's use formula 3 to change the denominator of our expression. Recall formula 3 from earlier in this chapter:

$$\text{Contribution margin per unit} = \text{Sales price} - \text{Variable cost}$$

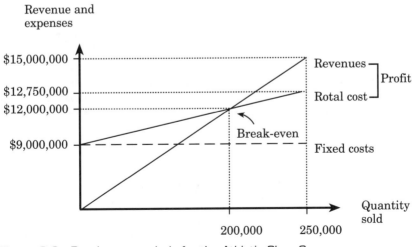

Figure 3.2 Break-even analysis for the Athletic Shoe Company

Substituting the right side of this equation into the denominator, the formula becomes

$$\text{Break-even point in dollars} = \frac{\text{Fixed costs}}{\text{Sales price} - \text{Variable cost}}$$

In our shoe company example, then,

$$\text{Break-even point in units} = \frac{\$9,000,000}{\$60 - \$15} = 200,000 \text{ units}$$

This shoe manufacturer needs to sell 200,000 pairs of shoes to break even. (Remember, the Athletic Shoe Company produced 250,000 pairs, so it did better than break-even—it made a profit.)

This type of analysis can also be used to calculate the amount of sales in dollars needed to break even. To determine how many dollars in sales are needed to break-even, we use a different formula:

Formula 8: Break-even Point (in Dollars)

$$\text{Break-even point in dollars} = \frac{\text{Fixed cost}}{1 - \dfrac{\text{Variable cost}}{\text{Selling price}}}$$

$$\text{Break-even point in dollars} = \frac{\$9,000,000}{1 - \dfrac{\$15}{\$60}} = \$12,000,000$$

These formulas are closely linked, and conversions from break-even in units to break-even in dollars (or vice versa) are straightforward. For example, break-even in units can be translated to break-even in dollars in the following manner:

$$\text{Break-even in dollars} = \text{Break-even in units} \times \text{Sales price}$$
$$\text{Break-even in dollars} = 200,000 \times \$60 = \$12,000,000$$

Break-even analysis can be used to help organizations set a price for their product. Let's assume the shoe company is going to sell all of the shoes it produced (250,000 pairs). The calculation for the break-even price is

Formula 9: Break-even Price

$$\text{Break-even price} = \frac{\text{Total cost}}{\text{Units sold}} = \frac{\$9,000,000 + (\$15)(200,000)}{200,000} = \$60$$

Since the break-even point is $60, we may, depending on price elasticity (how sensitive customers are to price), want to set our price for shoes above $60 in order to make a profit. Alternatively, if consumer demand allows, we may choose to produce and try to sell more shoes.

Profit Target

The break-even formula can be modified slightly to include a profit target. Suppose, in the shoe example, management decides it wants to make $2,250,000 profit. How many shoes would need to be sold to make $2,250,000? The formula looks similar to the break-even formula, but the profit target is added:

Formula 10: Profit Target

$$\text{\# Units to achieve profit target} = \frac{\text{Profit target} + \text{Total fixed costs}}{\text{Contribution margin per unit}}$$

$$\text{\# Units to achieve profit target} = \frac{\$2,250,000 + \$9,000,000}{\$45} = 250,000$$

In this example, we would need to sell 250,000 pairs of shoes at $60 to achieve the goal of $2,250,000 profit.

Profit-target calculations can also be estimated in terms of sales levels. The following formula helps decide what level of sales is needed to make $2,250,000.

Formula 11: Sales Level

$$\text{Sales level to achieve profit target} = \frac{\text{Profit target} + \text{Fixed costs}}{1 - \dfrac{\text{Variable cost}}{\text{Sales price}}}$$

$$\$15,000,000 = \frac{\$2,250,000 + \$9,000,000}{1 - \dfrac{\$15}{\$60}}$$

Thus, the company would need to have sales of $15,000,000 to reach its profit objective of $2,250,000.

Market Share

Market share, given as a percent, is the dollar amount of sales made by the firm in relation to all sales in the industry. It is useful to compare a company's market share with that of similar companies.

Formula 12: Market Share

$$\text{Market share} = \frac{\text{Company sales}}{\text{Total market sales}}$$

In our shoe example, suppose we estimated the market we competed in to have an annual sales volume of $300,000,000. Given our level of sales ($15,000,000), this would translate into 5% market share.

$$\text{Market share} = \frac{\$15,000,000}{\$300,000,000} = 5\%$$

Market-share analysis has a direct link with break-even analysis. Break-even sales levels can be translated into a percentage of market share. In our example, for instance, the break-even sales level in units was 200,000 units, which at $60/pair would generate sales of $12,000,000. In a total market with sales of $300,000,000, that sales level ($12,000,000) represents a 4% market share.

Elasticity

Although break-even analysis is an extremely useful tool in determining how many units must be sold for a company to remain solvent or achieve a profit target, it does not consider how many units can actually be sold. When evaluating sales, profits, and pricing strategies, we need to consider the important relationship between demand and price. Although economic theory describes this relationship in terms of a downward-sloping demand curve, managers still need to assess the impact on the total contribution margin resulting from price changes. The tool used to measure price sensitivity and market demand is called *elasticity*. Elasticity is a measure of how sensitive demand for a product is to a change in price.

A product is said to be *elastic* when a change in price causes a relatively large change in demand. Alternatively, a product is inelastic when a change in price causes a relatively small change in demand.

Formula 13: Elasticity of Demand

$$\text{Elasticity of demand} = \frac{\text{Percent change in quantity demanded}}{\text{Percent change in price}}$$

Elasticity of demand is an important concept to examine when price changes are contemplated. The following equation shows how the contribution margin is related to total contribution.

Total contribution margin = (Sales price per unit − Variable cost per unit)
× Quantity sold

In our example,

$$\text{Total contribution margin} = (\$60 - \$15) \times 250,000$$
$$= \$45 \times 250,000$$
$$= \$11,250,000$$

If a manufacturer increases price, the contribution margin increases, but the quantity sold will likely decrease. Price elasticity determines the extent to which an increase in price will affect total contribution. If consumers are insensitive to price increases (as represented by a price-inelastic demand curve), then slight decreases in the quantity sold will be offset by the increased margin per unit, resulting in an increased total contribution margin.

Margins

The difference between the retail sales price and the manufacturer's sales price (also called *wholesale price* or *cost price*) is called the *margin*. *Markup* is another word commonly used for margin. Often, margins are used to determine the retail sales price of a product.

Formula 14: Margin

$$\text{Margin} = \text{Sales price} - \text{Cost price}$$

Or, to write it another way,

$$\text{Sales price} = \text{Cost price} + \text{Margin}$$

In our example, this would be calculated as a $60 margin:

$$\text{Margin} = \text{Sales price} - \text{Cost price}$$
$$= \$120 - \$60$$
$$= \$60$$

Margins are often expressed as percentages. You can use either the sales price or the cost price as the base for calculating the percent margin. As an example, in determining a pricing structure a retailer might desire a 100% markup on cost. In this case let's say a shoe retailer bought shoes from the Athletic Shoe Company for $60. In order to achieve a 100% markup on cost we would calculate a sales price of $120 as follows:

Formula 15: Sales Price

$$\text{Sales price} = \text{Cost price} + (\text{Cost price} \times \% \text{ Margin})$$
$$= \$60 + (\$60 \times 100\%)$$
$$= \$120$$

However, margins are traditionally expressed as a percentage of the sales price. Thus, the shoe retailer is trying to determine a sales price for his product, where the wholesale price is $60. If the retailer wants a 50% margin on sales on shoes, he will use the following formula to calculate a selling price of $120:

$$\text{Margin on sales price: } \$ \text{Sales price} = \frac{\$ \text{ Cost price}}{1 - \% \text{ Margin}}$$

$$\$120 = \frac{\$60}{1 - .50}$$

Financial Ratios

Financial ratios are an important tool in business decision making because they help summarize the relationships among information on a financial statement. Ratios provide a quick way to compare the company under review with other companies in similar industries or with bench marks that have been provided for companies in general. Bench marks for the given ratios are a very general approximation of where a healthy company would be financially. However, industry ratios vary widely, so what is considered a good bench mark in one industry may not be in another. Ratios are also used as a method of tracking a company's financial progress over time.

There are four categories of ratios that are important for managerial decision making. The following section will provide a brief overview of the purpose of each category. For your future reference, Table 3.1 provides the computation for each ratio, accompanied by a brief description of the information being provided.

Measuring the Ability to Pay Current Liabilities

Ratios in this category are used to measure a business's ability to meet its short-term obligations (liabilities) with its current assets. Current assets minus current liabilities is referred to as **working capital.** Companies with large amounts of working capital are better able to meet current obligations and are in a stronger financial position. Two ratios, based on working capital, are the **Current Ratio** and the **Acid-Test Ratio** (see Table 3.1 for details).

Measuring the Ability to Sell Inventory and Collect Receivables

The business cycle consists of translating cash to inventory, then to receivables (through sales), and then back to cash (through collection).

Table 3.1 Financial ratios for managerial decision making

Ratio	Formula	Purpose
I. MEASURING THE ABILITY TO PAY CURRENT LIABILITIES		
Current ratio	$\dfrac{\text{Current assets}}{\text{Current liabilities}}$	Measures ability to pay current liabilities from current assets
Acid-test ratio	$\dfrac{\text{Cash + short-term investments + net current receivables}}{\text{Current liabilities}}$	Indicates ability to pay current liabilities from most liquid assets
II. MEASURING THE ABILITY TO SELL INVENTORY AND COLLECT RECEIVABLES		
Inventory turnover	$\dfrac{\text{Cost of goods sold}}{\text{Average inventory in days}}$	Shows ability to sell inventory
Accounts receivable turnover	$\dfrac{\text{Net credit sales}}{\text{Average net accounts receivable}}$	Measures collectibility of receivables
Day's sales in receivables	$\dfrac{\text{Average net accounts receivable}}{\text{One day's sales}}$	Indicates how many days it takes to collect accounts receivable
III. MEASURING THE ABILITY TO PAY LONG-TERM DEBTS		
Debt ratio	$\dfrac{\text{Total liabilities}}{\text{Total assets}}$	Measures percentage of assets financed by borrowing
Times-interest-earned ratio	$\dfrac{\text{Income from operations}}{\text{Interest expense}}$	Indicates ability of operating income to cover interest expense
IV. MEASURING PROFITABILITY		
Rate of return on net sales	$\dfrac{\text{Net income}}{\text{Net sales}}$	Shows the percentage of each sales dollar earned as net income
Rate of return on total assets	$\dfrac{\text{Net income + Interest expense}}{\text{Average total assets}}$	Measures profitability of asset utilization

Given this cycle, selling inventory and efficiently collecting accounts receivable are fundamental to business success. Three ratios measure a company's success in this endeavor: **Inventory Turnover, Accounts Receivable Turnover,** and **Days-Sales-in-Receivables** (see Table 3.1 for details).

Measuring the Ability to Pay Long-Term Debts

In order to finance ongoing operations or capital expenditures, most businesses incur long-term debt. Two ratios serve as tools to measure a company's ability to pay the principal and interest on these loans. These ratios are the **Debt Ratio** and the **Times-Interest-Earned Ratio.**

Measuring Profitability

The most important ratios for making business decisions (at least those required in case analysis) are those measuring profitability. Given that the primary goal of business is to earn a profit, the importance of these ratios cannot be overstated. Two ratios assist managers in measuring profitability, **Rate of Return of Net Sales** and **Rate of Return on Total Assets.**

Financial Statements and Projections

To compare alternative strategies, it is useful to create pro-forma financial statements. These are estimates of the profitability of different business choices. Three statements that are of particular use are

- Profit and loss statements
- Balance sheets
- Cash flow projections

The key to producing sound pro-forma statements is estimating future sales and future costs. If you are given current and/or past financial statements in a case, you can use expenses as a percentage of sales to predict future expenses based on estimated sales. When creating a pro-forma balance sheet, you may need to plug in (calculate) a figure to get Assets = Liabilities + Owner's Equity. Typically, either cash or long-term debt is used as the plug-in figure; therefore, adjust this number upward or downward in order to balance the basic accounting equation (A = L + OE).

Insufficient cash flows is a major problem for companies that either have widely fluctuating sales, rapid growth, or a capitalization problem (lack of investment funds). Having enough cash on hand to pay current bills is essential to the survival of a company. Preparing a cash flow pro-forma analysis, therefore, is useful even for a healthy, growing firm. The cash flow formula is straightforward:

Ending cash balance
+ Future cash inflows
− Future cash outflows
= Future cash flow

The cash flow pro-forma analysis is done for a specified period of time, such as a month, quarter, or year, and usually for multiple periods. The tricky aspect of cash flow is remembering that inflows and outflows deal strictly with the cash situation, not sales; if sales are made on credit, there is no cash flow until the account has been paid. Likewise, cash outflows are not equal to accounts payable; the only payables are those that come due and are paid during the period in question.

Summary

The goal of this chapter has been to provide the student of sport marketing with the analytical tools to perform a successful case analysis. Increasingly, the world of sport is paying more attention to the bottom line. The analytical tools introduced in this chapter should help with cases that require financial analysis to support the conclusions of your analysis. The use of these tools, when appropriate, will help you avoid the mistake of making judgments purely on hunches and intuition—which in many cases can lead to costly errors.

In the next chapter we will present an example case that use some of the tools presented in this chapter.

CASES

4

Example Case and Analysis

George R. Milne and Mark A. McDonald

Introduction

The case method is based on the learning principle that knowledge is best acquired through experience. However, before a student attempts to analyze his or her first case, it is useful to see an example of how a case is analyzed.

The four-step case analysis framework introduced in Chapter 2—identify problem(s), analyze the situation, develop solutions, and choose the best solution—will be used in this analysis. This will help clarify the purpose of each of these steps by providing a hands-on example.

The case we analyze in this chapter, "Haigis Hoopla," is different from other cases in this book because the subject matter is about *students*. In this case, the students were part of an organization making strategic decisions about running a sports event called the Haigis Hoopla, in which people of all ages play basketball against other teams from all over the region. By analyzing this case, we hope you will be able to identify with the organizers' situation (as students and business people) and use the facts from the case to arrive at a proposed solution.

The remaining cases in the book are about managers in sport organizations. Our goal for future cases is to get you as comfortable identifying with sport managers as you were identifying with students. In many respects, the cases in this book can be thought of as tools for transforming you from students to future sport managers.

As you will soon discover, the case in this chapter has numerous issues to be resolved and, like most cases, has no single "correct" answer. In an effort to demonstrate the analytical process, we will present one way of writing up the case.

We suggest studying this chapter in four steps:

1. Read only the Haigis Hoopla case.
2. Prepare your own analysis based on the framework and tools presented in Chapters 1–3.
3. Review the analysis of Haigis Hoopla provided at the end of this chapter.

4. Compare your analysis with the one in the chapter. (Remember, no one analysis is correct—just make sure to support your ideas with quantitative and qualitative reasoning.)

Case Study: Haigis Hoopla[1]

Introduction

As Mike Perez, executive director of Haigis Hoopla, carefully walked along the icy February sidewalk to his car, he reflected upon the presentation by Minutemen Marketing and the follow-up meeting he had with the Haigis Hoopla team. Noting the sun was setting later at night, Perez was reminded that the April 21 event was quickly approaching. The joint-venture concept presented by Minutemen Marketing was an interesting opportunity that could enhance the annual 3-on-3 basketball event and reflect positively on the Department of Sport Studies. On the other hand, as the Haigis team had pointed out in a heated one-hour discussion, there were distinct potential downsides to such a partnership. Haigis Hoopla, now in its fifth year, had evolved into a very successful event, and straying from the proven formula could hurt this year's efforts. Perez was left to decide whether he would pursue the partnership and, if he did decide to, how he could structure an agreement that would be beneficial to both Haigis Hoopla and Minutemen Marketing.

Haigis Hoopla

Haigis Hoopla is a 3-on-3 basketball tournament held in late April on the Haigis Mall at the University of Massachusetts in Amherst. The inaugural tournament in 1991 represented the first time that an outdoor basketball tournament of any magnitude had been held in the Pioneer Valley. The first year's event had over 100 teams competing, with approximately 1,000 spectators. By 1994, the annual tournament had grown to 281 teams with over 4,000 spectators (see Table 4.1). Although the basketball tournament is the main focus of the event, there are also other attractions for spectators. The weekend festival has featured a three-point shoot out, a free-throw contest, a slam-dunk

---

1. The case was written by George R. Milne and Mark A. McDonald. Copyright © 1996 by George R. Milne and Mark A. McDonald. Some of the names and figures have been disguised.

Table 4.1 Haigis Hoopla event growth

Year	Teams	Spectators
1991	109	1,000
1992	214	2,500
1993	210	3,000
1994	281	4,000

contest, and free giveaways provided by Haigis sponsors. Also, holding the event on a weekend in April on such a spacious campus common permits the spectators to enjoy the sunshine, music, and refreshments from event vendors as well as exciting basketball action (see Figure 4.1).

The basketball tournament attracts male and female players of all ages from the Pioneer Valley and surrounding areas (see Table 4.2). There are thirteen divisions: Girls 8–10 yrs, Girls 11–12 yrs, Women's Open, Boys 8–10 yrs, Boys 11–12 yrs, Boys 13–14 yrs, Boy's High School, Men's Couch Potatoes, Men's Weekend Warriors, Men's Hot Shot, Men's Top Gun, Men's Masters (over 35 yrs), and Media. Entrants pay $15 per person (about 25% pay $18 per person for late registration) to enter the tournament, with competitions structured as either double-elimination or round-robin, depending on division size. The registration fee entitles players to participate in the event and receive the official Haigis Hoopla T-shirt and a bag of other promotional goodies donated by sponsors. The event spans three days over the course of a weekend, starting with the registration party on Friday evening. Half of the teams registering to participate in the event have three players; the other half has four players (one being a substitute). Play begins Saturday morning and ends late Sunday afternoon with the division finals. In case of inclement weather, play is postponed until the following weekend.

Games are played on half courts (35′ × 40′) with a portable basket created on cement walkways of the Haigis Mall and adjacent parking lots (see Figures 4.2 and 4.3). Players call their own fouls, with court monitors and referees ready to step in and resolve disputes. A completed game occurs when a team makes 14 points with a 2-point lead up to 17 points, or until the 30-minute time limit expires. During the semis and finals, games are extended to 21 points. The play of the game is wide open, with fouls counted only when either team gets 8 points or the game enters the last 5 minutes of the contest. No dunking is allowed; dunking or hanging on the rim results in a technical foul. Baskets made within the 20′ line count 1 point; those baskets made outside the line count for 2 points. The ball changes possession after each score and the ball is cleared and checked beyond the 2-point line. Jump ball

Figure 4.1 Haigis Hoopla event

situations are handled with even-odds. Substitution is unlimited when the ball is not in play. Finally, there is an implicit 30-second clock, requiring the offensive team to draw iron or give the ball up to the other team.

Table 4.2   Haigis Hoopla 1994 participant demographics

AGE		GENDER		RESIDENCE	
Under 12	5%	Male	87%	Amherst	50%
12–17	20%	Female	13%	Pioneer Valley	90%
18–24	65%				
25–29	7%				
30+	3%				

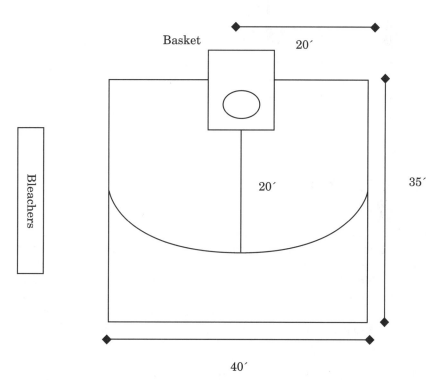

Figure 4.2   Basketball court dimensions

Managing the Event

In 1991, an event management course was added to the sport management curriculum at the University of Massachusetts at Amherst. This course was a practical application course to be taken during the spring semester by both undergraduate and graduate students. Since its inception, the course has been offered every year. Enrolled students are responsible for planning, organizing, and operating a 3-on-3 basketball tournament. This event is seen as critical to the Sport Management Department—to enhance the department's reputation across the uni-

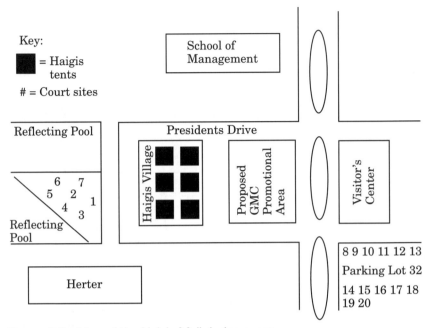

Figure 4.3 Map of the Haigis Mall during event

versity community and the Pioneer Valley by providing community outreach as well as providing quality educational experience to sport management students.

Haigis Hoopla is a nonprofit organization. A member of the faculty serves as the executive director, chairman of the board, and the instructor of the sport event management course. This faculty member has ultimate responsibility for Haigis Hoopla and leads a board of directors (consisting of all full-time sport management faculty) in creating and implementing policies with respect to the event.

This was the first year that Mike Perez had held the executive director position. His responsibilities included the management of day-to-day operations and direct supervision of students organized into the following functional management teams: financial management, resource management, marketing, public relations, operations and services, hospitality, and tournament operations. Other faculty members served as consultants to these teams. A total of 23 students enrolled in the sport event management course and served as the Haigis Hoopla staff in 1995.

The financial goal of Haigis Hoopla 1995, as with all previous years, was to be self-sufficient. Any excess of revenues over expenses would be contributed to a scholarship fund established to benefit a senior sport management student. Historically, revenues had been acquired through registration fees and corporate sponsorships. Table 4.3 shows the revenues and costs for the 1994 event. In addition to the cash sponsorships, many businesses donated products or services to be used as giveaways or to help reduce cash outlays to run the event. No T-shirt sponsor had ever been found, thus costing Haigis $3.93 per shirt. Most of the other costs were fixed in nature but changed from year to year. For example, while advertising was a fixed cost, Haigis management had tended to spend up to 25% of the cash value in servicing the sponsorship to fulfill an obligation to sponsors. In addition, some expenditures contained both fixed and variable costs, such as the portable hoops, which need to be depreciated to account for eventual replacement. Hoops cost Haigis $225 each, and each hoop can service 18 teams for the tournament with an expected life of three years. At the end of 1994, Haigis Hoopla had an inventory of 13 hoops.

As the event had grown in popularity, sponsorship support had also increased. Corporate sponsorship had traditionally been offered at four levels: Title, Partner, Associate, and Patron. Table 4.4 depicts the amount of sponsorship support provided annually from 1991 to 1994. Table 4.5 shows the benefits and costs of each of these levels for the 1994 event. The number of cash sponsors dropped in 1994, resulting

Table 4.3   Haigis Hoopla 1994 revenues and expenses

Revenues:	
Sponsorship fees	$ 2,250
Participant registrations*	$12,534
Total revenues	$14,784
Expenses:	
Advertising	$ 600
Equipment:	
Tent rental	750
Public address system rental	25
Other	1,250
T-shirts**	5,000
Copies	500
Supplies	550
Security	950
EMT	100
Photographer	250
Portable toilets	400
Participant awards	500
Gas	50
Other	100
Total expenses	$11,025

*Registration fee was $12 per person, $15 late registration, in 1994.
**Total T-shirt expenses include the cost of shirts given to 275 volunteers, staff, and supporters of Haigis Hoopla.

in the Haigis staff landing only $2,500 in cash sponsors (see Table 4.6). More importantly, this was a dramatic reduction from the $9,250 in sponsorships during the 1993 campaign. One of Perez's primary goals was to push sponsorship revenue back to pre-1994 levels. As Perez noted,

> After a disappointing year in 1994 for sponsorship solicitation, I put tremendous pressure on myself and the students to bring this key revenue source back to 1993 levels. While registration fees cover all of our operating expenses, sponsorship dollars make continued donations to the scholarship fund possible. We always try to donate at least $5,000 each year from Haigis proceeds. Not only did I want to reach this goal in 1995, I wanted to make up for any shortfall in 1994. With this goal in mind, we extended our sponsorship procurement process from being limited to the spring semester to an entire year of sustained effort. Six students pounded the streets during the fall to get sponsors. While we still have no committed cash sponsors, we are confident that the hard work will pay off in the end.

When the Haigis event started in 1991, many of the sponsors viewed the sponsor fee largely as a contribution to the community and corporate public relations. Since Haigis had grown in size and reach, the decision to become a Haigis Hoopla sponsor had become increasingly driven by bottom-line considerations. This placed more pressure on the event organizers to quantify the marketing value attached to a given sponsorship level. (See Table 4.7 for a report on industry-wide growth in sponsorship.)

For the Haigis Hoopla organization, the growth of the event has led to ever-increasing operational and legal risks. Although the event is insured through the university and participants sign a waiver and release of liability, there is always concern regarding potential lawsuits. In 1992, for example, a student staff member was injured while helping to run the tournament. This incident led to a lawsuit, which was eventually settled out of court by the Commonwealth of Massachusetts. Operationally, there is concern that the event might become too large and

Table 4.4   Growth in Haigis Hoopla sponsorship 1991–1994

Year	Number of Sponsors	Cash	Donated Product Value
1991	6	$1,500	$5,500
1992	6	$5,600	$8,250
1993	12	$9,250	$15,000
1994	7	$2,500	$12,000

Table 4.5 Features by corporate sponsorship level (1994)

Sponsorship Feature	$7,000	$2,500	$1,500	$750
Community outreach	✔	✔	✔	✔
Tax deduction	✔	✔	✔	✔
Advertisement in event program	✔	✔	✔	✔
Coupon placement in goody bag	✔	✔	✔	✔
Novelty giveaways	✔	✔	✔	✔
Public address system announcements	✔	✔	✔	✔
Access to Haigis hospitality tent	✔	✔	✔	✔
Client/sponsor entertainment opportunities	✔	✔	✔	
Consumer education opportunities	✔	✔	✔	
Pre-event radio coverage	✔	✔	✔	
On-site merchandising/vending	✔	✔	✔	
Product sampling	✔	✔	✔	
Exhibition tent in Haigis Village	✔	✔	✔	
Access to participant lists and demos	✔	✔	✔	
Product exclusivity	✔	✔		
Event entitlements	✔	✔		
Identification on event posters	✔	✔		
Recognition on staff/participant T-shirts	✔	✔		
Local print advertising	✔	✔		
Signage in Haigis Village	✔	✔		
Event entitlements (contests/divisions/courts)	✔	✔		
Event day radio coverage	✔	✔		
Product drawings, demonstrations, & displays	✔	✔		
Identification on team entry forms	✔			
Championship court signage	✔			
Scoreboard signage	✔			
Inflatable opportunity	✔			
Use of cross-promotion marketing campaigns	✔			
First right of refusal offer	✔			

Table 4.6 Haigis Hoopla cash sponsors

1993	1994
Bart's	Bertucci's
BayBank	Black Sheep Deli
Bob's Stores	Coca-Cola
Coca-Cola	Princeton Review
Flowers A-La-Carte	
Hampshire Mall	
Mass, Inc.	
Princeton Review	
Rafters/The Pub	
Spalding	
Uptown Pizza	
Visa	

Table 4.7 Growth in global event spending 1992–1994*

Year	Amount Spent
1992	$3.20 billion
1993	$3.70 billion
1994	$4.25 billion

*The figures do not include additional spending (i.e., media buys) to promote the sponsorship investments. (*Source*: International Events Group.)

unwieldy for effective management by a student team with limited resources.

1995 Haigis Hoopla Plans and Goals

The overall goal of the 1995 Haigis Management team was to improve the quality of service delivery for all aspects of the event. The Haigis experience was to provide an exciting, safe, and fun event for participants, volunteers, and members of the community. Specifically, the objectives of the 1995 Haigis team were

1. To be professional and detail oriented in all phases of tournament operations including planning, site preparation, event operations, volunteer recruitment, financial management, and sponsorship solicitation/servicing;
2. To increase the diversity of participants with specific emphasis on increasing the children's division (18 and under) to represent 35%

of all participants and increasing the number of female teams to 50;

3. To successfully promote Haigis Hoopla to the university and Pioneer Valley communities and attract 5,000 spectators to the event in 1995;
4. To create a center-court area that would provide seating capacity (bleachers), signage opportunities for sponsors, and an attractive area for championship games to take place;
5. To generate cash sponsorship revenues of $8,500;
6. To secure in-kind sponsorships valued at $9,000 retail;
7. To recruit and train 125 volunteers to work both prior to and during the event;
8. To complete set-up of the Haigis Mall area by 3:00 p.m. on Friday, April 21, 1995 and the set-up of the auxiliary areas by 11 p.m. Friday night;
9. To arrange the taping and editing of a Haigis Hoopla video for use in future public relations and sponsorship solicitation efforts; and
10. To have a sports celebrity appearance at Haigis Hoopla.

Minutemen Marketing[2]

Minutemen Marketing was an advertising agency comprised of 22 University of Massachusetts School of Management undergraduates and one faculty member. This organization was formed in January 1995 as part of the students' participation in the General Motors Marketing Internship (GMMI) program, which was established by SRO Prom Associates in 1990. Originally, this program was called the Pontiac Undergraduate Internship program. Undergraduates from three California schools earned academic credit and gained business experience marketing Pontiac cars to their respective campuses. By 1991, the program expanded to ten campuses in California. Because of the program's success, the internship expanded to include all six divisions of General Motors in 1992 and was subsequently called the General Motors Marketing Internship (GMMI). By the start of 1995, GMMI had expanded to include seven states and 110 campuses, one of them the University of Massachusetts.

The assignment for Minutemen Marketing was to promote GMC trucks for the Don Lorenz, Inc., car dealership in Greenfield, Massachusetts. Don Lorenz, Inc., was a second-generation automotive dealer that had been in business for over 40 years. Steve Lorenz took over the dealership in 1990 as a five-line dealership, including GMC trucks.

---

2. Much of this material was adapted from Minutemen Marketing's report, *Lorenz GMC Jamboree,* April 4, 1995.

The dealership first sold the GMC truck line in 1972. The Lorenz dealership stresses customer service and satisfaction. By participating in the GMMI program, Lorenz hoped to better understand campus perceptions in selecting a dealership and increase visibility and awareness for the Lorenz dealership.

Minutemen Marketing was given a budget of $2,500 by GMMI to promote GMC trucks (the Jimmy and Sonoma models) to the primary target market of UMass undergraduate students, graduate students, faculty, and staff, and the secondary target market of communities local to UMass and Don Lorenz, Inc. Minutemen Marketing's objectives were to

1. Stimulate dealership traffic at Don Lorenz, Inc., in Greenfield, MA;
2. Create a high participation level at the Don Lorenz, Inc., event;
3. Create interaction between spectators and vehicles at the event; and,
4. Extend Don Lorenz, Inc.'s customer base south to reach Amherst, Hadley, Northampton, Pelham, Sunderland, and Whately (the towns surrounding the university).

In January, Minutemen Marketing considered several promotion concepts. One of the ideas was to hold the event at the annual "Spring Concert." This rock concert, held on Mother's Day weekend in May, historically had large crowds. There was no research available on the demographics of the concert attendees, although it was thought to be primarily students. A second concept was to create a concert called the Lorenz GMC Jam that Minutemen Marketing would manage. There were potential problems with gaining administrative approval, however. A third idea was aligning with Campus Fest—a semiannual, week-long promotional event during which companies displayed their goods to the UMass community. A disadvantage of using this event was that there was already another car dealership involved. The fourth idea was to partner with Haigis Hoopla.

The Presentation and Follow-up Meeting

In late February, Minutemen Marketing contacted Haigis Hoopla executive director Mike Perez to set up a meeting to discuss the possibility of a joint venture. Minutemen Marketing account planners, Julie Jones and Amy Dawson, along with their faculty advisor, Nancy Chin, met with Perez to discuss the possible partnership. After each party conveyed how they could help each other out, Perez suggested that representatives from Minutemen Marketing make a formal presentation to the Haigis Hoopla management team. A few days later, Julie Jones and Bill Arnold delivered the presentation to Perez and the Haigis group.

At the time of the presentation, Minutemen Marketing explained that they were not able to provide a cash contribution for the sponsorship opportunity. They argued, however, that by having the GMC event within the Haigis event, Haigis would benefit by the advertising dollars GMC would spend on event promotion since all GMC advertising could also promote Haigis. Further, Minutemen Marketing suggested they could provide Haigis with research and advertising capabilities and skills (such as desktop publishing and video) that would help Haigis with their current and future efforts. With respect to the event, Minutemen Marketing pointed out that trucks and on-going contests could add to the festival atmosphere of Haigis. During this meeting, Perez suggested that Minutemen Marketing consider offering a shooting contest where an individual would have the chance of winning a GMC Jimmy truck if they made a lay-up, free throw, three-point shot, and a half-court shot in 30 seconds. This could add excitement and likely increase the number of participants. Minutemen Marketing, in return, was looking for the benefits usually afforded to a partner sponsor (see Table 4.5).

After the representatives from Minutemen Marketing exited the room, a heated discussion erupted. Tom, the leader of the sponsorship group, set the tone: "Why should we let Minutemen Marketing take advantage of our event? We have worked too hard building this tournament from scratch to give it away for nothing!" Peter, another student from the sponsorship group, piped in: "You are right. We have been pounding the streets, making cold calls, sending letters since September to sign on sponsors—why let this group have a free ride? How can we justify charging other companies $2,500 to become partners, when this group is giving us zilch?"

Perez knew he had to gain control of the situation quickly: "Settle down guys," he said. "Let's try to look at the big picture. One of our key goals for this year is to increase spectatorship at Haigis, right? Wouldn't having Minutemen Marketing spending upwards of $1,500 on advertising help us reach that goal? Also, they bring some serious resources to the table, such as 23 students, desktop publishing skills, and video production capability."

One obvious drawback in the proposed partnership was the lack of cash for the sponsorship benefits. Haigis would be offering Minutemen Marketing sponsorship benefits valued at $2,500. Although Minutemen Marketing would bring some benefits to the table, there was doubt as to the actual value. Was there any way for Minutemen Marketing to contribute directly to the Haigis event? Additionally, there was the risk that the GMC event would distract from the basketball tournament and that Minutemen Marketing would simply take advantage of what the Sport Management Department had spent four years to develop. Also, if Minutemen Marketing decided to get sponsors for its GMC promotion, the Minutemen Marketing activities could hurt the Haigis team's efforts to gain sponsors by creating confusion in the local market-place. Lastly, working with Minutemen Marketing on the GMC promotion would only serve to further complicate the job of organizing and operating Haigis Hoopla.

Perez was left to consider the Haigis team's feedback. There were obvious benefits, including the long-term benefits of assisting another university program with its educational objectives. Perez realized that growing the event was aligned with the Haigis mission and that adding the GMC promotion could have indirect benefits. On the other hand, there were equally as many downsides. Perez was under pressure to meet his financial goals as well as the marketing objectives. The final decision to go forward rested on whether an agreement could be struc-tured to make Minutemen Marketing commit some of their resources to help Haigis. But, since Minutemen only had $2,500 to spend on all their marketing, this could be difficult. Several questions raced through Perez's mind. Should Haigis go forward with the joint venture? How could an agreement be structured so that it would benefit both Haigis and Minutemen Marketing? If a partner-level sponsorship was given away for far less than $2,500, how would this affect the event's ability to break even? With these thoughts, Perez put on his coat and headed out into the cold February weather.

Case Response

Problems

The primary problem of this case centers on whether Mike Perez, executive director of Hagis Hoopla, should agree to a strategic partner-ship with Minutemen Marketing. On the one hand, a partnership would provide resources and would advance the position of the Sports Studies Department on the campus. On the other hand, Minutemen Marketing has little money to contribute, and there is the perception that Min-utemen Marketing would be getting a free ride on the event that the Sport Marketing Department had invested plenty of time and energy developing. In evaluating this major dilemma, two other problems arise. First, how would a partnership help or hurt Hagis Hoopla in meeting its marketing objectives? Second, if an agreement was to be developed, how could it be structured so that it would be beneficial to both Haigis Hoopla and Minutemen Marketing?

Situation Analysis

Haigis Hoopla is a 3-on-3 basketball tournament that is run by the Sport Management Department in conjunction with a sport management course. The purpose of the event is to educate students about how to run a sporting event. The financial objective is to cover costs and raise money for a scholarship fund. Individual entry fees from the tournament participants and cash sponsors generate revenue.

As Table 4.1 shows, the event that was started in 1991 has seen the number of teams grow by 157% and the number of spectators by 300%. In 1994 the event made $3,759 (Table 4.3: $14,784 – $11,025 = $3,759), which was roughly $1,250 short of the scholarship fund goal. The positive revenue was primarily driven by an increase in the number of participating teams (Table 4.1), since cash generated from sponsorship fell by $6,750 from 1993 levels. As a result, there is pressure on Perez, the executive director, to increase the level of cash sponsors back to 1993 levels while also growing the event in terms of participants and spectators.

In 1994, fixed expenses were roughly $7,225 ($11,025 – $3800 for participant T-shirts). Given the goals of improving operations (adding bleachers, etc.) and adding advertising support, it is reasonable to assume 1995 fixed costs to be $8,750.

A break-even analysis is useful to estimate the number of teams the event needs to cover fixed costs.

Variable expenses:

> *T-shirts:* $3.93/player × 3.5 players per team = $13.76
> *Hoops:*

18 teams/hoop			
Current inventory	= 13 hoops (recently purchased)		
Cost per hoop	= $225		
Expected life of hoop	= 3 yr		
Depreciation expense/			
year/hoop	= $225/3 yr	=	$75/yr
Current capacity	= 13 hoops × 18 teams/hoop	=	234 teams
Variable expense/team	= $75/18 teams	=	$4.16 team

Variable Revenue:

> early registration: $15/player × 3.5 players/team × .75 = $39.38
> late registration: $18/player × 3.5 players/team × .25 = $15.75
> $55.13

Break-even Calculation:

> BE = (Fixed Costs)/(Variable revenue – variable expenses)
> 236 = $8,750 / ($55.13 – $17.92)

Thus, Haigis needs 236 teams to sign up to break even. (Note this analysis did not count the additional fixed cost of $225 for purchasing additional rims. To cover this additional cost, they will need a couple of additional teams to sign up.)

If the 1995 Haigis event tournament is as large as the 1994 event (assuming the same costs), it will break even. However, to meet the scholarship goal of $5,000, Haigis needs to either increase the number of participants and/or increase the level of sponsorship. The following table shows how various combinations of participants and cash sponsorship affect the contribution to the $5,000 scholarship fund. In calculating these figures, the level of fixed costs was increased to $10,000 ($8,750 + $1,250) to make up for the $1,250 scholarship fund shortfall in 1994. For example, if 275 teams showed up, and $2,500 in cash sponsorship was obtained, $2,732.75 would be earned for the 1995 scholarship fund: [275 × ($55.13 − $17.92)] + $2,500 − $10,000.

Contribution toward shcolarship fund sponsorship cash received

# Teams	$0	$2,500	$5,000	$7,500
275	232.75	2,732.75	5,232.75	7,732.75
300	1,163.00	3,663.00	6,163.00	8,663.00
325	2,093.25	4,593.25	7,093.25	9,593.25
350	3,023.50	5,523.50	8,023.50	10,523.50
375	3,953.75	6,453.75	8,953.75	11,453.75
400	4,884.00	7,384.00	9,884.00	12,384.00

For 1995, Haigis had a goal of acquiring $5,000 for the scholarship fund and getting cash sponsorship levels up over $8,000. If this level of sponsorship is obtained, there would be no need to grow the number of participants. However, 1994 efforts only brought in a cash sponsorship of $2,500. With last year's entrant levels (281 teams), this would fall short of the scholarship goal. Assuming a 50% growth rate in number of teams (especially given the diversity goals), this would result in roughly 375 teams. At this level, total sponsorship of $2,500 would help the event meet its scholarship goal.

Early in February, Haigis was contacted by Minutemen Marketing to conduct a joint venture. Minutemen Marketing wanted to run an event within the event. They promised to provide advertising support. In turn, Minutemen Marketing wanted to gain the benefits from a $2,500 sponsorship without making the cash contribution. At this point, Haigis had not yet landed a sponsor, but its team had spent the prior six months courting possible sponsors.

The decision maker for the case is Mike Perez. He needs to decide whether Haigis should go forward with this partnership and how to structure the deal if he does decide to go forward.

SWOT Analysis

This SWOT Analysis examines the question of whether Haigis should form a partnership with Minutemen Marketing.

STRENGTHS

- The partnership would provide Haigis with increased marketing muscle. All the advertising that Minutemen Marketing conducts would also mention the Haigis event.
- The GMC promotion could add excitement to the event—especially if there was a contest to shoot baskets and win a free truck.
- A partnership with the School of Management could provide Haigis with superior department resources. The School of Management could provide desktop publishing and video capabilities.
- The strategic partner would be relatively independent and would not need to be managed day-by-day.

WEAKNESSES

- An event within an event could confuse the marketplace.
- Another entity other than Sport Management would be capitalizing on the campus event.
- The GMC promotion run by Minutemen Marketing could create inequities in the sponsorship base since it would be receiving sponsorship benefits and not paying for them.

OPPORTUNITIES

Going forward with the joint venture would

- Strengthen departmental linkages on campus
- Provide Sport Management with potential long-term access to resources
- Provide leverage to attract another exclusive car dealership sponsor in future Haigis events.

THREATS

- Minutemen Marketing's skill at running an event is untested.
- Haigis would have to give up control over the entire event.
- The experience of the event could be potentially changed.
- There is a possibility of resentment by those members of the Haigis team whose six months of soliciting sponsors would be undercut by allowing Lorenz, Inc., to affiliate at no charge.

Evaluation of Alternatives

ALTERNATIVE #1—NO DEAL

One alternative is not to go forward with the partnership. Based on the break-even analysis, it appears as if Haigis could break even. It is not apparent whether Haigis would achieve its scholarship goals, however. The case reports that the Haigis team has been working six months to get sponsors, so it is likely this hard work will pay off. With the trends pointing toward increased corporate involvement in sponsorship (Table 4.7), it is likely that sponsors will be available.

Both the short-run and direct benefits do not lend support to a partnership. The main issue is that Minutemen Marketing does not have the cash. Further, the long-run benefits are not certain and come with some downsides. If Perez listens to his team he will be supporting their position. This could build morale and energize his team.

ALTERNATIVE #2—ACCEPT DEAL ON MINUTEMEN MARKETING'S TERMS

Despite the arguments above, the long-term and indirect alternatives do hold some promise. In particular, by forming a partnership with the School of Management, Sport Management would potentially have access to additional resources. Further, having a car sponsor could be an educational benefit for Haigis in the future. Even if the relationship between Haigis and Minutemen Marketing did not continue more than a year, there is the possibility that Haigis could convince another local car dealership to promote its cars at a future event. In addition, Minutemen Marketing agreed to promote Haigis in all its advertising. Since Minutemen Marketing needs to communicate to the community, Haigis would be guaranteed positive exposure.

ALTERNATIVE #3—PROPOSE A DEAL WHERE MINUTEMEN MARKETING COMMITS ADDITIONAL RESOURCES AND IS FACED WITH RESTRICTIONS

If one takes a long-run perspective, another reasonable alternative is to structure the deal so that it is a win–win situation. Minutemen's initial proposal stressed that it could provide additional advertising for the Haigis event. Thus, all Minutemen Marketing advertising would mention Haigis. This is a big plus; however, there is no guarantee *how* Minutemen will spend its money. Given that it has a total of only $2,500 to spend, it might not spend be a great deal of money on *effective* advertising. Further, the ad placements might not be made in media channels that would benefit Haigis. An approach to ameliorating these shortcomings would be to direct Minutemen Marketing to place advertising dollars in areas that would benefit Haigis.

Another aspect of the Minutemen Marketing proposal that needs evaluating is the contention that displaying trucks would add to the festive atmosphere of the event. This may be true, but there are no guarantees that Minutemen Marketing will not attract additional sponsors to the event. There is the danger that the GMC Jamboree that is being planned will grow so large that it might overtake the Haigis event. Some controls need to be placed on the GMC event.

Decision

The Haigis team appears to have strong opposition to the partnership despite the numerous long-term and indirect benefits. The downsides to the partnership are not likely to happen, and if the worst occurs, the downside risk to Haigis is very minimal. At minimum, Haigis will still break even since they only need 268 teams to sign up. To make the partnership more palatable, Perez needs to get some guarantees from Minutemen Marketing.

Because Minutemen Marketing has a limited $2,500 budget, it is not reasonable to expect them to pay directly for a partnership. However, it is possible to direct Minutemen Marketing to spend its advertising dollars in a way that benefits Haigis. One approach might be to have Minutemen Marketing spend its advertising dollars with the same advertising vehicle that Haigis is using. This would give Haigis more clout and possibly lead to a lower cost-per-ad rate. Haigis should also retain control and have approval over the way the event is mentioned in advertising.

In addition to directing advertising expenditures, Haigis should consider putting restrictions on the type of sponsors that Minutemen Marketing could solicit. One restriction that seems reasonable is to deny Haigis the right to solicit any sponsors. A lesser restriction would be to limit their solicitation to in-kind solicitations that are approved by Haigis.

Another consideration is to have Minutemen Marketing pay for insurance surrounding their car give-away contest. Because this expense is tied directly to the Minutemen Marketing promotion, it makes sense that this group should assume this expenditure. Additionally, this is a tangible benefit ($) that can help seal the agreement.

Most importantly, Haigis should get Minutemen Marketing to sign an agreement of understanding. This agreement should specify the responsibilities of both parties, assuring benefits while providing protection. Therefore, Alternative #3 is the best solution: Propose a deal where Minutemen Marketing commits additional resources and is faced with restrictions.

Reebok (A)

Andy Rohm

Introduction

Reebok International Ltd. began its fiscal year 1997 with a positive shift in brand momentum and in trade and retail brand perception. Made up of three principal operating units—the Reebok Division, The Rockport Company, and the Greg Norman Collection—Reebok ended the 1996 fiscal year with a #2 market share position, flat revenues of $3.5 billion, and declining net earnings. However, at year-end 1996, the Reebok Division, a world-wide designer, marketer, and distributor of sports, fitness, and casual footwear, apparel, and equipment, had also seen its global apparel business growing. Its 3,000 athletes had performed well at the 1996 Atlanta Games, and its footwear range (long held as the true barometer of success in the athletic footwear industry) had benefited from fresh, new designs and innovative new technologies.

Reebok was certainly not expecting to repeat its phenomenal growth levels of the 1980s (it reached a #1 market share in 1987, a growth path that Reebok's chairman, Paul Fireman, would later describe as "pure white vapor"), yet the company did see promise and growth potential in the years ahead within the arenas of athletic footwear, apparel, and related equipment. Would 1997 be different from the past three years (1994–1996), in which the Reebok Division saw its U.S. combined footwear and apparel revenues drop 3.5% and its footwear market share drop 11.8%? Reebok management seemed to think so, as evidenced by Chairman Paul Fireman's remarks to Reebok employees and shareholders in its 1996 *Annual Report:*

> I look back on fiscal 1996 as a year that was disappointing financially yet rewarding operationally, as we made steady progress toward improving our company's long-term prospects and financial outlook. Total revenues for the year remained flat at $3.5 billion while net earnings declined. However, we made gratifying headway in managing our brands against the key objectives that I outlined in last year's annual report.

The Reebok® brand—which is the largest and most visible of the brands managed under the Reebok International corporate umbrella—has been re-focused on building quality market share and improving operational efficiencies. In 1996, we made good progress in the long-term rehabilitation of the Reebok brand—a return to cutting-edge thinking and true product innovation. We unveiled a number of new footwear products in the latter half of 1996. Early results indicate that these products have been well received by both retailers and consumers, as evidenced by recent strong sell-throughs and increased future bookings.

The mission of the Reebok brand is to create innovative products that make a difference to athletes and consumers. At this point, I can say with confidence that we are no longer caught up in the cycle of searching for the latest breakthrough. Instead, we are developing a continuous stream of evolving products based on well-researched technological and design platforms, opening up a host of possibilities for the Reebok brand as we look ahead.[1]

In sum, Reebok's upper management, specifically Chairman Paul Fireman and President Bob Meers, were not at all pleased with the Reebok brand's recent performance. The past four years had been difficult for Reebok as 1996 revenues remained flat at $3.5 billion while a formidable competitor based on the other coast, Nike, saw its 1996 revenues reach over $6 billion. Furthermore, several shareholder groups had recently called for the resignation of Fireman, the founder and catalyst of modern-day Reebok, who was regarded as one of the industry's product and marketing visionaries, in part due to the company's past poor performance in comparison to Nike's. Mr. Fireman had boldly offered to step down as chairman in 1998 if the company's fortunes did not improve.

As the company looked to the year 2000 and beyond, Reebok management, led by Fireman and Meers, faced four challenges: (1) the athletic footwear and apparel consumer market of the 1990s was becoming increasingly sophisticated, exhibiting substantially more dynamic and varied buying patterns and behaviors than in years past; (2) the growth of the U.S. athletic footwear market had begun to mature, possibly reaching a saturation point; (3) the investment levels required to sign select professional athletes and teams were higher than ever; and, (4) Reebok's traditional core consumer base (the 35+ consumer) was no longer the "sweet spot" in terms of athletic footwear and apparel purchase volume and frequency.

---

1. *Source:* Reebok International Ltd. 1996 Annual Report.

Reebok's Background

Reebok International Ltd. actually began as the J.W. Foster Company in 1895 in Bolton, England. At that time, a good pair of running shoes was difficult to find. Joseph William Foster, a young and dedicated runner and member of the Bolton Primrose Harriers track club, was determined to run faster. So, Foster stitched together a pair of "running pumps" with spikes nailed through the soles and found that these handmade "racing spikes" actually enhanced his performance on the track. Thus, in 1900 Foster founded the J.W. Foster Company, a producer of custom-made cross-country spikes for a majority of England's top runners. Before long, Foster was building shoes for England's elite runners, including Harold Abrahams and Eric Liddle of the Academy Award-winning *Chariots of Fire* fame, both of whom won gold medals wearing "Fosters" in the 1924 Paris Games.

By 1933, the J.W. Foster & Sons factory, known as "The Olympic Works," was producing several types of athletic shoe, ranging from running, cross-country, cycling, and road-walking shoes to boxing, soccer, and rugby "boots." Over the years that followed, the J.W. Foster & Sons Company formed close relationships with the local English running clubs and athletes, subsequently building the foundation for what is now Reebok International Ltd.

Then, in 1958, two Foster brothers, Joe and Jeffrey, founded their own company and called it *Reebok*, after a fleet African gazelle. Between 1965 and 1979, in the midst of the U.S. running boom, Reebok's Joe Foster searched for a distributor for Reebok in North America, yet discussions and arrangements with distributors produced disappointing results. In 1979, however, Foster and a young entrepreneur named Paul Fireman met at a Chicago trade show, and soon Fireman received the distribution rights for Reebok in North America.

Modern-Day Reebok

Although its roots and heritage are grounded in the running market dating back to 1895, modern-day Reebok experienced terrific success throughout the 1980s by introducing not a running shoe, but the first athletic shoe designed for women, the Freestyle™ aerobics shoe. In 1982, with U.S. sales at $1.3 million, Reebok strategically shifted its production from running shoes to the Freestyle to catch and ride the popularity wave of aerobics as an emerging exercise form, particularly among women. Between 1987 and 1989, Reebok was the world's #1 athletic footwear brand, having overtaken both Nike and the global brand known as *adidas*. Reebok's revenues reached $1.8 billion in 1989, and by 1992, the Freestyle had become the industry's #1 selling athletic shoe. Reebok sales reached over $3 billion from a level of less than $1 million back in 1980.

Reebok's yearly growth was fueled by footwear like the Freestyle that met the needs of a fast-growing and opportunity-filled fitness market, as did the original "Fosters." This growth occurred within three general footwear segments—women's fitness, walking, and a comfort casual category called "Classics"—and Reebok subsequently captured the #1 market share position during the mid-1980s. Reebok had a "bond" and relationship with the female fitness enthusiast that was second to none.

Reebok's Current Market Position

Reebok's modern-day strengths, developed during the fitness boom of the 1980s, also led to a broad consumer perception that the Reebok brand did not equate to "true" and "authentic" performance. By 1990, Nike had regained the #1 share of the U.S. athletic footwear market, with a combination of exciting and timely product, excellent operational logistics in customer service, inventory management, and inspirational, compelling communications ("Just Do It"), supported by athletes and icons such as Michael Jordan, Andre Agassi, and others.

In response to Nike's growing market share, Reebok reorganized in 1992 around two major activity groups to boost its global performance sports *and* fitness positions:

1. **Performance sports:** including baseball, basketball, football, soccer, tennis, preseason, cross training and running; and,
2. **Fitness:** including women's fitness, walking, and classics, among others.

By 1996, in order to take full advantage of the growth in women's sport participation, Reebok had further segmented its women's business to concentrate on women's sport, focusing on basketball, volleyball, and softball; and women's training, focusing on more cutting-edge health club activities such as step aerobics, an indoor cycle training program called *Cycle Reebok*, and fitness walking. A department called *Reebok University* provided key industry instructors, trainers, and influencers with up-to-date training programs and instruction in support of the women's sport and training businesses. Other programs that evolved from Reebok's women's training category included a concept called *Versatraining* that attempted to capture the myriad and diverse training routines in which women were participating with an integrated footwear, apparel, and fitness-training marketing concept.

That same year, Reebok continued its corporate focus on the soccer category as well as a renewed emphasis on the running/track & field category, particularly with the 1996 Atlanta Games around the corner. These two categories epitomized sports performance Reebok management believed; they were seen as critical to boosting Reebok's long-term domestic and global position as a true sports performance brand.

The Total Footwear Market

The total 1996 U.S. athletic footwear retail market reached $14.1 billion, or 342 million pairs of shoes sold, an increase of 6% and a decline of −1%, respectively, versus 1995 levels (Exhibit 5.1). Reebok's 1996 share of the U.S. athletic footwear market was 17.7% (Exhibit 5.2), #2 behind Nike's 34.7% share. Several other companies had gained momentum and market share in recent years, including adidas, Con-

Exhibit 5.1 Total market performance/total U.S. athletic footwear

	1992	1993	1994	1995	1996
Pairs					
(millions of pairs)	292	311	325	344	342
Dollars					
(billions of dollars)	$11.7	12.1	12.4	13.3	14.1

Source: 1996 NPD/SMART Consumer Panel.

Exhibit 5.2 1996 market share/U.S. athletic footwear market.

Chg.	'96 Overall (%)	'95 Overall (%)	% Vol
Nike	34.7	29.4	25%
Reebok	17.7	18.9	−1
Asics	1.6	1.8	−5
Saucony	0.8	0.7	9
New Balance	2.5	2.1	23
adidas	2.5	2.0	35
Fila	3.6	2.8	37
LA Gear	1.7	2.0	−28
Converse	1.7	2.1	−14

Source: 1996 NPD/SMART Consumer Panel.

verse, and Fila, as did several smaller, niche specialty brands, such as Saucony, New Balance, Asics, and Brooks.

Basketball led all industry footwear categories in 1996 with 20.1% of the overall market, followed by cross training at 17.0%, running at 11.4%, sport casual at 10.8%, hiking at 7.8%, and tennis at 7.2%. While accounting for only 9% of the U.S. population, the 12–17 male and female consumer age category led basketball, running, and cross-training purchases, with 17% of total purchases in 1996. Seasonal sales trends showed that March, August (during back-to-school time), and the December holiday season accounted for the greatest proportion of footwear sales (NPD/SMART Consumer Panel). Exhibit 5.3 shows Reebok's market share by footwear category.

Recent market trends pointed to three footwear categories as having the most success at the retail level: basketball, cross training, and running (Exhibit 5.4). Further, the walking footwear category contin-

Exhibit 5.3   Reebok market share by category total (1996).

Total	Dollar Share (%) 17.1	Unit Share (%) 15.9
Aerobic	51.9	52.0
Walking	26.9	23.9
Tennis	21.6	17.1
Cross Training	18.5	19.7
Basketball	14.9	17.0
Baseball	13.7	13.5
Running	9.3	11.9
Sport Sandals	4.7	3.9
Hiking	4.5	4.6

Source: 1996 NPD/SMART Consumer Panel.

Exhibit 5.4   Category volume by gender/1996 dollar %

Males 12+ (%)		Females 12+ (%)	
Basketball	25.0	Cross Training	22.2
Cross Training	18.9	Walking	14.9
Running	12.7	Running	13.0
Hiking	8.3	Aerobics	10.7
Athleisure	7.9	Athleisure	10.6
Walking	6.0	Tennis	7.1
Tennis	5.4	Basketball	6.8
Sport Sandals	1.7	Hiking	5.4
Baseball	1.6	Sport Sandals	2.8

Source: 1996 NPD/SMART Consumer Panel.

ued to grow, even among a younger 18–24 consumer age category, and almost all local and regional road races now contained walking divisions. The tennis category, one of Reebok's perennial strengths, had been flat over the past several years. Other trends and sales figures pointed to an increase in up-and-coming or alternative sports—soccer, in-line skating, snowboarding, mountain biking, and BMX riding—sports that were capturing increasing shares of the critical youth market's (ages 12–17) share of participation and spending.

Whereas during the 1970s and 1980s the athletic footwear market centered primarily around a few core categories—basketball, tennis, running, and fitness shoes—the levels of product segmentation had exploded between the late 1980s and 1997, and now one could find a "sneaker" for every conceivable sport or activity, from cross-training and preseason football training to run/walk, Versatraining (Reebok) and Total Body Conditioning (Nike). As the U.S. athletic footwear market matured, companies began to attempt to capture larger shares of this maturing consumer base by segmenting their product offerings based upon more specialized consumer needs.

The rapid development and acceptance of new footwear technology, led by the introduction of Nike Air in 1979, led to a proliferation of technical developments in the 1980s and 1990s. Almost every athletic footwear brand had some type of proprietary system: Reebok introduced technologies such as Hexalite in the 1980s, the Pump® in 1990, and DMX 2000 in early 1997; other key technologies included Nike Air, adidas Feet You Wear, Asics Gel, Saucony GRID, and Brooks HydroFlow. Although these brands found it difficult to quantify the direct benefits of their technologies in terms of an athlete's performance, these proprietary technologies did help to separate their products from the influx of sport fashion brands, creating a barrier to entry in this sports performance product segment.

New sport fashion brands entering the athletic footwear market included well-known companies such as Tommy Hilfiger, Ralph Lauren and Polo Sport, Nautica, and Donna Karan (DKNY). These brands all had significant fashion and apparel strengths and were now entering the sport performance domain of Reebok, Nike, adidas, and Fila. They were well positioned to capitalize on the broad and growing consumer appeal of athletic footwear as fashionable and "cool." In response to this trend, Reebok, in April 1996, signed a licensing agreement with Ralph Lauren to design and distribute footwear under the Ralph Lauren and Polo Sport labels. Salomon Brothers, Inc., projected that U.S. wholesale revenues from these brands alone would reach $580 million by year-end 1999.[2]

---

2. "The Athletic Footwear and Apparel Industry," Brett Barakett, December 3, 1996, Salomon Brothers Inc.

The Consumer

In the 1990s, as athletic footwear became more of a popular culture symbol of fashion, status, and "cool," it also became clear that in general only 20% of athletic footwear purchased in the United States was actually being used for the activity for which it was designed. Basketball, cross-training, and running shoes, and sport sandals were worn widely for style and comfort, not for their particular intended use. Although this phenomenon helped significantly to widen the potential consumer base, it also added complexity and scope to the marketing of these products. Because of the increased fashion element of the athletic footwear purchase, the consumer evolved into a much more fickle and dynamic moving target.

Purchase activity and frequency also began to shift, from the traditionally stronger consumer groups—the 25–39 and 40–59-year-old consumer having the largest share of disposable income—to the increasingly powerful 12–17 and 18–24-year-old consumer, who exhibited the highest purchase frequency and who bought footwear more for style and status than for the actual sport-specific activity. This shift in purchase behavior and frequency, in part attributable to Nike's successful line of Air Jordan footwear introduced in 1985, raised the ante in what had been a fairly straightforward game of reaching the consumer: focus on the sport, build a product around it, communicate a relevant message, and associate it to a relevant athlete or team. Exhibit 5.5 details industry market share by brand and consumer age group, and Exhibit 5.6 shows the average retail price paid for athletic footwear by gender and by age group.

Exhibit 5.5   Brand performance by age/1996 dollar %

12–17 (%)		18–24 (%)		25–34 (%)	
Nike	55.7	Nike	49.2	Nike	36.5
Reebok	12.2	Reebok	13.3	Reebok	21.1
Fila	6.2	Fila	5.1	Fila	3.3
adidas	5.2	adidas	3.3	Asics	2.2
Airwalk	2.7	Timberland	1.9	New Balance	2.1
35–44 (%)		**45–54 (%)**		**55+ (%)**	
Nike	28.2	Reebok	23.7	Reebok	20.3
Reebok	23.3	Nike	19.3	Nike	11.1
New Balance	3.7	New Balance	5.8	Easy Spirit	9.5
Fila	2.4	Easy Spirit	4.4	Rockport	5.6
Asics	2.4	Rockport	3.6	New Balance	4.9

Source: 1996 NPD/SMART Consumer Panel.

Exhibit 5.6 Average price profile/total athletic footwear 1996

Age						
4–11	**12–17**	**18–24**	**25–34**	**35–44**	**45–54**	**55+**
$29	$53	$51	$43	$41	$42	$39

Gender	
MALES	FEMALES
$45	$38

Source: 1996 NPD/SMART Consumer Panel.

By the 1990s, the stakes had become even higher. As consumer purchases grew, more and more footwear styles were developed to meet the demand, or to create new avenues of demand, and the marketing programs behind those products became more expansive and complex. A basketball, running, or cross-training shoe had to do more than perform; it had to trigger an emotional or culture-based attachment that placed it above the myriad of other footwear available. This meant a greater emphasis on the total marketing package in support of the shoe, including the marketing element of athlete, sports marketing, and advertising and retail presence. The cost of athlete, team, and league sponsorships skyrocketed, yet these elements became increasingly critical to reaching the 12–17 market. The investments were high, yet one *absolutely had to play* in this game to effectively reach that critical consumer base.

Reebok's share of this important 12–17 consumer segment had fallen since 1994. Its product range was seen as stale, its athletes were not as inspirational or recognized as Nike's, and as Bob Meers stated regarding it's "Planet Reebok" and "This Is My Planet" advertising campaign:

> It [Planet Reebok] succeeded in raising the profile of key Reebok endorsers, extending our involvement beyond traditional sports and reconnecting with our core fitness constituency. However, it failed to ignite a passion for the brand among our target consumers: young, physically active men and women and trend-setting teens.[3]

Further, Reebok's share of the 18–34 consumer also had fallen since 1994. This consumer group placed a higher level of importance on the specific performance attributes of a footwear model than did the 12–17 segment. Reebok's past heritage, exemplified by the successes of its Classics category (Reebok's line of sport casual footwear, including the

---

3. *Source:* 1996 Reebok International Ltd. Annual Report.

Freestyle), did not fully support its desired sports performance image with this 18–34 consumer, as evidenced in the brand perception map illustrated in Exhibit 5.7 and based upon recent 18–34-year-old consumer focus groups. Exhibit 5.8 reports brand performance by gender and Exhibit 5.9 reports age distribution in percentage of dollars spent on U.S. athletic footwear.

The Competitive Arena

Nike dominated the U.S. athletic footwear market with a 34.7% share in 1996, followed by Reebok's 17.7% share, then Fila at 3.6%, and

Exhibit 5.7   Brand perception map

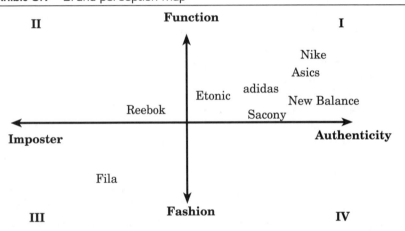

Source: Reebok Marketing, Consumer Focus Groups.

Exhibit 5.8   Brand performance by gender/total U.S. athletic footwear market 1996 dollar %

Males 12+ [%]		% Vol. (+/−) 96/95	Females 12+ [%]	% Vol. (+/−) 96/95
Nike	40	19	30	26
Reebok	15	−8	22	0
New Balance	4	19	2	27
Fila	4	27	3	50
Converse	2	−14	NA	NA
adidas	4	36	2	40
Asics	2	0	NA	NA

Source: 1996 NPD/SMART Consumer Panel.

Exhibit 5.9 Age distribution in percentages of $ spent/total U.S. athletic footwear

Age	% Spent of Total
<12	11.9
12–17	17.4
18–24	10.5
25–34	20.7
35–44	15.5
45–54	11.1
55 +	11.7

Source: 1996 NPD/SMART Consumer Panel.

adidas at 2.5%. Several second-tier companies (Asics, New Balance, Avia, Puma, Saucony, Etonic, and Brooks) carved out successful niche businesses in various performance segments, particularly the running category. Other companies placed great emphasis on styling and fashion appeal and less on performance, including LA Gear and British Knights; these brands had seen sharp declines in market share performance during the mid-1990s as consumer tastes shifted from pure fashion to both style *and* function.

Nike

Nike's successes and growth stemmed from several areas:

- Its product and technology strengths and well-planned product and technology evolutions, such as its Air product;
- Its athlete stable, which contained some of the world's most talented and identifiable sports personalities;
- Its advertising communications, which were not only innovative, but entertaining and relevant to its consumer targets;
- Its retail presence, which commanded a greater percentage of prime in-store real estate than did its competition with eye-catching point-of-purchase displays; and,
- Its operational strengths, from customer service to distribution, which were world class.

Based upon 1996 media numbers, it also significantly outspent its competitors in TV, print, outdoor, and radio advertising. Nike was the market leader and had shown no signs of its business and brand popularity slowing down.

adidas

adidas, for many years, was the global leader in the athletic footwear and apparel business and still presently holds a #1 share within specific markets, such as Germany. Founded by Adolph Dassler in the 1920s, adidas developed sport-specific shoes for elite athletes in dozens of sports (much like Foster & Sons), from running and soccer to fencing and weightlifting. In the early 1990s, U.S. retailers, due to its world-wide market strengths, financial assets, and relative underperformance in the United States, looked at adidas as a "sleeping giant." By 1993, adidas had upgraded its footwear line and styling in running, tennis, adventure sports, cross training, and basketball, and its U.S. business subsequently began to pick up. The distribution problems that had plagued adidas U.S.A. began to subside, and the "retro" look so popular in the mid-1990s elevated adidas, because of its authentic sports heritage, to one of the most sought-after footwear brands.

adidas recently launched a global line of footwear, including running and basketball shoes, behind the "Feet You Wear" technology concept (according to specialty retailers in the United States, however, this launch has experienced limited success). adidas also recently signed several major sports marketing assets in the Unitd States, including a $90-million/10-year-plus deal with the New York Yankees and collegiate agreements with schools such as Notre Dame.

Fila

While Fila did not have the performance history of Nike or adidas, it too made its initial mark on the sports scene in performance sports as an upscale Italian tennis footwear and apparel brand. Fila became a hot fashion item during the late 1980s and 1990s among 12–24-year-old consumers in urban markets such as Detroit and Atlanta. However, to protect its revenue stream from the vagaries of fashion, style, and status, Fila began seeking out and signing high-profile endorsees such as Jamal Mashburn, Jerry Stackhouse, and Grant Hill of the NBA, and world-class runners such as Cosmos Ndeti and German Silva. Products for these athletes now contained a footwear technology that Fila had been aggressively promoting: the Fila 2A cushioning system. Fila had also recently expanded its push in the women's market with a multiple-page print insert featuring female athletes and compelling photography in core women's magazines. To further its sports-authenticity push, Fila recently opened a satellite design studio in Boulder, Colorado, to focus on products for the adventure and outdoor sports enthusiast.

Asics

Asics has seen its U.S. revenues grow substantially since 1985 due to its strengths with the serious running enthusiast. Its running product line was embraced by the running community; runners and Asics devotees provided Asics with the type of sports credibility that makes a brand "cool" and accepted within the 12–24 age segment. Asics attempted to branch off into other footwear categories in the United States, including cross training and basketball, but with limited success, in large part due to these categories' significant barriers of entry, including sports marketing and advertising investment requirements.

Second-Tier Companies

The smaller and more specialized second-tier companies, such as New Balance, Saucony, Avia, Etonic, Puma, and Brooks, have gained niche followings among the sport-specific consumer who looks to these brands for specialized benefits. New Balance, for instance, specializes in width sizing; Saucony maintains a popular fit in its running shoes, especially among women; Avia has in the past developed a strong women's fitness following; and Etonic, Puma, and Brooks have concentrated on the running enthusiast to the exclusion of other categories, except for the addition of soccer by Puma and walking and golf by Etonic.

Brand Positioning

To better track brand positioning, Brett Barakett, equity analyst for Salomon Brothers, developed two measures illustrating the relative position of the major athletic footwear brands within the performance–athletic/fashion–athletic continuum. The first measure shows the spectrum of athletic brands on the performance/fashion scale:

Performance Athletic   **Fashion Athletic**

◄───►

Nike   Reebok   Fila   Polo Sport   Adidas   Nautica
                                                          Tommy Hilfiger
                                                          Donna Karan

The second is Salomon Brothers' Fashion Risk Factor (FRF), which rates the brands' risk levels associated with the changing tides of fashion. A lower FRF rating means that less of a company's revenues are tied to fashion, thus lowering the risk of the brand being suddenly found out of style or out of fashion. Reebok was rated the lowest FRF at 40%; Nike's FRF was rated at 50% and Fila's at 80%.

Exhibit 5.10 shows brand performance by retail price.

The Retail Channels

NPD/SMART Consumer Panel data showed that all key sales channels in which Reebok competed experienced growth in 1996, with athletic specialty stores showing the largest increase (+12%) over 1995 levels. The distribution of athletic footwear volume by U.S. retail channel is outlined in Exhibit 5.11. The athletic specialty channel was up 12% versus 1995 levels, pro shops were down 1%, discount chains were down 4%, department stores were up 5%, and family shoe stores gained 7%. Reebok's 1996 volume distribution is shown in the following table:

Channel	Reebok % of Revenues	% Chg. vs. '95
General sporting goods	11	−7
Pro shops	1	−30
Discount stores	8	−6
Department stores	37	−6
Athletic specialty	16	−9
Family shoe	7	+2
All other	20	N/A

Exhibit 5.10   Brand performance by retail price/1996 unit %

$30–$40		$40–$50		$50–$60	
Nike	26.0%	Nike	32.1%	Nike	38.5%
Reebok	24.9	Reebok	13.3	Reebok	24.0
LA Gear	3.9	Fila	3.5	Fila	4.4
Converse	3.3	adidas	3.3	adidas	3.5
Keds	3.3	LA Gear	2.2	New Balance	3.0
$60–$70		$70–$85		$85–$100	
Nike	43.7%	Nike	48.0%	Nike	53.3%
Reebok	19.5	Reebok	12.4	Reebok	8.3
Fila	4.9	Fila	6.4	Fila	5.2
New Balance	3.8	Easy Spirit	5.3	New Balance	3.7
Easy Spirit	3.2	New Balance	4.3	Timberland	3.4

Source: 1996 NPD/SMART Consumer Panel.

Exhibit 5.11 Distribution of brand volume by channel/total U.S. athletic footwear

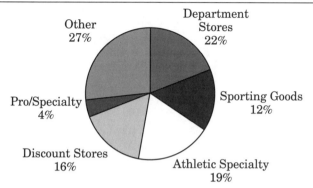

Source: 1996 NPD/SMART Consumer Panel.

Exhibit 5.12 shows the average brand retail selling price. Exhibit 5.13 shows the average retail price by retail channel, and Exhibit 5.14 details the distribution of brand volume by retail channel. The general sporting goods and athletic specialty channels were most frequented by the 12–17 and 18–24 age groups, the department store channel by the 35–44, 45–54, and 55+ age groups.

Experience showed that the national athletic specialty chains (such as Footlocker, Footaction, and Finish Line), catering to a younger, fashion-driven and typically "nonathletic" consumers, looked to a brand's performance image as a barometer of success and appeal within this younger 12–24-year-old market. This national athletic trade

Exhibit 5.12 Average brand retail selling price—overall

Brand	Selling Price ($)
Nike	57.82
Reebok	45.72
New Balance	57.70
Asics	52.32
Converse	37.01
adidas	46.14
Fila	55.29
LA Gear	29.66
Market Average	**41.20**

Source: 1996 NPD/SMART Consumer Panel.

Exhibit 5.13 Average price within retail outlet/total 1996 athletic footwear

Retail Channel	Average Retail Price ($)	% Chg. 96/95
Total market	41.20	7
General sporting goods	50.97	6
Athletic specialty	59.86	3
Pro shops	62.97	2
Department stores	43.63	6
Discount stores	21.55	4
Family shoe stores	46.23	12

Source: 1996 NPD/SMART Consumer Panel.

Exhibit 5.14 Distribution of brand volume by retail channel/total 1996 athletic footwear dollars

	adidas	Fila	Nike	Reebok
General sporting goods	20%	11%	18%	11%
Athletic specialty	30	39	33	16
Pro shops	6	3	NA	NA
Department stores	16	15	20	37
Discount stores	8	6	5	8
Family shoe stores	5	9	6	7
All other	15	17	16	20

Source: 1996 NPD/SMART Consumer Panel.

channel represented a significant level of footwear volume and Reebok felt it was therefore a critical channel to reach. Exhibit 5.15 highlights brand performance by retail channel.

Both Reebok and Nike also operate their own retail stores, which include brand concept stores that feature new and complete product lines and merchandising systems, and outlet stores that allow for excess inventory to be sold in a controlled environment. Not only do these brand-specific retail stores allow for more control over the selling process and environment they also deliver higher company profit margins on products sold, as the third-party retailer is eliminated from the distribution chain. Reebok owns and operates approximately 100 outlet stores, whose stated and primary objectives are to help liquidate excess inventory and to enhance the Reebok brand. Reebok also has several brand concept stores, including four in New York City and one in King of Prussia, Pennsylvania. Nike operates several "Niketown" concept stores in major markets, such as Chicago, San Francisco, New York, Boston, and Portland (Oregon), that have proved to be more than merely

Exhibit 5.15   Brand performance by retail channel/1996 dollar %

General Sporting Goods		Athletic Specialty Stores	
Nike	48.4%	Nike	57.6%
Reebok	15.2	Reebok	14.5
adidas	4.0	Fila	7.0
Asics	3.7	adidas	3.8
Fila	3.0	New Balance	3.0
Department Stores		**Pro Shops**	
Nike	31.9%	Nike	23.1%
Reebok	29.3	Foot-Joy	6.5
Keds	4.1	Reebok	5.9
Easy Spirit	3.9	New Balance	4.9
Fila	2.4	adidas	4.3

Source: 1996 NPD/SMART Consumer Panel.

retail locations; in many cases they are viewed as veritable sports museums (Niketown Chicago is one of that city's top tourist draws). By nature of its retail stores, Nike finished 1996 as the thirty-fourth largest sporting goods retailer in the United States. The downside of the brand-operated concept and outlet store is that each potentially takes sales away from the core retailer base; in essence, pitting the supplier against the retailer.

Reebok's Marketing Elements

Product

Reebok designs and markets sports, fitness, and casual footwear, apparel, and equipment sold in approximately 170 countries. Footwear and apparel categories are sport specific and include

- Basketball
- Cleated (baseball, soccer, football, and rugby)
- Women's sports (volleyball, softball, and basketball)
- Women's training and walking
- Running and track & field
- Cross training
- Tennis
- Classics
- Adventure sports (mountain biking, trail running, hiking)
- Kids

Reebok's largest volume categories in the United States include classics, basketball, cross training, women's sports, and women's fitness. Typically, Reebok will market over 600 individual styles of footwear in a particular season and even more styles of apparel. In addition, special make-ups—shoes developed with custom colors or designs that offer key national or regional accounts a special product point-of-difference—account for over 100 seasonal styles as well. Suggested retail prices for Reebok's footwear range from $30 to $120, depending on the specific style. Competitive brands' suggested retail pricing windows include: Nike, $30 to $180; adidas, $40 to $100; Fila, $30 to $125; Asics, $30 to $125.

A common retailer issue with Reebok's technology introductions is that Reebok historically has had a portfolio of too many technologies. Technology introductions over the years include Dynamic Cushioning, Hexalite, Viz Hex, Radial Hex, Suspended Hex, Hytrel, DMX, DMX Series 2000, 3D Ultralite, The Pump, Graphlite, and Hexliner. Past technologies, such as Dynamic Cushioning used in Reebok's walking category, were developed outside the company, thus requiring Reebok to pay royalties on each pair sold. The Reebok Development Center, a multimillion dollar design, development, and manufacturing facility in Stoughton (completed in 1996), now enables Reebok to control its own technology development. An Advanced Technologies Group is responsible for creating and commercializing future technologies, generally working within a 2–3 year development window. This facility also allows Reebok to test new manufacturing techniques for use with its Far East production sources.

Reebok's footwear production sources consist of independent factories (not company owned) in China, Indonesia, Thailand, Korea, the Philippines, and Vietnam. Reebok also operates a development center in Korea, as well as production offices in each country where its footwear is sourced. These factories produce footwear to the design and development specifications provided by the U.S.-based Reebok Design and Development departments.

The development process actually begins with a product brief created by Reebok's product marketing team (in some cases with the added input of specific endorsed athletes). Then, several designs are created based upon that brief, and the designers and developers work with the factories to "commercialize" the actual product (including sample development, fit testing, costing, and final production). In the past, the initial hand-drawn designs were manually transferred to blueprints. These blueprints were then sent by mail to the development office in the Far East to begin production tooling. Prototype samples were produced, modified, and wear tested so that the final sample could be confirmed (correct colors, materials, dimensions, and fit) for retail production. Depending on the complexity of the product, the development window from product brief to retail introduction was eighteen months to three years. Inherent in this process were the many iterations and quality checkpoints required within the product design and development cycle arising from manually drawn blueprint accuracy and language barriers between the United States and the Far East, new pilot production processes, and the actual time spent shipping prototypes back and forth between the Far East development offices and Reebok U.S. Between their newly completed development center and investments in computer-aided design and manufacturing equipment, Reebok management hopes to improve upon this design, development, and production process through further investments in technology.

Advertising

Over the past ten years, Reebok launched over seven advertising campaigns, unlike Nike, whose "Just Do It" campaign was long lived. Due to this frequent turnover of campaigns, themes, and messages, it was widely held in the industry that Reebok's lack of advertising message consistency led to a mixed and unclear consumer and retailer perception of what the Reebok brand stood for. Following is a list of the seven advertising campaigns:

1987   "LIFE IS NOT A SPECTATOR SPORT"
Helped reaffirm Reebok's commitment to, and strength within, the women's fitness movement.

1989   "UBU"
Critically acclaimed for stand-out creativity, "UBU" was launched in 1989 and received positive remarks for its unique TV and print executions, yet the campaign also lacked integration with the industry backdrop of sports performance.

1990   "LIFE IS SHORT. PLAY HARD."
Consumer feedback and campaign recognition was positive, and in-store displays tied in well with the print and TV advertising. "Life Is Short . . ." helped launch The Pump in 1990 with the "Sky Surfer" TV spot showing a surfer released from a plane firmly attached to his board, thanks to his Pump footwear. In addition, the "Bungee" TV spot featured two bungee jumpers, one who survived the jump, one who did not, implying that the non-Pump wearer slipped off the end of his bungee cord. The bungee spot was subsequently pulled from the air after numerous viewer complaints.

1992   "I BELIEVE . . ."
The "I Believe . . ." campaign, focusing on the female fitness enthusiast, did reach the target consumer with what was viewed as a meaning-

ful message with impact. This campaign was especially popular with the female consumer.

1993 "PLANET REEBOK"
The Planet Reebok campaign sought to create a truly global and integrated advertising platform, in which Reebok markets around the world would execute a common platform, with minimal customization or departure from this theme. Subsequent brand-image studies, however, showed that the "Planet Reebok" concept did not reach the consumer, young or old, with a resonant and compelling reason to buy Reebok.

1995 "THIS IS MY PLANET"
Reebok's 1994 U.S. revenues and market share had fallen from the previous year and, based upon studies showing that "Planet Reebok" was not delivering a compelling and personal reason to choose Reebok, the "This Is My Planet" campaign was introduced to deliver the human and personal element that Reebok management felt was lacking. It helped elevate Reebok endorsers in the minds of the consumer, yet combined with relatively weak product offerings, it failed to jump-start the brand as management had hoped.

1997 "REALITY"
In 1997, Reebok began to roll out what the company referred to as "Reality" spots. These TV and print ads were developed to shift the brand message to one of substance and credibility. Athletes were shown in settings natural to their personas, whether it was Allen Iverson getting ready to play his first game as a Philadelphia 76er, or Shaquille O'Neal riding around L.A. with his friends in the back seat of a convertible.

1996 saw a dramatic increase in total athletic footwear industry advertising spending, in part attributable to heavy television spending around the Olympic Games. Industry and Reebok brand spending totaled $328.4 million and $89.1 million, respectively, as illustrated in the following chart:[4]

Industry Spending	1993	1994	1995	1996
Industry	$261.9 MM	$258.7 MM	$261.6 MM	$328.4 MM
Reebok	$62.2 MM	$59.7 MM	$58.9 MM	$89.1 MM
Nike	$130.4 MM	$128.6 MM	$138.8 MM	$182.6 MM

---

4. *Source:* Leo Burnett and Adviews, 1996 Competitive Spending.

Other brands' 1996 advertising spending was as follows: adidas at $15.5 MM, Fila at $14.9 MM, LA Gear at $5.7 MM, Converse at $5.2 MM, and New Balance at $2.6 MM. adidas' 1996 spending increased 188%, Fila's spending increased 9%, and Converse's spending fell 59% from the previous year (1995). Industry spending was allocated to TV, followed by print, radio, and outdoor expenditures. Reebok's media mix paralleled the total industry: TV (75%), print (23%), radio (2%), and outdoor (1%).

Sports Marketing

Beginning in 1991 and 1992, Reebok's senior management dramatically shifted the "playing fields" on which Reebok was competing. Nike had overtaken Reebok as the industry's #1 U.S. athletic footwear and apparel marketer in 1989 and was widely seen as THE sports performance brand for athletes of all ages. Nike had the athletes—Michael Jordan, Andre Agassi, John McEnroe, and multisports personality Bo Jackson—along with a solid and technical product line. In response, Fireman issued a decree that, by 1996, Reebok would have become a major player on the playing fields and running tracks of the world. The strategy was to dramatically shift Reebok from a fashion athletic to a performance athletic brand through sports marketing investment in high-profile athletes, teams, and leagues.

One of the athletic footwear industry's significant barriers to entry has always been the tremendous investment needed to sign, support, and promote high-level athletes, teams, and leagues. Only a handful of companies in the industry have this capability, and Reebok was one of them. Over the next four years, between 1992 and 1996, Reebok invested heavily in sports marketing assets:

Football

Athletes	Emmit Smith, Herman Moore, John Elway, Greg Lloyd
NFL Teams	Detroit Lions, San Francisco 49ers, New Orleans Saints, New York Giants

Basketball

Athletes	Rebecca Lobo, Saadia Roundtree, Jennifer Azzi
Leagues	A.B.L. and WNBA (Women's Professional Basketball Leagues)

Baseball

Athletes	Roger Clemens, Mo Vaughn, Frank Thomas, Mark McGuire

Soccer

Athletes	Eric Wynalda, Julie Foudy, Michelle Akers
Teams	New England Revolution (MLS), Liverpool Soccer Club, Argentina national team

By 1996, Reebok was able to outfit 3,000 athletes at the Atlanta Games in contrast to the year 1992, in which 200 Olympians were outfitted in Reebok footwear and apparel in Barcelona. The level of investment was high, particularly in comparison with the athlete investment levels of the 1970s and early 1980s, when a company might pay an athlete hundreds or thousands of dollars to compete in its shoes. By the 1990s, the costs to compete in this sports marketing arena had risen dramatically, as evidenced by the following:

- Multimillion dollar shoe contracts commanded by athletes such as Tiger Woods, Michael Jordan, Allen Iverson, and Grant Hill
- Soccer sponsorships such as the Italian national team (Nike $20 million/four years), Manchester United (Umbro $90 million/six years), Liverpool ($38 million/five years), Argentine national team (Reebok $60 million/eight years) and Brazilian national team (Nike $220 million/ten years)
- Team sponsorships such as the adidas/New York Yankees deal, which reportedly would cost adidas $90 million over ten years

Another element to be considered in these aforementioned investments was the return that the brands could generate by selling licensed team merchandise, such as replica jerseys and apparel with the team logos. For example, Reebok booked over $40 million of orders for Liverpool replica jerseys during the first year of their contract.

Retail Presence

A critical element in an athletic footwear brand's ultimate retail success and consumer image is how that brand appears at the retail, or store, level. Purchase behavior studies have shown that it is here at the retail point-of-purchase where the consumer's brand associations, in many cases, are confirmed, confused, or contradicted. Brands such as Nike, adidas, Fila, and Reebok invest heavily in generating in-store displays that support both the brand image and the product on the store wall. The primary objective is to create a brand-concept zone within the store in which to better communicate the brand's unique selling proposition and image by way of athlete, product, technologies, and coordinated footwear and apparel collections. As a result of their market share and retail-presence investments, Reebok and Nike are able to command significant store presence with "store-within-a-store" concept zones. This ability to create strong retail presence at the store level potentially amounts to another competitive barrier of entry.

Furthermore, several companies (including Reebok, Nike, and adidas) have employed technical representatives (tech reps), whose roles are to educate the retail sales associate regarding new products and technologies, athlete and product associations, and new marketing/advertising programs. These "brand-builders" also conduct retail associate clinics and attend events such as road races or soccer tournaments to directly convey their brand's message to both the retailer and consumer.

Summary

From a company with its roots and beginnings dating back to 1895, Reebok International had experienced a tremendous modern-day growth rate. Sales had risen to $3.5 billion in 1996 from $1.3 million in 1982. Yet, neither Reebok management nor the investment community was satisfied. Since 1994, revenues had remained flat and net income had declined. Equally disturbing was the drop in market share within critical consumer segments. Other competitors, including Nike, adidas, and Fila, had gained momentum and market share over the past several years, in part at Reebok's expense, and while the retail community saw promise and potential, as of 1996 it still remained skeptical of Reebok's ability to regain both its past strengths and its share of consumers' feet.

Obviously, Reebok Division senior management faced several challenges and subsequent decisions that would help shape the brand's image and determine its growth and profitability towards the year 2000 and beyond. In the context of a maturing market, an increasingly sophisticated consumer, rising advertising and sports marketing investment levels, and increased competition, the athletic footwear "game" was certainly being contested on a playing field much different from the one on which Fosters & Sons had competed back in 1895, and this new playing field had shifted even more in recent years.

Reebok management believed that the direction it had recently charted for the brand on this new playing field would indeed return it to profitability and growth in the years ahead.

6

Reebok (B): The Reebok Running Category

Andy Rohm

Introduction

Sharon Golden gazed out at the company's basketball and tennis courts from the fourth-floor conference room window at Reebok International Ltd. headquarters. She and her colleagues were finalizing the Running category's marketing plans for 1997, plans that she had to present to Reebok's brand marketing senior management in five days. It had been weeks since Sharon had made it outside at lunch for a run or a game of tennis and she mused to herself that she was letting work get in the way of her passion for sports.

Not quite so amusing was the issue at hand—the upcoming presentation and how Reebok Running (RR) was going to strengthen its image and position during the coming year among serious running consumers, consumers who had placed Reebok a distant #5 in recent running brand-preference and ownership studies.

One of Golden's and her team's goals was to elevate Reebok to a top three preference and ownership position among serious runners by the end of 1998. Golden's job was to ensure that RR's planned 1997 marketing mix would deliver the "impact" needed to elevate the current perception of RR as one of a credible and legitimate running brand. She and her team also needed to decide how RR was going to foster a solid relationship with running consumers and convert them into long-term "Reebok Running advocates." And, given Reebok's history and current market position, Golden asked herself whether RR was focusing the necessary yet finite resources to meet its objective of delivering the most effective and breakthrough marketing elements possible. In the face of these difficult "marketing mix" decisions that lay ahead, Sharon again fixed her thoughts back on her team's final and critical 1997 marketing strategy planning session.

Background

The world's #2 athletic footwear and apparel brand, Reebok originally began as the J.W. Foster Company in 1895 in Bolton, England. Joseph William Foster, a young and dedicated runner and founder of the J.W. Foster Company, produced custom-made cross-country spikes for a majority of England's top runners. Before long, Foster was building shoes for England's elite runners, including Harold Abrahams and Eric Liddle of Academy Award-winning *Chariots of Fire* fame, who won gold medals wearing "Fosters" in the 1924 Paris Games. Over the years, the J.W. Foster Company formed close relationships with local English running clubs and athletes, subsequently forming the foundation for what is now Reebok International.

Modern-Day Reebok

Although its roots and heritage were grounded in the running market dating back to 1895, modern-day Reebok, as detailed in the Reebok (A) case, experienced terrific success throughout the 1980s by introducing not a running shoe, but the first athletic shoe designed for women, the Freestyle™ aerobics shoe. By 1992, the Freestyle had become the industry's #1 selling athletic shoe as Reebok sales reached over $3 billion from a level of $1.3 million back in 1982.

Reebok's yearly growth was fueled by footwear like the Freestyle that, as had the original "Fosters," met the needs of a fast-growing and opportunity-filled fitness market. This growth occurred within three general footwear segments: (1) women's fitness; (2) walking; and (3) a comfort–casual category called "Classics." Reebok captured the #1 market share position during the mid-1980s. Reebok held a "bond" and relationship with the female fitness enthusiast that was second to none.

Reebok Running's Current Market Position

Modern-day Reebok's competitive strengths, developed during the fitness boom of the 1980s, also led to a broad consumer perception that the Reebok brand was not connected to true and authentic performance. During the same period, Nike in 1989 had regained the #1 share of the U.S. athletic footwear market—34.7% share versus Reebok's 17.7% (NPD/SMART Consumer Panel)—with a combination of exciting, timely product and inspirational, compelling athletes such as Michael Jordan.

In 1996, approximately $1.7 billion in running footwear was sold in the United States at retail (NPD/SMART Consumer Panel). Reebok's 1996 market share of this running footwear market was 11.9% (Exhibit 6.1), #2 behind Nike's 44.8% share. In addition to being far behind Nike in overall running share, of equal concern to Golden was that Reebok currently held only a #5 share within the *performance* running footwear segment, defined as footwear at $75+ retail (Exhibits 6.2 and 6.3).

Golden and her team felt that RR had to aggressively re-establish a legitimacy- and credibility-based relationship with two targets: (1) the serious running enthusiast and (2) the running specialty dealer. Golden also believed that the independent running-specialty dealer

Exhibit 6.1 1996 market share U.S. athletic footwear market

	Overall (%)	*Running (%)*
Nike	34.7	44.8
Reebok	17.7	11.9
Asics	1.6	8.8
Saucony	0.8	7.0
New Balance	2.5	7.0
adidas	2.5	3.8
Fila	3.6	1.5

Source: 1996 NPD/SMART Consumer Panel.

Exhibit 6.2 Last running brand purchased

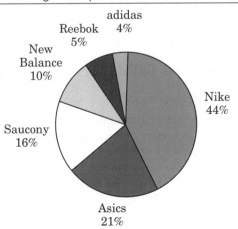

adidas 4%
Reebok 5%
New Balance 10%
Saucony 16%
Asics 21%
Nike 44%

Source: 1996 *Runner's World* Subscriber Study.

Exhibit 6.3 Current running brand ownership

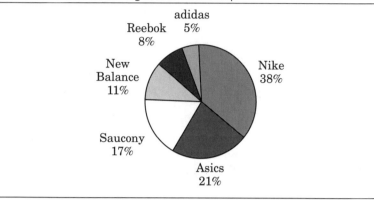

Source: 1996 *Runner's World* Subscriber Study.

network, with a base of approximately 350 stores in the United States, served as a critical conduit to the target running enthusiast and consumer.

Moreover, experience showed that the national athletic specialty chains such as Footlocker, Footaction, and Finish Line (to name a few), catering to a younger, fashion-driven, and typically "nonrunning" consumer, looked to a running brand's performance image as a barometer of success and appeal within these younger 12–17- and 18–24-year-old markets. This national athletic trade channel represented a significant level of running footwear volume and RR felt it was therefore a critical channel to reach.

The Target Consumer

Golden and her RR team spent several weekends a year at road races and events such as the Boston and New York marathons, talking with and getting to know their target consumers, primarily the 25–44-year-old male/female active runner and, secondarily, the 14–22-year-old high school and collegiate runner. Based upon their findings, Golden developed a target consumer attribute hierarchy shown in Exhibit 6.4 that helped illustrate the three tiers of running consumer and their associated mindsets. Also, through industry publication-subscriber studies, focus groups, and one-on-one interviews, RR was able to identify several target consumer findings. They found that the core running consumer

- Is hesitant to change her/his running shoe if it performs to expectations;
- Keeps an eye out for new technologies and innovations;

Exhibit 6.4 The running consumer hierarchy

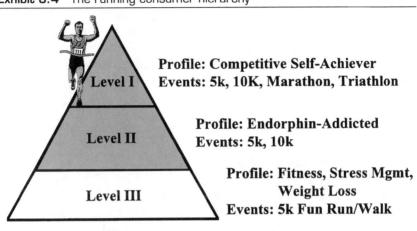

Profile: Competitive Self-Achiever
Events: 5k, 10K, Marathon, Triathlon

Profile: Endorphin-Addicted
Events: 5k, 10k

Profile: Fitness, Stress Mgmt, Weight Loss
Events: 5k Fun Run/Walk

Level I

Level II

Level III

Objective: Convert & Own Levels I & II

Source: Reebok Running Category.

- Is influenced in purchasing decisions by peers, magazine running shoe reviews, specialty running store recommendations, credible advertising, and brand presence at races and events;
- Feels that manufacturers change running styles too quickly, often for fashion's sake, not the runner's sake.

Exhibit 6.5 details the results of *Runner's World* magazine's 1996 subscriber study on running shoe purchase decision criteria, based upon surveys with their active runner/subscriber base.

Exhibit 6.5 Running shoe purchase decision criteria

Attribute	% Influenced
Fit & comfort	97.2
Injury prevention	83.5
Performance/Technology	83.2
Weight	49.1
Brand	42.9
Price	35.1
Appearance	23.5
Sales recommendation	22.8
Athlete sponsorship	<10.0

Source: 1996 *Runner's World* Subscriber Study.

After evaluating her team's findings gained from focus groups and interviews conducted at numerous events and races, Golden decided to "map" these findings based upon the target running consumer's brand perceptions and specific relationship-building Reebok "contact points" (Exhibits 6.6, 6.7, and 6.8). In theory, she felt that by knowing more about her target, she would be able to develop more impactful and relevant marketing plans that would "speak" more directly to her consumer.

The Total Footwear Market

The 1996 U.S. athletic footwear retail market reached $14.1 billion, or 342 million pairs of shoes sold, a growth of 6% in dollars and a decline of 1% in units as compared with 1995 levels. Basketball led all footwear categories with 20.1% of the market, followed by cross training at 17.0%, running at 11.4%, casual at 10.8%, hiking at 7.8%, and tennis at 7.2%. (Exhibit 6.9 shows 1996 brand performance by gender within this total athletic footwear market.) Exhibits 6.10–6.16 provide additional background information about the atheletic footwear market.

Exhibit 6.6   "Running" relationship contact map

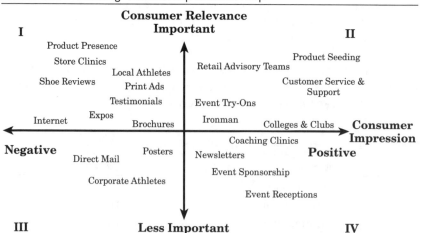

Quadrant I indicates elements of higher consumer importance that resulted in a negative consumer impression (i.e., Reebok fell short of the consumer's standard); *Quadrant II* indicates elements of higher consumer importance that resulted in a negative consumer impression; *Quadrant III* indicates elements of lesser consumer importance that resulted in a negative consumer impression; and *Quadrant IV* indicates elements of lesser consumer importance that resulted in a positive consumer impression.

Source: Reebok Running Category.

Exhibit 6.7 Brand perception map

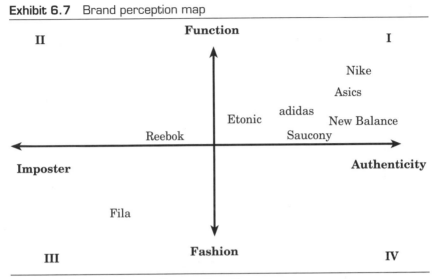

Source: Reebok Running Category, Consumer Focus Group.

Exhibit 6.8 Brand perception map

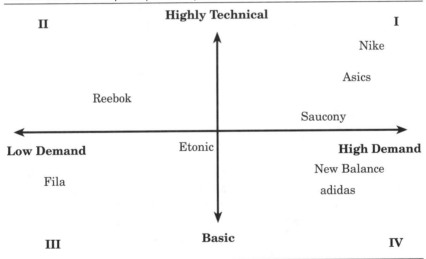

Source: Reebok Running Category, Consumer Focus Group.

Market Trends

The recent reports of a "second running boom," the first having occurred in the late 1960s and early 1970s, combined with increased participation in races such as the New York and Boston marathons, indicated

Exhibit 6.9   Brand performance by gender/total U.S. athletic footwear market/1996 dollar %

Males 12+		% Vol (+/−) 96/95	Females 12+	% Vol (+/−) 96/95
Nike	40%	19	30%	26
Reebok	15	−8	22	0
New Balance	4	19	2	27
Fila	4	27	3	50
Converse	2	−14	NA	NA
adidas	4	36	2	40
Asics	2	0	NA	NA

Source: 1996 NPD/SMART Consumer Panel.

Exhibit 6.10   Age distribution in percent of $$ spent/total U.S. athletic footwear

Age	% Spent of Total
<12	11.9
12–17	17.4
18–24	10.5
25–34	20.7
35–44	15.5
45–54	11.1
55+	11.7

Source: 1996 NPD/SMART Consumer Panel.

to RR that the market demand for performance running footwear would not lessen in the near future. However, other trends and sales figures pointed to an increase in up-and-coming or alternative sports—soccer, in-line skating, snowboarding, mountain biking, and BMX—sports that were capturing increasing shares of the younger market's (ages 12–24) participation and spending.

Even though running and track and field was still the #2 participatory sport in high schools across the United States, if these alternative sports trends continued, an entire generation of consumers would conceivably soon enter their prime spending and sports-participation years unaccustomed to running, track and field, or triathlon as sports and participatory activities. RR's 1997 marketing plan needed to somehow address this fact of dwindling running activity and interest within the active 12–24 consumer segment.

Exhibit 6.11   Reebok Running marketing spending by percentage
of total 1996/U.S. category budget

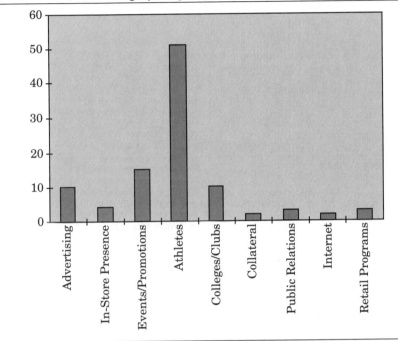

Source: Reebok Running Category.

Exhibit 6.12   Distribution of brand volume by channel/total U.S.
athletic footwear

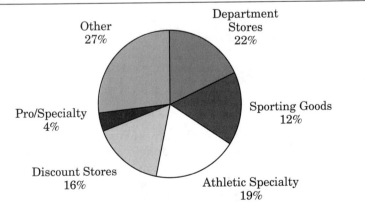

Source: 1996 NPD/SMART Consumer Panel.

Exhibit 6.13   Average brand retail selling price—running shoes

Brand	Selling Price
Nike	$63.85
Reebok	42.56
New Balance	62.61
Asics	57.51
Saucony	53.16
adidas	53.22
Fila	51.06
Market Average	54.43

Source: 1996 NPD/SMART Consumer Panel.

Exhibit 6.14   Running shoes purchased in last 6 months

# of Pairs	% Who Purchased
1–2	41.6%
3–4	32.3
5–6	13.5
7+	5.6

Source: 1996 *Runner's World* Subscriber Study.

Exhibit 6.15   *Running shoe purchase locations*

Channel	% Purchased
Running specialty	31.4%
Athletic specialty	26.4
Mail order	17.6
Sporting goods	9.2

Source: 1996 *Runner's World* Subscriber Study.

RR's Marketing Elements

Advertising

While on a run around New York's Central Park several months earlier with *Runner's World*'s advertising manager, Golden came upon an idea that fell directly in line with RR's mission to generate running credibility and legitimacy within the enthusiast market. In the face of a product miscue the year before that saw RR sales decline within the running and athletic specialty channels, Golden felt that something had to be done in the current year to communicate an RR message of running credibility and legitimacy. The result of this run–conversation was a

Exhibit 6.16 Running shoe retail price point distribution

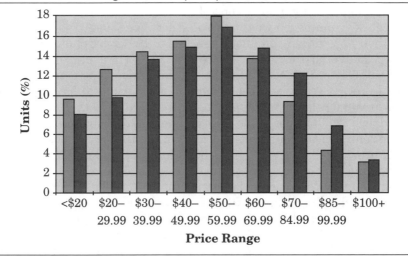

Source: 1996 NPD/SMART Consumer Panel.

three-part print advertisement series highlighting (1) Reebok's roots in running; (2) the role of Reebok's athletes in running product development; and (3) Reebok's running and track and field athletes and their preparation for the 1996 Atlanta Games.

Later in 1996, it was decided to shift the focus to a product-specific print execution. During subsequent meetings between RR and Advertising, the discussions centered around the long-term need for image-building advertising versus the immediate need for product-specific ads to generate retail sales. Golden asked the two groups: "Can we achieve both? How long would it take to build back credibility with the target consumer? Was advertising (print, TV, or outdoor) the most effective medium in which to rebuild this credibility base?"

Product

One of the key drivers of success within the U.S. athletic footwear industry is the extent to which specific brands' footwear introductions are received by the 12–17 male/female consumer and core 25–44 running consumer groups. RR's U.S. footwear volume had fallen 14% between 1993–1994, 16% between 1994–1995, and 20% between 1995–1996. To help reverse these lagging running bookings and consumer demand, major new technology and running product launches were slated for 1997. In support of this renewed focus on technology and innovation, Reebok had recently completed a multimillion dollar Reebok Development Center (RDC) with which to pioneer new technologies and manufacturing processes while quickening the prototype cycle and enhancing quality control.

Reebok's running footwear was priced between $30–$95 suggested retail; their new running products launched in 1997 were planned to have a suggested retail price of between $60 and $110. The average retail price for a pair of Reebok shoes was at the low end versus its primary competition. In recent years, no Reebok running shoe had sold for more than $100 except for the Instapump model introduced in 1992–1993 that retailed for $125. Because of the price and narrow distribution, the Instapump running shoe had limited success in the United States, although it performed well in several of Reebok's international markets such as France and Japan due to its technical nature and looks.

On average, Reebok would carry a running model a minimum of six months and a maximum of twenty-four months on the market. The trade off between the need to introduce fresh new styles versus the importance of listening to the demands of the core running consumer, who preferred consistency in running shoes, was a critical and difficult balance to achieve.

Retail Programs

One painfully obvious fact, revealed by RR's frequent visits to the field, was that Reebok had neither the confidence of, nor shelf space with, the running specialty dealer. Dealer comments were candid and direct regarding their perceived need for more attention and better service from Reebok. Their comments ranged from the need for more consistent products (to meet the demands of their customers) to better inventory management of key styles for reorders. The dealers felt that in general Reebok's higher-volume national accounts received a higher level of service and inventory priority. Reebok was viewed by these specialty dealers as a potentially powerful player in the running market, yet had to address several critical areas first.

In 1996, RR held three specialty dealer summits to gain input and ideas on how to work with and support this channel better. At one of the three summits, RR's designers and developers attended to listen and take note of the dealers' feedback. Also in 1996, RR attended over two dozen national or regional road races or triathlons, approximately 25% of which involved local retailers. Regarding sales programs, RR's trade discount programs were competitive. Several competing brands had specialty inventory programs that reserved "fill-in" inventory for running dealers; Reebok restocked the running dealer from a general inventory pool available to all other distribution channels. Finally, RR had recently instituted a road-race support program to further support the running dealer and the various local races with which they were involved. On the other hand, it was also evident that the running specialty channel was looking for RR to succeed, based upon past product successes, past and current athletes, and relationships with past and current RR personnel.

With all this in mind, Golden had to wonder if her team was doing enough for this specialty retail base. She wondered if the specialty retailer summits that RR conducted were productive tools to furthering partnerships with the dealers. Were they being executed correctly? Would RR's involvement with retailers at local events pay dividends?

Events/Promotions

The role of running, track and field, and multisport events and promotions within RR's relationship marketing process was two-fold:

1. To communicate directly with the running enthusiast, to exhibit new products, and to partner with a local retailer *at a local and regional level;*
2. To broadcast an image-building message on a larger scale, utilizing print and TV advertising, athletes, course signage, clinics, licensed product sales, product exhibits, and retail partnerships *at a national/ global level.*

Investment levels for local, regional, and national events varied widely, from hundreds of dollars on up at the local level to five- and six-figure investments at the national and global levels. Specific events that RR participated in during 1996 and Reebok's investment levels ($ = low; $$ = $10,000+; $$$ = $100,000+) included

Event	Sponsorship Level	Media Type
• Ironman World Championships (Exhibit 6.17)	$$$	National TV/print
• NYC Marathon	$$	Regional TV/print
• Boston Marathon	$$	Regional TV/print
• Mrs. T's Triathlon (Chicago)	$	Local TV/print
• Dallas White Rock Marathon	$	Local print

Golden's concern, one that she had voiced several times over, was that it was easy to invest finite budget dollars on events, yet seemingly difficult to measure the event return-on-investment. And it came as no surprise to Golden that event opportunities such as these, and the subsequent decisions as to whether to invest in the event, arose quite frequently. She felt that in too many instances, these decisions were made solely by intuition and not based on the end impact on the target running consumer.

Exhibit 6.17 Ironman® World Championships *Event Summary*

Location:	**Kona, Hawaii**
Event:	**2.4-mile ocean swim; 112-mile bike leg; 26.2-mile marathon run**
Timing:	**October**

Reebok's Involvement:

- Locensed Ironman performance footwear product
- A stable of world-class triathletes competing in the event and employed in the development and promotion of the Ironman footwear line
- On-site joint local retailer/Reebok store
- Course signage and banners
- Product expo and new product try-ons
- Key national account promotions
- Reebok athlete clinics and autograph sessions
- Press reception
- National network coverage on NBC's tape-delayed telecast
- Commercial units on NBC telecast
- Hospitality and VIP programs

Ironman sponsorship measurables include on-site retail store sales, total numbers of event attendees that visited our expo and try-on areas, press reception attendance and subsequent editorial features, race course banner placements, national account promotion sell-through results, quarterly Reebok Ironman product sales and futures bookings supported by direct mailings to all Ironman participants, and Ironman telecast ratings. The 1995 and 1996 national two-hour tape-delayed NBC broadcasts earned a 2.6 and a 2.2 rating, respectively (similar in scope to a Senior Skins Game broadcast).

Athletes, Colleges, and Clubs

Another critical question facing RR was whether its resources spent on athletes, college track and cross-country teams, and running clubs were sufficiently impacting the target 25–44-year-old and 14–22-year-old running consumer. Reebok's U.S.-sponsored athletes consisted of two to three world-class sprinters (100 m–800 m), several national class distance runners (1500 m–marathon), and five to six world-class triathletes. In addition, forty "local hero" runners and triathletes throughout the United States and six to seven national college teams were supported by product-only deals. Finally, four regional running clubs—one in the Northeast, one in Texas, one in Colorado, and one in California—received equipment support as well. Faced with industry research showing that "elite" athletes tended to appear lower on the target consumer's scale of purchase influences, RR had some tough decisions to make regarding athlete investments and how those assets translated into building stronger target consumer relationships.

Collateral

Collateral materials and spending within RR typically went toward items such as bi-yearly product brochures, quarterly newsletters, and athlete posters, all distributed at key specialty stores and events. In focus groups, these items did not appear to significantly impact consumers' purchase decisions. Yet did these items at least enhance the consumer's perception and image of RR? In past team discussions and meetings, the opinions as to their impact on consumers' brand perceptions were clearly mixed.

New Media

A relatively new addition to the RR marketing mix involved the expansion of the Internet as a marketing tool. Reebok, along with most of its major competitors, maintained a web site featuring current products, dealer listings, athlete and event profiles, athlete "live chats," and other communications of interest. Golden and RR were approached frequently by various media partners pitching web-site advertising and site-to-site hyperlink opportunities.

Initial research by *Runner's World* indicated that 25% of their subscriber base had access to and spent time on the Internet. The growth in number of "hit rates" among national and regional running publications' web sites also indicated increased Internet activity and access, yet did these web-site "hits" necessarily equate to a captive audience receptive to and influenced by specific Internet advertising messages? Golden raised the question of whether there were additional Internet opportunities that could maximize some of RR's current marketing programs and assets. Golden wanted her team to look closely at these potential opportunities and marketing elements prior to next week's 1997 marketing plan presentation.

RR's Market Research

Market research conducted by and for the Running category included primary research in the form of formal and informal consumer focus groups and individual and group consumer interviews, as well as secondary research gained from outside companies hired to provide market size, share, and growth by brand, age, gender, ethnicity, and region.

In several qualitative focus groups with active running enthusiasts, RR elicited some interesting responses regarding Reebok's running brand image. For example, questions were posed asking the subjects to relate certain running brands to various other popular product categories, such as automobile brands. Whereas Nike equaled BMW, adidas equaled VW, Asics equaled Porsche, Reebok equaled automotive brands ranging from Hyundai to Oldsmobile.

Other commissioned research focused on more qualitative trend and attitude studies within younger age segments. Of particular interest to the RR team were the results of several studies examining the growing options and popularity of alternative sports such as snowboarding, in-line skating, mountain biking, and BMX. Recent successful made-for-TV programs such as the *ESPN X-Games* were examples of the sport and fitness alternatives now available to the 12–24-year-old youth segment. The concern was that as these options increased, running as a participatory sport and fitness activity would find its popularity diminishing within this critical youth market. Mirroring the concerns of many specialty running dealers, Golden felt that if this market did not take up running in its youth, it might be less disposed to take it up in later years as well.

RR's Marketing Mix Decisions

As Golden quickly shifted her attention away from the tennis courts outside and back to the planning session at hand, she was struck by the complexity and magnitude of her team's final decisions and recommendations. It was clear that not all elements of the potential marketing mix were on equal footing when it came to their ability to influence, impact, and build lasting relationships with the target consumer. The one key question her team had to answer in its upcoming presentation to senior management regarded which elements were most critical to impacting consumer purchase behavior and developing long-term loyalty. Athletes? Events? College teams? Retail programs? Product? New media? Advertising? Others yet to be defined? And should its plans include a renewed focus on the elusive yet critical 12–24-year-old consumer in the face of numerous alternatives and waning running participation within that segment?

And, given this set of marketing elements, how could she begin to measure and evaluate their impact on RR's target consumer? As she prepared to address the RR team in front of her, she knew that her team must deliver to management via a critical and evaluative thought process a Running category marketing plan that J.W. Foster himself would be proud of—one that would continue Reebok's climb back into running credibility and legitimacy.

Sources

1. *Runner's World* 1996 Subscriber Study.
2. "Running" Relationship Contact Map.
   Dr. Lisa Fortini-Campbell, presentation on "Integrating Communications and Communications Strategy: Managing Communications for the Changing Marketplace," Kellogg School of Business Executive Education Seminar, September 1996.
3. NPD SMART/Consumer Panel Research, 1996 Study.

Avid Sports

Mark A. McDonald and George R. Milne

Introduction

In the middle of racquetball with his chief programmer, Dave's mind started to wander . . .

Where would Avid Sports be four years from now? Has the company built up substantial barriers to entry? Were there technological innovations on the horizon that would make their system obsolete? Should they go public and sell the company? Should they expand into international markets, women's sports, and/or lower-level markets such as Division II colleges or high schools? Should Avid Sports seek out additional strategic partners? How would any of these alternatives impact short and long term profitability?

. . . Smack! "Ouch!" exclaimed Dave as the ball hit him squarely in the forehead. Dave silently reminded himself to always keep an eye on the ball, and never lose focus.

Nonlinear Sports Editing and the Avid System

In 1946 Cleveland Browns' coach Paul Brown was the first to film sports plays so that they could be studied later by coaches and players. This innovation changed the way National Football League (NFL) teams prepared for upcoming games. The practice of using film to record games continued until 1986, when the league converted to the use of videotapes.

Today, football coaches will spend up to sixty hours a week viewing tape to analyze player and team tendencies. This analysis can include, for example, breakdowns by type of play, formation, field position, time of game, down, yards for first down, and so forth. To ensure that teams are on equal footing, NFL rules require teams to deliver Sunday game tapes to the next three opponents by Monday morning. Teams must also send a copy to the league and make copies for the coaches and players. The video director for the Chicago Bears estimates that he may make 350 different video tapes for each game, totaling over 3,200 tapes per season. At $10 apiece, this is not only a time-intensive activity but also costly. Additionally, the entire process requires extensive use of commercial flights and courier services. Once a tape arrives, it can take the team's video editor about eight hours to dub, cut, and splice together different versions for analysis.

In December of 1994, Avid Technology introduced a revolutionary nonlinear digital editing system for the sports market (see Exhibit 7.1). Avid's SportsPro system significantly improved the way teams create cutups for scouting, player development, and game preparation. Instead of splicing together film, or fast forwarding through videotape to create cutups, video directors can use the instant access capabilities of the SportsPro system. The process involves digitizing game footage into the system, logging the video, matching game statistics to the video, and then running "filters" that create hours-long cutups in seconds.

To facilitate this process, the software includes an autolog, which looks for a shot of the scoreboard and uses this picture as a delimiter to mark the start and end of each play. This automatic process of breaking video up into plays is made possible by shooting video footage showing the scoreboard, followed by the play. With football and baseball

Exhibit 7.1   Picture of Avid SportsPro video editing screen

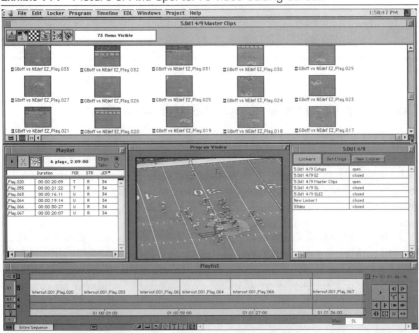

the plays are quite discrete. However, with basketball, soccer, hockey, and volleyball and the like, play is more fluid. The definition of plays is left to the user of the editing system. In basketball, a play may start when the ball reaches half court or changes possession; in soccer, shots on goals or touches; in hockey, when the puck crosses mid ice or the blue line.

With the plays delimited and digitized, statistics are then imported into the database from a game analysis program. Professional football teams, for example, might have 100 variables logged in or associated with each play (see Exhibit 7.2). The user of the system has random access to the plays based on the queries put to the database. The user establishes filters of the database depending on what he wants to view. Thus, the order of the plays is not in the linear, sequential fashion in which they occurred. For example, if a coach wanted to see all the third-down plays with more than ten yards to go, they come up instantly.

The evolution of analog video to digitized video could change the role of coaching. The power and speed of the system can be used for real-time analysis. Some National Basketball Association (NBA) teams shoot first-half video, digitize it, analyze it, and then create strategy changes prior to the second half of play.

History of Avid Sports

Avid Technology, Inc., was founded in 1987. The company, based in Tewksbury, Massachusetts, manufactures a wide range of video editing equipment. Avid's products are used to edit music videos, feature films, and television shows. Avid Technology is divided into three core areas:

- *Post production:* television shows, commercials, and film
- *Broadcast:* news gathering
- *Professional audio:* soundtracks, special effects, and television

Exhibit 7.2 Example of database criteria for NFL team logging

Play	Ball carrier	Deployment
Down	Number	Penalty
Distance	Front	Fumble
Field position	Coverage	Hash
Set	Result	Quarter
Strength	Per	Time
Motion	Sub	Red
Code	Stunt	Nickle
Gain	Blitz	Dime

The company grew quickly, employing over 100 employees by 1992. In 1994, John Barkley, Bob Simmons, and David Grandin were all working in the desktop group, a department entrusted with developing industry applications for vertical markets. Within this group, David was responsible for marketing, Bob concentrated on channel management, and John was in engineering.

In January of 1994, John and Bob presented nonlinear video editing at the American Football Coaches Association (AFCA) conference. This presentation, covering the potential application of this technology to the sport industry, garnered great enthusiasm. A number of coaches in attendance were very interested in improving their game preparation using this video technology. A month later, the first nonlinear video editing product created specifically for coaching staffs was unveiled at the annual NFL Scouting Combine, held in Indianapolis.

By the end of 1994, the desktop group, in a joint venture with equipment reseller SportsTech, developed a major new product called SportsPro. This digital video editing product dramatically reduced the time it took to search through footage and splice video segments together. Teams could analyze opponent tendencies and game situations in a matter of minutes. Mike Stoeber, Video Coordinator at the University of Florida, says, "the whole idea about using digital was about being able to get our jobs done faster while turning out a better product." Other early adopters of this new technology included the following professional and collegiate teams:

- Chicago Bears
- Green Bay Packers
- Cleveland Browns
- Duke University
- University of Miami

By late 1995, the number of employees at Avid Technology had reached 1,000. However, as reflected in back-to-back quarters in the red, Avid began to experience its first growing pains. Externally, segment profitability was leading to increased industry competition and shrinking profit margins. Some of these competitors were Data Translation (later changed to Media 100), ImMix, and Lightworks. Internally, the company experienced major turnover in its executive ranks, including bringing in a new CEO, CFO, and Vice President of Sales. Other strategic moves were a shift from direct to indirect sales channels, and a move from low-volume/high-margin products to higher-volume/lower-margin products. However, spending was racing out of control as the company started to lose focus on its core businesses. In response, company officials decided to sell off businesses that were not considered part of its core. The sports business, marketing a high-margin product to a relatively small niche market using direct sales, was an obvious target for divestiture.

In June 1996, Avid Technology sold (via a secured loan) to fourteen employees controlling interest in products that pro and college coaches utilized to edit and view game films. Avid Technology kept a minority stake and a seat on the board of the new company, Avid Sports LLC. According to D.J. Long, director of business development, "It's definitely related to our need to focus on markets that have been part of our historical distinctive competency. It's part of an attempt to perform better, which we need to do." At the point of the spin-off, twenty-two professional teams and twenty-five colleges had purchased Avid equipment. These sales, when placed in the context of Avid Technology's 1995 sales of $407 million and earnings of $15 million, were relatively insignificant. These numbers did not deter David Grandin, Avid Sports' president: "Given a different business model, there is a great opportunity to have a lot of fun while making a respectable profit."

Current Position

Internal Organization and Company Culture

Avid Sports had, as of May 1997, twenty full-time employees and paid five additional independent contractors. The company had plans to hire more employees to keep up with its growth. The quarterback of the company was Dave Grandin, an energetic and passionate sports fan (see Exhibit 7.3). The culture of Avid Sports was a cross between a start-up high-tech company and a sports club. Avid Sports was comprised of dedicated employees who enjoyed sports and their jobs. A banner from the last superbowl was on the wall, and baseball caps of various teams were propped up on cubical walls. Headquarters also featured a pool table where 9-ball was played during breaks. Since the company had been established as an LLC, all employees were considered members and participated in some profit sharing as a result. Additionally, the company had a 401(k) retirement matching plan.

Product Line Description

The Avid Sports line consists of the SportsPro digital video analysis systems, SportsView™ coaching Stations, and the Avid Sports Network Solution. The SportsPro product line provides editing capabilities that replace traditional tape-based systems. SportsPro allows sport organizations to create video-linked databases for opponent scouting, self-scouting, player development, and game preparation. The SportsView Coaching Stations make it easy to view the video databases created

Exhibit 7.3   Avid Sports organization chart (1997)

David Grandin
President

Bob Simmons		John Barkley	Karen Dapkus	Mike Moniz		
Customer Service	*VP, Sales & Marketing*	*VP Engineering*	*Director of Administration*	*Integration Manager*	*Product Manager*	*Finance*
•Field support team leader	•Account managers (4)	•Principal engineer		•Technician		•Consultant
•Field support (2)	•Sales/Mkt coordinator	•Software engineer				
•Phone support team leader	•Mkt consultant	Sr. software specialist (2)				
•Phone support coordinator		•Sr software specialist/QA eng.				
		•Tester				
		•Intern				
		•Document-contractor				
		•Eng. contractor				

Note: ---- represents temporary direct responsibilities.

by the SportsPro video analysis systems. The SportsView can be run with a mouse or by using a push-button hand control unit. By pressing buttons, coaches can review plays forward or backward. Coaches with SportsView can analyze video using clear slow motion in forward or reverse and display statistics over full-motion video.

Recently introduced is the Avid Sports Network Solution, which connects the SportsPro video director's station with SportsView Coaching Stations and storage drives. A network allows multiple users to access the same information from a database at the same time. In addition, the network establishes a platform for teams to share information with the league and for teams to access the league database and download information from the league.

Clients of Avid believe the digital solution is beneficial because of its speed and quality. The SportsPro systems allow teams to edit and view video more efficiently. It allows teams to analyze video faster because of instant random access, its flexibility, and changes in the way film is reviewed: there is no rewinding, dubbing, wrapping, or shuttling tapes; users just point to the plays they want to see for immediate access. It is flexible—coaches can ask for any scenario and see it instantly. Also, it saves time and promotes teamwork when the systems are linked together in networks consisting of multiple editing stations, SportsView Coaching Stations, and classroom projection. The quality of the Avid system is notable. The video quality is crisp, there is no extra footage before or after plays, and the video never degrades.

A major source of Avid Sports' competitive advantage is its technological capabilities. Avid Sports, in its agreement with its parent company, has the right to license proprietary technology. In essence, Avid Sports as a subsidiary of Avid Technology has access to thousands of man years that have gone into developing the technology, which would be very difficult to duplicate by a new entrant or a stand-alone entrant. The close relationship between Avid Technology and Avid Sports guarantees Avid Sports access to updates on software engines and other developed technologies.

Pricing/Service Contracts

The SportsPro models, pricing, and target markets are listed below.

SportsPro 2200: The high-end model geared toward football and baseball. Without storage, it sells for $75,000 with a profit margin of 65%. Clients also pay 7%–8% of the sales price annually for customer service. This is quite favorable given that the industry standard for customer service is 10%–15% of the sales price. The break even for service is about 6%.

SportsPro 2000: The next tier of the SportsPro product is aimed at the NBA, NHL, and NCAA basketball. Without storage, this system sells for $49,000 with a profit margin of 60%. Clients also pay 7%–8% of the sales price annually for customer service.

SportsPro 1500: The low end SportsPro product is targeted at tier II NCAA football teams (Ivy league, Big Sky conference, etc.). Without storage, it sells for $29,000 with a profit margin of 50%. This product has much reduced client servicing when compared to the SportsPro 2200 and SportsPro 2000.

The main differences among the products are the sophistication of the software and product utilization by end users. Football teams typically have one week to prepare for their next opponent, whereas basketball teams have one or two days. In addition, the events in a football game (first down, second down, etc.) are more structured than in basketball or hockey. Therefore, the way statistics are logged and cutups are created in each sport is different.

In addition to the editors, Avid Sports also sells SportsView Coaching Stations, video storage units, and Network Solutions.

SportsView Coaching Station: Coaching stations are user-friendly access terminals specifically designed for use by coaches. Coaches are able to quickly and easily view digital game tape using a hand-held remote control. Each SportsView Coaching Station sells for $25,000.

Magnetic Disk Storage Towers: Each storage tower holds eight 3 1/2″ drives or four 5 1/4″ drives. These units feature hot-swap drives, dual power supplies, and fans. Eight hours of magnetic storage costs approximately $18,000.

Network Solution: The Network Solution eliminates the need for video-tape by instantaneous sharing of data and video over the network. Over 100 devices can be connected to the network at once. The Net-work Solution sells for $20,000.

The other key element Avid offers is their Service Contracts (see Exhibit 7.4). These contracts are key to making clients feel comfortable with their hardware investment. The contracts also are a source of long-term revenue for the company.

Exhibit 7.4 Service contract

Service Contract

We believe that the true value of any product is defined by the caliber of the support provided to the customer. Support is critical to customer satisfaction and a superior support team is a winning element that develops lasting relationships with customers and products that are honed to fit their needs. Avid Sports has built its foundation on world-class support with a reputation for quick response and solutions. We work closely with our customer and are proud of our record. We encourage potential customers to contact our current users as to the reliability and quality of our support.

The Avid Sports Maintenance Plan is designed to be flexible in content and price to best fit the needs of our diverse customer base. There are three components that make up the Avid Sports Maintenance Plan. A Premium Package designed for users who need round the clock support and immediate hardware turnaround. A Basic Package that contains all the essential support tools yet is streamlined to fit the budgets of smaller institutions. And a Hardware Package that gives users the ability to stay current technologically at a substantial discount.

Avid Sports requires users to be on either the basic or premium package. By remaining current with software releases we are assured of being able to provide the highest standard of support. While the hardware package is not a required support program, it is a recommended one. It provides the easiest way to minimize down time by providing an extended warranty on Avid Sports supplied printed circuit boards and it is the only way to insure against obsolescence by providing upgrades to hardware platforms and peripherals at a substantially reduced cost.

The Premium Package

- Toll-Free Phone Support—7 × 24 × 365 including holidays. Phones will be manned in the office from 9 AM to 6 PM (EST).
- 24 hour turnaround on software or hardware that is under warranty. (Our best effort will be for 24 hour turnaround. We will guarantee 48 hour turn around).
- All software upgrades, documentation updates, and version releases (software only)*.

Exhibit 7.4 Continued

- A minimum of 25% discount for software add-on programs.
- Timbuktu access and support
- Remote access to Avid Sports' Web page with technical notes, product information, and more.
- Free registration on the Avid Sports annual conference.

Note: Hardware may be new or refurbished at Avid Sports' discretion.

The Basic Package

- Technical assistance through unlimited toll-free telephone support Monday through Friday 9 AM to 8 PM (EST). Phones will be manned in the office from 9 AM to 6 PM (EST). From 6 PM to 8 PM (EST) there will be beeper coverage provided with a 20 minute response time.
- All software upgrades, documentation updates, and version releases (software only)*.
- Remote access to Avid Sports' Web page with technical notes, product information and more.
- Free registration on the Avid Sports annual conference.

Note: In the event of a hardware failure, hardware under warranty will be replaced once the suspected part has been returned to Avid Sports and has been verified defective. Hardware replacement parts may be new or refurbished at Avid Sports' discretion.

The Hardware Maintenance Package

The Hardware Maintenance Plan is purchased on a yearly basis. It is not required but is recommended. It is intended as an insurance plan that enables customers to save on the cost of upgrades and on hardware replacement. The hardware warranty part of this package is available to any customers requiring Avid Sports supplied printed circuit boards that are out of warranty.

- Extended Warranty Coverage on hardware.
- 50% discount on hardware upgrades, both system and peripheral.

Based on the following model, it is easy to see the worth of such a plan.
EX. A team purchases two editors and 4 towers in 1996. In 1997, they decide to upgrade their two systems to networkable fiber channel technology. They purchase 6 of the new chassis and 32 new removable drives. The cost of the hardware would be $112,410. With the 50% discount they save $56,205!

Note: Hardware replacement parts may be new or refurbished at Avid Sports' discretion.
*only applies to software that operates on the users current configuration.

Promotion

Avid Sports has been very successful selling its products, partly because of strong word of mouth. Once video directors have tried the Avid system, they do not want to return to the old, linear, tape-based approach. If there is a difficulty in selling the system, it is usually overcoming some sport organization member's fear of technology or a political hurdle of some sort. Avid makes a great effort in its communications to stress the user-friendly nature of the product. For example, on some brochures the point "you don't have to be a computer geek" is made.

Testimonials, both unsolicited and solicited are very effective in the selling efforts. Kentucky Wildcats' basketball coach Rick Pitino (the first NCAA basketball adopter of Avid Sport technology) provided an interesting unsolicited testimonial for the system. In a 1996 *Sports Illustrated* article describing Kentucky's dramatic final-four victory over the top-rated and once defeated UMass basketball team, Pitino noted that the University of Massachusetts basketball team only ran six basic plays, which were always signaled for (hand signal) in the same way. Thus, Kentucky players always knew in advance, by watching the play being called by the UMass point guard, what play was being run by the UMass basketball team. Clearly, this discovery was a big payoff of the Avid SportsPro system. Other coaches and marquee teams have lent their testimonials to the Avid SportsPro promotional materials.

> **Avid SportsPro is a great teaching tool. It gives me all the information I need quickly.**—Rudy Tomjanovich, Head Coach, Houston Rockets, 1994–95 NBA Champions.
> **Avid's system really works. They're the first company to put it all together realistically.**—Tom Osborne, Head Coach Nebraska Cornhuskers, 1995–96 NCAA Football Champions.
> **It's one of the best investments we ever made.**—Rick Pitino, Head Coach, Kentucky Wildcats, 1995–96 NCAA Basketball Champions.
> **Every NFL coach will want one.**—Mike Holmgren, Head Coach, Green Bay Packers, 1996–97 NFL Super Bowl Champions.
> **Avid Sports' system of quickly breaking down video has proven extremely beneficial to the Gators.**—Steve Spurrier, Head Coach, University of Florida Gators, 1996–97 NCAA Football Champions.

Grandin notes that, as more and more teams adopt the product, "it is not so much that having this system gives a team an advantage, it is more that not having the system could put the team at a disadvantage relative to competitors who have already made the investment." Grandin goes on to say, "College teams, for example, would hate to lose a top recruit by not having the state-of-the-art equipment." In order to strengthen the link between the Avid Systems and on-field success, Avid Sports commissioned a research study entitled "What's winning worth?" (see Exhibit 7.5). This research calculated the average revenues for winning and losing teams in five sports leagues: the NFL, NBA, NHL, and NCAA Division I Football and Division I Basketball. The results clearly quantified the impact of a winning record and/or post-season appearance in millions of dollars.

Perhaps the biggest promotional thrust of the company is the two annual conferences that Avid runs each year for sports organizations.

Exhibit 7.5 What's winning worth? Additional average annual team revenue earned by winning teams compared to losing teams for 1991–1994 seasons

	NFL	NBA	NHL
Gate receipts	$1.9 MM	$3.7 MM	$5.0 MM
Media revenue	$1.7 MM	$2.2 MM	$0.9 MM
Total revenue	$5.0 MM	$5.0 MM	$6.3 MM
Franchise value	$6.9 MM	$12.0 MM	$11.4 MM

The Avid Sports Conference provides Avid and their strategic partners an opportunity to educate current and potential customers on product use. Conference sessions include basic to advanced training, technology updates, and roundtable discussions. In addition, the conference provides plenty of opportunity for relationship building among the conference participants.

Current Clients

Avid Sports currently services over seventy clients (see Exhibit 7.6). Avid initially developed and marketed digitized video systems for the football market. It is not surprising, therefore, that collegiate and professional football teams and leagues (thirty-eight clients) lead the list of clients. By customizing products for basketball video directors and coaches, Avid Sports has also been successful in cornering a sizable portion of that market. In addition to NBA officiating, thirteen NBA teams and six NCAA basketball teams have purchased Avid Sports products to date. Avid has also made inroads into the NHL (five clients) and the stadiums and arena industry (four clients).

Potential Clients

Exhibit 7.7 depicts Avid Sports' growth by market segment and subsequent remaining United States market potential. Clearly, traditional target groups such as National Football League and National Basketball Association teams have been largely tapped. Likewise, the number of remaining NCAA Division I football teams with both the financial resources and inclination to purchase digital editing equipment and software are limited. The greatest growth opportunities for Avid Sports are in the following areas:

- *International:* The development of top-level competition in the sports of soccer and basketball globally serves as an emerging market for Avid products (see Exhibit 7.8). In Europe, countries such as Italy,

Exhibit 7.6   Avid Sports clients (as of 5/8/97)

NCAA Football	*National Basketball Association*
Air Force Falcons	Chicago Bulls
Arkansas Razorbacks	Cleveland Cavaliers
Auburn Tigers	Detroit Pistons
Boston College Eagles	Houston Rockets
Duke Blue Devils	Los Angeles Lakers
Florida Gators	Milwaukee Bucks
Florida State Seminoles	Minnesota Timberwolves
Fresno State Bulldogs	Orlando Magic
Georgia Tech Yellow Jackets	Philadelphia 76ers
Iowa Hawkeyes	Phoenix Suns
Iowa State Cyclones	San Antonio Spurs
Kentucky Wildcats	Seattle Supersonics
Miami Hurricanes	Vancouver Grizzlies
Michigan State Spartans	NBA Officiating
Michigan Wolverines	
Minnesota Golden Gophers	*NCAA Basketball*
Nebraska Cornhuskers	
New Mexico Lobos	Florida State Seminoles
Northwestern Wildcats	Kentucky Wildcats
Ohio State Buckeyes	Miami Hurricanes
Purdue Boilermakers	Michigan State Spartans
Rutgers Scarlet Knights	Iowa Hawkeyes
Tennessee Volunteers	Indiana Hoosiers
Texas A&M Aggies	
Texas Longhorns	*National Football League*
USC Trojans	
Utah Utes	Baltimore Ravens
Virginia Tech Hokies	Buffalo Bills
	Chicago Bears
National Hockey League	Detroit Lions
	Green Bay Packers
Chicago Blackhawks	Kansas City Chiefs
Dallas Stars	Miami Dolphins
Vancouver Canucks	Philadelphia Eagles
Edmonton Oilers	San Francisco 49ers
NHL Productions	NFL Officiating
Stadium/Arena	*NCAA Volleyball*
Shea Stadium	Florida State Seminoles
Orlando Arena	Nebraska Cornhuskers
Palace At Auburn Hills	*Major League Baseball*
Rupp Arena	
	Kansas City Royals

Great Britain, Spain, Greece, and Germany all house top-notch basketball and/or soccer leagues. Professional baseball and the J-league (baseball) represent untapped markets in Japan.

- *Lower-margin/high-volume markets:* Avid Sports has traditionally focused on distributing high-margin (60%–70%) products on a low-volume basis. For example, the SportsPro 2200 has a profit margin

Exhibit 7.7 Growth of U.S. markets and market potential

Leagues	1994	1995	1996	1997*	Market Potential**
National Football League	1	4	7	9	31
National Basketball Association	0	4	10	13	31
National Hockey Association	0	1	1	4	29
Major League Baseball	0	1	1	1	31
NCAA Basketball	0	1	4	6	60
NCAA Football	4	8	26	28	110

*As of May 6, 1997.
**Total number of teams in each league.

Exhibit 7.8 International market potential.

Soccer Leagues	Market Potential*
Austria	10
Belgium	16
Bulgaria	16
Croatia	16
Cyprus	14
Czech Republic	16
Denmark	12
English (1st Division)	24
English (Premier)	20
French (Premier)	20
German	18
Greek	18
Italy	18
Netherlands	18
Irish	8
Norway	14
Poland	18
Portugal	18
Ireland	12
Russia	18
Scotland	10
Spain	22
Sweden	14
Switzerland	8

Exhibit 7.8 Continued

Soccer Leagues	Market Potential*
Turkey	18
Ukraine	16
Yugoslavia	12
Finland	10
Romania	18
Hungary	18
Israel	16
Puerto Rico	18
Basketball Leagues	
Australia	12
Greece	14
Italy	14
England	13
Germany	14
Spain	18
China	12
France	16
Taiwan	6

*Total number of teams in each league.

of 65% and is marketed primarily to the NFL (thirty total teams) and NCAA football teams. By targeting Division II/III collegiate teams, high schools, and/or women's sport teams, Avid could greatly expand the number of potential clients. However, these segments do not have the financial resources of the major professional sport leagues or major Division I collegiate athletic teams. New lower-end products and different sales approaches would have to be developed to service these markets. Additionally, with such a large client base, it would be difficult to ensure the high levels of customer service on which Avid has built a reputation.

- *Other niche markets:* While Avid Sports has focused its products and marketing on the sport industry, expansion into other niche markets such as the medical market, law enforcement and security, and training videos is a viable option. The medical market, for example, having a crucial educational and training component, could benefit from digitizing video of surgical procedures to be accessed by other practitioners and medical students. Random access to video of different procedures or the same procedure executed by different surgeons has the potential to save time and enhance depth of understanding.

Competitors

Avid Sports has faced minimal competition in the business of selling digital editing products to sport teams and leagues. Currently, there are three competitor firms battling against Avid's dominance in this industry:

- *Montage (About Sports):* Montage has sold systems to the University of Wisconsin and the University of West Virginia.
- *Dixon Sports (principal: Mike Dixon):* This company has focused its efforts on major league baseball. Three teams are Dixon Sports clients: the Cleveland Indians, Atlanta Braves, and Anaheim Angels. Dixon Sports is now trying to enter the football market.
- *Webb Electronics (principal: Joel Krause):* Webb Electronics is not a major competitor in the high-end markets of major professional sports or Division I collegiate athletics. Their only system sold at this level is to the Utah Jazz, and they also have a strong relationship with the Dallas Cowboys. Instead, selling efforts have focused on small colleges and women's sport teams.

Why the dearth of competition in this potentially lucrative market? The case of Home Team Advantage (HTA) of Palo Alto, California, an early entrant into this market provides some insight. HTA produced a user-friendly product named Touch 'N Go. This system, designed specifically for coaches, required no prior computer skills to operate. Touch 'N Go was sold initially to college teams in a variety of sports, with planned expansion into the NFL and other major professional leagues. The long-term goal of HTA was to work closely with collegiate and professional teams to edit footage of their sport events and then to sell the digital content over the information superhighway to individual consumers. HTA, however, faced formidable obstacles to reaching its goals. Glenn DeKraker, founder of HTA, underestimated the technological challenge inherent in developing an inexpensive system for storing and retrieving digital video.

Strategic Partners

In order to facilitate easy access to video and data by entire leagues and conferences, Avid Sports is partnering with leading companies in digitized recording and fiber optic transmission. These strategic alliances will eliminate the delays associated with duping tapes, relogging games, and using courier services. On May 24, 1996, Avid Sports, in partnership with Vyvx International Video Services Company, tested the viability of transferring digitized game video over a Vyvx-owned nationwide fiber optic network. Digitized video, logged into plays with game information, was successfully transferred between the New England Patriots and the Kansas City Chiefs of the NFL. This event previews the day when fiber optic lines will be utilized to transmit analysis video and game data to multiple sites upon completion of games.

Avid Sports has also forged partnerships with Sony and Panasonic. Both Sony and Panasonic offer DV technology that replaces the Beta format, enhancing digital quality and lengthening recording times by compressing digital component video signals to one-fifth their original size. Panasonic and Sony have developed entire product lines including recorders, players, cameras, and archiving equipment.

Future Opportunities

Given the rapid rate of technological change, Avid Sports is faced with a myriad of strategic opportunities. Opportunities include developing product extensions, expanding platform options, Internet distribution, erecting structural barriers to entry, expanding strategic partnerships, and/or executing an exit strategy.

Developing Product Extensions

Although Avid Sports' current line of products has been used primarily in pregame preparations, extensions could allow for self-scouting and scouting players. IBM has developed data-mining software, which has

Exhibit 7.9 Schematic of Avid Network system

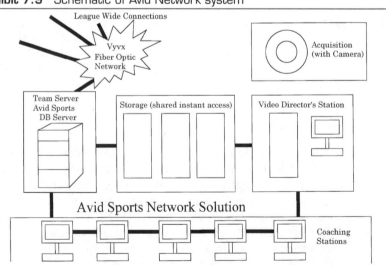

been adopted by several NBA teams. This software helps detect patterns in data indicating player or team tendencies. One use of this software would be to search for combinations of players coming off the bench who have been especially effective on offense or defense. Avid could incorporate a data-mining feature into its system.

Another possible product extension would be an add-on player scouting database to analyze potential draft picks or free agents. In addition to text database information on a player, personnel evaluators would have access to attached video of that player performing against various opponents and in different game situations. Avid Sports has already attempted, to no avail, to partner with a number of scouting services (for example, Sportsol and Hockey Scout). This leaves the opportunity to develop this add-on product in house.

Expanding Platform Options

All digital video editing products currently sold by Avid Sports operate exclusively on Apple computers. To date, Avid Sports has lost only one potential client due to reliance on the Apple platform. The Portland Trailblazers, owned by Paul Allen, one of the cofounders of Microsoft, would not purchase a product that wouldn't run on the PC platform. However, the poor recent performance of Apple has raised some red flags for Avid. If Apple continues its downward spiral, it may impact sales of digital video editing software running on this platform. Long-run stability for the company may depend on expanding platform options for customers.

Internet Video Distribution

Almost all industries are exploring delivering products and services via the Internet. The digital video editing industry is no exception. Grandin views "Internet delivery systems as being the wave of the future." As many users have experienced firsthand, transferring video on the Internet is slow and cumbersome. However, if the digital video is sent as files (preferably logged as lockers), the Internet could be utilized as an expedient delivery mechanism. For this type of system to be implemented throughout a sport league, an independent server would be required. Other major issues to consider are throughput and data security.

Erecting Structural Barriers to Entry

By capturing the business of many of the teams in the NFL and the NBA, Avid Sports has begun to create barriers to entry for potential competitors. Teams in leagues are in constant communication regarding technological advancements. Strong word-of-mouth regarding Avid's software innovations and superior customer service acts to discourage teams from seriously considering competitor products.

Avid has the opportunity to further enhance structural barriers to entry through development of league-wide network solutions (see Exhibit 7.9). In the future, a network established among teams in a league would make obsolete the current system of shipping tapes, allowing for instantaneous transmission of digitized video. Additionally, given the high cost of storage space ($18,000 to hold eight hours of video), a league-wide storage facility with teams sharing in the expenses would be a logical next step.

According to Al Treml, Green Bay Packers Video Director and co-chairman of the NFL Video Director's Committee, "a long-term goal of the system is to have a network setup with the league office and all other teams in the NFL, in addition to a touch screen menu. If Coach (Mike) Holmgren wants to analyze the Vikings' blitz, he can do so by using a touch screen, tapping on Vikings, defense, blitz and get the information." By partnering with Vyvx International Video Services Company, a leading fiber optic transmission company, Avid has taken the first step in helping entire leagues and conferences to leverage the power of digital video technology.

Expanding Strategic Partnerships

As reviewed earlier, Avid Sports is in the process of partnering with a number of companies such as Vyvx, Sony, and Panasonic. These strategic alliances require, to some degree, Avid to share control and proceeds. One positive outcome of this strategy is that it allows Avid to play a coordinating role when dealing with potential clients. Therefore, while some control and profits are shared with partner firms, some of the growing customer servicing pressures will also be transferred to these partners.

Executing an Exit Strategy

Although all the above opportunities merit consideration, Avid Sports' executives could always choose to execute an exit strategy. As has been done by a number of other high-tech companies, taking the company public has the potential to reap large financial rewards for executives and employees of Avid Sports. Given the attractiveness of both the sport and high-tech industries, investors are likely to pay a hefty premium in excess of the value of company assets.

Dave Grandin's backhand killshot slammed into the left corner of the front wall. All Fady could do was watch and weep. Point, game, and match for the company president. "Yes, indeed, keeping focused is the key," thought Dave, "but four years seems a long way off. . . ."

8

Smugglers' Notch Resort

Rod Warnick

Introduction

At a recent staff meeting, Bill Stritzler, managing director and now owner of Smugglers' Notch Resort, North America's #1 family resort, raised the question about the future. "What should we do with Smugglers' over the next five, ten, to twenty years?" Staffs had met and outside network teams had presented issues on a number of occasions for the resort to consider. "We need to make tough decisions about expansion and market focus." Bill, an avid fisherman, noted that spring was just around the corner. Spring was, in his mind, a time to renew and begin with fresh plans. The local community and the ski industry applauded his purchase of the resort in Northern Vermont in November. But, deep down he knew that he just could not settle for maintaining the status quo and advocating no change in Smugglers' master planning and marketing. He and others were concerned about the consolidation in the ski industry, especially Les Otten's acquisition of a number of ski areas and the creation of the American Ski Company. Smugglers' had room for expansion unlike other resorts, but does it keep to a family theme, does it venture into new markets, does it maintain the Vermont image and continue to serve the local community, does it try to hold the family market, which is likely to change greatly in years to come? All were nagging questions. His staff had varying opinions. However, Bill was always one to consider the market research carefully. What does it tell management? He awaits the staff's discussions about the future direction of Smugglers' and ponders how the resort and its markets should and will change in the years ahead. However, the question remained, "What should we do with Smugglers' over the next five, ten, to twenty years?"

History of Smugglers' Notch Resort

The resort was founded as Smugglers' Notch Ski Ways in 1956 when local residents built a surface lift on Sterling Mountain. Tom Watson, the renowned owner of IBM who was also an avid skier, purchased it eight years later and held it until its sale to Stanmar, Inc., of Sudbury, Massachusetts in 1973. Stanmar, Inc., is a major construction firm and also owns a resort on Martha's Vineyard. It decided to sell Smugglers' Notch in 1996 because company president, Stanley Snider, was retiring. The current managing director and chief executive officer, William P. Stritzler, purchased the resort in November of 1996. Smugglers' Notch Resort (SNR) celebrated its fortieth anniversary in the 1995–1996 ski season.

SNR has 4,800 acres and is made up of three different mountains—Sterling, Madonna, and Morse—and has a vertical drop of 2,610 feet, one of the biggest elevation drops in the East. The resort has five chair lifts, three surface lifts, and approximately sixty trails of which 21% are considered easier, 56% intermediate, 22% expert and 5% extreme. In recent publications SNR indicates it is the only ski area in the East to have a triple black diamond ski run, the most difficult of all ski terrain. In addition to the ski area, the resort has 412 condominiums, adding a number in recent years, a village center with restaurants, an award-winning child care center, an indoor swimming area, indoor tennis facility, and central business building. SNR daily passes cost $38 for adults midweek and $42 during the weekend. Daily lift passes for children ages 7 to 12 cost $26. Children age 6 and under ski for free. In addition to the winter ski season, SNR runs a full summer program from June through September. It operates two outdoor swimming pools, three water slides, two children's swim areas, twelve tennis courts, and a fully staffed children's and youth day camp program. Smugglers' has over the years evolved into a year-round family vacation destination. However, there is room for expansion at the resort. Approximately 1,000 acres are not currently developed. The expansion that has occurred over the last decade has centered on building new condominiums and refurbishing old ones. New amenities and facilities have been added such as more snowmaking, a new children's lift, a new bathhouse, and a children's swimming area. The addition of more condominiums has put more pressure on the existing recreational facilities and infrastructure.

Today, SNR has become know as "America's Number One Family Resort" (as voted by *Family Circle Magazine* over three previous years), "America's Family Resort," and "The #1 Family Resort in North America" (as voted by the editors of *Skiing Magazine* in 1996). All slogans are attributed to reviews and rankings by various ski and

family publications and are proudly promoted by SNR in its paid advertisements and mailings.

Current Conditions in National Ski Trends

The ski industry has reached a mature stage in its life cycle. To continue
to grow and be prosperous, the industry must find new ways to attract
existing markets and/or to build new markets. The ski industry enjoyed
substantial growth in the sixties, seventies, and into much of the eighties. However, the industry began to slow as the bulk of skiers, the
Baby Boomers, aged and moved into the busy family stage of life in
the nineties. But new markets are emerging in the nineties—
snowboarding, show shoeing, winter camping, telemarking, and cross-
country skiing all appear to be enjoying some degree of growth- with
each appearing to have mini-growth spurts. Some industry officials
believe that a number of these trends are fads and will not drive the
market in any commanding manner. Others believe that improved
technology in terms of shaped skis and improvements in the design of
snowboards will retain, reintroduce, and reinvigorate both skiing's and
snowboarding's existing markets in addition to creating new markets.
Traditionalists still believe, however, that the core and success of the
ski industry rest in the downhill ski market. Nevertheless, there is a
greater diversity in the choices of winter recreation enthusiasts.

Nationwide, ski areas are going out of business or consolidating in
nearly all areas of the United States. The number of ski areas has
shrunk from 745 in the mid-1970s to about 520 in 1996 according
to Michael Berry, president of the National Ski Areas Association of
Lakewood, Colorado. "It's almost like regional malls, if you will," says
Berry, "the mom and pop stores are gone and regional malls have
replaced them." This is the analogy for what has happened to the ski
industry. Others believe it is a case of economies of scale and the market
demands of the skiing public. Alpohonse Gilbert, professor of ski area
management at the University of Vermont's School of Natural Resources, says the bigger ski areas offer better rental equipment, better
accommodations, and better instruction. Big ski areas get a name for
themselves through marketing and recognition in ski publications:
"These big areas get a name that helps attract people, also. That's part
of skiing . . . where you ski. All of those things play a role. When
people go skiing today, they don't expect to hit a rock and they are
surprised when they do," says Gilbert (Allen, 1997).

Industry analysts say that the disappearance of small ski areas
and the consolidation of others are the result of the affordability of
snowmaking, high-speed chair lifts, insurance costs, and the other amenities that most skiers want today. Michael Berry indicates that this

creates a dilemma for the ski industry. The decline of the smaller ski areas, especially those nearer to large metro areas, does not help those that remain. Certainly some of the market will be absorbed by the remaining areas, however the bulk of the skiing population learn to ski and snowboard at smaller, inexpensive areas near home. The larger ski areas depend on these areas to create new skiers who then move on to the larger areas as their skiing ability improves. "As they (smaller areas) go out of business it becomes a more complex task to become a skier and a snowboarder . . . the industry is very concerned with it," says Berry. He also indicates that the larger areas will continue to do well since they can provide a busy visitor with an all-inclusive ski vacation to those people who have plenty of money but very little time, and demand an absolute guarantee of fun and quality skiing for their quality time and investment (Allen, 1997).

Proof of the maturity and indications of decline of the ski market also appear in national statistics. For example, Simmons Market Research Bureau's *Study of Media and Markets* (1979–1994) indicates that the percentage of all American adults who ski has remained relatively constant at about 3 to 5% over the past decade and a half. However, even more important in these statistics are the facts that there are fewer new skiers, fewer young adults who traditionally ski more, and growth only in the heavy or frequent ski market. SGRnet (1996–1997), which provides a broader range of skier profiles, including those aged seven and above, indicates in its most recent review that downhill skiing has also matured. Although the trends in the mid-nineties were positive for the youth markets (profile percentages were up for those under 12), the trends for most of Vermont's prime markets were not positive. Overall downhill skiing numbers were down. Profiles of SNR's prime markets—including skiers from metro areas (down 9.3%), households with at least one child under 18 (down 4.9%), and regional participants (New England down 6.3% and Mid-Atlantic down 1.0%)—all appeared to be declining. These are definite signs of a maturing market. See Table 8.1 for ski trends in the nineties for demographic segments gathered by SGRnet (1996–1997).

Trends in the Northeast and New England

Certain regions of the country have more skiers due in large part to their proximity to ski areas and the winter weather. The bulk of skiers typically live within a three- to five-hour drive time of major ski areas. Such areas as the Northeast, Colorado, and Northern California/Washington all have major ski markets within easy commuting time of their resorts. Bit trends in even the ten most active metropolitan ski markets in the United States do indicate patterns of decline in these market

Table 8.1 Selected demographic trends for downhill skiing: 1993–1995

	1993	1994	1995	Change Rate (%)
Overall participation (millions):				
All participants	10.5	10.6	9.3	−5.7
Frequent participants (20+ days/yr)	1.0	0.9	0.8	−10.6
Infrequent participants (<20 days/yr)	9.5	9.7	8.5	−5.1
Gender:	(Profile Percentage Below)			
Male (48.6% of U.S. pop.)	61.6	59.9	60.7	−0.7
Female (51.4% of U.S. pop.)	38.4	40.1	39.3	1.2
Age:				
7–11 (8.0% of U.S. pop.)	4.3	6.1	6.6	25.0
12–17 (9.4% of U.S. pop.)	14.8	18.5	16.8	7.9
18–24 (10.8% of U.S. pop.)	26.4	23.5	17.2	−18.9
25–34 (17.7% of U.S. pop.)	26.7	25.3	25.8	−1.6
35–44 (17.9% of U.S. pop.)	16.2	15.3	17.7	5.1
45–54 (12.8% of U.S. pop.)	8.8	8.8	9.5	4.0
55–64 (9.0% of U.S. pop.)	2.2	1.6	4.2	67.6
65–74 (8.1% of U.S. pop.)	0.7	1	1.7	56.4
75+ (6.2% of U.S. pop.)	NA	NA	0.5	0
Children in household:				
At Least 1 Under 18 (48.6% of U.S. pop.)	NA	54.8	52.1	−4.9
None under 18 (51.4% of U.S. pop.)	NA	45.2	47.9	6.0
Regional participation:				
New England (4.9% of U.S. pop.)	9.8	9.4	8.6	−6.3
Middle Atlantic (15.2% of U.S. pop.)	21.2	13.6	18.2	−1.0
East North Central (17.0% of U.S. pop.)	12.0	14.4	13.7	7.6
West North Central (7.1% of U.S. pop.)	8.7	4.5	5.9	−8.6
South Atlantic (17.7% of U.S. pop.)	9.4	12.6	13.1	19.0
East South Central (6.5% of U.S. pop.)	2.5	4.3	2.1	10.4
West South Central (10.8% of U.S. pop.)	5.9	5.4	3.7	−20.0
Mountain (6.1% of U.S. pop.)	9.6	13.1	11.8	13.3
Pacific (14.8% of U.S. pop.)	20.9	22.6	23.0	5.0
Household income:				
Under $15,000 (19.6% of U.S. pop.)	6.4	7.0	5.3	−7.5
$15,000–$24,999 (15.3% of U.S. pop.)	6.9	8.3	7.0	2.3
$25,000–$34,999 (14.3% of U.S. pop.)	8.5	11.0	8.9	5.2
$35,000–$49,999 (17.3% of U.S. pop.)	17.0	18.9	16.8	0.0
$50,000–$74,999 (19.9% of U.S. pop.)	28.9	27.1	32.1	6.1
$75,000 & over (13.6% of U.S. pop.)	32.3	27.6	30.0	−2.9

Table 8.1 Continued

	1993	1994	1995	Change Rate (%)
Metrosize area:				
Non-MSA (22.8% of U.S. pop.)	15.9	14.8	18.1	7.7
50,000–499,000 (20.3% of U.S. pop.)	20.3	24.8	19.4	0.2
50,000–499,000 (20.3% of U.S. pop.)	20.3	24.8	19.4	0.2
500,000–999,999 (10.8% of U.S. pop.)	8.7	10.6	10.3	9.5
1,000,000–2,499,999 (21.8% of U.S. pop.)	25	23.2	27.4	5.5
2,500,000+ (24.3% of U.S. pop.)	30.2	26.6	24.8	−9.3

Source: NSGA 1996–1997, SGRnet.

areas (see Tables 8.2, 8.3, and 8.4). Furthermore, the number of families with children who ski are also declining according to SRDS *Lifestyle Market Analyst*, and the numbers of prime family markets in the Northeast are also declining.

In Vermont, the ski industry has evolved and consolidated over the past decade and a half. Over ten years ago, eighty ski areas existed in Vermont; today, only eighteen ski areas exist. Several ski areas decided not to open in the 1996–1997 season and other areas are in some form of bankruptcy and, although still operational, their businesses may be considered marginal. The consolidation trend that has emerged is one of takeover and purchases by larger ski holding companies. American Ski Company, for example, now owns and operates Sugarbush, Killington, Pico, Mt. Snow, and Haystack. See Table 8.5, which indicates how ski areas in Vermont have recently changed hands and been consolidated. Vermont's ski areas stand at a crossroads according to the Vermont Ski Areas Association. Growth trends in the ski industry have flattened out and competition has intensified. The future for many is uncertain but does hold promise. Industry officials believe that advanced snowmaking and targeted marketing can carry the industry into a more predictable and sustainable future (VSAA, 1996). Some ski areas are working hard to attract new people to the sport, both at home and out of state, through free or low-cost learn-to-ski or snowboard programs. The advent of "shaped" skis will likely help more people learn and enjoy the sport. Snowboarding, already about 17 percent of the ski business nationwide, shows promise for future business in attracting more young people to the ski slopes. The challenges for each of the ski areas in Vermont are formidable, however. The number of people skiing and snowboarding in Vermont has actually declined over the past ten years from a peak of 5.2 million skier visits in 1986–1987 to 4.1 million skier visits in 1995–1996 (see Table 8.6).

Table 8.2 Size of ten largest U.S. ski markets, 1994–1996

Market Areas	Number of Households in Metro Areas			Number of Household Who Ski			Household Participation Ski Rates (%)		
	1994	1995	1996	1994	1995	1996	1994	1995	1996
Northeast:									
New York	6,854,209	6,904,481	6,918,846	589,462	559,263	539,670	8.6	8.1	7.8
Boston	2,133,422	2,131,504	2,148,405	313,613	296,279	281,441	14.7	13.9	13.1
Philadelphia	2,695,387	2,680,541	2,672,314	202,154	198,360	187,062	7.5	7.4	7.0
Washington, DC	1,883,420	1,903,000	1,927,789	152,557	152,240	146,512	8.1	8.0	7.6
Subtotal Northeast Markets:	13,566,438	13,619,526	13,667,354	1,257,786	1,206,142	1,154,685	9.3	8.9	8.4
Midwest:									
Denver	1,099,314	1,136,652	1,158,689	245,147	254,610	245,642	22.3	22.4	21.2
Chicago	3,127,701	3,149,712	3,151,762	209,556	207,881	198,561	6.7	6.6	6.3
Minneapolis-St. Paul	1,397,057	1,408,515	1,425,918	148,088	145,077	139,740	10.6	10.3	9.8
Subtotal Midwest Markets:	5,624,072	5,694,879	5,736,369	602,791	607,568	583,943	10.7	10.7	10.2
West:									
Los Angeles	5,091,822	5,123,041	5,139,253	544,825	496,935	467,672	10.7	9.7	9.1
San Francisco-Oakland-San Jose	2,337,392	2,350,077	2,373,487	280,487	274,959	268,204	12.0	11.7	11.3
Seattle-Tacoma	1,472,895	1,497,837	1,513,272	210,624	211,195	205,805	14.3	14.1	13.6
Subtotal West Markets:	8,902,109	8,970,955	9,026,012	1,035,936	983,089	941,681	11.6	11.0	10.4
Total Top Ten US Ski Markets	28,092,619	28,285,359	28,429,735	2,896,513	2,796,799	2,680,309	10.3	9.9	9.4

Source: SRDS *Lifestyle Market Analyst,* 1994–1996, Wilmette, Il.

Table 8.3 Families with children who ski, 1994–1996

Family Type	Number of Households			Number of Household Who Ski			Percent of Households Who Ski		
	1994	1995	1996	1994	1995	1996	1994	1995	1996
Single	42,955,692	43,274,153	43,372,589	3,479,618	3,402,430	3,252,457	8.1	7.9	7.5
Married	52,927,550	53,319,939	54,093,903	3,769,586	3,745,599	3,667,664	7.1	7.0	6.8
Single, any child at home	6,328,294	7,341,151	7,407,453	420,454	493,209	477,488	6.6	6.7	6.4
Married, child age under 13	12,560,705	12,460,638	12,475,711	1,196,119	1,172,266	1,148,740	9.5	9.4	9.2
Married, child age 13–18	9,204,791	9,273,033	9,454,250	753,917	750,536	754,293	8.2	8.1	8.0
Dual income, child under age 13	7,095,360	6,954,778	7,212,520	732,170	714,796	712,772	10.3	10.3	9.9
Dual income, child age 13–18	5,944,761	5,988,834	6,237,855	514,693	521,801	525,929	8.7	8.7	8.4
Dual income, no children	12,944,238	13,040,202	13,547,842	1,268,611	1,265,189	1,231,782	9.8	9.7	9.1

Source: Standard Rate and Data Service, 1994–1996. *Lifestyle Market Analyst,* Wilmette, Il.

Table 8.4 Family types in the Northeast market, 1994–1996

	Number of Households		
FAMILY TYPES NATIONWIDE	1994	1995	1996
Single	42,955,692	43,274,153	43,372,589
Married	52,927,550	53,319,939	54,093,903
Single, any child at home	6,328,294	7,341,151	7,407,453
Married, child age under 13	12,560,705	12,460,638	12,475,711
Married, child age 13–18	9,204,791	9,273,033	9,454,250
Dual income, child under age 13	7,095,360	6,954,778	7,212,520
Dual income, child age 13–18	5,944,761	5,988,834	6,237,855
Dual income, no children	12,944,238	13,040,202	13,547,842
FAMILY TYPES IN NORTHEAST	1994	1995	1996
Single:			
Boston	1,032,575	1,027,386	1,033,381
New York	3,406,524	3,424,626	3,424,828
Philadelphia	1,291,093	1,278,617	1,272,020
Washington	890,855	900,117	907,989
Married:			
Boston	1,100,844	1,104,120	1,115,020
New York	3,447,667	3,479,861	3,494,016
Philadelphia	1,404,300	1,401,922	1,400,291
Washington	992,560	1,002,878	1,019,800
Single, any child at home:			
Boston	117,338	144,942	143,943
New York	424,961	517,837	525,832
Philadelphia	177,896	209,082	213,785
Washington	114,888	131,307	134,945
Married, child under age 13:			
Boston	268,811	270,701	266,402
New York	815,651	828,538	830,261
Philadelphia	331,533	329,706	320,677
Washington	252,378	256,904	256,396
Married, child age 13–18:			
Boston	177,074	176,915	178,317
New York	575,754	593,786	595,021
Philadelphia	242,585	243,929	245,853
Washington	171,391	175,076	183,140
Dual income, child under age 13:			
Boston	166,407	161,994	165,427

Table 8.4 Continued

FAMILY TYPES IN NORTHEAST	Number of Households		
	1994	1995	1996
New York	431,815	434,983	463,563
Philadelphia	191,373	187,638	189,734
Washington	158,207	156,046	156,151
Dual income, child age 13–18:			
Boston	125,872	125,759	128,904
New York	370,127	372,842	380,536
Philadelphia	161,724	163,513	168,356
Washington	118,655	119,889	127,234
Dual income, no children:			
Boston	334,947	317,594	326,557
New York	987,006	945,915	968,638
Philadelphia	374,660	361,873	371,451
Washington	308,880	300,673	304,591

Source: SRDS, 1994–1996. *Lifestyle Market Analyst,* Wilmette, Il.

The Dilemma—The Future, What Markets?

Bill Stritzler convenes the staff meeting in April of 1997. He has asked his staff to come prepared to discuss the future planning and marketing issues before them. The fundamental concern is still the key question— "What should we do with Smugglers' over the next five, ten, to twenty years?"

Some believe it would be best simply to continue to be a family resort, a market niche approach. Those on the staff who believe this is the best strategy think that this market can be penetrated further. Jill Perdue, SNR marketing associate, believes that there are a number of smaller tier or secondary markets that SNR can penetrate:

> We often just go after the big markets—Boston, New York, and Hartford. I believe we should continue to maintain our image and seek to penetrate a whole set of second-tier cities. This would include such places as Albany, Syracuse, and Buffalo, New York; Harrisburg, Pittsburgh, and Scranton/Wilkes Barre, Pennsylvania; New Haven, Connecticut; and Providence, Rhode Island. Perhaps we should also seek out new markets in Ohio and Indiana. Furthermore, we should not overlook the Philadelphia, Baltimore, and Washington, D.C. metro areas. Besides, I believe if we are really "America's Family Resort" we should market our resort to more of America. People who live in these cities ski, we just need to get

Table 8.5 Transactions in Vermont's ski areas

Ski Area	Type of Transaction
Ascutney Mountain Resort	Went bankrupt; purchased and reopened by Steven and Susan Plausteiner, September 1993. (Location: Brownsville, VT)
Bolton Valley Ski Resort	Emerged from bankruptcy in September 1995, owned by the DesLauriers family of Bolton. (Location: Bolton, VT)
Burke Mountain Ski Area	Emerged from bankruptcy, sold in December 1996 to Northern Star Ski Corporation. (Location: East Burke, VT)
Haystack Ski Area	Purchased by SKI Ltd in November 1984, then merged with LBO Enterprises in February 1996. (Location: Wilmington, VT)
Jay Peak Ski Area	Purchased by Mt. Saint Sauveor International of Montreal, Canada. (Location: Jay, VT)
Killington Ski Area	Owned by SKI Ltd., part of the merger with LBO Enterprises in February 1996. (Location: Sherburne, VT)
Pico Ski Area	Sold in November 1996 to American Ski Company. (Location: Rutland, VT)
Mad River Glen Ski Area	Purchased by a cooperative and in final financing arrangements in 1996–1997 ski season. (Location: Waitsfield, VT)
Smugglers' Notch Resort	Purchased by William P. Stritzler, November 1996, from Stanmar, Inc., of Boston. (Location: Jeffersonville, VT)
Stratton Mountain Ski Area and Resort	Purchased by Intrawest in September 1995. (Location: Stratton Mountain, VT)
Sugarbush Ski Area	Purchased by LBO Enterprises in May 1995. (Location Warren, VT)

Ski LTD and LBO Enterprises have recently renamed the conglomerate to American Skiing Company. The source of this information was the Vermont Ski Areas Association and the *Burlington Free Press*.

more of them to come here. Not only are these areas potentially good ski markets but they also may be good markets for our summer business.

Bob Beemer, financial controller for the resort, believes that this approach is loaded with risks:

We have tested some cities in Ohio and more distant locations before and they have not been responsive. It is just too far to come for a winter vacation. Plus people have more choices for a winter vacation. If they want to ski there are plenty of places in the Mid-Atlantic States to ski—the Poconos, Western Pennsylvania, West Virginia, and even Virginia have ski areas within easy commutes. The last thing someone from the Midwest

Table 8.6 Vermont ski areas skier day comparisons and New England market share

Skier Day Comparison

YEAR	VERMONT	NEW HAMPSHIRE	MAINE	NORTHEAST*	U.S. TOTAL
1988–1989	4.5	2.2	1.0	12.7	53.3
1989–1990	4.6	2.0	1.1	13.3	50.0
1990–1991	4.1	1.6	1.1	11.1	46.7
1991–1992	3.8	1.9	1.2	12.2	50.8
1992–1993	4.2	2.1	1.2	13.2	54.0
1993–1994	4.3	2.2	1.3	13.7	54.6
1994–1995	3.7	1.9	1.2	11.4	52.5
1995–1996	4.1	1.9	1.3	12.5	54.0
Change rate	−0.9%	−1.2%	4.0%	0.4%	0.3%

Market Share Comparisons [%]

YEAR	VERMONT MKT SHARE (NORTHEAST)	VERMONT MKT SHARE (U.S.)	NH MKT SHARE (NORTHEAST)	NH MKT SHARE (U.S.)	MAINE MKT SHARE (NORTHEAST)	MAINE MKT SHARE (U.S.)	NORTHEAST MKT SHARE (U.S.)
1988–1989	35.4	8.4	17.3	4.1	7.9	1.9	23.8
1989–1990	34.6	9.2	15.0	4.0	8.3	2.2	26.6
1990–1991	36.9	8.8	14.4	3.4	9.9	2.4	23.8
1991–1992	31.1	7.5	15.6	3.7	9.8	2.4	24.0
1992–1993	31.8	7.8	15.9	3.9	9.1	2.2	24.4
1993–1994	31.4	7.9	16.1	4.0	9.5	2.4	25.1
1994–1995	32.5	7.0	16.7	3.6	10.5	2.3	21.7
1995–1996	32.8	7.6	15.2	3.5	10.4	2.4	23.1
Change rate	−0.9%	−1.1%	−1.6%	−1.9%	4.4%	3.9%	−0.1%

*Northeast includes Connecticut, Massachusetts, Maine, New Hampshire, New York, and Vermont.
Source: Vermont Ski Areas Association, 1996. Montpelier, Vermont.

wants to see on a winter vacation is more snow and cold weather. They can go to Disney or the islands or on a cruise. I believe we should stay close to our market and that is the regional Northeast markets of Boston and New York.

Jill Perdue had been able to collect data from Standard Rate and Data Services' *Lifestyle Market Analyst* (Table 8.7 profiles SNR's geographic markets) to support her point of view, but these data will need to be carefully reviewed and include participation rates by households. Bill Stritzler knows that the ski market is the bread and butter of their winter business. He asks if anyone knows what the future projection will be for the Northeast markets. No one has these data, but a staff associate says that the *U.S. Statistical Abstract* should contain the information and Mr. Stritzler asks that it be collected. He points out that they really need to know if possible what the population of children (those under age 18) and young adults (18 to 44) will be in 2000, 2005, 2010, and beyond in New England and the Northeast.

Peter Samuelson, director of the ski schools and summer mountain operations, believes that grabbing and building new markets are essential to SNR's long-term growth.

> Listen, we know that the skiing market is not growing. We have to work to create new skiers and offer more winter experience products. I believe we have missed part of the snowboarding market. This is where the growth in our industry is today. This is a natural for us—we have always done the very best in teaching the whole family how to ski. We know that many of the children we taught how to ski now snowboard. We cannot just be a place to ski, we must also be a place to snowboard. We must embrace this new trend and keep those families who learned how to ski together also coming back to ski and snowboard together. We have created a built-in market, let's evolve as our markets evolve. I know our surveys have indicated that the traditional skiers do not like the snowboarders. However, this will require education and clever marketing on our part. We know that snowboarders are primarily the youth and very young adult market, but we are now seeing some older adults and parents beginning to try snowboarding. I believe one of our best investments would be to create a Snowboard Park, we could call it the "Morse Monster" or the "Madonna's Hang Out," link it to our Smugglers' theme and run with it.

Peter Samuelson had been able to collect the latest statistics on snowboarding from the National Sporting Goods Association, and they will need to be carefully reviewed by the management team (see Table 8.8).

Lynn Lillis, associate director of the ski school, supports Peter's idea of product development with the emphasis on snowboarding. However, she does not believe it goes far enough:

Table 8.7 Geographic markets—Key markets for SNR's recreation and sport activities

Geographic Region	Golf	Tennis	Ski	Bike
National rates	19.6% (G)*	5.4% (D)	7.1% (D)	16.7% (D)
All New England mkts (prim., sec., tert.)	20.2% (SD)	6.4% (D)	8.1% (D)	16.0% (G)
1. Primary markets	16.5% (D)	6.7% (D)	9.1% (D)	16.0% (D)
Albany	22.2 (D)	5.5 (D)	12.2 (S)	17.2 (G)
Bangor	14.1 (D)	3.3 (D)	11.6 (G)	15.8 (G)
Boston	20.6 (D)	6.7 (D)	13.1 (D)	18.0 (G)
Hartford/New Haven	20.8 (D)	6.5 (D)	9.8 (D)	15.4 (G)
New York City Metro	15.1 (D)	7.6 (S)	7.8 (D)	16.2 (G)
Portland/Auburn	16.5 (D)	4.5 (D)	14.4 (D)	16.7 (S)
Providence/New Bedford	19.2 (D)	5.3 (D)	8.8 (D)	17.0 (S)
Springfield	20.0 (D)	4.7 (D)	10.1 (D)	17.5 (G)
2. Secondary markets	18.7% (S)	5.3% (D)	7.0% (S)	14.9% (G)
Harrisburg, Pa.	18.8 (D)	4.6 (D)	5.3 (G)	12.9 (D)
Philadelphia	18.2 (S)	6.1 (D)	7.0 (S)	15.9 (G)
Scranton-Wilkes Barre	16.5 (G)	3.2 (D)	6.3 (G)	11.0 (S)
Syracuse, NY	24.9 (D)	4.4 (D)	10.2 (D)	16.4 (G)
3. Tertiary markets	20.1% (G)	5.9% (G)	6.5% (G)	15.6% (G)
Baltimore	16.1 (D)	6.2 (D)	6.5 (D)	15.9 (G)
Cleveland	25.5 (S)	4.3 (G)	5.3 (G)	15.9 (G)
Pittsburgh	22.5 (G)	4.0 (G)	6.1 (G)	11.7 (G)
Washington, D.C.	16.7 (G)	8.0 (D)	7.6 (S)	17.5 (G)

*Participation rate noted is for most recent year, 1996, and rates are household participation rates. "(n)"—indicates trend of 1994–1996: (D) = Decline; (S) = Stable; (G) = Growth; (SD) = Stable/Decline and (SG) = Stable/Growth.
Source: SRDS, 1994–1996. *Lifestyle Market Analyst,* Wilmette, Il.

Table 8.8 Selected demographics of snowboarding, 1993–1995

Overall Participation	1993	1994	1995	Change Rate (%)
Number of participants (millions)	1.8	2.1	2.3	13.1
Frequent participants 10+ days/yr (millions)	0.6	0.7	0.7	8.3
Gender:	(Profile Percentage Below)			
Male (48.6% of U.S. pop.)	79.1	81.8	73.1	−3.6
Female (51.4% of U.S. pop.)	20.9	18.2	26.9	17.4
Age:				
7–11 (8.0% of U.S. pop.)	15.8	10.2	18.2	21.5
12–17 (9.4% of U.S. pop.)	38.7	41.4	34.4	−5.0
18–24 (10.8% of U.S. pop.)	27.4	26.4	20.9	−12.2
25–34 (17.7% of U.S. pop.)	7.1	12.5	15.6	50.4
35–44 (17.9% of U.S. pop.)	7.6	5.1	7.8	10.0
45–54 (12.8% of U.S. pop.)	1.5	1.7	1.3	−5.1
55–64 (9.0% of U.S. pop.)	0.8	0.8	1.5	43.8
65–74 (8.1% of U.S. pop.)*	1.0	1.9	0.3	2.9
75+ (6.2% of U.S. pop.)	NA	NA	NA	
*65 and over data combined in 93–95				
Geographic region:				
New England (4.9% of U.S. pop.)	8.7	7.5	8.8	1.8
Middle Atlantic (15.2% of U.S. pop.)	15.4	15.1	15.4	0.0
East North Central (17.0% of U.S. pop.)	22.0	9.4	18.5	19.8
West North Central (7.1% of U.S. pop.)	10.6	6.8	2.9	−46.6
South Atlantic (17.7% of U.S. pop.)	6.0	7.3	10.5	32.8
East South Central (6.5% of U.S. pop.)	1.7	3.7	3.1	50.7
West South Central (10.8% of U.S. pop.)	4.9	NA	5.9	20.4
Mountain (6.1% of U.S. pop.)	6.1	11.2	7.6	25.7
Pacific (14.8% of U.S. pop.)	24.7	29.0	28.3	7.5
Presence of children in household:				
At least 1 under 18 (48.6% of U.S. pop.)	NA	76.7	71.2	−7.2
None under 18 (51.4% of U.S. pop.)	NA	23.3	28.8	23.6
Household income:				
Under $15,000 (19.6% of U.S. pop.)	15.1	11.7	9.0	−22.8
$15,000–$24,999 (15.3% of U.S. pop.)	5.8	11.3	15.6	66.4
$25,000–$34,999 (14.3% of U.S. pop.)	17.4	9.4	14.2	2.5
$35,000–$49,999 (17.3% of U.S. pop.)	24.0	20.4	18.4	−12.4
$50,000–$74,999 (19.9% of U.S. pop.)	20.0	23.1	20.7	2.6
$75,000 & over (13.6% of U.S. pop.)	17.7	24.1	22.2	14.1
Metro size:				
Non-MSA (22.8% of U.S. pop.)	21.3	16.6	16.9	−10.1
50,000–499,000 (20.3% of U.S. pop.)	16.8	17.7	19.7	8.3
500,000–999,999 (10.8% of U.S. pop.)	10.0	10.9	14.3	20.
1,000,000–2,499,999 (21.8% of U.S. pop.)	14.3	23.1	26.0	37.0
2,500,000+ (24.3% of U.S. pop.)	37.6	31.7	23.1	−21.4

Source: NSGA, 1996–1997. SGRnet.

I believe we should go further with this product development. Listen, winter sports and the search for winter experiences are expanding. We should not just think of ourselves as the ski place or even the snowboard place for families. More people want to experience ice fishing, winter camping, snowshoeing, glade skiing, cross-country skiing, and telemarking. I believe we have too much tunnel vision and only want to consider what everyone else is doing. I believe we should be a total winter destination resort and offer variety for the family. Remember, we always promote the idea of "freedom for parents, fun for kids"; let's give them new experiences and new sources of fun. We can offer new experiences without major new capital-intensive facility investments. We could even contract out some of these new experiences. We should at least try to be more broadly based in our winter experiences; I believe this would offset the downturn in the traditional downhill ski market.

Peter Samuelson indicated that he was also able to come by some recent statistics on cross-country skiing and shared them with the management team after Lynn made her recommendation about other winter recreation opportunities. Lynn was able to acquire statistics on cross-country skiing and snowshoeing from SGRnet (see Tables 8.9 and 8.10). Unfortunately, little or no trend data or national/regional data appears to exist on ice fishing, winter camping, or telemarking.

Ed Padulsky, director of the ski pass department, believes that they had been overlooking one of their most precious markets—the local area ski market. Ed says,

Listen, part of our problem is we need to connect more to the local community and those who ski. We know that there are fewer opportunities for citizens of Vermont to ski locally. I know many people who just will not go to those big mountain areas like Killington, Stratton, or Mt. Snow, or even Stowe. They seem to be seen as the place for the rich and famous. The blue-blood Yankee skier and many who live nearby still perceive us as different, as more local, more family oriented, well, just more Vermont. Don't we also know that more people are moving to Vermont to pursue an outdoor lifestyle?

We also know that a number of ski areas have closed or failed to open in recent years, places like Maple Valley, Magic Mountain, Whaleback in New Hampshire. We also know that a number of other areas are still struggling—Burke, Ascutney, Bolton Valley, and Jay Peak. Let's concentrate on the local Vermont ski market. It could offset those markets that are declining, introduce our resort to a number of new locals, and create a new market for us. It makes us a community resort, too. Plus, we know that many people visit relatives and family and friends in Vermont during the ski season. We also could capture these people if we market cleverly and we would not need to make the major investments in new condos and other new amenities. We could then just reinvest into making this the real Vermont skiing experience. If we eventually have enough money, let's buy one of those smaller ski areas like Maple Valley

Table 8.9 Demographic trends in cross-country skiing, 1993–1995

Overall Participation	1993	1994	1995	Change Rate [%]
All participants (millions)	3.7	3.6	3.4	−4.1
Frequent participants (20+ days/yr) (millions)	1.1	1.1	1	−4.5
Non-frequent participants (millions)	2.6	2.5	2.4	−3.9
Gender:	(Profile Percentage Below)			
Male (48.6% of U.S. pop.)	46.6	48.1	51.2	4.8
Female (51.4% of U.S. pop.)	53.4	51.9	48.8	−4.4
Age:				
7–11 (8.0% of U.S. pop.)	8.0	6.0	8.4	7.5
12–17 (9.4% of U.S. pop.)	12.6	12.9	12.8	0.8
18–24 (10.8% of U.S. pop.)	7.3	10.9	12.9	33.8
25–34 (17.7% of U.S. pop.)	14.2	16.5	16.2	7.2
35–44 (17.9% of U.S. pop.)	29.1	23.8	23.4	−9.9
45–54 (12.8% of U.S. pop.)	15.6	14.3	14.0	−5.2
55–64 (9.0% of U.S. pop.)	8.4	10.9	8.7	4.8
65–74 (8.1% of U.S. pop.)*	4.8	4.9	1.7	−31.6
75+ (6.2% of U.S. pop.)	NA	NA	2.0	NA
Note: '93 & '94 include 65+ rate.				
Presence of children in household:				
At Least 1 under 18 (48.6% of U.S. pop.)	NA	50.7	47.6	−6.1
None under 18 (51.4% of U.S. pop.)	NA	49.3	52.4	6.3
Region:				
New England (4.9% of U.S. pop.)	14.9	10.9	11.2	−12.0
Middle Atlantic (15.2% of U.S. pop.)	18.9	20.8	24.5	13.9
East North Central (17.0% of U.S. pop.)	26.9	29.9	26.1	−0.8
West North Central (7.1% of U.S. pop.)	8.3	7.6	5.4	−18.7
South Atlantic (17.7% of U.S. pop.)	5.7	5.5	9.1	31.0
East South Central (6.5% of U.S. pop.)	0.6	1.8	1.7	97.2
West South Central (10.8% of U.S. pop.)	1.6	0.8	0.8	−25.0
Mountain (6.1% of U.S. pop.)	12	11.6	10.7	−5.5
Pacific (14.8% of U.S. pop.)	11	11.1	10.4	−2.7
Household income:				
Under $15,000 (19.6% of U.S. pop.)	7.8	9	14.9	40.5
$15,000–$24,999 (15.3% of U.S. pop.)	8.5	4.1	5.9	−3.9
$25,000–$34,999 (14.3% of U.S. pop.)	12.4	11	10.9	−6.1
$35,000–$49,999 (17.3% of U.S. pop.)	19.3	32.3	13.5	4.6
$50,000–$74,999 (19.9% of U.S. pop.)	28.5	23.3	28.1	1.2
$75,000 & over (13.6% of U.S. pop.)	23.5	20.3	26.7	9.0
Metro size:				
Non-MSA (22.8% of U.S. pop.)	28	28.9	23	−8.6
50,000–499,000 (20.3% of U.S. pop.)	20.5	24.8	20	0.8
500,000–999,999 (10.8% of U.S. pop.)	9.8	8.7	12.1	13.9
1,000,000–2,499,999 (21.8% of U.S. pop.)	15.9	14.9	21.7	19.7
2,500,000+ (24.3% of U.S. pop.)	25.9	22.8	23.2	−5.1

Source: NSGA, 1996–1997. SGRnet.

Table 8.10 Selected demographics of snowshoeing, 1995

Overall Participation	1995
Number of participants (millions)	0.6
	(Profile %)
Gender:	
Male (48.6% of U.S. pop.)	65.3
Female (51.4% of U.S. pop.)	34.7
Age:	
7–11 (8.0% of U.S. pop.)	5.1
12–17 (9.4% of U.S. pop.)	12.1
18–24 (10.8% of U.S. pop.)	13.9
25–34 (17.7% of U.S. pop.)	13.3
35–44 (17.9% of U.S. pop.)	18.0
45–54 (12.8% of U.S. pop.)	21.4
55–64 (9.0% of U.S. pop.)	10.6
65–74 (8.1% of U.S. pop.)	5.5
75+ (6.2% of U.S. pop.)	NA
Presence of children:	
At least 1 under 18 (48.6% of U.S. pop.)	25.8
None under 18 (51.4% of U.S. pop.)	74.2
Region:	
New England (4.9% of U.S. pop.)	17.8
Middle Atlantic (15.2% of U.S. pop.)	18.5
East North Central (17.0% of U.S. pop.)	19.7
West North Central (7.1% of U.S. pop.)	5.3
South Atlantic (17.7% of U.S. pop.)	5.3
East South Central (6.5% of U.S. pop.)	1.1
West South Central (10.8% of U.S. pop.)	4.0
Mountain (6.1% of U.S. pop.)	13.8
Pacific (14.8% of U.S. pop.)	14.7
Household income:	
Under $15,000 (19.6% of U.S. pop.)	21.7
$15,000–$24,999 (15.3% of U.S. pop.)	14.4
$25,000–$34,999 (14.3% of U.S. pop.)	5.8
$35,000–$49,999 (17.3% of U.S. pop.)	16.8
$50,000–$74,999 (19.9% of U.S. pop.)	23.7
$75,000 & over (13.6% of U.S. pop.)	17.7
Metro size:	
Non–MSA (22.8% of U.S. pop.)	44.5
50,000–499,000 (20.3% of U.S. pop.)	15.5
500,000–999,999 (10.8% of U.S. pop.)	3.4
1,000,000–2,499,999 (21.8% of U.S. pop.)	23.3
2,500,000+ (24.3% of U.S. pop.)	13.2

Source: NSGA, 1996–1997. SGRnet (trend data in '90s not available for snowshoeing).

or an area closer to the markets and make it the learn-to-ski place or the "Vermont Community Ski Place." Look at the stats of those areas where there are ski areas which are either in trouble or did not open. There is potential there—with disappointment comes opportunity. We should not let American Ski Company just push us out. We have a real opportunity here.

Ed was able to secure statistics, although dated, on the number of skiers by local zip codes. He has begun the process of reviewing the information for market potential (see Tables 8.11 and 8.12).

Finally, Roy Hobbs, director of guest relations, spoke about his belief that the great American ski decades have come and gone:

> Listen, I believe that the markets are changing and we cannot just depend on skiing as our bread and butter anymore. Look at who skis— those under the age of 35 and there are simply fewer and fewer of these folks. Those who are participating in winter sports in the youngest categories are snowboarding. We have let the other areas become known as the snowboard places. It will take investments to overtake them, plus they are big and have just better economies of scale . . . they can outinvest us. Younger people are into "showtime" in this activity and our image is "family." Snowboarders are rebels—"showtime" and "hot dogging" do not necessarily match the family image we have built over the years. I say we diversify beyond skiing and look to the summer months and our summer season to build our markets.
>
> There are at least three activities we should consider for the investment of our time and energy. Each are good family activities or could be and we have the property to make some investments in these areas. I say we focus on golf, mountain biking or biking in general, and in-line skating. Let me explain why I feel this way. First, the two warm weather activities that have grown the fastest in the nineties have been mountain biking and in-line skating. More and more people will be drawn into it. We also know how successful the Stowe Bike Trail has been and the Green Trail in Jeffersonville will happen. We could easily invest and develop various levels of trails within our property and connector trails to other trails nearby, which would make these activities wonderful family activities. It would serve to connect us to the community and to the environment and get people around the resort. I believe we should have a number of levels of trails—developed, semideveloped, and rough or natural. We would then be able to serve the in-line skaters and pleasure bikers on the developed trails and the real mountain bikers on the other trails.
>
> Furthermore, I do not believe we should overlook golf, but I believe we should put a different twist on it. This Tiger Woods phenomenon is for real. A whole new generation of golfers may now come to the game. Look at how Nike is advertising this—"I'm Tiger Woods" is a good indication of the major thrust by the golf industry. Golf, just like skiing, needs a feeder system; we could position a golf complex to teach people how to

Table 8.11 Vermont ski communities

Communities Potentially Losing Ski Areas

COMMUNITIES	NUMBER OF HOUSEHOLDS	PERCENT WHO SKI	NUMBER OF SKIING HSHLDS	PERCENT OF HSHLDS WITH CHILDREN LIVING AT HOME	HOUSEHOLDS WITH CHILDREN LIVING AT HOME
Ascutney Ski Area, Brownsville	785	53.9	423	44.1	346
Bolton Valley Ski Resort, Waterbury	1,988	26.3	523	37.7	749
Maple Valley Ski Area, Newfane	527	28.7	151	25.0	132
Burke Mtn. Ski Area, Lyndonville	2,012	27.1	545	35.9	722
Jay Peak Ski Area, Newport	2,600	15.3	398	35.2	915
Norwich Ski & Outing, Norwich	1,200	43.8	526	41.1	493
Magic Mountain Ski Area, Londonberry	502	51.9	261	24.0	120
Problem communities	9,614	29.4%	2,826	36.2%	3,479

Vermont's Top Ski Communities

COMMUNITIES	NUMBER OF HOUSEHOLDS	PERCENT WHO SKI	NUMBER OF SKIING HSHLDS	PERCENT OF HSHLDS WITH CHILDREN LIVING AT HOME	HOUSEHOLDS WITH CHILDREN LIVING AT HOME
Killington	616	80.1	493	26.2	161
Waitsfield	1,429	63.8	912	34.6	494
Stowe	2,924	61.9	1,810	31.7	927
Pittsfield	322	59.6	192	19.8	64
Warren	818	59.5	487	27.4	224
Chittenden	510	54.8	279	31.7	162

	Number of Households	Percent Who Ski	Number of Skiing Hshlds	Percent of Hshlds with Children Living at Home	Households with Children Living at Home
Brownsille	785	53.9	423	44.1	346
Londonberry	502	51.9	261	24.0	120
Stockbridge	69	49.2	34	20.6	14
Univ. of Vermont	66	48.4	32	3.3	2
South Woodstock	166	48.1	80	29.2	48
Barnard	92	46.5	43	35.7	33
Bridgewater	239	44.9	107	28.4	68
Wilmington	1,048	41.0	430	30.5	320
Total	9,586	58.2%	5,582	31.1%	2,984

Vermont's Largest Communities

Communities	Number of Households	Percent Who Ski	Number of Skiing Hshlds	Percent of Hshlds with Children Living at Home	Households with Children Living at Home
Burlington	14,259	28.3	4,035	22.8	3,251
Rutland	10,519	21.2	2,230	34.0	3,576
Brattleboro	6,917	18.7	1,293	32.6	2,255
Bennington	6,361	17.2	1,094	37.4	2,379
Colchester	6,292	29.8	1,875	36.9	2,322
Montpelier	5,724	21.7	1,242	34.7	1,986
Essex Junction	5,709	27.5	1,570	41.8	2,386
Barre	5,650	16.1	910	38.0	2,147
Total largest comm.	61,431	23.2%	14,250	33.0%	20,303

Source: SRDS, 1991. Zip Code Market Analyst, Wilmette, Il.

Table 8.12 Communities within SNR local market area

Communities Within 20 Miles of SNR

COMMUNITIES	NUMBER OF HOUSEHOLDS	PERCENT WHO SKI	NUMBER OF SKIING HSHLDS	PERCENT OF HSHLDS WITH CHILDREN LIVING AT HOME	HOUSEHOLDS WITH CHILDREN LIVING AT HOME
Burlington	14,259	28.3	4,035	22.8	3,251
South Burlington	5,212	30.7	1,600	31.5	1,642
Winooski	2,781	24.6	684	27.1	754
Univ. of Vermont	66	48.4	32	3.3	2
Alburg	622	9.2	57	45.4	282
Bristol	2,118	23.4	496	40.9	866
Cambridge	633	24.8	157	37.3	236
Charlotte	950	35.3	335	43.4	412
Colchester	6,292	29.8	1,875	36.9	2,322
Enosberg Falls	1,485	14.5	215	35.9	533
Essex Junction	5,709	27.5	1,570	41.8	2,386
Fairfax	821	22.0	181	45.9	377
Grand Isle	581	26.6	155	40.3	234
Highgate Center	556	12.1	67	48.2	268
Hinesburg	914	30.9	282	35.7	326
Huntington	1,057	28.1	297	41.5	439
Jeffersonville	841	33.7	283	41.7	351

Jericho	1,226	36.8	451	44.8	549
Milton	4,082	20.1	820	49.1	2,004
North Ferris	527	26.8	141	45.7	241
Richford	973	18.7	182	47.3	460
Richmond	1,665	40.4	673	44.9	748
St. Albans	4,872	17.8	867	40.3	1,963
Shelburne	2,379	35.2	837	36.5	868
Sheldon	622	28.8	179	62.2	387
South Hero	446	35.4	158	39.2	175
Starksboro	509	30.4	155	39.3	200
Swanton	2,924	19.3	564	40.8	1,193
Underhill	1,159	37.5	435	43.0	498
Vergennes	2,219	17.2	382	36.8	817
Westford	259	40.0	104	36.0	93
Williston	2,100	36.1	758	40.9	859
Total Local Market	70,859	26.9%	19,028	36.3%	25,737

Source: SRDS, 1991. *Zip Code Market Analyst,* Wilmette, Il.

golf. Many people and their children would like to learn how to play golf better and together if they have a place to play. This is particularly important in metro areas. I would propose a golf learning center targeted to families and learn-to-golf types. This could extend our season on either end by as much as four to six weeks. We might even have a totally different crowd coming to the resort in late April, May, and early June and September into October, but that's all right. We have the amenities they could use and we could really move more of those timeshare weeks. Look at the demographics. The Baby Boomers are golfing and we should get some of that market.

Furthermore, we have made some investments in tennis. No one has said anything about tennis. I know the trends are down in tennis; but we have a good complex here and it may very well come back in the future with the Baby Boomers' children. Let's not forget about our investment in tennis. It should figure into our future plans, too.

Roy Hobbs had been able to collect stats on the golf market and a number of the other recreational activities he mentioned including off- and on-road mountain biking, in-line skating, and tennis (see Tables 8.13–8.17). Golf, in-line skating, and mountain biking are entirely new ventures for SNR and will need careful consideration.

Table 8.13 Selected demographics of off-road mountain biking, 1993–1995

Overall participation	1993	1994	1995	Change Rate (%)
Number of participants (millions)	4.6	5.7	5.7	12.0
Frequent participants 30+/yr (millions)	0.3	1.3	1.7	182.1
Infrequent participants: <30/yr (millions)	4.3	4.4	4.0	−3.4
Gender:	(Profile Percentage Below)			
Male (48.6% of U.S. pop.)	72.5	66.6	65.3	−5.0
Female (51.4% of U.S. pop.)	27.5	33.4	34.7	12.7
Age of population:				
7–11 (8.0% of U.S. pop.)	12.5	7.7	9.2	−9.5
12–17 (9.4% of U.S. pop.)	14.1	16.4	11.2	−7.7
18–24 (10.8% of U.S. pop.)	23.3	23.2	21.4	−4.1
25–34 (17.7% of U.S. pop.)	25.9	30.9	30.7	9.3
35–44 (17.9% of U.S. pop.)	14.3	11.3	18.1	19.6
45–54 (12.8% of U.S. pop.)	3.0	6.4	6.0	53.5
55–64 (9.0% of U.S. pop.)	3.7	2.8	2.3	−21.1
65–74 (8.1% of U.S. pop.)*	3.1	1.2	0.8	−47.3
75+ (6.2% of U.S. pop.)	NA	NA	0.3	NA

*65 and over data combined in 93–94

Table 8.13 Continued

Overall participation	1993	1994	1995	Change Rate (%)
Geographic region:				
New England (4.9% of U.S. pop.)	4.5	7.8	7.3	33.5
Middle Atlantic (15.2% of U.S. pop.)	16.9	11.7	16.3	4.3
East North Central (17.0% of U.S. pop.)	12.1	13.0	12.2	0.6
West North Central (7.1% of U.S. pop.)	6.2	7.3	7.5	10.2
South Atlantic (17.7% of U.S. pop.)	11.9	15.4	11.7	2.7
East South Central (6.5% of U.S. pop.)	4.1	2.5	2.9	−11.5
West South Central (10.8% of U.S. pop.)	7.5	6.8	7.6	1.2
Mountain (6.1% of U.S. pop.)	8.9	11.8	12.2	18.0
Pacific (14.8% of U.S. pop.)	27.9	23.7	22.3	−10.5
Children present in household:				
Child under 18 in household	NA	49.2	46.3	−5.9
None under 18 in household	NA	50.8	53.7	5.7
Household Income:				
Under $15,000 (19.6% of U.S. pop.)	19.2	17.2	17.2	−5.2
$15,000–$24,999 (15.3% of U.S. pop.)	11.2	12.9	11.4	1.8
$25,000–$34,999 (14.3% of U.S. pop.)	13.6	13.4	16.6	11.2
$35,000–$49,999 (17.3% of U.S. pop.)	21.7	19.5	15.3	−15.8
$50,000–$74,999 (19.9% of U.S. pop.)	20.8	22.2	21.3	1.3
$75,000 & over (13.6% of U.S. pop.)	13.6	14.8	18.1	15.6
Metro size:				
Non-MSA (22.8% of U.S. pop.)	21.2	20.8	16.6	−20.2
50,000–499,000 (20.3% of U.S. pop.)	16.8	25.7	23.4	−8.9
500,000–999,999 (10.8% of U.S. pop.)	8.6	8.2	10.4	26.8
1,000,000–2,499,999 (21.8% of U.S. pop.)	22.4	20.1	23.4	16.4
2,500,000+ (24.3% of U.S. pop.)	30.9	25.2	26.2	4.0

Source: NSGA, 1996–1997. SGRnet.

Table 8.14 Selected demographics for on-road mountain biking, 1993–1995

Overall participation	1993	1994	1995	Change Rate (%)
Number of participants (millions)	10.5	9.0	10.5	1.2
Frequent participants (50+ days/yr; 110+ days in 1993) (millions)	1.1	1.8	2.1	40.2
Infrequent participants (<50/yr and <110/yr in 1993)	9.4	7.2	8.4	−3.4

Table 8.14 Continued

Overall participation	1993	1994	1995	Change Rate [%]
Gender:	(Profile Percentage Below)			
Male (48.6% of U.S. pop.)	58.8	57.7	58.3	−0.4
Female (51.4% of U.S. pop.)	41.2	42.3	41.7	0.6
Age:				
7–11 (8.0% of U.S. pop.)	14.5	6.9	9.4	−8.1
12–17 (9.4% of U.S. pop.)	15.9	13.8	12.5	−11.3
18–24 (10.8% of U.S. pop.)	17.0	21.1	18.4	5.7
25–34 (17.7% of U.S. pop.)	25.4	30.3	25.4	1.6
35–44 (17.9% of U.S. pop.)	15.4	15.3	18.4	9.8
45–54 (12.8% of U.S. pop.)	7.2	8.3	6.3	−4.4
55–64 (9.0% of U.S. pop.)	2.8	2.8	2.8	0.0
65–74 (8.1% of U.S. pop.)*	1.8	1.4	1.5	−7.5
75+ (6.2% of U.S. pop.)	NA	NA	0.1	
*65 and over data combined in 93–94				
Region:				
New England (4.9% of U.S. pop.)	5.3	7.0	6.2	10.3
Middle Atlantic (15.2% of U.S. pop.)	12.0	9.7	12.7	5.9
East North Central (17.0% of U.S. pop.)	15.7	15.3	16.7	3.3
West North Central (7.1% of U.S. pop.)	7.3	6.8	7.1	−1.2
South Atlantic (17.7% of U.S. pop.)	11.1	14.9	11.5	5.7
East South Central (6.5% of U.S. pop.)	3.4	1.7	3.4	25.0
West South Central (10.8% of U.S. pop.)	5.5	9.2	8.4	29.3
Mountain (6.1% of U.S. pop.)	9.4	12.1	11.3	11.1
Pacific (14.8% of U.S. pop.)	30.3	23.3	23.0	−12.2
Children present in household:				
At least 1 under 18 (48.6% of U.S. pop.)	NA	50.6	52.2	3.2
None under 18 (51.4% of U.S. pop.)	NA	49.4	47.8	−3.2
Household income:				
Under $15,000 (19.6% of U.S. pop.)	15.0	14.2	15.3	1.2
$15,000–$24,999 (15.3% of U.S. pop.)	12.2	12.9	10.3	−20.2
$25,000–$34,999 (14.3% of U.S. pop.)	14.9	14.2	16.0	12.7
$35,000–$49,999 (17.3% of U.S. pop.)	21.1	19.3	18.0	−6.7
$50,000–$74,999 (19.9% of U.S. pop.)	23.8	21.3	23.1	8.5
$75,000 & Over (13.6% of U.S. pop.)	13.0	18.1	17.3	−4.4
Metro size:				
Non-MSA (22.8% of U.S. pop.)	18.8	19.9	18.8	−5.5
50,000–499,000 (20.3% of U.S. pop.)	19.1	22.5	24.9	10.7
500,000–999,999 (10.8% of U.S. pop.)	8.7	9.6	9.9	3.1
1,000,000–2,499,999 (21.8% of U.S. pop.)	25.1	23.3	21.5	−7.7
2,500,000+ (24.3% of U.S. pop.)	28.3	24.7	25.0	1.2

Source: NSGA, 1996–1997. SGRnet.

Table 8.15 Selected demographic trends for in-line skating, 1993–1995

Overall participation	1993	1994	1995	Change Rate (%)
Number of participants (millions)	12.4	19.5	23.9	39.9
Frequent participants +30 days/yr (millions)	5.6	5.8	8.0	20.8
Infrequent participants <30 days/yr (millions)	6.8	13.7	15.9	58.8
Gender:	(Profile Percentage Below)			
Male (48.6% of U.S. pop.)	52.2	52.2	49.7	−2.4
Female (51.4% of U.S. pop.)	47.8	47.8	50.3	2.6
Age:				
7–11 (8.0% of U.S. pop.)	36.8	35.9	33.6	−4.4
12–17 (9.4% of U.S. pop.)	29.3	27.1	28.6	−1.0
18–24 (10.8% of U.S. pop.)	11.8	13.0	12.6	3.5
25–34 (17.7% of U.S. pop.)	12.0	13.0	13.5	6.1
35–44 (17.9% of U.S. pop.)	6.4	7.2	7.8	10.4
45–54 (12.8% of U.S. pop.)	2.7	2.2	2.1	−11.5
55–64 (9.0% of U.S. pop.)	0.7	0.6	0.7	1.2
65–74 (8.1% of U.S. pop.)*	0.3	0.9	0.4	72.2
75+ (6.2% of U.S. pop.)	NA	NA	0.8	
*65 and over data combined in 93–94				
Region:				
New England (4.9% of U.S. pop.)	5.2	5.9	4.0	−9.4
Middle Atlantic (15.2% of U.S. pop.)	14.2	15.0	15.8	5.5
East North Central (17.0% of U.S. pop.)	18.4	20.2	18.0	−0.6
West North Central (7.1% of U.S. pop.)	8.5	6.4	7.5	−3.8
South Atlantic (17.7% of U.S. pop.)	14.2	14.4	15.7	5.2
East South Central (6.5% of U.S. pop.)	3.3	2.4	4.0	19.7
West South Central (10.8% of U.S. pop.)	9.0	10.3	10.2	6.7
Mountain (6.1% of U.S. pop.)	6.2	7.5	6.2	1.8
Pacific (14.8% of U.S. pop.)	20.9	17.8	18.0	−6.9
Presence of children in household:				
Child under 18 in household	NA	80.4	79.0	−1.7
None under 18 in household	NA	19.6	21.0	7.1
Household Income:				
Under $15,000 (19.6% of U.S. pop.)	12.0	11.1	12.4	2.1
$15,000–$24,999 (15.3% of U.S. pop.)	11.3	9.7	10.2	−4.5
$25,000–$34,999 (14.3% of U.S. pop.)	13.1	15.0	14.4	5.3
$35,000–$49,999 (17.3% of U.S. pop.)	18.6	20.7	19.9	3.7
$50,000–$74,999 (19.9% of U.S. pop.)	28.4	25.9	26.0	−4.2
$75,000 & over (13.6% of U.S. pop.)	16.7	17.6	17.1	1.3

Table 8.15 Continued

Overall participation	1993	1994	1995	Change Rate (%)
Metro size:				
Non-MSA (22.8% of U.S. pop.)	16.4	13.2	16.6	3.1
50,000–499,000 (20.3% of U.S. pop.)	17.5	18.4	19.6	5.8
500,000–999,999 (10.8% of U.S. pop.)	9.1	10.5	11.4	12.0
1,000,000–2,499,999 (21.8% of U.S. pop.)	20.8	25.0	22.8	5.7
2,500,000+ (24.3% of U.S. pop.)	26.1	32.9	29.5	7.9

Source: NSGA, 1996–1997. SGRnet.

Table 8.16 Selected demographic participation trends for golf, 1993–1995

Overall participation	1993	1994	1995	Change Rate (%)
All participants (millions)	22.6	24.6	24.0	3.2
Frequent participants (40+ days/yr) (millions)	4.9	4.6	4.5	−4.1
Infrequent participants (<40 days/yr) (millions)	17.7	20.0	19.5	5.2
Gender:	(Profile Percentage Below)			
Male (48.6% of U.S. pop.)	76.0	76.0	75.2	−0.5
Female (51.4% of U.S. pop.)	24.0	24.0	24.8	1.7
Age:				
7–11 (8.0% of U.S. pop.)	3.7	2.7	3.6	3.2
12–17 (9.4% of U.S. pop.)	7.5	7.7	8.4	5.9
18–24 (10.8% of U.S. pop.)	13.6	11.7	10.2	−13.4
25–34 (17.7% of U.S. pop.)	22.9	24.4	23.8	2.0
35–44 (17.9% of U.S. pop.)	20.4	20.0	20.5	0.3
45–54 (12.8% of U.S. pop.)	14.1	13.4	15.3	4.6
55–64 (9.0% of U.S. pop.)	8.6	9.0	7.6	−5.5
65–74 (8.1% of U.S. pop.)*	9.2	11.2	6.8	−8.8
75+ (6.2% of U.S. pop.)	NA	NA	3.6	NA
*65 and over data combined in 93–94				
Children in household:				
At least 1 under 18 (48.6% of U.S. pop.)	NA	44.0	47.9	8.9
None under 18 (51.4% of U.S. pop.)	NA	56.0	52.1	−7.0
Region:				
New England (4.9% of U.S. pop.)	4.2	4.2	4.3	1.2
Middle Atlantic (15.2% of U.S. pop.)	15.0	13.8	14.9	−0.0
East North Central (17.0% of U.S. pop.)	22.4	20.7	22.4	0.3
West North Central (7.1% of U.S. pop.)	9.0	8.8	8.7	−1.7

Table 8.16 Continued

Overall participation	1993	1994	1995	Change Rate (%)
South Atlantic (17.7% of U.S. pop.)	15.9	16.8	17.1	3.7
East South Central (6.5% of U.S. pop.)	4.2	4.7	4.3	1.7
West South Central (10.8% of U.S. pop.)	8.7	8.9	7.8	−5.0
Mountain (6.1% of U.S. pop.)	6.8	7.6	7.7	6.5
Pacific (14.8% of U.S. pop.)	13.7	14.6	15.3	5.7
Household income:				
Under $15,000 (19.6% of U.S. pop.)	6.4	8.2	6.6	4.3
$15,000–$24,999 (15.3% of U.S. pop.)	8.5	9.8	8.4	0.5
$25,000–$34,999 (14.3% of U.S. pop.)	11.8	12.6	13.2	5.8
$35,000–$49,999 (17.3% of U.S. pop.)	18.4	20.1	17.1	−2.8
$50,000–$74,999 (19.9% of U.S. pop.)	32.4	29.0	29.7	−4.0
$75,000 & Over (13.6% of U.S. pop.)	22.5	20.3	25.0	6.7
Metro size:				
Non-MSA (22.8% of U.S. pop.)	19.7	18.0	18.4	−3.2
50,000–499,000 (20.3% of U.S. pop.)	22.4	20.9	20.2	−5.0
500,000–999,999 (10.8% of U.S. pop.)	10.1	13.1	12.9	14.1
1,000,000–2,499,999 (21.8% of U.S. pop.)	21.6	24.8	21.6	1.0
2,500,000+ (24.3% of U.S. pop.)	26.3	23.2	26.3	0.8

Source: NSGA, 1996–1997. SGRnet.

Table 8.17 Selected demographic trends for tennis, 1993–1995

Overall participation	1993	1994	1995	Change Rate (%)
All participants (millions)	14.2	11.6	12.6	−4.8
Frequent participants (30 + days/yr) (millions)	3.5	2.3	2.6	−10.6
Infrequent participants (<30 days/yr) (millions)	10.7	9.3	10.0	−2.8
Gender:	(Profile Percentage Below)			
Male (48.6% of U.S. pop.)	58.5	56.4	54.2	−3.7
Female (51.4% of U.S. pop.)	41.5	43.6	45.8	5.1
Age:				
7–11 (8.0% of U.S. pop.)	7.1	8.1	9.2	13.8
12–17 (9.4% of U.S. pop.)	17.4	18.0	17.9	1.4
18–24 (10.8% of U.S. pop.)	23.8	18.6	19.7	−8.0

Table 8.17   Continued

Overall participation	1993	1994	1995	Change Rate (%)
25–34 (17.7% of U.S. pop.)	21.7	22.9	21.6	−0.1
35–44 (17.9% of U.S. pop.)	16.6	14.9	16.7	0.9
45–54 (12.8% of U.S. pop.)	7.7	10.1	8.5	7.7
55–64 (9.0% of U.S. pop.)	3.9	4.1	4.1	2.6
65–74 (8.1% of U.S. pop.)*	1.9	3.3	2.0	17.1
75+ (6.2% of U.S. pop.)	NA	NA	0.2	
*65 and over data combined in 93–94				
Children in household:				
At least 1 under 18 (48.6% of U.S. pop.)		55.1	57.3	4.0
None under 18 (51.4% of U.S. pop.)		44.9	42.7	−4.9
Region:				
New England (4.9% of U.S. pop.)	5.7	5.5	4.4	−11.8
Middle Atlantic (15.2% of U.S. pop.)	18.0	13.6	18.0	4.0
East North Central (17.0% of U.S. pop.)	17.3	17.8	15.0	−6.4
West North Central (7.1% of U.S. pop.)	6.3	5.4	6.6	4.0
South Atlantic (17.7% of U.S. pop.)	19.1	18.3	20.1	2.8
East South Central (6.5% of U.S. pop.)	5.4	5.6	4.2	−10.6
West South Central (10.8% of U.S. pop.)	10.1	10.1	9.2	−4.5
Mountain (6.1% of U.S. pop.)	5.5	6.0	5.7	2.0
Pacific (14.8% of U.S. pop.)	12.5	17.7	16.9	18.5
Household income:				
Under $15,000 (19.6% of U.S. pop.)	11.8	10.8	11.2	−2.4
$15,000–$24,999 (15.3% of U.S. pop.)	9.8	12.9	11.9	11.9
$25,000–$34,999 (14.3% of U.S. pop.)	12.3	9.1	10.6	−4.8
$35,000–$49,999 (17.3% of U.S. pop.)	18.2	17.0	16.3	−5.4
$50,000–$74,999 (19.9% of U.S. pop.)	26.5	29.8	25.5	−1.0
$75,000 & Over (13.6% of U.S. pop.)	21.4	20.4	24.4	7.5
Metro size:				
Non-MSA (22.8% of U.S. pop.)	14.6	12.6	16.7	9.4
50,000–499,000 (20.3% of U.S. pop.)	23.5	18.9	18.9	−9.8
500,000–999,999 (10.8% of U.S. pop.)	9.8	13.8	12.0	13.9
1,000,000–2,499,999 (21.8% of U.S. pop.)	21.4	21.8	21.8	0.9
2,500,000+ (24.3% of U.S. pop.)	30.9	33.0	30.6	−0.2

Source: NSGA, 1996–1997. SGRnet.

Conclusion

Bill Stritzler requests a careful review of the statistics collected. He especially wants to know if he should be worried and what proposals for overall marketing strategy the management teams might have for the future. So, Bill is faced with a planning and marketing dilemma. Does he pursue a new direction at the resort? Does he maintain the status quo, even though he knows the market may decline and change? Does he invest in new product development—new activities at the resort—or does he invest in growing his current markets by seeking out new, more-distant markets through advertising or capitalizing on the failures or shortcomings of other areas? Does he move the resort to connect more aggressively with the growing local Vermont community? Or does SNR completely diversify into totally new activity and product offerings and invest heavily in new major infrastructure improvements?

Bibliography

Allen, Anne Wallace, January 5, 1997. "Vermont's Small Ski Areas Going Downhill Fast." *Springfield Sunday Republican*. Business Section, Section D1-D2.

Geggis, Anne. November 5, 1996. "Smugglers' Notch Resort Sold." *The Burlington Free Press*. 1A-2A.

National Sporting Goods Association, 1996–1997. SGRnet: http://www.sgrnet.com.

Simmons Market Research Bureau. 1979–1994. *Study of Media and Markets, Sports and Leisure*, Vol. P10. New York, New York.

Sneyd, Ross. November 5, 1996. "Longtime Manager Buys Smugglers' Ski Resort." *The Times Argus*. pp. 1,8.

Standard Rate and Data Service. 1994, 1995, 1996. *Lifestyle Market Analyst*. Wilmette, Illinois.

Vermont Ski Areas Association. 1996. *Vermont Ski Industry . . . State of the Industry*. Montpelier, Vermont.

9

Pier 39 Licensed Products Stores

Susan C. Milne and Ronald P. Courtney

Introduction

Chris N. Sharkey strode confidently down the aisles of Atlanta's Super Show, the largest wholesale apparel convention in the United States featuring licensed sports products. "Starter has a great display this year with their new line of 49er T-shirts," Chris thought as he contemplated the success of his three retail stores located on Pier 39 in San Francisco. His stores, the NFL (National Football League) Shop, the MLB (Major League Baseball) Shop, and The College Shop carried apparel and gift items featuring popular professional football, professional basketball, and college sports teams. Chris purchased a good deal of the upcoming year's inventory for his stores during this four-day event that showcased 3,000 vendors from nearly 100 countries.

Chris's buyer purchased most new product lines at conventions like Atlanta's Super Show. A small portion of new items were found through catalogs or when sales representatives called on the store. One reason for attending the show was to meet the vendors in person. Having a good relationship with a vendor was important. There were times when a certain product was selling like crazy and it was critical to have orders filled while the oftentimes short-lived fads were still hot. In general, retailers put a lot of trust in their suppliers to guide purchases. Chris often bought large quantities of stock based solely on the advice of a sales representative. If Chris asked for the top-five-selling items of a particular company, he had to trust that he would be given good information and not be duped into buying some over-stocked junk the supplier wanted to get rid of. Because these vendors controlled the supply of products and influenced many purchases, Chris had tried to develop good relationships with all of his key contacts.

All of Chris's major vendors had booths at the Super Show. Champion was pushing a new line of tank tops. "That will be a major loser," he thought. In the next aisles he saw the exhibit by the company Sports Spectacular. Last year's sales of their hats had been better than expected. As he turned the corner to enter the middle of the convention center, he saw the Nike display and his smile quickly faded. He had been unsuccessful at his attempts to get an appointment with the national account representative from Nike, one of his largest and most important vendors, who supplied some of his store's best-selling cloth-ing. Annoyed that his sales weren't large enough to warrant a meeting with Nike's account representative, Chris began to wonder whether he was maximizing the potential of his three stores. He had long toyed with the idea of merging his three sports apparel and gift stores into one big store selling goods from all major professional and college sports. With the availability of a large retail space in close proximity to his current stores, he now had the opportunity to make a decision that would determine the future of his company. His choice could lead either to success and profits or could drive the company into financial ruin.

Licensed Products

Chris felt fortunate to be selling licensed products at a time when sales of these products were increasing. Licensed sports merchandise is defined as products for sale that bear the logos of sports teams and leagues. Licensees are entities that buy contractual permission to use a trademark under the licensor's (the league's) supervision and control. These contracts require manufacturers to meet certain standards when creating and selling products, pay advance fees (money paid by a li-censee to obtain a license), and guarantee royalties for the use of the trademark. Professional leagues have done a great job maximizing licensing opportunities and helping create interest in fans to tout their favorite teams. Total sales of all licensed products in the four leagues was more than $6 billion in 1992 (see Table 9.1). There are thousands of officially licensed products available, ranging from standard T-shirts to outlandish boxer shorts with prints of baseball scenes and slogans. One of Chris's best-selling items was a jersey with an authentic repro-duction of a professional team's logo.

In the four major professional leagues (football, baseball, basketball, and hockey), merchandising is coordinated by a central "properties" division. For example, professional baseball's Major League Baseball Properties (MLBP) is in charge of licensing and marketing MLB prod-ucts. For items sold through these channels, proceeds from sales of team merchandise are pooled and divided evenly among the league teams. In 1991, MLBP had over 300 licensees. The 300 licensees of the MLBP sell over 3,000 products with "official" baseball team logos and

Table 9.1 1992 Retail sales of licensed products for the four major sport leagues in North America*

League	Total Sales (billions)
National Football League	$2.5
Major League Baseball	2.0
National Basketball League	1.0
National Hockey League	0.5
Total Sales	$6.0

*Source: "What's next: Raider's deodorant?" by Elizabeth Lesly, *Business Week*, November 30, 1992, p. 65.

designs. The standard royalty rate is 8.5% on gross production. In 1992, the MLBP generated almost $170 million in licensing royalty revenues for the major league baseball teams.

Sales of goods licensed by major league baseball grew from $200 million in 1987 to $2 billion in 1992. Even minor league baseball was trying to create interest in merchandise with their logos and had recently become involved in licensing. Chris had not yet tried selling any minor league merchandise, but he wondered if there was potential interest in local teams. Similarly, the National Football League Properties is the branch charged with controlling and promoting licensed merchandise in the NFL. Chris purchased many of his preprinted clothes for The College Shop from vendors who were licensed through the Collegiate Licensing Company.

Licensed products were the key to sales in Chris's three stores. He began selling licensed products in 1980 when many department stores had small sections devoted to licensed product clothing depicting the popular "home" teams for the local geographic area. He had been able to capitalize on the phenomenal growth of licensed products in the past decade. For instance, National Football League revenues from souvenirs increased nearly 400% since 1980, and Chris had read predictions that sales would exceed $3 billion by 1993 (Compte, 1989). However, Chris was always skeptical of economists' predictions and wondered if sales from licensed products had reached their peak. Sales most likely would not continue to grow at such a phenomenal pace. Would this be the year that sales would begin the downward trend that happens to most products that become so enormously popular? If so, the industry (and, more importantly, his own profits) could experience a huge decline if fashion trends changed and wearing team-related clothes went out of style.

The NFL Shop, the MLB Shop, and The College Shop

Chris's three stores carried many items that were similar except that they bore the logos of their respective sports. Hats (baseball caps), jackets, T-shirts, and sweatshirts with various team logos were sold in all the stores. To supplement the basic sales items, there were products unique to each store, such as football helmets sold in the NFL Shop and old uniforms sold in the MLB Shop. The San Francisco Giants and the Oakland A's were the most popular teams in the MLB Store. Similarly, local college logos such as Stanford and Berkeley sold well in the College Shop.

Chris had worked hard to create his three licensed-products stores on Pier 39. The NFL Shop was his largest and most successful. Chris was one of the first in the country to create a store specializing in sports clothing for professional and college teams. In the 2,100-square-foot store, he sold products featuring the teams and popular players of the National Football League. Anything you could imprint with a team logo could be found at the NFL Shop: T-shirts with a picture of Joe Montana throwing a touchdown pass, black towels blaring RAIDERS in silver letters, baseball hats with the red and gold 49er emblem embroidered on the front, and even Dallas Cowboy cheerleading outfits for toddlers. In a small section of the store, he carried a few NBA (National Basketball Association) products, but there was not enough room in the store to carry a more complete NBA line.

Similarly, his two other stores on Pier 39 featured sports products. The MLB Shop was filled with licensed products from major league baseball teams. Locals enjoyed buying and wearing items identifying them with the Oakland A's and the San Francisco Giants. Items for other popular teams, such as the New York Yankees and the LA Dodgers, were sold to people traveling to San Francisco from other parts of the country and Europe. The College Shop appealed to sports fans, students, and alumni looking for paraphernalia from their favorite colleges. Some of the best-selling teams included the University of San Francisco, Stanford, and the University of California at Berkeley. Predicting sales for The College Shop was the most difficult because the best-selling teams always depended on who was winning at the moment. They could always count on increased sales of items depicting the winners of the Final Four (basketball) and NCAA (football) tournaments.

One unusual feature of The College Shop was a sewing machine for stitching pre-embroidered letters onto clothing. This allowed people to custom-order shirts or sweatshirts with whatever college name they chose. Set up as an attraction in the middle of the store, this machine took up a bit of floor space (32 square feet), but it also provided some entertainment as people watched the embroidery process while others in their group shopped. Each time a college's name was sewn onto a shirt, a 6% royalty fee was paid to that college. When premade shirts were sold in this store or the other licensed-products stores, the royalty fee was included in the price paid to the vendor.

The biggest and best-selling product by far in all of the three stores was anything that depicted the local San Francisco 49er football team or their quarterback Joe Montana. Fortunately, the 49ers, having been labeled the "Team of the Decade" in the eighties, had been extremely successful in the past few years. By 1992, average game attendance was 61,824 and the franchise was valued at $139 million (see Table 9.2). As the 49ers star quarterback, the enormously popular Joe Montana was named sportsman of the year in 1990 after leading his team to the Superbowl four times. Other titles earned during his incredible career included three Superbowl MVPs (Most Valuable Player awards), two NFL MVPs, and eight Pro Bowl stars. Chris could not have chosen a more perfect location to sell 49er paraphernalia to out-of-town fans. However, he tried not to forget that fans were fickle. If the 49ers suddenly stopped playing well and had a few bad seasons, or if Joe Montana got hurt, traded, or retired, store sales would suffer greatly.

The popularity of the local professional sport teams, combined with the location of his stores on Pier 39, was good for Chris's business. His three stores were successful to varying degrees. The NFL Shop was the most profitable, with sales of $1.1 million last year generating a

Table 9.2 San Francisco 49ers football team statistics

Year	Record WINS	Record LOSSES	Attended Playoffs
1980	6	10	No
1981	13	3	Yes
1982*	3	6	No
1983	10	6	Yes
1984	15	1	Yes
1985	10	6	Yes
1986	11	5	Yes
1987	13	2	Yes
1988	10	6	Yes
1989	14	2	Yes
1990	14	2	Yes
1991	10	6	No
1992	14	2	Yes

*Strike season.

profit of $81,210. Next, the MLB store had sales of $800,000 and a yearly profit of $58,880. The College Shop was in last place with a smaller sales figure of $600,000, and $20,310 in profits (see Table 9.3).

Chris relied on his intuition, feedback from his managers, and guidance from his vendors to determine which products to buy. He had a general idea of the financial contribution of general groupings of his products. He and his staff created a monthly report depicting products by class with key financial measurements such as ROI (return on investment), percent gross profit, and percent of total dollars sold (see Table 9.4). One measurement Chris watched carefully was the turnover at cost. This liquidity ratio gives him a good indication of which products are selling and which are just taking up precious floor space. Slow inventory turnover is a serious red flag that the items that make up

Table 9.3 NFL Shop profit & loss statement

Income	Year-to-Date Actuals
Gross sales	$1,100,000
Cost of Goods Sold	
Clothing	283,800
Merchandise gifts	42,570
Caps/Hats	132,440
Freight	14,190
Total cost of goods sold	$ 473,000
Gross profit	$ 627,000
Rent Expenses	
Base rents	72,000
Percent of sales rent	66,000
Property tax	12,000
Common area maintenance	29,000
Promotion fund	22,000
Total rent expenses	$ 201,000
Operating Expenses	
Insurance	16,500
Equipment—rental	14,300
Credit card fee MC/VISA/AMEX	13,200
Utilities	13,200
Contract labor	12,000
Fixtures/Display	9,900
Office & store supplies	8,800

Table 9.3 Continued

Telephone	6,050
Repair/Maintenance	5,500
Travel expense (shows, etc.)	5,500
NSF check charges	4,950
Bank charges	4,290
Accountant fees	3,300
Postage	2,530
Depreciation	2,000
Interest expense	1,750
Total operating expenses	$ 123,770

Payroll Expenses

Wages	192,640
Health insurance	8,580
Payroll taxes (FICA, FUI, SUI)	19,800
Total payroll expense	$ 221,020
Total all expenses	$ 545,790
Net Profit	$ 81,210

MLB Shop profit & loss statement

Income	Year-to-Date Actuals
Gross sales	$800,000

Cost of Goods Sold

Clothing	181,360
Mdse. gifts	60,000
Caps/Hats	108,000
Freight	10,640
Total cost of goods sold	$360,000
Gross profit	$440,000

Rent Expenses

Base rents	50,000
Percent of sales rent	47,520
Property tax	6,000
Common area maintenance	14,500
Promotion fund	16,000
Total rent expenses	$134,020

Table 9.3 Continued

Income	Year-to-Date Actuals
Operating Expenses	
Insurance	12,000
Utilities	11,200
Equipment—rental	10,000
Credit card fee MC/VISA/AMEX	9,600
Supplies: Office & operating	5,920
Repair/Maintenance	5,360
Contract labor	5,000
Fixtures/Display	4,500
Telephone	4,400
Bank charges	4,070
NSF check charges	3,600
Accountant fees	3,300
Travel expense (shows, etc.)	2,800
Postage	2,240
Depreciation	2,000
Interest expense	1,750
Total operating expenses	$ 87,740
Payroll Expenses	
Payroll expense	138,560
Health insurance	6,400
Payroll taxes (FICA, FUI, SUI)	14,400
Total payroll expense	$159,360
Total all expenses	$381,120
Net Profit	$ 58,880

The College Shop profit & loss statement

Income	Year-to-Date Actuals
Gross sales	$600,000
Cost of Goods Sold	
Clothing	122,700
Mdse. gifts	38,330
Caps/Hats	71,160
Freight	6,960
2% royalty fee	6,850

Table 9.3 Continued

Total cost of goods sold	$246,000
Gross profit	$354,000

Rent Expenses

Base rents	42,000
Percent of sales rent	36,000
Property tax	4,200
Common area maintenance	10,150
Promotion fund	12,000
Total rent expenses	$104,100

Operating Expenses

Insurance	10,000
Supplies: Office & operating	11,400
Equipment—rental	9,580
Utilities	7,980
Credit card fee MC/VISA/AMEX	7,200
Repair/Maintenance	5,220
Fixtures/Display	4,440
Contract labor	4,230
Accountant fees	3,300
Travel expense (shows, etc.)	3,060
Bank charges	2,880
NSF check charges	2,880
Telephone	2,640
Depreciation	2,000
Interest expense	1,750
Postage	1,620
Total operating expenses	$ 80,180

Payroll Expenses

Payroll expense	133,560
Health insurance	4,800
Payroll taxes (FICA, FUI, SUI)	10,800
Total payroll expense	$149,160
Total all expenses	$333,690
Net Profit	$ 20,310

Note: Interest expense on $50,000 loan, accountant fees, salaries for buyer and bookkeeper are prorated among the three stores.

Table 9.4 NFL Shop at Pier 39: Class report

Class	%T$S	$Sold	$RcvC	Sold	%GP	TOC	ROI
Children's clothing	12.30	135,300	75,768	6,054	58.85	4.91	7.04
Gifts & novelties	17.80	195,800	79,691	30,434	62.10	5.32	8.71
Headwear	16.30	179,300	77,996	9,175	57.10	3.31	4.41
Jackets	16.20	178,200	81,259	1,864	51.30	3.84	4.04
Jerseys	8.10	89,100	49,540	1,407	54.50	2.20	2.63
Pants	1.30	14,300	5,606	631	60.10	7.76	11.70
Shirts	16.20	178,200	74,309	6,765	58.00	5.09	7.04
Sweatshirts	11.80	129,800	60,357	2,660	55.20	5.08	6.25
Total/Average	100.00%	1,100,000	504,525	58,990	57.14%	4.69	6.48

%T$S: Percent of total dollars sold
$SOLD: Dollar sold at retail
$RcvC: Dollars received at cost

SOLD: Units sold
% GP: Percent gross profit

TOC: Turnover at cost
ROI: Return on investment

MLB SHOP at Pier 39: Class report

Class	%T$S	$Sold	$RcvC	Sold	%GP	TOC	ROI
Children's clothing	13.60	108,800	52,224	6,162	57.75	3.49	4.95
Gifts & novelties	12.60	100,800	35,683	18,797	64.60	3.38	6.15
Headwear	32.40	259,200	110,678	14,178	58.60	2.23	3.16
Jackets	12.20	97,600	49,581	1,133	52.60	1.67	1.85
Jerseys	11.10	88,800	52,126	1,483	49.00	2.69	2.58
Pants	0.60	4,800	2,203	208	57.80	1.29	1.77
Shirts	16.9	135,200	58,406	5,318	57.40	3.94	5.31
Sweatshirts	0.60	4,800	1,272	128	52.80	4.78	5.35
Total/Average	100.00%	800,000	362,174	47,406	56.32%	2.93	3.89

The College Shop at Pier 39: Class report

Class	%T$S	$Sold	$RcvC	Sold	%GP	TOC	ROI
Children's clothing	0.36	2,189	1,116	147	61.00	6.00	9.39
Gifts & novelties	3.32	19,906	8,530	2,489	59.50	2.00	3.24
Headwear	13.81	82,852	30,739	4,230	61.84	3.37	5.59
Jackets	9.33	55,966	26,454	800	52.38	2.45	2.70
Jerseys	1.30	7,779	3,749	152	52.75	3.37	3.76
Miscellaneous	0.29	1,714	492	41	62.40	4.50	4.63
Pants	0.66	3,968	1,674	152	58.13	2.61	3.80
Production (letters & blank garments)	35.77	214,614	66,998	18,421	64.20	3.40	6.10
Shirts	18.93	113,604	49,782	5,576	58.86	3.31	4.77
Sweatshirts	16.23	97,409	48,232	2,518	51.92	3.96	5.15
Total/Average	100.00%	600,000	237,765	34,525	58.30%	3.50	4.91

The College Shop Class report: Percent of total dollars sold by conference

Class	Eastern Conference	Midwest Conference	Western Conference	Independents
Children's clothing	0.00	0.00	77.21	22.79
Gifts & novelties	0.57	0.43	15.58	83.42
Headwear	27.82	13.48	48.01	10.68
Jackets	18.53	17.56	46.45	17.47
Jerseys	46.99	23.24	21.40	8.36
Pants	12.87	7.02	73.39	6.72
Shirts	20.51	6.57	53.50	19.42
Sweatshirts	14.38	13.78	53.82	18.01

the product class are not selling well. He liked to see products turn over four times a year or more. Although Chris needed to rely on this information for planning future inventory purchases, he knew that it was not entirely accurate. Since there was no formal tracking system in place, the data was subject to his own biases and those of his workers. He needed to purchase a computerized inventory tracking system that would calculate the same information based on actual sales and not just on perceptions of what was sold. Also, with a computer system he would be able to track inventory at an individual product level and enable his buyers to track with accuracy what specific items were selling and which weren't. He had recently met with a local computer firm that offered a product suited to his needs at a cost of $33,000 for each store.

One of the ways Chris felt that he had a competitive advantage over large department stores selling merchandise similar to his was that as a small business owner he was able to keep his costs relatively low. Although he had little control over the high price of his leases because of their location in a high-traffic tourist area, he did try to keep a watchful eye on his other expenses. After inventory costs and rent, payroll was his third-highest yearly expenditure. One person was in charge of buying all the merchandise for the three stores. His salary and benefits totaled $38,000 per year. In addition, there was a book-keeper who managed the accounting for the Pier stores—accounts pay-able, payroll, and paperwork to comply with government regulations and pay royalty fees for The College Shop. Payroll expense for this worker was $30,000. One manager worked in each of the three stores. Each manager was in charge of scheduling his or her store's employees, hiring and firing, closing out the registers at the end of the day, creating window displays, as well as pitching in with the sales staff during busy times of the day. The remainder of his employees worked in the stores, spending most of their time ringing up sales and stocking the shelves at a cost of $6 to $7 per hour (see Table 9.5). Employee costs as a percentage of sales were relatively high in The College Shop because sewing on embroidered letters was labor intensive.

Table 9.5 Employee data for Pier 39 stores

Location	Number of Employees*	Manager's Salary
NFL Shop	7 to 10	$35,000
MLB Shop	5 to 6	$35,000
College Shop	5 to 6	$30,000

*The number of employees changes slightly during the year. The summer months (June through September) require more employees because of the increased tourist traffic while a smaller staff is more cost efficient for the slower winter months (December through March).

Another major expense for Chris was promotional money paid to Pier 39 from each store. The Pier 39 management spent a lot of money and time attracting tourists and locals to visit the Pier. The Pier required its tenants to pay 2% of the previous year's gross sales toward a promotional fund to finance advertising campaigns. The goal was to create an image of the Pier as a destination spot for people spending time in San Francisco and the Bay Area. The marketing department did a good job promoting the Pier. For instance, some of the promotional fund money was used to solicit a visit to the Pier as a side trip for various cruise lines, walking and bus tours, convention centers, and travel-agent-sponsored outings. The Pier advertised in free magazines and newspapers available to tourists in hotels and restaurants. During the winter holiday season, it purchased the largest evergreen tree in San Francisco and had a tree-lighting ceremony attended by some popular Walt Disney characters. All of the major TV networks covered the ceremony with praise and goodwill for the Pier. Since money for the promotional fund was charged to all the tenants on the Pier, albeit not in equal amounts, the advertising campaigns did not focus on any specific products or stores. Aside from the efforts made by the Pier, Chris had not spent any money advertising his own unique shops.

Despite some relatively large monthly expenses, Chris's stores were in a fairly good financial position. All three stores were showing a profit and he was happy with the managers and the sales staff. He was, however, determined not to become complacent about his stores and let them become stagnant. Chris was constantly trying to improve the stores: buying new types of merchandise to mix with the licensed products, creating new signs to attract shoppers' attention, and taking a strong interest in how the Pier used its advertising dollars.

Pier 39

Chris considered the location of his three stores, Pier 39, one of the major factors of his success in retail. Pier 39 was converted in 1978 into a festival marketplace featuring unique shopping and dining overlooking the picturesque bay of San Francisco. In addition to the more than 110 one-of-a-kind stores, Pier 39 is a destination spot where tourists and locals can enjoy breathtaking views of the Golden Gate Bridge and Alcatraz Prison, be entertained by street performers on an outdoor stage, take a ride on a beautiful Venetian carousel, or view the hundreds of sea lions that make the docks attached to the Pier their home. These and other attractions on and around the forty-five acre complex make Pier 39 one of the world's top five attractions (see Table 9.6).

Chris's stores were located in various sections of the Pier. A map of Pier 39 (see Figure 9.1) shows the prime retail spots on level 1 near

Table 9.6 The world's top five attractions*

Park, Location	1992 Attendance (millions)
Walt Disney World, Florida	25.1
Disneyland, California	13.0
Pier 39, San Francisco	**10.5**
Blackpool, Pleasure Beach	6.5
Sea World, Florida	4.5

*Source: The London Observer, March 1, 1992.

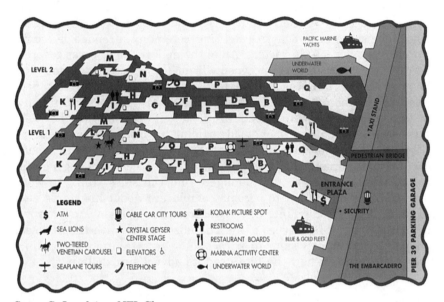

Space G, Level 1 = NFL Shop
Space N, Level 1 = The College Shop
Space P, Level 2 = MLB Shop
Space Q, Level 2 = The space available for lease
Figure 9.1 Pier 39 map

the entrance to the shops and restaurants. The NFL Shop, located in space G, was about three-quarters of the way from the entrance to the Pier. Although it did have the largest square footage of the three stores, the NFL Shop had a small display window and was set back a bit from the center aisles where most people walked. Chris had tried to compensate for the poor frontage with a large, bold sign to attract shoppers. The College Shop, in space N, had better frontage to entice potential customers to enter the store, but its small size limited the number of products that could be offered from the popular colleges.

The worst location was that of the MLB store (space P). Chris always felt that the anemic sales of the MLB Shop could be at least partly attributed to the location on the second floor, where foot traffic was much less than on the ground level.

Not only was location a factor in the profitability of the stores but the size and operating costs played a major role. As shown in Table 9.7, costs for leasing the stores was a major expense. Yearly expenses totaled $164,000 just to rent the spaces and that did not include other leasing costs such as property taxes (landlords typically pass on to their tenants the cost of taxes for the property they own and lease) and common-area maintenance fees. Another rental fee charged by most landlords is a fixed percentage of sales above a break-even rent amount. This fee is referred to as the percent of sales rent. In Chris's situation, he paid 12% of his monthly gross sales above a set sales figure called the monthly sales basis. The formula to determine the monthly sales basis of the 12% rent fee is

$$\text{Monthly sales basis} = \frac{\text{yearly base rent/12 months per year}}{12\% \text{ rent fee}}$$

For example, the yearly base rent for the NFL Shop was $72,000. The monthly sales basis is calculated as follows:

$$\$50,000 = \frac{\$72,000/12}{.12}$$

Therefore, the NFL Shop was required to pay 12% of all gross sales above $50,000 each month to Pier 39. If sales in August were $80,000 then the percent of sales rent would be $3,600 for that month. This is calculated by subtracting the monthly sales basis from gross sales for the month and multiplying the outcome by 12%.

$$\text{Monthly percent of sales rent} = (\text{monthly gross sales} - \text{monthly sales basis}) \times 12\%$$
$$\$3,600 = (\$80,000 - \$50,000) \times 12\%$$

In order to pay the high leasing fees charged by Pier 39, the stores needed to generate large sales. To accomplish this, Chris needed to attract customers into the store and also have the right mix of products to encourage spending. When trying to decide which products to sell and how best to display the merchandise, Chris tried to picture his typical customer. Who was buying clothes and souvenirs depicting professional and college sports? To find out who was coming to the Pier and why, Chris relied on a survey conducted by the Pier 39 marketing department (see Figure 9.2). The majority of people coming to the Pier were tourists. Local residents of San Francisco had a love/hate relationship with major tourist attractions like Pier 39 in their city.

Table 9.7 Pier 39 lease information

Location	Square Feet	Yearly Base Rent	Monthly Sales Basis of 12% Rent Fee	Year-to-Date Percent of Sales Rent	Property Tax	Common Area Maintenance	Lease Ending (Years)
NFL Shop	2,000	$72,000	> $50,000	$66,000	$12,000	$29,000	Now
MLB Shop	1,000	50,000	> $34,722	$47,520	$ 6,000	$14,500	Seven
College Shop	700	42,000	> $29,166	$36,000	$ 4,200	$10,150	Two

Visitors to Pier 39:
  51% Male
  48% Female

Visitor type:
  59% are tourists to the San Francisco Area
  26% are Bay Area residents
   9% are Northern Californians living outside the Bay Area
   6% are attending conventions or conferences in San Francisco

74% of those surveyed would return to Pier 39

Average length of stay is 2 hours and 45 minutes

Purpose of coming to Pier 39:
  39% General shopping or browsing
  37% Sightseeing
   7% Came for other reasons (i.e., bring friends, go out for a walk, people
      watch)
  17% Came to go to a specific attraction, restaurant, or store

Visitors came to Pier 39 in groups of:
  One: 8%
  Two: 28%
  Three: 18%
  Four: 23%
  Five: 10%
  Six or more: 12%

Attractions visited:
  Blue and Gold Fleet Bay Cruise (provides cruises around the Bay):   12%
  Center Stage: 46%
  Two-Tiered Venetian Carousel: 51%
  Namco Cyber Station Family Games Arcades: 20%
  Turbo Tours (motion theater adventure "ride"):   14%
  Sea lions: 68%
  Other: 32%

Eating at Pier 39:
  43% ate at our fast-food establishments
  32% ate at our full-service restaurants
  20% did not eat on the Pier

Transportation to Pier 39:
  42% via auto and used the Pier 39 parking garage
  15% via auto and did not park in garage
  10% via tour bus
   8% walked to the Pier
  10% used public transportation
   5% via taxi
   3% via ferry service
   6% via other (pedicabs)

Figure 9.2   Pier 39 survey information (Based on 241 surveys taken July 10th through July 15th)

Pier 39 ratings in the following categories:

	Excellent	Good	Average	Fair	Poor
Layout	71%	24%	4%		
Decor	63%	29%	5%	1%	
Pier safety	69%	23%	5%		1%
Variety of shops	59%	26%	7%		
Merchandise quality	54%	31%	8%	1%	
Variety of restaurants	57%	27%	9%		
Customer service	61%	25%	6%		2%

Money spent at Pier 39:
  3% spent nothing
  11% spent under $10
  30% spent $10 to $30
  26% spent $30 to $50
  17% spent $50 to $100
  12% spent $100 or more

Age of Pier 39 visitors:
  10% are 15–19
  21% are 20–29
  33% are 30–44
  11% are 45–54
  9% are 55–64
  12% are 65+

56% of Pier 39 visitors have children
37% of Pier 39 visitors brought their children with them

Education:
  7% have had less than a high school education
  2% have had some high school
  23% are high school grads
  5% have had vocational/technical school training
  24% are college graduates
  12% are post-college graduates

Where do Pier 39 visitors stay while visiting the city?
  29% reside in Bay Area homes
  27% stayed in hotels/motels in San Francisco
  12% stayed with friends or relatives
  9% visited the Pier from outside the San Francisco area
  5% stayed in other habitations (i.e., cruise ships and motor homes)

Previous visits to Pier 39
  49% were first time visitors to Pier 39
  29% had been to Pier 39 twice before
  9% had been to Pier 39 three times
  14% had been to Pier 39 four or more times

How did Pier 39 visitors hear about the Pier?
  22% were told by friends/relatives
  20% knew about the Pier from a previous trip
  12% were tour participants
  10% were told by their travel agent or concierge

Figure 9.2   Continued

9% read about Pier 39 from travel publications (*Rough Guide, AA Travel, Bay City Guide, Berlitz, Let's Go USA, Travel & Leisure, Poliglot Travel Guide*)
1% saw a newspaper ad
1% heard a radio ad
2% saw or heard something about Pier 39 on TV or radio

Income range of Pier 39 visitors:

Less than $15,000	13%
$15,000 to $24,999	9%
$25,000 to $34,999	20%
35,000 to $49,999	11%
50,000 to $74,999	14%
$75,000 or MORE	19%
REFUSED	14%

Figure 9.2 Continued

They complained loudly about the traffic jams created by people trying to drive and read a map at the same time. They were frustrated by not being able to get reservations at their favorite restaurants during the summer season, and they were particularly wary of Pier 39 because it was one of the bigger attractions and seen as crass and boldly commercial by some of the old-timers nostalgic for a Fisherman's Wharf that actually did trade in fish. Thirty-nine percent of people coming to the Pier were doing general shopping or browsing, while only 17% came to go to a specific restaurant or store. Chris concluded that most people who bought from his stores did not come looking for something specific, but rather "stumbled" into the store. Strolling shoppers were drawn into his stores because of the location, or because the name of the store on his sign and on the Pier directory piqued their interest.

There was no direct competition with Chris's stores at Pier 39. His were the only stores that sold items relating to professional and college sports. However, he was competing with other stores for shoppers who were looking for souvenirs and gifts to take home as mementos of their vacations or business trips to San Francisco. The variety of shops and specialty merchandise sold on Pier 39 was wide, including San Francisco souvenirs of all types, colorful kites, imported chocolates, hand-woven sweaters, high-fashion leathers, and even a store filled only with wind-up toys. Chris could not discount the fact that a tourist or business person only had so much money to spend and room in his or her suitcase for purchases made while away from home. Even though the other shops sold vastly different products, each store on Pier 39 was a potential competitor. Not only did shoppers have an incredibly wide variety of products from which to choose, many people coming to the Pier were mainly interested in dining. Pier 39 boasted that each of its ten full-service restaurants had a breathtaking view of the San Francisco Bay because of the unique feature of being surrounded by water on three sides. Thirty-two percent of people who came to the Pier ate at one of the full-service restaurants, while 44% chose to eat at the walkaway food shops that catered to those in a hurry or on a budget. Chris relied on diners to stroll through his shops and make impulse purchases on their way to or from their meals.

The Dilemma

During a Pier 39 Merchants' Advisory Committee meeting recently, the manager of the Pier, Brian Crowe, approached Chris with a proposition. A 7,800-square-foot restaurant, located on the second level in space Q, was going out of business, and Brian asked Chris if he would be interested in leasing the old restaurant's spot for a retail store. Whatever store took over the space would have to generate incredible sales just to pay the lease, thought Chris. The Pier was currently charging yearly fees of about $40 per square foot for rent. Monthly fees were costing approximately $1.5 per square foot for common-area maintenance fees and $0.50 per square foot for property taxes. The yearly rental expenses on a store this large would be immense. Not even the NFL store sales would generate the kind of cash flow needed to sustain the large rental fees. But wait . . . what if he combined the three sports apparel stores—the NFL Shop, the MLB Shop, and The College Shop—into one megastore with sports apparel and novelty items from all professional and college sports? A giant sports store could include products from basketball, hockey, soccer, Nascar racing, and perhaps even minor league baseball. However, sharing retail floor space among all of the sports could potentially take sales away from the popular NFL and MLB sales and hurt profitability. Was there enough interest in sports apparel to generate cash to pay for a store that was more than double the size of his current selling space and leave him with a reasonable profit? Chris called a meeting with his accountant to discuss the feasibility of his burgeoning idea.

Dawn Smith, CPA, considered one of her major roles as accountant and financial consultant to be playing devil's advocate to many of Chris's incredible schemes. She saw him as a great talent, having enormous intuition predicting trends in retail and sensing what the customers were going to buy, yet she was the one who was charged with handling the cash flow and was paid to worry about just how extended the business was financially. She was quite concerned when she heard about his plan to combine the three Pier stores into one, especially considering that they were about to spend about $100,000 on a new computer tracking system that she felt was desperately needed. She came to the meeting armed with the current balance sheet showing just where things stood (see Table 9.8).

Table 9.8 Balance sheet: Pier 39 shops

Current Assets			
Cash	54,400		
Till Money	600		
Inventory	304,000		
Total Current Assets		$359,000	
Fixed Assets			
Security Deposit	6,200		
Leasehold Improvements	105,000		
Equipment	35,000		
Total Fixed Assets		$146,200	
Total Assets			$505,200
Liabilities & Equity			
Loans	50,000		
Liability Miscellaneous	2,400		
Accounts Payable	47,600		
Sales Tax Payable	16,420		
Total Current Liabilities		$116,420	
Total Owner's Equity		$388,780	
Total Liabilities & Equity			$505,200

Chris, guessing that he was going to meet with opposition from Dawn about their cash situation, opened the meeting by discussing some of the benefits of creating a megastore. "By merging The NFL Shop, The MLB Shop, and maybe even The College Shop into one store, we could change the focus of our store. Until now we have been driven by the tourist-as-customer angle and haven't tapped into the locals who want to buy licensed merchandise. We could become an anchor store, with people coming to the Pier specifically to shop with us. Instead of just having a good summer season, we could sell more items as gifts and see an increase in sales for our traditionally slow Christmas season. Adding new sports like hockey and soccer would broaden our appeal to more types of customers. We could definitely do more with basketball by putting in a major NBA (National Basketball Association) section. Our increased sales would most likely justify the increase in expenses of the larger site." Chris also considered that a giant store with larger sales could increase his clout with major vendors like Nike. Chris felt that with a large sign, the new location was incredible. Although it was on the second level, it was the first retail store at the entrance of the Pier. There was potential to create a huge amount of traffic for the store, especially if they had a large, exciting sign that would encourage anyone interested in professional sports to climb up the stairs and wander through the shop. A big sign would be easy to see from the pedestrian bridge coming from the parking lot. An elevator was also conveniently located to bring customers wishing to reach the second level right to the entrance of the store. Chris was concerned about a trend he had recently noticed. Stores in shopping malls in the Bay Area, and presumably in other parts of the country, were selling more licensed products. They were beginning to offer products similar to those sold in his stores. In order to differentiate himself from the local mall stores, Chris felt that he needed to create something new and exciting. Otherwise, he was afraid his stores' concepts would become commonplace and people would stop buying from him. A new store would need to give the impression that this is THE PLACE to shop for professional sports apparel and gift items. A store that catered to sports fans of all popular sports, both local and those from out of town, might be the answer.

"What you say does make sense," countered Dawn, "but why take the risk of creating a new store with unknown sales when you have three viable, profitable stores? Let's consider some of the negatives of your suggestion." Dawn then proceeded to explain why she thought the megastore idea was a mistake. Dawn's major concern was the affordability of the project. Right now the three stores had fairly new fixtures, flooring, counters, etc. There were no foreseeable major renovating expenses coming in the next three years. In order to create the megastore, you would have to fund conversion of the restaurant into a store: new lighting, flooring, wall fixtures, counters, signs, moving the merchandise, etc. She estimated that it would cost approximately $100,000 to convert the existing restaurant into a new retail store. Inventory was another issue that concerned Dawn. Although they could pull the existing inventory from whichever stores they chose to merge into the megastore, they would still need about $100,000 to purchase new goods to fill the additional space. Right now they were able to keep up with payments to vendors, but with so much additional inventory to purchase, payments could lag behind the standard terms of net 30 days. She would hate to lose the good relationships they had built with the vendors because of a short cash position. Also, with a store the size of 7,800 square feet, it would be prudent to have a security system installed and/or extra people on the sales floor to watch for thieves. In their current stores, losses due to theft were increasing and she could imagine how much worse it would be in a huge store with lots of space not visible to the sales clerks working at the checkout counter. Dawn estimated they would need four employees ringing up sales and as many as eight people milling about to answer customer's questions, stock the shelves, check inventory, and protect the merchandise. Alternatively, she had been investigating an inventory security system they could lease for $250 per month for forty months that would ring an alarm if someone tried to leave the store without paying for an item.

Their existing cash would not be able to fund the restaurant conversion, a new security system, purchase of a computer tracking system, and the purchase of new inventory. Last year they had borrowed $50,000 on a five-year note at 10.5% interest, secured by a lien on the inventory. They would need to borrow more money if they decided to create a megasports apparel store. In addition to the cash flow problem, another major factor that worried Dawn was potential loss of sales. Right now someone unfamiliar with the Pier could look at the sign for any of the three stores and have a pretty good idea regarding the types of goods being sold inside. The NFL Shop would immediately interest someone who liked football and might want to buy or browse through items relating to professional football. What kind of name would you choose for a shop that sold all different types of professional and college sports items? If the store's name didn't immediately inform the casual shopper what was being sold in the shop, Chris could lose an incredible amount of customers. She did not think that any name for a giant store would be direct enough to convey all the products available, especially if they tried to combine professional sports items with college products. Also, Dawn felt that the three stores provided three different opportunities for people to find their stores and purchase their goods. She wondered if people spent more money if they didn't spend it all at one store. According to the Pier 39 survey, only 12% of people spent $100 or more. Many of the licensed products like jackets cost more than $100. She felt that they needed to maximize the potential to sell the big-ticket items with more than one location. It is probably easier to get a customer to spend $100 in three different stores than $300 in one store, she guessed.

If they decided to go forward with the megastore, they would need to broaden the focus of their target market to include local customers while keeping their current tourist customer base. The store would have to be interesting enough to help the locals overcome their negative attitudes toward shopping at a tourist-type location. Additionally, prices for similar goods were generally higher at the Pier than at local malls because of the high rent paid to the Pier. Would customers be willing to brace the crowds and traffic to buy a hard-to-find shirt featuring their favorite soccer team? Wouldn't they be just as likely to buy items during a game or at their local department store? Dawn was skeptical that they would have much success with local customers.

Would inventory turnover be higher, lower, or the same with a combination of offerings of professional and perhaps even college goods? Dawn's concern was that they would end up with lots of hard-to-find items that appealed to such a narrow market that turnover at the individual product level would decrease. Another argument that Dawn made during the meeting was the timeliness of the move. At the moment, the company was short on cash. They would need some major funds to create the new store. How much money would they need and at what cost to borrow the funds? It might be more prudent to wait until the company's cash flow improved a bit. Could they save enough over the next few years to pay for the expansion and then try to find a spot for the megastore? How long would it take?

Chris agreed with Dawn that there were some major issues that needed to be addressed. She had brought up some points that he had not considered, which did cause him to think that maybe he had been too rash in his initial enthusiasm for owning a giant sports apparel store. He was excited by the idea of creating something new and unique but worried that he might just be satisfying his ego to become the owner of the largest store on Pier 39 and perhaps the largest licensed products store in the United States. Maybe it would be best to combine only The NFL Shop and The MLB Shop to provide a focus of just professional sports products and leave The College Shop as a separate entity. He could hedge his risk a little by maintaining one smaller, profitable store. But would he be able to generate enough sales with just professional sports items? Another idea he considered would move the smaller College Shop into one of the larger spaces he was moving out of if he decided to focus on professional sports for the megastore. While he was certain the Pier would allow him to cancel any or all of his current leases if he would take over the restaurant space, he did have the option of to keeping any of the locations he currently occupied in addition to renting the new space.

During this brainstorming session he devised a few ways to try to reduce some costs of moving into the large store. Brian was going to have a hard time leasing the restaurant space because of its size. The Pier liked Chris as a tenant because he was a local business owner, was personally involved with his stores, and paid his rent on time. Chris was fairly sure that he could convince Brian to reduce the leasing fee to something between $30 and $40 a square foot. Also, he could include in the lease negotiations Pier assistance converting the restaurant into a store. If the landlord would agree to upgrade the spot to a "vanilla box" (all demolition work, painting, flooring, and ceiling complete) in move-in condition, he could save between $45,000 and $70,000. Another cost-saving area was in the purchase of the computer. Instead of buying three separate computers, he could purchase one large inventory-tracking system that would cost him between $50,000 and $75,000.

Chris suggested that they end their meeting and return in one week. He needed detailed analysis and compelling arguments to substantiate reasons why either combining the stores (all three or just the two professional sports stores) into a megasport store could be successful or why they should leave things the way they were.

10

Salt Lake City 2002 Winter Olympic Games—The Prevention of Ambush Marketing

Jay Gladden and David Shani

Introduction

As Alyssa Samson drove north out of Park City, Utah, on the Olympic Parkway, the mounting pressure of the 2002 Salt Lake City Winter Olympic Games troubled her. As the Director of Corporate Services for the Salt Lake Organizing Committee (SLOC), Alyssa was responsible for the fulfillment and implementation of the sponsorship packages sold to corporations for the 2002 games. Even though the games were several years away, Alyssa knew it was her responsibility to ensure that all sponsors were satisfied with their involvement with the Salt Lake City Olympics.

Alyssa was returning home to Salt Lake City after two days of meetings with representatives from the International Olympic Committee (IOC) and the United States Olympic Committee (USOC). One of the major thrusts of those meetings was how to curtail ambush marketing, the efforts of corporations to associate with events without obtaining sponsorship rights. At the 1996 Summer Olympic Games in Atlanta, ambushing corporations such as Nike were very successful at achieving a presence without paying for rights. This displeased both the IOC and the new leadership within the USOC.

Alyssa was so engrossed in thought that she nearly missed the exit for Interstate 80 West, which would take her the rest of the way home. However, she was troubled. The sponsorship fees for the Olympic Games had continued to escalate. With the increased financial commitment, corporations were seeking broader assurance that they would receive exclusive exposure within their product category. However, Alyssa also knew that the prevention of ambush marketing was no

179

easy task. This was particularly true in the United States, where the Constitution generally protected the freedom of commercial speech.

Alyssa was also wary of the widespread criticism that befell Atlanta in 1996 when thousands of nonsponsors attempted to achieve an association with the games. The IOC was openly derisive toward the lack of commercial control exercised by the Atlanta Committee for the Olympic Games (ACOG). The 2002 games represented the return of the Olympics to the United States. It rested upon Alyssa and the rest of the SLOC to prevent unauthorized commercial affiliation with the Olympics. Otherwise, the IOC would be very reluctant to award a U.S. city the Olympic Games for a long time. Thus, as Alyssa took the exit onto route 89 south back into Salt Lake City, she began to structure her plan for preventing ambush marketing.

Commercialism and the Olympic Games

Although it is often suggested that there are no commercial influences associated with the Olympic Games, this is not true. At the very first modern Olympic Games in 1896, financial pressures led organizers to sell souvenir stamps to raise money. From this point, corporate involvement grew slowly. In 1912, several photography companies were allowed to take pictures and sell the photographs. By 1924, corporations were paying to advertise within the Olympic Stadium. However, this so angered the leaders of the Olympic movement that such signage was permanently banished and remains so today.[1]

As time passed, the Olympic Games grew substantially. The increased number of athletes and countries competing in a wider variety of events drastically increased the costs associated with managing the games. Table 10.1 depicts the growth of the Winter Olympic Games during the second half of the twentieth century. Early on, IOC members provided a large portion of the financing for the Olympic Games. However, with the costs of running the Olympic Games reaching hundreds of millions of dollars by the 1970s, it was no longer possible for private financing solely to fund the Olympic Games.

In the United States, this problem is particularly acute, for it is the only country competing in Olympic sport that receives no funding from its federal government. The Amateur Sports Act of 1978 designated the USOC as the sole overseer of Olympic sport in the United States. Although initial drafts of the legislation mandated an initial payment

---

[1]History of commercialism in the Olympic Games was excerpted from S. Rozin, "Olympic Partnership, *Sports Illustrated,* July 25, 1995, pp. 37–76.

Table 10.1 Growth of the Olympic Games: 1952–1994

Year	Host City	Countries	Events	Athletes
1952	Oslo, Norway	30	22	732
1956	Cortina d'Ampezzo, Italy	32	24	819
1960	Squaw Valley, California	30	27	648
1964	Innsbruck, Austria	36	34	933
1968	Grenoble, France	37	35	1,293
1972	Sapporo, Japan	35	35	1,128
1976	Innsbruck, Austria	37	37	1,261
1980	Lake Placid, New York	37	39	1,283
1984	Sarajevo, Yugoslavia	49	40	1,490
1988	Calgary, Canada	57	46	1,634
1992	Albertville, France	64	57	1,801
1994	Lillehammer, Norway	67	61	1,844

Source: 1995 Fact Book: United States Olympic Committee.

coupled with yearly payments from the U.S. government to the USOC, the final legislation contained no such provision; therefore, the Olympic movement in the United States is funded completely with nongovernmental monies. This includes the hosting of the Olympic Games.

The necessity for private financing of the games became obvious following the 1976 Summer Games in Montreal. These taxpayer-financed games had a $1 billion deficit when the games were over (Helyar, 1996). However, the potential for commercially financing the games was not seen until the 1984 Summer Games in Los Angeles. Under the direction of Peter Ueberroth, those games raised $125 million in corporate sponsorships, which enabled the Los Angeles Organizing Committee to generate a $222 million profit.

IOC Cultivation of Commercialism

Based on the success of the Los Angeles Games, the IOC, which oversees the entire Olympic movement, decided that they would begin actively selling worldwide sponsorships. To do so, they created The Olympic Program (TOP). Instead of selling sponsorship rights for one Olympics, TOP sold sponsorships for four-year periods of time, called *quadrenniums*. Under the direction of President Juan Antonio Samaranch, the IOC was very successful in selling sponsorships, commanding $40 million per sponsorship for the quadrennium ending in 1996. Table 10.2 presents the revenue generated by the IOC through TOP sponsorship sales.

Table 10.2   TOP sales by qadrennium

Quadrennium	Sponsorship Sales ($M)
TOP I—1985–1988	$ 95
TOP II—1989–1992	$175
TOP III—1993–1996	$350
TOP IV—1997–2000 (projected)	$400

Source: The Wall Street Journal, July 19, 1996

Prior to 1985, the local organizing committees (LOCs) were the only entities selling sponsorships for the games. LOCs are created after a country has been awarded the Olympic Games and serve as the organizer and administrator of those games. Included in that responsibility is the construction and development of facilities. LOCs disband completely following the conclusion of the Olympics.

As depicted in Figure 10.1, the National Olympic Committee (NOC) within each country governs LOCs. Therefore, the SLOC is governed by the USOC. In addition, the NOCs (in this case the USOC) is governed by the IOC. Therefore, when the IOC decided that it wanted to begin selling worldwide sponsorships, the LOCs had no choice but to abide by its desires. However, with the IOC selling the premier worldwide

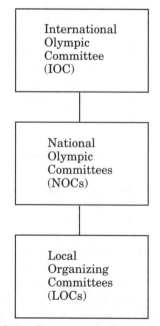

Figure 10.1   Olympic organizational structure

sponsorships, this detracted from a potentially lucrative revenue stream. The IOC only distributes 20% of its gross sponsorship sales to the LOC. The rest of the money is first used to cover the administrative expenses of the IOC and then spread across the NOCs and International Sports Federations in an effort to benefit the Olympic movement. As a result, the LOCs are forced to sell sponsorship packages below TOP. However, the LOCs are restricted in the rights that they can promise to sponsors. The IOC reserves the right to offer the most benefits because it oversees the Olympic movement. Ultimately, the LOCs are only able to offer a scaled-back version of benefits and thus are more limited in the amount of revenue that they can generate through sponsorship sales.

Although it is the IOC that has openly utilized and benefited from the sales of sponsorship, it has lately been suggested that there is too much commercialism associated with the Olympic Games. In particular, the Atlanta Olympic Games received harsh criticism for its extensive use of commercial money to fund the games.

The 1996 Summer Olympic Games—
Atlanta, Georgia, U.S.A.

The 1996 Summer Olympic Games in Atlanta were the largest Olympic Games ever. Fifteen thousand athletes and coaches from 197 countries competed in events covered by over 10,000 members of the media. While the games were the largest, for the first time in his tenure as president of the IOC, Juan Antonio Samaranch did not deem the games the "best ever"; instead, he referred to the games as "most exceptional."

Some of this rebuke was due to the operational glitches that occurred during the games. The computer system used to report results to broadcasters and the media malfunctioned early on, causing false results to be transmitted. In addition, the transportation of IOC officials, various visiting diplomats, and media members was poorly coordinated from the outset. Bus drivers were not properly trained, losing their way to some of the sporting venues. Furthermore, the bomb that was detonated in the Centennial Olympic Park certainly dampened the enthusiasm and enjoyment of all who were in Atlanta. These were some of the problems, but the IOC was even more disappointed with the rampant commercialism present at the 1996 games.

While the Atlanta games represented the largest games ever, they also represented the largest display of commercialism in conjunction with Olympic Games. Olympic sponsors attempted to maximize benefits from association with the games. Sponsors such as Coca-Cola, AT&T, and Budweiser created multiacre "villages" in downtown Atlanta in an effort to sell their products. Coca-Cola alone spent more than $250 million to support their $40 million TOP sponsorship. However, non-sponsors also spent lavishly attempting to associate with the Atlanta games. For example, athletic shoe and apparel manufacturer Nike spent $3 million purchasing and refurbishing an old garage near the Olympic Village in downtown Atlanta, ultimately creating a massive sports museum. In addition, Nike spent millions of dollars outfitting national teams competing in the games. In particular, the exposure Nike received from the shoes worn by Michael Johnson while winning the 200- and 400-meter dashes brought Nike immediate recognition with hundreds of millions of television viewers. Besides Nike, nonsponsors Lee Jeans and Volkswagen each spent more than $10 million to be "broadcast sponsors" of the Olympic Games on NBC.

In addition to the efforts of large corporations that did not sponsor the games, a number of Atlanta-based corporations attempted to benefit from the Olympic Games. In particular, the city of Atlanta hired a marketing firm to sell the merchandising and vending rights to portions of city parks and streets. So many businesses purchased rights that the streets of downtown Atlanta took on the appearance of a flea market during the games. Such efforts were blatantly inconsistent with the Olympic image (as portrayed by the IOC) and lessened the impact and exclusivity of actual Olympic sponsors.

ACOG's Financial Challenge

The Centennial Olympic Games were awarded to Atlanta largely due to the efforts of Billy Payne. A commercial real-estate lawyer, Payne left his law partnership in 1987 to pursue his dream of bringing the Olympics to Atlanta. Atlanta had never before submitted a bid to host the games; thus Payne had to work fast to formulate a bid that would defeat the 1896 host, Athens, Greece. This work included determining the construction that needed to be done and coordinating improvements with the city of Atlanta. Thus, the city of Atlanta did not coordinate the bid; rather, it was one of many groups that Payne worked with to create an attractive bid.

Once awarded the games, Payne was faced with the Herculean task of financing the games. First, the Atlanta Committee for the Olympic Games (ACOG) was formed. Again, the USOC oversaw the creation and implementation of this organization. In addition, the USOC worked with ACOG to create Atlanta Centennial Olympic Properties (ACOP), which served as the marketing organization for the Olympic Games. Under the agreement, all revenues generated through sponsorship and licensing (royalties from the sales of licensed merchandise) were to be split, with 70% going to ACOG and 30% going to the USOC. Although the USOC shared in the revenues, it provided virtually no personnel assistance to the ACOP effort. Thus, in addition to the minimal share ACOG received from TOP sales, ACOG was now forced to relinquish nearly one-third of the monies generated from local sales.

Hosting the largest Olympic Games also required spending the most money. The final expense budget for the 1996 games topped out at $1.7 billion. Table 10.3 presents the expenses associated with the games. The nearly $500 million in construction costs seems high, but that

Table 10.3 1996 Summer Olympic Games—Expenses

Type of Expense	$ thousands	%
Executive and Administrative		
Executive operations	29,989	1.8
Administrative and human resources	44,215	2.6
Financial and management services	69,938	4.1
Nondepartmental costs	52,328	3.1
Subtotal	196,370	11.5
Construction		
Sports facilities	467,727	27.4
Village	47,000	2.8
Subtotal	514,727	30.2
Functional operations		
Corporate services	68,092	4.0
Olympic programs and physical legacy	52,257	3.1
Centennial Olympic Park	18,000	1.1
Communications and governmental relations	25,365	1.5
Olympic ceremonies	31,215	1.8
Senior policy advisor and external relations	9,391	0.6
Operations	155,316	9.1
Accreditation	4,977	0.3
Technology	223,483	13.1
Venue planning management	23,532	1.4
Games services	98,362	5.8
Atlanta Olympic broadcasting	115,503	6.8
International relations	78,596	4.6
Sports	59,024	3.5
Subtotal	964,103	56.5
Contingency fund	30,000	1.8
Total	1,705,200	100

Source: The Wall Street Journal, July 19, 1997.

money was used to build a variety of structures that had a lasting impact on the Atlanta-area economy:

- The Olympic Stadium, which could later be used by baseball's Atlanta Braves;
- Dorms that would house 10,000 athletes during games and Atlanta-area students thereafter;
- The Georgia Tech Natatorium, a state-of-the-art swimming and diving facility that would serve as Georgia Tech's home pool after the Olympics; and,
- The Stone Mountain facility, which housed the tennis, rowing, canoeing, cycling, and archery competitions.

Payne and the organizers of the Atlanta games had promised to build these facilities in their bid to the IOC; thus, they had no choice but to do so.

The problem then became financing the more than $1.7 billion budget. Table 10.4 presents the revenue sources for the 1996 Olympic Games. Given the fact that ACOG received no money from the U.S. government, and only a portion of the TOP revenues and was forced to share 30% of all local sales with the USOC, the generation of sponsorships seemed difficult. Initially, the organizers attempted to sell $40 million packages. However, since the rights were not as far-reaching as the TOP package, many companies balked. Therefore, rather than sell a limited number of sponsorships for large amounts of money, ACOP ultimately sold numerous sponsorships for between $5 and $20 million.

In addition, ACOP entered into licensing agreements with hundreds of companies. Under these agreements, the licensees were allowed to place the Atlanta Olympic Games name and logo (torch above the rings) on merchandise for sale at retail. In return, ACOP was to receive a

Table 10.4   1996 Summer Olympic Games—Revenues

Source of Revenue	$ thousands	%
Broadcast rights	559,500	32.8
Sponsors and licensees	462,500	27.1
Ticket sales	422,000	24.7
IOC marketing program	77,600	4.6
Local merchandising	32,000	1.9
Other income	151,600	8.9
Total	1,705,200	100

Source: The Wall Street Journal, July 19, 1997.

royalty from every piece of logoed merchandise sold (usually between 7–10% of the wholesale price). In an effort to maximize licensing revenues, ACOP paid no attention to IOC desires that all licensees be consistent with the Olympic image. As such, licenses were sold to all sorts of companies, including the television game show "Wheel of Fortune."

Finally, part of ACOG's working agreement with the city of Atlanta for the games allowed the city to lease space outside of the Olympic Village to outside vendors. The outside marketing agency leased acres of space on streets and in parks, promising vendors the opportunity to reach 750,000 people as foot traffic proceeded through the city between Olympic attractions.

In all, high levels of corporate involvement, from both sponsors and nonsponsors, greatly detracted from the impact and awareness expected by the actual sponsors. With so many corporations present in one way or another, it was difficult to discern which companies had actually paid for the rights to advertise in association with the games. In a study completed during the Olympic Games, nonsponsor Nike was the third most recognized corporation sponsoring the games. Only Coca-Cola and AT&T had higher levels of recognition. Clearly, the Atlanta Games were very conducive to ambush marketing efforts.

Ambush Marketing Defined

Ambush marketing refers to activities by companies who, although not official sponsors, still attempt to capitalize on association with certain events.[2] Traditionally, ambush marketing is seen as one company's efforts to weaken a competitor's association with an event. For example, during the 1994 Olympic Games in Lillehammer, Norway, American Express ambushed VISA, a TOP sponsor, by running television ads that said, "If you're travelling to Norway this winter, you'll need a passport, but not a VISA." However, ambush marketing efforts are not solely geared toward weakening a competitor's involvement. As Nike demonstrated with its sports museum not far from Centennial Olympic Park, ambush marketing can simply attempt to capitalize on the goodwill associated with an event.

---

[2]For in-depth discussions of ambush marketing, see L. Bean, "Ambush Marketing: Sports sponsorship confusion and Lanham Act," *Boston University Law Review,* September, 1995, pp. 1099–1133, and S. McKelvey, "NHL v. Pepsi-Cola Canada, Uh-Huh! Legal Parameters of Sports Ambush Marketing, *Entertainment and Sports Lawyer,* Fall, 1992, pp. 5–18.

Unfortunately for the event promoter and sport sponsor, there are many forms of ambush marketing. Many of the forms go unrecognized by the general public because they are so subtle. In general, there are numerous ways to conduct ambush marketing. Four of the more prevalent tactics include:

- Purchasing broadcast time in and around event broadcasts;
- Conducting consumer sweepstakes or promotions utilizing the themes or locations of the event;
- Negotiating a smaller, less-inclusive sponsorship deal with a team, athlete, or organization that is competing in the competition; and,
- Advertising in and around the event venue(s).

The IOC sells the worldwide rights to advertise in association with the Olympic Games to a limited number of corporations, but it does not dictate who advertises on television. Therefore, as demonstrated in the American Express/VISA conflict above, one company can ambush the efforts of a competitor by purchasing advertising time during an event. In addition, the networks make such an option attractive by allowing their advertisers to promote themselves as "Official Broadcast Sponsors of the Olympic Games," even allowing such advertisers to use a specially designed logo in their advertising efforts. Thus, even though VISA paid $20 million to the IOC for worldwide rights, American Express successfully ambushed its involvement by purchasing network television time.

Conducting sweepstakes and promotions using an event's theme is another popular form of ambush marketing. For example, in 1990 Pepsi conducted a contest called the "Diet Pepsi $4,000,000 Pro Hockey Playoff Pool" in which fans examined bottle caps for the chance to travel to NHL playoff games (McKelvey, 1992). Pepsi successfully implemented this campaign even though it was not a sponsor.

Rather than purchase a large, all-encompassing sponsorship, corporations successfully ambush events by negotiating smaller sponsorship deals with a team, athlete, or organization that is involved with the event. For example, Nike was the sponsor for USA Track & Field at the 1996 Atlanta Summer Olympics. As such, Nike provided the uniforms for the U.S. track team. In doing so, they placed the company's popular trademark, the swoosh, on the chest of all U.S. track uniforms. Such exposure served to greatly enhance the casual spectator's awareness of Nike's corporate presence. In another case recently, Wendy's has agreed to a large sponsorship deal with the NHL and USA Hockey. This agreement covered the 1998 Olympics in Nagano, where Wendy's had the opportunity to ambush TOP sponsor McDonald's.

A final popular form of ambush marketing is to advertise in and around event venues. At the Atlanta Olympic Games, this tactic was extremely popular. Fuji Film purchased advertising space on eighteen billboards throughout Atlanta featuring eventual U.S. decathlon champion Dan O'Brien. Such billboards served to detract from the exclusive TOP sponsorship purchased by Kodak. The utilization of a city garage to create a Nike Sports Museum and Hospitality Center represents another example of this form of ambush marketing.

Legal Recourse for Event Promoters

According to U.S. law, there are several legal recourses that an event promoter can take to prevent ambush marketing. First, if an ambushing company uses a trademarked name, symbol, or logo of the event, the promoter can sue for trademark infringement. Under the Lanham Act, an ambushing company using a mark that is likely to cause confusion with respect to the corporate affiliation of the event can be held liable for damages. However, if the company does not use a registered trademark or symbol, then it is difficult for the event promoter to curb ambushing using the Lanham Act; such was the case with the Diet Pepsi Pro Hockey Playoff Pool.

However, the Amateur Sports Act of 1978 provides additional trademark protection for Olympic sponsors. In making the USOC the official organization for Olympic sport in the United States, it also granted the USOC power to bring civil action against unauthorized users of any of the Olympic symbols or marks. This includes the names "Olympics" and "Olympic Games," the Olympic symbol (five interlocking rings), the Olympic flame, and the Olympic torch. Thus, the USOC is empowered to sue any organization that uses these marks without the permission of the IOC or USOC.

A second legal remedy for event promoters is to sue ambushers for the misappropriation of goodwill. An event promoter or sponsor could sue an ambusher saying that a company falsely representing itself had wrongly used the sponsor's goodwill. Theoretically, this recourse would seem to apply in cases such as the Diet Pepsi Pro Hockey Playoff pool; however, U.S. courts have been reluctant to apply this law.

Reasons for the Prevalence of Ambush Marketing

There are numerous reasons that ambush marketing has thus far been relatively unimpeded. As the rights fees for sponsorship of the marquis sporting events have increased, the number of corporations seeking ways to subvert traditional sponsorship packages while still receiving the benefits of association has increased significantly. Although legal recourse does exist, it has not been successful at curbing this activity. There are four reasons why this is true:

- Most ambush marketing campaigns are short lived;
- Limited case law exists;
- Corporations have been successful in defending themselves; and,
- An adverse court decision could create an onslaught of ambush activity.

Because events occur over short periods of time, corporations' efforts to ambush events usually occur over a very limited time period. For example, at the 1996 Head of the Charles Regatta, Nike parked a HMMVV truck on the fringe of the grounds for the event from which it distributed logoed giveaway items. However, the event only lasted two days, hardly enough time for the organizers of the Head of the Charles to take legal action. Thus, with ambush campaigns usually occurring over a very short period of time, it is very hard for event promoters to utilize their legal recourse to curtail such activity.

Laws exist that are generally applicable to the problem of ambush marketing, but only a handful of cases have progressed through the judicial system. This is particularly true for challenges to ambush marketing using the theory of misappropriation. Legal battles require much time and effort, and thus far very few promoters or sponsors have brought suit against ambush marketers.

Another reason for the relative lack of prior ambush marketing cases may be due to the fact that corporations are extremely adept at protecting themselves from legal challenges for ambush marketing activity. For example, in the Diet Pepsi Hockey Playoff Pool, there was no mention of the National Hockey League or the Stanley Cup Playoffs, two registered trademarks. Instead, Pepsi adopted the common tactic of referring to the NHL playoffs generically. As such, the NHL could not sue Pepsi charging trademark infringement. In addition, disclaimers are a very popular strategy to defend against ambush marketing charges. In essence, if a company undertakes marketing activity that might be construed as an ambush campaign, it includes a disclaimer in all materials saying that the company is not an official sponsor and has not paid to affiliate with the event. The use of such a disclaimer also helped protect Pepsi.

Finally, and perhaps most practically, sports organizations are reluctant to bring suit against ambush marketers because they fear the repercussions of an adverse decision. Due to the lack of case law regarding ambush marketing, a court decision in favor of an ambushing company would set a precedent that could be used by every other company implementing an ambush campaign. As a result of such a scenario, the value of sponsorship rights would decline and the number of companies undertaking ambush campaigns would increase.

Repercussions of Successful Ambush Marketing Efforts

Although prevention is difficult, it is absolutely tantamount for any sports organization wanting to charge high sponsorship-rights fees. The corporate outlay of funds is only beginning when a sponsorship contract is signed. In order to receive the maximum benefits of association with the event, the corporation must spend millions more creating advertising and promotional campaigns to coincide with the event. Coca-Cola, which paid $40 million to be a TOP sponsor during the 1993–1996 quadrennium, spent $300–$500 million on its Olympic marketing program associated with the Atlanta Games (Thomas, 1996).

Ambush marketing campaigns devalue the gargantuan efforts of official sponsors such as Coca-Cola. To secure long-term, lucrative sponsorship deals, the sports organization must be able to offer category exclusivity; that is, the sponsor is assured that none of its competitors will be granted any advertising rights. Central to this benefit is the event organizers' ability to curtail ambush marketing activities. When ambush marketing campaigns are successfully implemented, the sports organization is unable to deliver on promised benefits. As a result, the sport sponsor may be displeased with its involvement with the event and choose not to renew its sponsorship. Poor renewal can ultimately undermine the financial viability of the entire event. Most events rely on sponsorship fees to underwrite a majority of operating expenses.

Public Awareness of Ambush Marketing

Another problem for event promoters is that the public is unaware of ambush marketing efforts. In a study of people who watched the 1996 Atlanta Olympic Games, nearly one-third of all respondents believed that only worldwide sponsors of the Olympic Games could advertise during the Olympic Games. Further, better than one-third of all respondents were not aware that ambush marketing even took place. In addition, even when aware, the public is generally indifferent to the practice of ambush marketing. Only one-half of all people studied felt strongly that ambush marketing was unethical. Further, only 45% of the respondents were annoyed by the fact that companies practice ambush marketing.

The lack of awareness and public indifference toward ambush marketing further enhances the difficulties facing event promoters. The event promoter is faced with the challenge of educating the public with respect to ambush marketing. If significant segments of the general public are unaware or indifferent to the practice, then a company employing ambush marketing tactics can be less concerned about negative public backlash associated with its efforts. Therefore, the burden appears to be on the event promoter to educate the general public with respect to the official sponsors of the event and the negative impact of ambush marketing.

Salt Lake City—2002 Winter Olympic Games

Unlike Atlanta, Salt Lake City campaigned for thirty years to host the Olympic Games. Their efforts began in 1966, when Salt Lake City was chosen by the USOC to be the U.S. nnominee to host the 1972 Winter Olympic Games (Sapporo, Japan, was ultimately awarded those games by the IOC). Following the 1966 bid, Salt Lake City was also the U.S. nominee for the 1976, 1992, and 1998 Winter Olympic Games. Finally, on June 16, 1995, in their fifth official attempt to host the Winter Olympic Games, Salt Lake City was successful, being awarded the 2002 event.

Planning and development began almost immediately. In June of 1995, SLOC was formed as a nonprofit, tax-exempt organization under the laws of Utah. By the time of the 2002 Winter Games, SLOC expects to have employed 600 people in various capacities. In addition, they estimate that 12,000 to 15,000 volunteers will help in managing the games.

In addition to employing a number of people to coordinate and manage the games, SLOC will incur a variety of other expenditures. Table 10.5 is a brief listing of SLOC's budgeted expenditures, which currently total $920 million. However, as with most projections, these expenses

Table 10.5 Budgeted expenses—Salt Lake City Winter Olympics

Description	Budgeted Expenditures ($M)
Venue permanent and temporary facilities	$171
Winter sports park and Utah Sports Authority projects	$ 59
Olympic Village and ceremonies	$ 36
Permanent operations legacy fund	$ 40
Games operations	$614
Total expenses	$920

Source: Salt Lake Organizing Committee, 1997.

Table 10.6 Budgeted revenues—Salt Lake City Winter Olympics

Description	Budgeted Revenue ($M)
Broadcast rights/fees	$435
International sponsorships (share of TOP)	$ 45
National/local sponsorships	$250
Tickets	$124
Licensed merchandise (net of royalty payments)	$ 35
Other	$ 31
Total	$920

Source: Salt Lake Organizing Committee, 1997.

are likely to grow. Such overruns may be largely due to extra costs incurred in the development of facilities. For example, a 13,000-seat multipurpose skating and hockey facility is being developed in West Valley City, Utah.

Although the SLOC budget is barely half of ACOG's budget, it still presents the challenge of raising nearly $1 billion. As depicted in Table 10.6, broadcast rights fees and disbursements from the IOC TOP program will help account for a little more than half of the $920 million needed. However, SLOC is depending on $250 million in national and local sponsorships.

In an effort to work closely with the USOC in the marketing of the Olympic Games, including the sales of sponsorships, the USOC and SLOC have created a joint venture called Olympic Properties of the United States (OPUS). The control and organization of OPUS will be different from that of ACOP. Most notably, USOC staff members will manage and coordinate all marketing activities. OPUS is attempting to sell eight-year sponsorship packages. Included in these deals would be sponsorship of the United States Olympic Team for the 1998, 2000, 2002, and 2004 Games as well as the 2002 Salt Lake City Games. Sponsors will pay more than $100 million for these rights, with part of the proceeds going to SLOC.

Conclusion

With the USOC so intricately involved with the marketing of the Salt Lake City Winter Olympic Games, they are very concerned with the threat of ambush marketing. The USOC knows the importance of not repeating the commercial fiasco that occurred in Atlanta. As a consequence, SLOC and its marketing employees are well aware of the need

to provide sponsors with exclusive exposure and rights during the Salt
Lake City Games.

As Alyssa pulled into the parking garage at 215 South State Street,
she knew a comprehensive plan with multiple strategies was needed
to combat ambush marketing at the Salt Lake City Olympic Games.

11

B³: The Bikes, Blades, and Boards Tour

Dan Covell

Introduction

"Coke, Pepsi, Gatorade, Perrier, Evian?" Bronwen Douglass looked up as if the waiter had been reading her mind. She had gone to the office restaurant to get a drink after her noontime workout: a twenty-mile in-line skating jaunt. "Oh, uh, Perrier, please. Thanks."

The waiter left to fetch her order. She was grateful for the days when the weather cooperated and allowed her to skate. The midday exercise always served to clear her head and get her ready for the rest of the day. Bronwen was beginning her first year as an account executive at ESPN after a year at Advantage International, a major sport marketing firm. She was about to embark on her first big project, one she felt she had been preparing for her whole life. While at Advantage, she had been working as an assistant to Clay Green, one of Advantage's most prominent account reps. Bronwen had taken a job at ESPN similar to that of Green's at Advantage, and her first task was to create a target list of potential sponsors for the B³ Tour, an "aggressive" sports competition for professional BMX stunt bikers, in-line skaters, and skateboarders, and then to draft a proposal to sell sponsorships. The sponsor category she had been given was "soda/beverage," a big-ticket item for any sport event, let alone B³. Not only was this her first real shot to make her mark in the company, but she was an avid in-line skater and had even won a few amateur competitions. She had also done some skateboarding during her high school and college days and had the scars to prove it.

As she sat in the restaurant at the company's headquarters in Bristol, Connecticut, she had been lost in thought, putting her ideas together about the project. The waiter's query had put the issue in arrestingly simple terms. She had been considering those five options to target for her sponsorship proposal, but she had yet to formulate a conclusion. She again ran over the questions in her mind: Which of the companies would provide a good sponsor–event match? What do

195

they need to know about this event, the participants, and the targeted demographic segment to get them on board? "I really have to make sure that the one I target has the product that is targeted for our demographic," she thought to herself. The waiter arrived and placed a bottle of Perrier and a glass with ice and a lime wedge on the table in front of her. With that, she had made her decision. "Hey, you've been a big help. Thanks a lot," Bronwen said. The waiter looked puzzled. "You're welcome, I guess," he replied. "What the hell is she talking about?" the waiter wondered as he turned and walked back to the kitchen.

B³: Bikes, Blades, and Boards

The Management Team: ESPN and Advantage International

B³ is an "extreme sports" competition for the world's top professional stunt bikers, aggressive in-line skaters, and skateboarders, with prize money totalling $50,000 split between the best in each of the three competitions. B³ was created by ESPN, the international leader in sports television and televising extreme sports. ESPN hired Advantage International to help manage B³. (See Exhibit 11.1).

ESPN's first foray into the extreme games market was in 1995, with the advent of the first Extreme, or "X" Games, held in Newport, Rhode

Exhibit 11.1 An overview of ESPN, Inc.

- Founded in 1979.
- The world's largest cable network.
- Reaches more than 68.4 million homes in the United States (71% of U.S. homes with televisions).
- Subsidiary of ABC, Inc., which is wholly owned by the Walt Disney Company.
- Holdings include: ESPN, ESPN2, ESPN International, the ESPN Radio Network, ESPN SportsZone, and ESPN Enterprises.
- Produces more than 11,400 hours of original and/or live programming each year involving more than sixty-five sports.
- Derives its revenue from advertising sales and affiliate fees and has more than 1,000 national sponsors.
- ESPN International, formed in January 1988, owns or has equity interests in fifteen networks and distributes American and international sports programs that reach 200 million homes in 198 countries and territories worldwide.
- Created ESPN2 in 1993 to reach fans interested in both traditional and emerging participatory sports. "The Deuce," with its contemporary feel and unique graphics, now reaches 33.4 million U.S. homes.

Island, June 24–July 1 (see Exhibit 11.2). In the summer of 1996, ESPN produced a tour similar to B³, "Destination Extreme," that visited six U.S. cities (including New York City and South Padre Island, Texas). "Destination Extreme" served as XGames qualifying trials for aggressive in-line skating, stunt biking, and skateboarding, built grassroots

Exhibit 11.2   The Summer Xgames

- An "Olympic"-type competition billed as the first global competition in extreme sports.
- Created by ESPN2 programmer Ron Semiao, in part to sell an event to sponsors that targeted young viewers with unformed brand loyalties, in part to capitalize on the growth in extreme sports.
- Involved 350 athletes who competed in twenty-seven events, including:
    street luge
    bungee-jumping
    sea kayaking
    sky-surfing
    BMX stunt biking
    aggressive in-line skating
    skateboarding
- Over $400,000 in prize money awarded in 1997.
- 1996 cable TV ratings averaged 1.0 (about 713,000 households).
- The following sponsors pay between $1 and $2 million each:
    Snickers
    Nike
    Taco Bell
    AT&T
    Mountain Dew
    U.S. Marines
    Chevrolet

A second XGames was held in Rhode Island the following summer rather than the planned two-year cycle to discourage rumored copycat events. The 1997 event was held in San Diego on June 20–29. An inaugural winter version of the XGames was held at Snow Summit ski area in Big Bear Lake, California, January 30–February 3, 1997.

- Events included:
    ice climbing
    snowboarding
    snow mountain biking
    super-modified shovel racing
- Sponsors included:
    Volkswagen
    Nike
    Taco Bell
    AT&T
    Pringles
    Mountain Dew

interest for extreme events, and enhanced extreme-event brand equity for ESPN.

Advantage International, a full-service sport marketing agency (and the second largest company of its kind in the world), brings significant expertise to B³, specifically in the areas of operations, sponsorship and ticket sales, licensing, public relations, hospitality opportunities, and promotion (see Exhibit 11.3).

The Event

Participation in extreme and aggressive sports has grown substantially in the United States in the 1990s. Consider in-line skating: There are currently 23 million in-line skaters, more than take part in mainstream sports such as soccer and football, and in-line skating is currently the most popular sport among children and teens. Also, BMX bike sales were up 28% in the first quarter of 1997, the only growth segment of the $2.3 billion bicycle industry. B³ was created to capitalize on the wave of growing interest and participation in the emerging sports of aggressive in-line skating, stunt-biking, and skateboarding and to build upon ESPN's XGames brand equity, which serves to bundle market the image of youth and enthusiasm to ESPN viewers, sponsors, and advertisers. The inaugural year of the tour was 1997, with stops in prominent high-profile, high-traffic locations. The kickoff event was held in New York City's Riverside Park on July 25–27, with a second event held at Seal Beach in Los Angeles, August 29–31. Stadium spectator seating capacity was 3,000 at each venue. "Blade Jam Only from Rollerblade," the world's largest interactive skating festival sponsored by Rollerblade, served as an interactive companion event to the B³ tour.

The tour featured the world's best bikers, bladers, and skateboarders in two-day competitions on the vertical ramp, half-pipe stunt chute, and a street obstacle course. The events yielded eight hours of original television programming on both ESPN and ESPN2: two-hour shows dedicated to each of the three competitions and two one-hour compilation shows featuring the best from the vertical ramp and street competitions.

Advantage International was responsible for the management of all facets of the tour. To reinforce the credibility of B³ with the athletes, TV viewers, live spectators, and sponsors, Advantage and ESPN sought the cooperation of the premier sanctioning bodies in each event (the Aggressive Skating Association [ASA], the Bicycle Stunt Series [run by Hoffman Promotions, an independent company], and World Cup Skateboarding [WCS]) to serve in technical and practical advisory roles. ASA, the sanctioning body for aggressive skating in the United States, boasts the world's largest in-line skating membership and is widely acknowledged as a key component in the worldwide boom of in-line

Exhibit 11.3. An overview of Advantage International

- Founded in 1983 by A. Lee Fentress primarily as an athlete representation organization. Fentress also founded ProServ, another management company, in 1976.
- 225 employees in fourteen offices on five continents, with company headquarters located in McLean, Virginia.
- Athlete representation is a vital component of the company. Current Advantage clients include:
  NBA stars Grant Hill, David Robinson, Sam Perkins, and Jerry Stackhouse
  Professional tennis standouts Steffi Graf, Zina Garrison Jackson, Jana Novotna, Todd Martin, Michael Chang, Richard Krajicek, and Mark Philippoussis
  Professional golfers Sandy Lyle, Mark McCumber, and J.C. Snead
  Olympic medalist speedskater Bonnie Blair and swimmer Matt Biondi
- The company is also an international leader in event management for corporate clients such as:
  American Express
  British Petroleum
  Black Enterprise Magazine
  Lexus
  Time magazine
  Kraft General Foods
  Downtown Athletic Club (Heisman Trophy Association)
- Managed events include:
  The Disney U.S. Men's Clay Court Championship
  The Senior PGA Tour Cadillac NFL Golf Classic
  The LPGA JAL Big Apple Classic
  The Continental Grass Court Championships
- Sells corporate sponsorships for:
  Pro Beach Soccer Tour
  Roller Hockey International
- Corporate sponsorship consultant 1996 Summer Olympic sponsorship activities for:
  IBM
  NationsBank
  Home Depot
  United Parcel Service
  Motorola
  General Mills
- Managed corporate "grassroots" sport sponsorship programs such as:
  The Coors Light /USA Softball World Series
  The Mercedez-Benz Trophy tournament for amateur golf in the United Kingdom

through its exhibitions and pro aggressive skating tour. WCS shares ASA's international organizing prominence and administers competition at the world's three largest skateboarding events: the XGames, the Slam City Jam in Vancouver, British Columbia, and the Munster Mash in Germany. Advantage will share event operations responsibilities with Hoffman Promotions (HP). HP, in addition to the Bicycle Stunt Series and B³, has also organized operations and competition components for the XGames, the XGames trials, and six additional professional extreme sports events.

The Target Sponsor

Bronwen took the stairs two at a time (with skates in tow), jogged down the hall, and burst into her office. Her office mate, Jim Dexter, who was working on the risk management plan for B³, had just returned from a planning session at the New York site. "Good workout?" Jim asked. "Better than I could have hoped," Bronwen replied. Jim gave her the same look the waiter had after delivering the bottle of Perrier, but Bronwen didn't notice. She went straight to her computer and opened her B³ file.

As she waited for the program to open, she leafed through her notes from her year of working at Advantage on sponsorship proposals for the Cadillac NFL Golf Classic and the Pro Beach Soccer Tour. Referring to these always served to focus her thoughts. She did this after hearing a motivational presentation from Pat Williams, general manager of the Orlando Magic. Williams had told of his first job with the Philadelphia 76ers when his boss told him: "This is what you should be thinking about: How can I make the 76ers a better team, and how can I sell more tickets? If you aren't doing one of these two things, you're off on a tangent." She continued to marvel at the simplicity and utility of that caveat.

She found the first component of her mantra: the definition for sport/event property; any sport or lifestyle entity that has name/event recognition, desirability, and perceived value and which chooses to offer itself for some type of affiliation. Bronwen then thought back to the sponsorship presentations she and Green had made. Green always made it clear to her: "Much of the success of our events hinges on corporate sponsorship sales. Corporations now spend over $4 billion annually on sport/special event sponsorships — and this number has tripled in the last decade. For most events such as tennis and golf tournaments, there are two primary revenue sources: ticket sales and corporate sponsorship sales." But the challenge for Bronwen was that admission to a made-for-TV event like B³, is free. For an event like B³ to be produced, sponsorships must be sold.

Sponsorships for B³ would not be cheap. Presenting sponsorships, the category for which the beverage sponsor would be solicited, would run well into six figures. Associated sponsorships, with fewer benefits provided, would cost roughly half the presenting sponsorships. Clearly the target sponsor would need to be a company with substantial corporate marketing expenditures. Bronwen knew the figures well and knew what was going on in the industry in terms of sponsorship:

- Cadillac reports that its Senior PGA Tour sponsorship has brought its dealers over $250 million in sales since 1990.
- VISA, Coca-Cola, Kodak, UPS, and IBM paid $40 million each for the right to claim the status of Official Worldwide Sponsors for the 1996 Summer Olympics. This fee did not include ad purchases. The total spent by all sponsors was $477 million.
- As part of its purchase of U.S. Olympic Team sponsorship status through 2008, General Motors expects to spend $500 million on media agreements with NBC and another $300 million in leveraging efforts. This does not include the sponsorship fee paid to the United States Olympic Committee.
- Reebok and the University of Wisconsin recently signed a five-year, $9.1-million deal where Reebok provides the Wisconsin athletic department footwear, uniforms, and warmup clothing for all varsity teams and contributes $2.3 million for scholarships and payments to coaches for the right to exclusively sell Wisconsin athletic apparel.
- Trans World Airlines inked a twenty-year deal to pay $1.3 million annually for the naming of the Trans World Dome in St. Louis, the home city for the airline.
- Valvoline, the oldest brand of Ashland Oil (which also owns Jiffy Lube and SuperAmerica gas stations and convenience stores) spent more than $11 million on promotions tied to the Indy Racing League as official sponsor of the PPG Indy Car World Series and NASCAR's Winston Cup series in 1996.

Bronwen then outlined the rest of the requirements for the project. From her mental list of potential sponsors, she needed to target one company that would be a strong prospective sponsor for B³. She would present a one-page company overview that included the following: company size, annual revenue, and advertising expenditures; the company's target market, including consumer demographic and psychographic information; the company sponsorship objectives; and the company's existing and projected sport and lifestyle sponsorships. She had to find out what kind of product they sold and what position in the marketplace they occupied. She also needed to determine the nature of their marketing structure: Who makes the marketing decisions, what are their general marketing approaches, what are their prior sponsorship experiences specific to sport and the outcomes of those sponsorships. This was the information she would use to understand the company needs and assess their ability to reach consumers through B³. Whichever company best fit these criteria would not only be the strongest potential sponsor for B³ but also would be a good fit to sponsor

Advantage's other emerging sport properties, such as Pro Beach Volleyball and Roller Hockey International.

But first things first, Bronwen thought. The review had served to get the juices going, but she focused back on B³. "OK," she concluded, "I've got most of the information I need, but I'll have to check a few more on-line sources to provide the company information and make a few more phone calls to confirm some things." She put down her notes, picked up the phone, and started dialing.

The Sponsorship Proposal

After five hours (and multiple voice-mail messages left and returned), Bronwen was slipping her skates back on. She had what she needed, but a new dilemma had presented itself. Jim returned from a meeting in the conference room.

"Getting ready for another 20 miles?"

"No, just going to head home."

"Get done what you needed to?"

"Yeah. I think I know where I want to go, but so many of these beverage companies try to reach so many different types of consumers by making and distributing so many different types of products, it's tough trying to decide which particular type of beverage, let alone a single company. Should I focus on a soda, a sport drink, a juice, or a water? If I decide on a soda, should it be regular or diet? If water is best, should it be spring or sparkling?"

"I know what you mean," Jim said. "I have that problem with deciding on which vendors to hire for things like tents, portable toilets, and private security personnel."

"I guess I need to go back and have another internal focus session. See you in the morning." With that, soliciting another puzzled look from Jim, Bronwen grabbed her notes, stuffed them in her backpack, and glided out of the office to the elevator.

After a quick dinner and clean-up, Bronwen sat on her couch and revisited her notes. "The sponsor is looking to achieve two key goals through sponsorship: a captive target market and a measurable, quantifiable sponsorship success, determined through television air time and a creative, on-site component," Green had said as they prepped for the Disney sponsorship rounds. "You need to create and convey a win-win strategy that characterizes a mutually beneficial relationship."

The target market for B³ was described as "alternative males," ages 13 to 18. ESPN and the sponsor wanted to increase revenues and exposure through B³ and make sure they reach the targeted segment. The difference with a made-for-TV event like B³ was that the sponsor is mainly concerned with the TV ad buys. The signage and presence at the event is of secondary importance. Bronwen then looked over the commercial buys provided to the beverage sponsor:

Multiple thirty-second ads in all eight original hours on ESPN
Multiple thirty-second airings of all original hours on ESPN2
Open or closing billboard in every airing on ESPN
Open or closing billboard in every airing on ESPN2

She then reviewed the on-sight elements, which could include banners, display booths, and or PA announcements. There were also additional elements to be provided, including program ads, hospitality opportunities, and corporate identification on all collateral event materials.

Bronwen knew that the sponsorship proposal had to be brief and to the point but comprehensive in detail. She again recalled her first days with Advantage. "Decision makers have neither the time nor the interest to read a novel. They see thousands of sponsorship proposals every year. Give them the facts and tailor your proposal toward that company. Everything they will receive needs to be presented clearly. Every available activity or opportunity should be clarified precisely," Green had repeated as he proofread her early proposal-writing drafts. "The sponsor needs to know about the company seeking the sponsorship and the event itself. Give them a full and accurate description of the event, including company histories and an overview of other activities. You also have some conceptual concerns on the part of companies: Do they want to do business with these companies? Are they reputable? Does this event reach our target audience? Are there sampling and sales opportunities? Are there timing issues regarding products and other promotional activities? Can this be a growth event for us? What is the long-term potential? There are three sure ways to get your proposal rejected: first, focus on the benefits to you, not the sponsor; second, focus on how much money you need, not the value to the sponsor; last, be unorganized and unclear."

As she looked again at the draft of her proposal, Bronwen felt she had the answers to these questions by determining the target company's objectives for sponsorship. Some look to demonstrate good citizenship and commitment to the community. Others are looking to generate favorable media interest and publicity. Others are looking to achieve sales objectives, to identify with a particular market segment, or to create an advantage over competitors through the sponsorship association. She just had to let them know what they would be getting for their investment, to present the objectives clearly, and to position the match between their corporate objectives and the opportunities available through the sponsorship of B³.

But even if all that is in place and on the mark, Bronwen knew that often the make-or-break element of the deal was the creative component. This is what distinguished your proposals from thousands of others out there. It could involve ideas and concepts concerning promotions, on-site couponing, whatever she thought would work best for the sponsor. It had to be original and also provide a means of measuring the effectiveness of the sponsorship to the sponsor. The corporation needs to be able to quantify the results, and ESPN needs to be able to show them how sponsoring this event helped them sell more.

She was ready to put it together. Bronwen had made her decision in the restaurant earlier that day, thanks to the assistance of the waiter. She pulled out her laptop, turned it on, and started to write her proposal.

Bronwen was back in the restaurant the next day after another noon workout. She had brought her proposal with her for a final review before she contacted her target sponsor but wanted to review the criteria on why she had chosen whom she had. She checked her notes on her list:

Coca-Cola

The giant in sport beverage sponsorship, with a worldwide market share of 42%. Coke dwarfs its closest rival, Pepsi-Cola, and spends $1 billion annually in advertising. It owns the following brands: PowerAde (beginning sponsorship with the NHL for the 1997–1998 season), Fruitopia, Minute Maid, Sprite, Nestea, and Mello Yello. Coke is also looking to get into the bottled water market and will likely test a product in the United States soon. The company spent $45 million to acquire international Olympic sponsorship, another $62 million in associated advertising, and is also an official sponsor for several U.S. Olympic sport-governing bodies. It holds official sponsorships with major league baseball, the National Football League (a five-year, $250-million deal including McDonald's as a promotional partner), the National Basketball Association, the National Hockey League, the International Hockey League, and the PGA Tour. Coca-Cola is also a NASCAR race title sponsor, the sponsor of the "Sky Field" activity area at the Atlanta Braves' Turner Field, has signage at numerous major and minor league venues, including the controversial Coke bottles fastened to a light tower atop the "Green Monster," Fenway Park's storied left-field wall. Although it is also active in amateur and youth sports, such as the Coca-Cola Youth Bowling Championship and the National High School Coaches Association national championships, Coca-Cola does not have a significant presence in the "aggressive" market.

Pepsi-Cola

The Winter XGames sponsors included Volkswagen, Nike, Taco Bell, AT&T, Pringles, and Mountain Dew. Both Mountain Dew and Taco Bell are owned brands of Pepsi. Other Pepsi beverage products include

Lipton teas and All-Sport sports drink. Pepsi also recently released a water product, Aquafina, with a stated goal of becoming the top-selling bottled water product in the United States. The company used mega-stars Shaquille O'Neal, Andre Agassi, and Ken Griffey, Jr., to promote All-Sport. They have a heavy investment in sport sponsorship and advertising, including aggressive and extreme events like the XGames and additional cycling and triathlon events. The company's annual global media spending is about $1.4 billion, so it could afford what B³ is asking. It has also shown a desire to position Pepsi and Mountain Dew as youth-oriented alternatives to their major rival Coca-Cola in their "Generation Next" and "Do the Dew" advertising campaigns. This fits well with our targeted demographic. It has also shown that it can buck the establishment with its subversion of the NFL's league sponsorship deals with Coca-Cola by signing individual sponsorship deals with the Dallas Cowboys and the New England Patriots to be the "official sponsors" of both teams' home venues. This creativity is also a good match with our alternative set. A strong option for B³, with either Pepsi, All-Sport, Aquafina, or Mountain Dew as a specific product sponsor choice.

GATORADE

Gatorade holds the enviable distinction of being the original sport drink, first created for athletes at the University of Florida in the late 1960s, then made available to the general public in the early 1970s. Gatorade's presence has slipped in the past few years from its high mark of controlling 93% of the total market in the late 1980s, due in part to the emergence of competing brands such as PowerAde and All-Sport. Gatorade is still the leader, however, thanks in part to the use of spokesperson Michael Jordan, the most recognizable athlete person-ality in the world. As the leader, Gatorade has been looking to strengthen its position as a mainstream youth brand, but the marketing efforts of Quaker Oats, Gatorade's parent company, have been muddled after the company acquired the Snapple brand in 1995 for $1.7 billion. Efforts to create cross-promotions and marketing relationships between the two brands were unsuccessful, and Quaker Oats sold Snapple in early 1997 for $300 million ($250 million less than its annual sales of $550 million) to Triarc, the beverage company that owns Mystic Iced Tea, RC Cola, and Diet Rite. Gatorade's recent Olympic advertising efforts did not elicit the level of response and recognition it had hoped.

Gatorade has leveraged its position through its involvement in sev-eral grassroots amateur sport events such as "Hoop-It-Up" (a national amateur 3-on-3 basketball tournament), the NFL's "Air-It-Out" adult touch football competition, Pop Warner Football, and Little League Baseball. It has done a little with extreme-type events but has not committed a significant effort to it. Although it has lost its official sponsorship of the NHL, Gatorade still holds official status with major league baseball, NASCAR (as well as a title sponsorship for two races), the NFL, and the NBA. Despite the fact that Gatorade's hold on the market has slipped, it is still the leader and is involved in mostly mainstream sport activities.

PERRIER

The Perrier Group, the U.S. arm of the eponymous French beverage company, is also a big player in the beverage market. Perrier has undergone some challenges in the United States, with a recall of product after concerns regarding the discovery of traces of highly toxic benzene in bottles of Perrier in 1990. Perrier owns 26.8% of the $3.6 billion U.S. bottled water market, with sales of $966.8 million in 1996. Perrier has captured this segment through sales of thirteen regional "sparkling" (carbonated) and "nonsparkling" (noncarbonated) brands, including Arrowhead, Calistoga, Deer Park, Great Bear, Ozarka, Poland Springs, and Valvert. Perrier is known more as a sparkling water company, but the Perrier brand itself controls only 2% of that market. Evian dominates the nonsparkling market, and Perrier introduced Valvert in 1995 to compete with Evian in the fast-growing premium-priced, nonsparkling market and to increase corporate sales. Perrier hopes to make Valvert a national brand this year. Perrier is not substantially involved in marketing through sport, although it has a strong presence at the French Open (signage at Paris' Roland Garros Stadium) and uses its regional brands as a promotional sponsor and in-stadium advertiser for pro clubs such as the San Jose Sharks (Calistoga), San Diego Chargers (Arrowhead), Boston Bruins (Poland Springs), and Washington Wizards and Capitals (Deer Park).

EVIAN

Evian, owned by Great Brands of Europe, a subsidiary of the multinational French food company Group Danone, is the top seller of bottled water in the world, with U.S. sales of $201.8 million in 1996. Great Brands also owns the Saratoga and Volvic brands. Evian holds only 5.6% of the total bottled water market in the United States, but as we have seen, owns a 50% share in the premium-priced, nonsparkling segment. Evian has been able to grab the top spot by targeting its Evian brand to the urban fitness market and the Volvic brand toward outdoor enthusiasts. Part of its strength lies in the fact that, unlike Perrier, Evian has fewer regional brands and can create stronger marketing approaches for its reduced product lines. Even so, Evian spends approximately $10 million annually in advertising.

Evian has defined its sport sponsorship involvement as looking to sponsor events where product consumption is a natural extension of sport participation, where the consumers involved match its target market: consumers who are upscale and purchase premium goods and services. As such, Evian is not heavily involved in sport marketing outside of tennis (official sponsor for the U.S. Open), volleyball (title sponsor for Women's Pro Beach Volleyball Tour, and the Indoor AVP Pro Beach Volleyball Championship), and cycling (title sponsor for the "Ride for the Wild," an eight-city off-road biking tour, and the Volvic/ PowerBar Cycle Team, a women's professional mountain biking team). Evian seems to be positioning itself as the high-end water for fitness-conscious yuppies.

The Decision

Although most people don't think of water as a great fit for extreme events, there is some potential for growth here. Pepsi is not getting significant competition from Coke in its control of this market. Pepsi has the XGames, and it probably feels that it is doing what it needs to do to position its brand against stodgy, traditional Coke. This is also not a big enough market for Coke to want to expend energy battling Pepsi for these consumers. It doesn't need this market, so it figures "let Pepsi have it."

There are some compelling reasons to choose Perrier. There has been strong growth in the U.S. bottled water market, which is growing 8% annually, twice the increase of other carbonated drinks. Sales of smaller-size bottles (16 ounces and smaller) alone are growing 30% annually. Perrier is looking to promote Valvert as a national brand to go head to head with Evian. Since Evian is the established leader, it makes sense for Perrier to position Valvert as an alternative to Evian. It also makes sense that a limited sponsorship to this highly defined target market, with sampling and promotional opportunities, can give Perrier a great read on what they need to do to present themselves as the alternative and make their mark. Also, as both Coke and Pepsi look to get into the bottled water market, this is an additional competitor that Perrier must consider.

The waiter who had served her yesterday approached her table. "Coke, Pepsi, Perrier, Evian?" he repeated.

"I'll have the usual," Bronwen replied, "I have a good feeling about that drink."

The waiter smiled, turned to retrieve her order, and thought to himself, "OK, whatever."

12

The Ladies Professional Golf Association (LPGA)

Mark A. McDonald and George R. Milne

Introduction

Joelle Dold, promotions assistant for the Ladies Professional Golf Association (LPGA), sat pensively in her office contemplating her new job with the LPGA. Prior to accepting this position, she had never really given the LPGA much thought. Being an avid golfer and follower of sports on television, she knew of the exploits of Greg Norman, Jack Nicklaus, and even John Daly but still was not at all versed in the happenings and personalities on the LPGA Tour. Of one thing she was certain, however, her success on this new job required a comprehensive knowledge of the inner workings of the LPGA. Many challenging questions entered her thoughts: How sound is the relationship between the LPGA and its corporate partners? What is the LPGA doing to shape key stakeholder perceptions of women professional golfers? Is the LPGA exercising enough control of local tournaments to ensure the continued growth of the LPGA brand? Has enough been done to promote high-profile women golfers on tour? How does the performance of the LPGA compare to the competition, PGA events?

Joelle knew that a keen understanding of these issues could only help her career at the LPGA, but where to start? As she mulled this question around in her mind, she couldn't help smiling to herself as one thought kept creeping into her consciousness—those who forget the past are bound to repeat it! Of course, as her sport sociology professor had hammered into her in college, to truly understand a complex issue, always start with the past. Fortunately, Joelle had developed fantastic computer skills over the years. She typed in www.lpga.com and began surfing through the history of the LPGA.

History of the LPGA

The history of the LPGA was heavily influenced by promotions in the 1930s and 1940s. Two promoters of men's and women's golf, George S. May and Fred Corcoran, developed distinct approaches to running women's golf tournaments. With the goal of making money for his country club, in 1943 May started the first professional monied women's golf tournament, the All-American Open. Taking his lead from noted entrepreneurs Spalding (sporting goods) and Comiskey (professional sports), May's approach called for facility ownership, producing events, and making profits from gate and concession sales. May promoted golf as entertainment, focusing his energies on catering to admission-paying spectators.

In contrast, Corcoran viewed golf tournaments as a medium to garner valuable exposure for athletes, manufacturers, charities, and the town. This perspective was in line with manufacturers such as Wilson and Spalding who already hired golf professionals to travel and conduct demonstrations and clinics. Since many tournaments were already financially supported by benevolent organizations, sponsoring a tour was more cost efficient than sponsoring individual athletes. By focusing on the golf tournaments, however, manufacturers risked losing control of the players. In response, these companies continued to support a stable of the highest-profile athletes and funded the salary of the tournament director.

Fred Corcoran was hired as tournament director of the men's golf circuit in 1937. In this capacity, by shifting responsibility to the community to come up with the purse, he ran the first financially self-sufficient tournament. Another major contribution of Corcoran was converting professional golf into a charity. Through witnessing Bing Crosby's celebrity pro-am tournaments to raise money for charities during the 1930s, Corcoran saw firsthand the benefits of increased attendance and exposure for the game of golf. During World War II, golf was again used to raise funds, this time for the Red Cross. At the completion of the war, Corcoran seized the opportunity to leverage the power of golf to stimulate civic pride and raise money for hospital and youth program charities. Golf as a charity was good business. With donations to charitable organizations being fully tax deductible, local businesses were more willing to make contributions to tournaments. Hundreds of volunteers were also willing to donate their time to help a good cause. Additionally, a properly selected charity, along with the involvement of these volunteers, served to further promote a tournament. Essentially, by operating golf as a charity, Corcoran successfully converted a labor-intensive undertaking into a no-cost venture.

While Fred Corcoran was becoming proficient at operating men's golf as a charity, women's professional golf was emerging. In 1944, Hope Seignious, Betty Hicks, and Ellen Griffin established the Women's Professional Golf Association (WPGA) with the primary purpose of organizing and promoting professional tournaments for women. This organization, however, got off to a rocky start. Amateur women's golf associations influenced country clubs not to host WPGA events, forcing the professional tournaments onto public courses. Likewise, the men's professional organization and the manufacturers were equally unhelpful to this struggling organization. A 1945 proposal for the WPGA to become part of the PGA Tour was rejected, and the powerful Golf Manufacturers Association turned down a request for aid. On the positive side, the president, Seignious, was able to successfully operate the first three United States Opens. The women's tour, at this point, was completely run by the golfers, who served on committees to manage the various aspects of the tournaments.

The downfall of the WPGA can be traced to a membership meeting held in March of 1947. In this meeting, tensions arose between players representing manufacturers and tournament players, who wanted pay for performance. Given that the WPGA was established to promote the game of golf, and not golf products, debate between these factions stabbed at the heart of the association. The financial support this group badly needed was to come from the manufacturers. In 1948, Wilson Sporting Goods began to back the ladies tour, and Fred Corcoran was offered a job organizing a professional tour for women.

In May of 1949, the Ladies Professional Golf Players Association (LPGPA) was created, lead by Corcoran and the manufacturers. By 1950, the WPGA, while still on the books, was clearly defunct as the organizing body for women's golf. In 1950, the LPGPA was renamed the Ladies Professional Golf Association (LPGA) and established its headquarters in Atlanta, Georgia. Key to the success of the LPGA in the early years were the personalities of women golfers such as Babe Zaharias, Patty Berg, Peggy Kirk, Louise Suggs, and Betsy Rawls. In the first year, Babe Zaharias earned $14,800 over nine events to lead the LPGA in prize money (Table 12.1). By the end of the 1950s, more than twenty tournaments were offered, with total prize money of $200,000. The LPGA Teaching Division, later renamed the LPGA Teaching and Club Professional (T&CP) Division, was established in 1959.

The growth of golf nationally and the emergence of television led to the rapid growth of the LPGA in the 1960s. In 1963, during the final round of the U.S. Women's Open Championship, the LPGA received its first television coverage. The number of tournaments grew to more than thirty, with prize money tripling to $600,000. Golf equipment demand by women also aided in overall growth. By assisting tournaments financially and sponsoring players, golf industry manufacturers

Table 12.1   Annual total prize money distributions*

Year	Money Leader	Winnings ($)	Total Tournament Prize Money	Total Member Tournament Events
1950	Babe Zaharias	14,800	50,000	9
1951	Babe Zaharias	15,087	70,000	14
1952	Betsy Rawls	14,405	150,000	21
1953	Louise Suggs	19,816	120,000	24
1954	Patty Berg	16,011	105,000	21
1955	Patty Berg	16,492	135,000	27
1956	Marlene Hagge	22,235	140,000	26
1957	Patty Berg	16,272	147,830	26
1958	Beverly Hanson	12,369	158,600	25
1959	Betsy Rawls	26,774	202,500	26
1960	Louise Suggs	16,892	186,700	25
1961	Mickey Wright	22,236	288,750	24
1962	Mickey Wright	21,641	338,450	32
1963	Mickey Wright	31,269	345,300	34
1964	Mickey Wright	29,800	351,000	33
1965	Kathy Whitworth	28,658	356,316	33
1966	Kathy Whitworth	33,517	509,500	37
1967	Kathy Whitworth	32,957	435,250	32
1968	Kathy Whitworth	48,379	550,185	34
1969	Carol Mann	49,152	597,290	29
1970	Kathy Whitworth	30,325	435,040	21
1971	Kathy Whitworth	41,181	558,550	21
1972	Kathy Whitworth	65,063	988,400	30
1973	Kathy Whitworth	82,864	1,471,000	36
1974	JoAnne Carner	87,094	1,752,500	35
1975	Sandra Palmer	76,372	1,742,000	33
1976	Judy Rankin	150,374	2,527,000	32
1977	Judy Rankin	122,890	3,058,000	35
1978	Nancy Lopez	189,814	3,925,000	37
1979	Nancy Lopez	197,489	4,400,000	38
1980	Beth Daniel	231,000	5,150,000	40
1981	Beth Daniel	206,988	5,800,000	40
1982	JoAnne Carner	310,400	6,400,000	38
1983	JoAnne Carner	291,404	7,000,000	36
1984	Betsy King	266,771	8,000,000	38
1985	Nancy Lopez	416,472	9,000,000	38
1986	Pat Bradley	492,021	10,000,000	36

Table 12.1 Continued

Year	Money Leader	Winnings ($)	Total Tournament Prize Money	Total Member Tournament Events
1987	Ayako Okamoto	466,044	11,400,000	36
1988	Sherri Turner	350,851	12,510,000	36
1989	Betsy King	654,132	14,190,000	36
1990	Beth Daniel	863,578	17,100,000	37
1991	Pat Bradley	763,118	18,435,000	37
1992	Dottie Mochrie	693,335	21,325,000	39
1993	Betsy King	595,992	20,400,000	35
1994	Laurie Davies	687,201	21,975,000	37
1995	Annika Sorenstam	666,533	24,400,000	37
1996	Karrie Webb	1,002,000	26,500,000	40

*Data were compiled from the *1996 LPGA Player Guide.*

started to form solid alliances with the LPGA. The availability of prize money and tournaments, however, still paled in comparison to the men's tour, the Professional Golfers Association (PGA).

The 1970s were a critical time for women's professional golf. There was a dramatic shift from being primarily a player-run organization to a professionally managed business, as exemplified with the hiring of its first commissioner in 1975, Ray Volpe, and the movement of its headquarters to New York. National and international corporate support helped increase prize money to $4.4 million. Volpe courted corporations by creating sponsorship packages that incorporated targeted advertising, employee functions, and entertainment options. Sponsorship dollars accounted for 40% of the LPGA's revenues in 1978, up dramatically from 10% in 1975. LPGA players, such as Nancy Lopez, JoAnne Carner, Jan Stephenson, and Amy Alcott capitalized on the power of television to enhance their recognition and the credibility of the LPGA. This decade truly belonged to Nancy Lopez, as she set a new record in 1978 by winning nine tournaments, including a record five in a row.

The growth of women's sports programs in high schools and colleges, spurred by Title IX legislation, resulted in an influx of new young stars into the LPGA during the 1980s. This decade was also a time of dynamic growth and change for the LPGA. Prize money grew to over $14 million, and the association began developing charitable programs for youth, primarily girls and minorities. Change came in the form of the LPGA headquarters moving twice, finally ending up in its current location of Daytona Beach, Florida. The LPGA also funded, with $400,000, the first nonteam sport retirement system in 1981.

Growth in women's golf has shown no signs of slowing in the 1990s. The LPGA has developed five tournaments with purses exceeding $1 million each and has increased total prize money to over $30 million. The LPGA, Women Professional Golfers' European Tour (WPGET), and Karsten Solheim of Karsten Manufacturing Corporation joined in 1989 to develop the premier international women's golf competition, The Solheim Cup. First played in 1990, this is a biennial trans-Atlantic team match play competition between European members of the WPGET and United States members of the LPGA. Lastly, during this decade, the LPGA became the first professional golf organization to partner with an official national charity, the Susan G. Komen Breast Cancer Foundation.

During this decade, the LPGA was also involved in creating the first Women in Golf Summit in 1991 (held also in 1993 and 1995). This conference focused on defining and addressing current issues in women's golf. In 1991, the LPGA in conjunction with Mazda initiated a series of clinics and seminars for women in business. Since then, Gillette has taken title to this series, with 1998 marking the sixth year of the LPGA Gillette Golf Clinics for Women.

The history of the LPGA was certainly intriguing, thought Joelle. Clearly, the LPGA had already evolved beyond many people's expectations. The LPGA and women's golf had gone through tremendous struggles to reach its current level of professionalism and earn the respect of networks, corporations, and golf consumers. Joelle began to wonder how the LPGA organized its business operations to operate efficiently and foster continuing growth.

LPGA Business Issues

The LPGA Board of Directors is responsible for the overall direction of the organization. The board is comprised of five independent members and the LPGA Tour Executive Committee (six tour players). The commissioner of the LPGA serves ex-officio. A representative of the Teaching and Club Professional Division is invited to all board meetings. Responsibilities of the board of directors include long-range planning, policy development, advising on legal, corporate, member, and sponsor-relationship issues, evaluation of LPGA management, and other areas as mandated by the LPGA Constitution.

The management of the LPGA is entrusted to the commissioner and his staff (deputy commissioner, vice president, and general counsel). The commissioner's office supervises approximately fifty staff members in the areas of marketing, communications, accounting/finance, tournament operations, and the Teaching and Club Professional Division. Jim

Ritts was appointed as the LPGA commissioner-elect in June of 1995 and officially began his duties in January 1996.

The LPGA is comprised of five integrated entities: the LPGA Tour, the Teaching and Club Professional (T&CP) Division, Women, Junior Golf, and Charitable Organizations. The following sections review each of the parts of the LPGA.

LPGA Tour

The LPGA Tour consists of the LPGA tour events, LPGA touring professionals, and the corporate partners, who financially support the tour. The LPGA schedule for 1997 included forty-three events (Table 12.2), with four being new tournaments. Total tournament purses ranged from $500,000 at the Susan G. Komen International to $1.5 million for the J.C. Penney Classic held in early December. Total prize money for the forty-three tournaments held in 1997 was over $30 million. This represents tremendous growth in purses over the past century. In 1950, for example, the tour schedule was comprised of only nine events, with a total purse of $50,000. The leading money winner that year, Babe Zaharias, earned $14,800. Karrie Webb, in comparison, led the 1996 LPGA Tour with winnings of $1,002,000 (see Table 12.1).

Table 12.2 1997 Tournaments and total purses*

Dates	Tournament	Total Purse
January 9–12	Chrysler-Plymouth Tournament of Champions (Sports Channel/NBC)**	700,000
January 17–19	Healthsouth Inaugural (ESPN)	600,000
February 6–9	Diet Dr. Pepper National Pro-Am (TCG)	500,000
February 13–16	Los Angeles Women's Championship	650,000
February 20–22	Cup Noodles Hawaiian Ladies Open	650,000
February 27–March 2	Alpine Australian Ladies Masters	650,000
March 13–16	Welch's/Circle K Championship	500,000
March 20–23	Standard Register PING (ESPN)	700,000
March 27–30	Nabisco Dinah Shore (ESPN2/ABC)	900,000
April 3–6	Longs Drugs Challenge (TCG)	500,000
April 17–20	Susan G. Komen International (TCG)	500,000
April 25–27	Chick-fil-A Charity Championship (TCG)	550,000
May 1–4	Sprint Titleholders Championship (CBS)	1,200,000
May 9–11	Sara Lee Classic	675,000
May 15–18	McDonald's LPGA Championship (TCG/CBS)	1,200,000
May 22–25	LPGA Corning Classic (TCG)	650,000
May 24–25	J.C. Penney/LPGA Skins Game (ABC)	540,000
May 29–June 1	Michelob Light Classic (TCG)	600,000

Table 12.2 Continued

Dates	Tournament	Total Purse
June 5–8	Oldsmobile Classic (ESPN)	600,000
June 13–15	First Bank Presents the Edina Realty LPGA Classic (Regional)	600,000
June 19–22	Rochester International	600,000
June 27–29	ShopRite LPGA Classic (Regional)	900,000
July 3–6	Jamie Farr Kroger Classic (TCG)	700,000
July 10–13	U.S. Women's Open (ESPN/NBC)	1,200,000
July 17–20	JAL Big Apple Classic (NBC)	750,000
July 25–27	Giant Eagle LPGA Classic (TCG)	600,000
July 31–August 3	du Maurier Classic (ESPN/ESPN2)	1,000,000
August 7–10	Friendly's Classic (TCG)	550,000
August 14–17	Weetabix Women's British Open	900,000
August 22–24	Star Bank LPGA Classic in conjunction with The Children's Medical Center	550,000
August 30–September 1	State Farm Rail Classic (ESPN2)	600,000
September 5–7	The Safeway LPGA Golf Championship (Regional)	550,000
September 11–14	SAFECO Classic	550,000
September 18–21	PING Welch's Championship	550,000
September 25–28	Fieldcrest Cannon Classic	550,000
October 2–5	CoreStates Betsy King LPGA Classic	600,000
October 9–12	Samsung World Championship	525,000
October 31–November 2	Nichirei International	675,000
November 7–9	Toray Japan Queen's Cup	750,000
November 20–23	ITT LPGA Tour Championship (ESPN/ESPN2/ABC)	750,000
December 4–7	J.C. Penney Classic (ESPN/ABC)	1,500,000
December 12–14	Diners Club Matches (ESPN/ABC)	700,000
December 20–21	Wendy's Three-Tour Challenge (ABC)	650,000

*Data were compiled from www.lpga.com (4/21/97).
**Television network airing event in parentheses.

The LPGA received increasing media coverage during the 1990s. In 1997, twenty-nine events were televised—twelve on network TV, fourteen on cable, and three on regional channels (Table 12.3). This is a significant increase over 1990, when seventeen tournaments were televised, six on network television. The growth of cable television

Table 12.3 LPGA growth in the 1990s*

Year	Tournament Attendance	Televised Events	Annual Charitable Donations
1990	N/A	16 (5 network)	N/A
1991	N/A	17 (6 network)	N/A
1992	N/A	19 (10 network)	$6,730,000
1993	N/A	15 (9 network)	$6,863,682
1994	1.73 million	17 (11 network)	$6,346,722
1995	1.60 million	25 (10 network)	$7,142,994
1996	1.64 million	29 (12 network)	$7,761,712
1997	TBD	30 (12 network)	TBD

*Data were obtained directly from the LPGA.

and the establishment of The Golf Channel (a twenty-four hour cable television network) in 1995 have increased TV coverage of the LPGA.

Negotiations of fees for television rights for the LPGA are very different from those for other sport properties. The men's tour, the Professional Golf Association (PGA), for example, receives rights fees directly from the networks to cover its tournaments. The networks are responsible for selling the commercial time for the PGA Tour telecasts. In contrast, LPGA tournaments must buy all the commercial and programming time from the networks, pay all production costs necessary to televise the tournament, and pay a rights fee to the LPGA Tour. These tournaments must then recover these time-buy, production, and rights-fees costs through the sale of commercials and sponsorships. The networks and the LPGA Tour are in a no-risk situation for the tournament organizers bear responsibility for selling the commercial spots.

Although media coverage of the LPGA continues to grow, attendance at LPGA events has remained steady during this decade (Table 12.3). In 1996, 1.64 million people attended LPGA tournaments. This represents very little change from 1994, when 1.73 million spectators graced the fairways of LPGA events. Attendance at tournaments varies depending on size of market, scheduling, marketing acumen, and weather conditions. Jim Ritts, commissioner of the LPGA, notes, "The game is expanding its appeal to a larger spectrum of people, including women, minorities, and younger people."

The LPGA has signed promotional agreements with a number of corporate sponsors. These agreements serve a variety of purposes. For the LPGA, these relationships provide financial or in-kind support, help promote the association and its events, and enhance the overall image of women's golf and the LPGA. Corporate partners, in return, benefit from being associated with the premier women's sport organization, receive local, regional, national, and international exposure, and have unique advertising and promotional opportunities. Table 12.4 provides a list of 1996 LPGA promotional partners and licensees. These include such notables as Eastman Kodak (official film and photographic consultant), Eli Lilly and Company (official sponsor of the Lilly Legends Series), Anheuser-Busch (official sponsor), and Mercury (official car). In 1996, the LPGA signed sponsorship agreements with Texas Instruments as the "official computer of the LPGA" and AGT Sports as the "official technology partner of the LPGA." These partnerships will advance the LPGA into new areas of leading-edge technology.

Licensing fees range from $100,000–$400,000 annually, depending on the extent of the program. Title to an LPGA tournament typically averages three times the tournament purse (i.e., $500,000 purse = $1.5 million sponsorship). This financial commitment, however, is not inclusive of any television time purchased ($600,000–$700,000 for cable, $1 million+ for network) or production costs. As a result of partnering with over thirty companies, licensing revenues grew by 170% from 1993 to 1997. This growth includes a 55% increase from 1994 to 1996, with a projected increase of 27% in 1997.

The LPGA has created multifaceted relationships with its promotional partners. Smucker's, for example, sponsors the LPGA Child Development Center. This center travels to about thirty LPGA tournaments annually, providing care for the children of the more than thirty-five moms competing on the LPGA Tour. This center is the first traveling childcare center in professional sports, and affords LPGA professionals the opportunity to balance family life with their careers. LPGA corporate partners do not limit their financial involvement to golf tournaments. Crayola is title sponsor of the LPGA Tour Junior Golf Clinic Program, held at twenty-six LPGA tournaments. The purpose of this program is to provide a rewarding golf experience for juniors. In addition to this program, Crayola also provides product for the Smucker's LPGA Child Development Center, the LPGA Urban Youth Golf Program, and the LPGA Girls Golf Club in partnership with the USGA and Girl Scouts USA.

The LPGA has actively developed and implemented new concepts in the 1990s. In 1994, the home course of the LPGA, LPGA International, opened at Daytona Beach, Florida. This course also serves as the site of the $1.2 million Titleholders Championship and LPGA Academy resort currently being developed. A new state-of-the-art LPGA headquarters was opened in 1996. That same year, the LPGA launched an official merchandise program and web site (www.lpga.com). The LPGA Fan Village that also debuted in 1996 kicked off a ten-tournament tour in 1997 with a presenting sponsorship of Target stores. This unique, mobile, interactive fan exhibit brings tournament spectators "inside

Table 12.4   1996 LPGA promotional partners and licensees*

Company	Category
Alabama Sports Medicine	Official sponsor of the LPGA fitness van
All Sport	Official sports beverage of the LPGA
American Sports Medicine Institute	LPGA fitness van
Anheuser-Busch: Michelob Light	Official sponsor of the LPGA
Bausch & Lomb	Official sunglasses of the LPGA
Beverley Willey	LPGA beauty/hair and fashion consultant
Budget Rent a Car	Official car rental company of the LPGA
Buena Vista Hospitality Group	Official golf development and management company of the LPGA
Continental Airlines	Official airline of the LPGA
Crayola	Official sponsor of the LPGA
The du Maurier Ltd. Classic	Official sponsor of the LPGA fitness van
Eastman Kodak Company	Official film and photographic consultant of the LPGA
Eli Lilly and Company	Official sponsor of The Lilly Legends Series
Golf Magazine	Official magazine of the LPGA
HEALTHSOUTH Corporation	Official sponsor of the LPGA fitness van
IZOD Club Golf and Tennis	Official apparel of the LPGA
Lincoln-Mercury	Official car of the LPGA
MBNA America	Official credit card company of the LPGA
Mead Corporation	Official trash receptacle of the LPGA
Merrill Lynch	Official shootout sponsor of the LPGA
Paul Arpin Van Lines	Official mover of the LPGA
Rolex Watch U.S.A.	Official timepiece of the LPGA
7UP	Official soft drink of the LPGA
The J.M. Smucker Co.	Official child development sponsor of the LPGA
Square Two Golf	Official golf club manufacturer of the LPGA
Sunderland of Scotland	Official rainwear of the LPGA
Target	Presenting sponsor of the LPGA Fan Village
Titleist and Foot-joy Worldwide	Patron company of the LPGA
Worldtek Travel, Inc.	Official travel agency of the LPGA

*Data were compiled from *1996 LPGA Player Guide.*

the ropes" through player autograph sessions, video swing analysis, LPGA historical timeline, and photo fantasy station. According to Jim Ritts, "Our goal is to try to capitalize on the growing sense of momentum of the LPGA. We see women as an important economic force."

Another important element of the Tour is the LPGA Hall of Fame. With some of the toughest eligibility standards in all of sport (thirty wins with two majors; thirty-five wins with one major; or forty wins), entrance into the Hall represents the pinnacle of a professional women golfer's career. Since its beginning in 1950, the LPGA has inducted fifteen individuals into its Hall of Fame (Table 12.5). In 1951, four of the founding members were inducted: Patty Berg, Betty Jameson, Louise Suggs, and Babe Zaharias. The last player to make the Hall was Betsy King in 1995.

In managing its events, the LPGA partners with the Tournament Sponsors Association (TSA), an association of tournament organizers and promoters with the common mission to improve the quality of their events and to further the growth of women's golf. In this role, these promoters have a responsibility to both the LPGA and the designated charity to properly market and manage their golf tournaments. An elected board of directors, which meets regularly with the LPGA commissioner and his staff, governs this association.

Table 12.5 Members of the LPGA Hall of Fame*

Year Inducted	Player	Number of Career Victories
1951	Patty Berg	57
1951	Betty Jameson	10
1951	Louise Suggs	50
1951	Babe Didrikson Zaharias	31
1960	Betsy Rawls	55
1964	Mickey Wright	82
1975	Kathy Whitworth	88
1977	Sandra Haynie	42
1977	Carol Mann	38
1982	JoAnne Carner**	42
1987	Nancy Lopez**	47
1991	Pat Bradley**	31
1993	Patty Sheehan**	34
1995	Betsy King**	30
1994	Dinah Shore	Honorary member

*Data were compiled from the *1996 LPGA Player Guide.*
**Current player as of 1996.

LPGA Teaching and Club Professional (T&CP) Division

The LPGA T&CP Division (1959) has the largest membership of women golf professionals in the United States. Membership comprises head and assistant professionals, teaching professionals, golf directors and administrators, owners of golf schools and driving ranges, and high school and college coaches. Total membership exceeds 1,000, more than a 25% increase since 1992. The number of applicants has increased by 78% during that time span. Members have an opportunity to play in the country's premier competition for women teaching and club professionals, the *Golf for Women Magazine* LPGA Teaching and Club Professional Championship, reintroduced by the LPGA in 1992. LPGA headquarters is responsible for all administration, marketing, and educational programs for this division. T&CP Division members, in conjunction with the LPGA and LPGA Tour players, are involved in a number of innovative teaching, educational, and special event programs to help "grow the game of golf." One of these educational programs is the LPGA National Education Program.

LPGA NATIONAL EDUCATION PROGRAM

Planned to launch in 1997, this is a comprehensive five-day golf education program series. All new members of the T&CP Division will be required to attend the three-tiered program. Each program will focus on developing an effective teaching model, understanding the learning process, and creating effective learning programs.

The T&CP Division is supported by a number of corporations, including Cobra Golf, *Golf for Women Magazine,* Prize Possessions, Spalding, Square Two Golf Company, Scorecards U.S.A., Taylor Made, Rolex, Titleist and Foot-Joy Worldwide, and Callaway Golf Company.

Women

Another area of emphasis for the LPGA is enhancing playing opportunities and creating programs for women. Getting more women involved in the game and teaching them how to network and conduct business on the golf course is important for the continued growth of women's golf, and so the LPGA has created programs for businesswomen. One program that has met with success is The Gillette LPGA Golf Clinics for Women.

THE GILLETTE LPGA GOLF CLINICS FOR WOMEN

The Gillette Clinic is a nationwide series (fourteen cities) of golf clinics for professional women. These clinics help women become more comfortable with the game of golf as well as teach them the benefits of utilizing golf to help build and maintain important business relationships. Clinics include personalized golf instruction and skills demonstrations.

Junior Golf

In addition to promoting the benefits of golf to professional women, the LPGA also strives to create opportunities for youth, particularly girls, to participate in the game of golf. Part of this mission is to utilize golf to educate and instill positive values in young girls. To this end, the LPGA has developed several programs specifically geared to the youth market, two of which are the LPGA Girls Golf Club, in partnership with the USGA and Girl Scouts USA, and the LPGA Urban Youth Golf Program.

LPGA GIRLS GOLF CLUB

Started in Phoenix in 1989, the LPGA Girls Golf Club is now in seventy U.S., three Canadian, and fifteen Australian/New Zealand communities. In March 1997, the LPGA formed a unique partnership with the USGA and Girl Scouts USA that strengthened this program. The program encourages girls aged 7–17 to compete and build friendships in a nonthreatening environment.

LPGA URBAN YOUTH GOLF PROGRAM

This program was launched in Los Angeles in 1989 and has since spread to three more cities: Detroit, Michigan; Portland, Oregon; and Wilmington, Delaware, with a fourth to open in Atlantic City, New Jersey, in 1998. This program is designed to expose minority and underprivileged urban youth to the positive qualities that golf can bring to a child's life. A grant from the Amateur Athletic Foundation provided funding to establish this program.

Charitable Organizations

In addition to managing tour events and the T&CP Division, the LPGA is also involved in charitable activities. The LPGA requires that every tournament have an identified local or national charity as the event beneficiary. These charities may elect to create events in association with the tournament in order to raise funds. Charity contributions from LPGA tournaments totaled $7.76 million in 1996 (Table 12.3).

From 1981 to 1996, the total funds raised for charity was approximately $86 million. In addition to assisting charities in their local markets, the LPGA designated the Susan G. Komen Breast Cancer Foundation as its official national charity in 1992. This charity was chosen because of the relevancy of this foundation for women and how the LPGA family had been directly affected by breast cancer. Several notable LPGA members died from this disease, underscoring the need to better inform women of all ages about its causes and treatments. Specifically, LPGA Tour players Heather Farr and Kathy Ahern died of breast cancer after fighting courageous battles, and Tour player Shelly Hamlin and LPGA Director of Tournament Operations, Suzanne Jackson are breast cancer survivors. The LPGA is the only professional golf association that has one "official national charity."

In 1991, the LPGA established The LPGA Foundation. The Foundation is a nonprofit charitable organization that provides a vehicle for making donations to the charitable efforts of the LPGA. Funds from this source have been used to build a catastrophic illness fund for LPGA members and others in the golf industry, to help develop junior golf programs across the country, and to provide academic scholarships for junior golfers.

Through expanding playing opportunities and purses, enhanced media coverage and corporate involvement, and proactive programs for club professionals and administrators, businesswomen, and youth, the LPGA has done extremely well during the 1990s. The true measure of this success, however, requires benchmarks for comparison, thought Joelle. What better point of comparison than the competition in the golf market, the Professional Golf Association (PGA) and its three golf tours, the PGA, Senior PGA, and the Nike tours.

The Competition

The PGA Tour

The PGA Tour has experienced tremendous growth in the number of players, number of events, television coverage, prize money, and charitable contributions. There are three main reasons for the success of the PGA Tour: the image of the players and the game, the growth in popularity of golf, and the structure of the sport.

The primary purpose of the PGA Tour is to provide financial opportunities for their players and to protect the integrity of the game, with a secondary mission of raising money for charity. Since its first contribution in 1938, PGA Tour events have raised about $300 million for charity, with $164 million of this total coming in the 1990s. In 1996 alone, PGA Tour events contributed $35 million. This money flows directly back to the communities where the tournaments are played.

Attendance at PGA Tour events has been climbing in recent years. Based on the first twelve tournaments held in 1997, average attendance has been 126,000, ranging from a low of 39,500 to a high of 421,095. Several factors account for the wide variance in attendance figures, including population of the surrounding metropolitan market, the tradition and the prestige of the event, commitment of the local community, and marketing of the event.

While attendance has been growing, global TV coverage has also been on the upswing. In 1996, golf was televised in more than 140 countries around the world, with over 700 hours of golf aired in the United States. According to Tim Finchem, PGA Tour commissioner, "We know that television is changing and that viewers' choices are going to expand rapidly in the coming years" (*Business Week*, May 1, 1995). This expansion is evidenced by the new television package for the years 1999 to 2002. Golf tournaments will be covered extensively by three broadcast partners and three cable partners. CBS will televise seventeen events per year, ABC will have eleven, and NBC will carry the remaining five. The three cable partners will be responsible for coverage of early rounds. ESPN will cover nineteen events and USA Network will have twelve. The Golf Channel/Fox Sports Net, in addition to covering eleven events, has exclusive rights to one full event. This new television contract will increase rights fees from the current $40 million a year to more than $100 million annually (*Wall Street Journal*, May, 12, 1996).

Also included in this new broadcast package was the new World Championship Series (WCS), co-sanctioned by the five-member tours of the PGA Tours International Federation. CBS will broadcast the World Series of Golf, with ABC televising the WCS Stroke-Play Championship and the WCS Match-Play Championship. When commenting on the TV schedule, PGA Tour Commissioner Finchem noted: "We have successfully segmented the schedule in a way that we think is going to increase the visibility of the Tour in different parts of the year and, as a consequence, create more value for the sponsors. Suffice it to say that gross revenues from all television sources we expect now to double, and it would not be unreasonable to expect that by the year 2000, our official purse at PGA Tour events will average in excess of $3 million" (www.pgatour.com). The PGA Tour is anticipating purse increases in 1997 to $75 million in official money. Finchem added the following on the impact of this broadcast deal on PGA Tour sponsors: "If you look at it from the standpoint of the sponsors, we're going to have more valuable programming, a little more programming, it's going to be scheduled better so there's more promotion involved, and the sponsors are going to have a more valuable product to invest in" (www.pgatour.com).

The PGA Tour has been actively involved in golf course management, with continuing growth in the Tournament Players Club (TPC) Network. Clubs that are part of this network are owned and operated by the Tour. The first such club, the Tournament Players Club at Sawgrass, opened in 1980 and introduced the concept of stadium golf, which provides more seating options around greens and improved sight lines. Over the past ten years, the players clubs have generated $50 million in savings to tournaments that play on those sites because the tournaments play rent-free and are subsidized. Also, increased ticket sales and corporate hospitality opportunities generate more tournament revenues at the Players Clubs. New Players Clubs have been developed in Heron Bay and Summerlin, and construction is underway at Myrtle Beach and Jasna Polana in Princeton.

The PGA Tour has also been very active in the international arena. Finchem worked with golf's five world governing bodies in 1996 to form the PGA Tours International Federation. The PGA Tour, working with this new international organization, is developing new match-play, stroke-play, and team play events for 1999. The President's Cup will be held in Australia in 1998, and the PGA Tour has developed the International Tournaments Players Clubs (ITPC) in Japan, Thailand, and China. Growth is expected in the ITPC network as interest in golf continues to boom overseas.

Working in conjunction with the world's major golf entities, including the LPGA, the biggest business venture undertaken by the PGA Tour is the development of the World Golf Foundation. The mission of the foundation is to introduce golf to young people and through golf promote academic achievement, community service, and positive values. The foundation oversees the World Golf Village and the World Golf Hall of Fame. The first phase of construction of The World Golf Village, located near St. Augustine, Florida, will be completed in Spring 1998. This village will include the World Golf Hall of Fame, the World Golf Hotel and Conference Center, three golf courses, a golf academy, the new headquarters of PGA Tour productions, an IMAX theatre, a Mayo Clinic facility, and the World Golf Village Library and Resource Center. The founding partner of the World Golf Village is Shell Oil Company.

How bright is the future of the PGA Tour? Judging from the positive impact of new players like Tiger Woods, who has garnered worldwide media attention, the Tour continues to be a growing sport organization. Tiger has brought new excitement to the Tour, helping grow ticket sales by 25% and television ratings. Finchem concurs, "I think he has all the potential to have a profound impact on our sport as an entertainment sport. I mean, we are selling more tickets. He is increasing television ratings. And, he has taken us into an exposure dimension beyond where we were in the media" (www.pgatour.com).

Senior PGA Tour

The PGA Tour is also responsible for developing and managing the Senior PGA Tour, designed for players over the age of 50. The Senior PGA Tour debuted in 1980 with just two events and prize money totaling $250,000. By 1993, players competed in forty-three events (twenty-seven televised) for $26.3 million in prizes. Today, the Senior PGA Tour is widely recognized as one of the most successful sports ventures launched in the 1980s. Currently, based on twenty-four Senior tournaments' reporting figures, average event attendance is 75,000. Attendance varies widely, depending on location and event prestige, from a low of 25,000 to a high of 187,259. The 1997 Senior Tour schedule included thirty-five official events and a number of unofficial events. Unofficial events often have special playing formats, such as the Senior Skins Game and the Senior Slam. Thirty-one of the 1997 Senior events are at least partially covered by one of the cable networks. The major networks (ABC, NBC, or CBS) televised nine tournaments. The major carrier of Senior events is ESPN, which broadcast twenty-seven Senior events during the year 1997.

Why has this tour become so successful in such a short time span? The primary factor involves demographics. The greying and financially healthy individuals playing on the Senior Tour are a good match with the customers of corporations utilizing the Tour to sell their products and services, so it is not surprising that corporate sponsors have displayed great interest in the Senior Tour. One major sponsor, for example, is Cadillac. About 8% of Cadillac's advertising and marketing budget goes into the PGA Tour, with the largest commitment to the Senior Tour, where twenty events come under the heading of The Cadillac Series. All twenty events are televised on ESPN with Cadillac as the sole automobile sponsor. According to Alex Morton, executive vice president of advertising at DMB&B, "It's been wildly successful. We have sold $230 million worth of product directly attributable to our involvement with the Cadillac Series. My feeling is that we actually generate a lot more sales than this" (*Business Week,* May 1, 1995). In addition to spurring product sales, the Senior Tour also represents an excellent hospitality opportunity for corporations. Based on its prestige, for example, the 1995 U.S. Senior Open was able to charge $85,000 for a private, air-conditioned hospitality tent for 100 people.

Nike Tour

The Nike Tour started in 1990 (as the Hogan Tour) serves as the PGA Tour's minor league. In 1993, Nike signed on to be the sponsor of the Nike Tour for an amount rumored to be at least $20 million. The top fifteen money winners from the Nike Tour automatically earn PGA Tour playing privileges for the following year. Another avenue to the PGA Tour is by winning three events in 1997. To date, twenty-two Nike Tour graduates have won twenty-nine events of the PGA Tour.

The 1997 Nike Tour schedule included thirty events. Nine of these tournaments were shown on The Golf Channel (TGC); the year-ending

Nike Tour Championship, held at the Grand National Golf Club, aired on ESPN. Since its inception in 1990, prize money has more than doubled from $3 million to $6.225 million in 1997. Total charitable contributions of the Nike Tour total $9.5 million.

Joelle leaned back in her chair and, contemplated all that she had learned about the LPGA. Insight into business issues impacting the LPGA served to further excite her about the new job and the role she was to play in promoting women's golf worldwide. As she reviewed her "to do" list in preparation for the day ahead, she reminded herself to never lose sight of the larger issues affecting her organization.

The LPGA Fan Village

William A. Sutton and Cindy Davis

Introduction

Bill Alvarez struggled with mixed emotions as he walked through a misting rain on his way to the Friday evening LPGA clambake. He was excited to see the implementation of his Fan Village concept, while at the same time the actual exhibit and area were not quite as he had envisioned. Pondering as he walked, he recalled how the concept of a fan village began.

The Ladies Professional Golf Association (LPGA) undertook a qualitative research project to measure fan (defined as attendees of LPGA events) interests and attitudes during the summer of 1994. Results from this research were to be used to support the unveiling of a new merchandising program. The LPGA employed Event Satisfaction Unlimited, a sport and lifestyle marketing agency headquartered in Amherst, Massachusetts, to conduct this research. Bill Alvarez, vice president of consumer services, was responsible for this account and recommended using focus groups because he planned on using examples of logos and merchandise for the participants to respond to and critique. The focus groups, which were acceptable to the LPGA, were conducted at LPGA events in Rochester, New York, Boston, and Stratton Mountain in Vermont.

The first focus group was conducted on June 18, 1994, during the Rochester International, an annual LPGA tournament conducted in Rochester, New York. The focus group was designed to probe merchandise-purchasing practices and assess the reactions of the participants to a planned merchandise line, which was to be produced in conjunction with Izod club and J.C. Penney. To evaluate the strength of the LPGA merchandise concept, various merchandise samples and LPGA logoed items were available as visual aids in the focus group setting. The focus group participants, who consisted of nine females and three males, mirrored actual LPGA attendance of 66% female and 37% male, were between the ages of 30 and 65, and included tournament volunteers, novice golfers, and avid golfers. The focus group was conducted in a room in the clubhouse at Locust Hills Country Club, site of the

Rochester International, and lasted approximately two hours and fifteen minutes.

As the focus group began, Alvarez introduced himself and asked each participant to do the same. After the introductions had been made, Bill explained how focus groups worked and thanked the participants on behalf of the LPGA for their time. It was at this point that one of the participants, Stan, a 63-year-old avid golfer and tournament volunteer, interrupted and blurted out: *"What exactly is the LPGA?"* This initial question caused quite a stir within the group. The majority of the participants also indicated that they were unfamiliar with the LPGA and its connection to the golf tournament held in Rochester. With these questions it was apparent that conducting research into an LPGA merchandising program was premature with this group. To capitalize on the group's interest in the LPGA, Alvarez redirected the group to determine the fans' knowledge of the LPGA and its objectives for supporting and sanctioning events such as the Rochester International.

The questions posed by the participants and the ensuing discussion revolved around the following key areas:

1. Event attendees were unaware of what the LPGA stood for, its mission, and relationship to the Rochester International (and LPGA Tour events in general).
2. Attendees noted that with the exception of the Tour players, there was no LPGA presence at Tour events.
3. Since awareness and comprehension of the LPGA was low, an attempt to build an LPGA merchandise venture targeted at attendees was premature.
4. LPGA players are the most visible extension of the LPGA Tour.

Based on the feedback received from this initial focus group, Alvarez recommended the LPGA use the planned focus groups to determine event attendees' awareness and comprehension of the LPGA instead of as a tool to evaluate a new merchandising program. Building on this suggestion, Alvarez and the LPGA concentrated focus group questions on how the LPGA could use its tournaments to promote and publicize the LPGA and its mission. Specifically, each focus group participant was asked the following:

1. In your own words, what is the LPGA?
2. An image can be defined as the manner in which something (person, place, and organization) is viewed. In your mind what is the current image of the LPGA?
3. Based upon our discussion and the information we have shared with you, do you feel the LPGA is headed in the right direction?

4. What action(s) do you feel that the LPGA should initiate or undertake to better position itself and convey a more accurate portrayal of its mission?

At the conclusion of the focus group, Alvarez met with LPGA personnel to discuss his findings and to suggest a course of action. The key findings from the group researched were

- Respondents did not understand the role of the LPGA in relationship to the tournament they were attending.
- None of the participants had ever heard of the LPGA Teaching and Club Professional Division.
- The perception of the LPGA relates directly to the perception of its players—which is highly positive.
- LPGA fans wish to know more about the LPGA and its players on a regular, accessible basis.
- The LPGA is missing an opportunity to communicate and educate its target market by not having an established medium in place at LPGA Tour events.

Course of Action

Alvarez, now functioning in his original role as a consultant, compiled and presented his final report to the LPGA. He recommended the creation of an area where fans could interact with the organization. This area would consist of a variety of exhibits and activities designed to increase awareness, comprehension, and interest in the LPGA as well as promoting loyalty and increased fan involvement.

Alvarez had firsthand experience in observing and evaluating these events. Through his work with Event Satisfaction Unlimited, he had evaluated fan festivals and profiled the attendees for all of the major sport leagues. Major league baseball was the first to create a fan experience by developing "Fan Fest" to be held in conjunction with its annual All-Star Game in July. The National Football League followed in 1992 by creating the "NFL Experience" to be held prior to the Super Bowl. The National Basketball Association created the "Jam Session" in 1993, and the National Hockey League began the "NHL FANtasy" in 1996, both electing to conduct events in conjunction with their respective All-Star Games. These fan festivals include a myriad of interactive activities and exhibits particularly appealing to the under-24 age group. All promote the respective corporate sponsors, encourage the sale of licensed merchandise, and include a card/memorabilia area. These events help grow their respective sports by providing the fan a unique experience regardless of income level. At the same time, these fan festivals provide a opportunity for sponsors to leverage their involvement and better position their products/services with the sports league.

Although the interactive nature of these events form the "core" in terms of activities and things to do for the fans, Alvarez through previous research knew player participation was essential for the event's success. Knowing that LPGA fans held LPGA Tour players in high regard and that they were also very interested in meeting them, Bill felt an on-site LPGA fan event would be the best forum to bring the fans closer to the LPGA pros. It would also serve to entertain and to educate event attendees about the LPGA, both on-site as well as nationally, through the publicity generated around the event. Unlike the festivals hosted by other professional sports leagues at their annual premier event, Bill envisioned an LPGA festival that could be repeated at twenty-five or more LPGA Tour events annually (traveling through the United States, Canada, and possibly to Japan and other venues). Thus, in a meeting with LPGA Vice President Alice Newly, Alvarez recommended the LPGA create an interactive presence at each Tour event to disseminate information about the LPGA and its various program elements:

- the LPGA Teaching and Club Professional Division
- LPGA Junior Girls Golf Program
- the LPGA's national charity, the Susan G. Komen Breast Cancer Foundation
- LPGA tournaments' involvement with charities

and also to accomplish the following:

- gather data about attendees through surveys or contests and merchandise giveaway registrations
- showcase LPGA Tour professionals
- provide an area for LPGA sponsors and licensees to promote their products
- entertain fans and provide corporate hospitality to corporate partners in an area designed to be informative
- create a retail opportunity to sell LPGA merchandise and souvenirs
- establish an educational component and utilize video, interactive computers, and other displays to inform attendees about the history and growth of the LPGA
- initiate a vehicle to create a LPGA fan database
- provide a revenue source through sponsorship opportunities
- offer stage/interview areas for the media to meet with LPGA Tour players

Alvarez felt all of this could best be accomplished by creating an LPGA Village at each tournament. This village would be a highly visible, self-contained area designed to entertain and educate fans about the LPGA and its programs.

Implementing the Concept

Alvarez's concept developed into a traveling exhibit and staging area by Make An Impression, Inc., of Stratford, Connecticut. The LPGA Fan Village, as this exhibit was called, made its debut in 1996 at the McDonald's LPGA Championship in Wilmington, Delaware (see Figure 13.1). The premise of the LPGA Fan Village in its initial year was threefold: information, entertainment, and merchandising. The LPGA Fan Village was staged a second time in 1996 at the State Farm Rail Classic in Springfield, Illinois. The purpose of these two test sites, prior to the roll-out of a national tour in 1997 was multifaceted:

- to gain consumer reaction and feedback
- to provide potential sponsors with a model for building sponsorship in 1997
- to encourage LPGA tournaments to host the fan village

FIGURE 13.1 The LPGA Fan Village
Photo Credit: George R. Milne

FIGURE 13.2 LPGA Fan Village at 1996 McDonald's LPGA championship.
Photo Credit: George R. Milne

These Fan Village test sites included the following elements and activities:

- video presentations
- special fan/player photo opportunities (sponsored by Kodak)
- player autograph sessions
- LPGA web site access
- forty-foot pictorial LPGA historical timeline
- merchandise from the "Authentic LPGA Collection"

Consultant Evaluation and Consumer Reaction

During the 1996 McDonald's LPGA Championship, a team of consultants from Alvarez's new company, Audience Profiling International (API), was employed to assess LPGA attendees' reactions to the LPGA Fan Village (see Figure 13.2). API's job scope also included analyzing the present state of the LPGA Fan Village and making recommendations for the 1997 Tour. During the consultant's visit, the 1997 Fan Village tour was anticipated to consist of ten to fifteen events. The consultants conducted mini-interviews that were videotaped and lasted ten to fifteen minutes (see Appendix for research results). Those interviewed included couples, groups, and individuals and they were asked their opinions regarding the following topics:

- the location of the LPGA Fan Village in relation to other activities at the McDonald's LPGA Championship
- the internal elements of the LPGA Fan Village
- possible additions/improvements to the LPGA Fan Village
- what they liked best about the LPGA Fan Village
- how the LPGA could use the LPGA Fan Village to increase awareness and understanding regarding its mission and programs
- their feelings regarding the LPGA Fan Village as a touring event

LPGA Fan Village Market Research Results

Being a new concept, an area large enough for the LPGA Fan Village was not included in the traditional site plan for the McDonald's LPGA Championship. The tournament and the LPGA decided to place the LPGA Fan Village tent in an area lined with sampling tents. These sampling tents created a corridor of merchants leading to the Fan Village entrance. The consultants observed numerous attendees who looked interested in visiting the Fan Village turn away because they did not wish to go through the corridor of sampling tents.

The LPGA Fan Village in its initial state and size cost $250,000. In addition to the development costs, travel and set-up costs averaged $18,000 for each site. To continue in this format or to expand in size and scope would require a title and possibly a series of presenting or participating sponsors.

The most popular activity in the Fan Village was the opportunity for fans to meet and interact with the LPGA Tour players. This came as no surprise to the survey team, as it mirrored what they saw in other professional sports. The survey team also felt it was the area where the LPGA had its strongest advantage over the other sports leagues. The LPGA players are unique among professional athletes, known for their willingness to sign autographs and meet and interact with their fans. With no players union to forbid or limit such player involvement, the LPGA and its Tour players could maximize autograph sessions with both the on-site fans and the media.

There was no seating area for fans around the Fan Village (there was seating for twenty-five inside the Fan Village). Although food and beverages were sold at various points throughout the tournament, there were no such outlets in the Fan Village. When referring to the Fan Village in the interview process, several respondents indicated that the term *village* was perhaps an overstatement and that *fan tent* would be a better description.

As Alvarez left the clambake, he retraced his steps and walked by the LPGA Fan Village. The rain had stopped and he paused at the entrance. As he stood there, his mind raced back to his original vision and he compared that to the fan festival in front of him. Understanding that all good ideas take time to develop, he still felt that the initial presentation fell short of his expectations. Walking back to his car, he found himself caught in the excitement of ideas and how he could improve the LPGA Fan Village for the 1997 season. He became determined to create a final product that would be more in line with his initial vision—fans, athletes, staff, and sponsors creating an atmosphere of education, interaction, and entertainment for both the serious golfer and the casual fan. He was ready to begin work immediately developing a list of recommendations to take the LPGA Fan Village to the next level. As Alvarez drove away from the course, he knew that although the LPGA Fan Village had not yet reached the heights that he had dreamed about, his vision was attainable with creativity and hard work.

Appendix

Group Interviews

For purposes of describing the fans in these interviews, the following groups and brief descriptions and comments from the interviews were recorded. The comments will basically include how they came to learn about the Fan Village concept, their impressions, and suggestions for improvement.

GROUP 1—TWO WOMEN IN FORTIES, FIRST-TIME ATTENDEES OF THE LPGA EVENT

Learn about Fan Village.   First-time attendees at the event. Not currently golfers, but "certainly would consider golf as a possibility for the second half of their lives."

Impressions.   No knowledge of fan village beforehand. Did not check out laptops, video, or merchandise purchasing opportunities. Major impression. Autograph stations were extremely positive.

Suggestions.   Why is it here? Needs orientation session. Pre-explanation? Maybe fan village should be used in conjunction with pre-event publicity for the tournament (for example, place the village in local malls to build up interest and curiosity in the LPGA and upcoming tournament).

GROUP 2—THREE PEOPLE IN GROUP; ONE MALE & TWO FEMALES IN FIFTIES

Learn about Fan Village. First time saw it here, were curious. Follow LPGA and past attendees.

Impressions. Autographs were viewed in a very positive light. Good opportunity to get up close and personal with the women golfers. Did not have any expectations prior to entering the fan village.

Suggestions. Should provide golf lessons at the fan village; hourly golf tips from the pros; great opportunity to provide instruction; fan village lacks excitement; great need for interactive activities; putting contests. Where is the signage? They should pass out some free things to help the fans get into the swing of things." Merchandise is much too pricey. "Why doesn't the LPGA publicize more that this (the LPGA Championship) is the largest charity tournament in the world?" Major concerns with access to the Fan Village were expressed . . . too hard to get to, too muddy, etc.

GROUP 3—TWO WOMEN IN FORTIES; THIRD-TIME ATTENDEES OF THIS LPGA EVENT

Learn about Fan Village. Knew about the fan village ahead of time, tried to find it at the tournament site.

Impressions. Did not notice or participate in the Kodak booth. Did not notice the video. Thought the fan village was generally well laid out. Was very impressed and interested in the history of LPGA display.

Suggestions. Need more signage, events, and excitement; availability of the player guide has not been advertised by the LPGA. Note— "Many fans would be very interested in getting their hands on a player guide." Would like to see retired professionals at the village; this would tie nicely into the emphasis placed on LPGA history within the village.

GROUP 4—MALE/FEMALE COUPLES, IN FORTIES, PAST ATTENDEES OF LPGA EVENTS

Learn about Fan Village. Walked through very quickly; were here last year and saw a new tent (i.e., the Fan Village Tent), that is partly why they stopped by . . . curious.

Impressions. Why did you attend this event? Because of the players. Women players are much more accessible than male players; great to talk with them. The women play a game I can relate to.

Suggestions. Better signage.

GROUP 5—THREE WOMEN IN THIRTIES, FIRST-TIME THIS TOURNAMENT BUT ATTEND MANY LPGA EVENTS

Learn about Fan Village.   From Connecticut and with no prior information about the village.

Impressions.   All three individuals were attracted by the sign regarding autographs. How about the Fan Village? Wondered what was it about? Very interested in the history of the LPGA; found it "neat" that players were signing.

Suggestions.   Needs more publicity.

GROUP 6—TWO WOMEN IN THIRTIES, FIRST TIME TO THIS LPGA EVENT

Learn about Fan Village.   Saw it and decided to check it out.

Impressions.   Noted the web site (will check out later in the day); did not, however, notice the video or Kodak station. Will return over the weekend to the course to purchase hats. All three individuals were attracted by the sign regarding autographs.

Suggestions.   The basic concept of the fan village is great . . . village needs to be personalized with skill competitions. Should keep in mind that free stuff attracts the older people. Restrooms would be very nice.

GROUP 7—TWO WOMEN IN THIRTIES AND EARLY FORTIES, FIRST TOURNAMENT, FOLLOW LPGA

Learn about Fan Village.   Read about Fan Village in local paper, described the village well.

Impressions.   Like idea of players inside and available for fans to meet. Had no real expectations, set up nicely, staff very friendly. Not in Fan Village—more products and services specifically for women. Would like training program for women. Would like to know which companies, show support for women . . . Like to see a listing of these companies so we could support those companies through our purchasing. Membership program interest—sounds interesting. What group did in Fan Village—watched videos, technology very interesting.

Suggestions.   Came away with different perception of LPGA; however, knew a great deal about LPGA already. Very supportive of LPGA, women's movement and athletics for women.

Missing.   More history about tournaments and particular history of this specific tournament would be nice. Merchandise was reasonable, did not see all aspects of the Fan Village. Thought Fan Village could be bigger. What to add—more interactive stations such as interactive golf and also make it a place to meet people. Recommend better directional signage.

GROUP 8—RETIRED COUPLE IN MID SIXTIES, BEEN TO LPGA EVENTS BEFORE

Learn about Fan Village. Saw and decided to take a break and come see what it was. Like following women golfers, watch and follow LPGA on TV. Do play golf and would like to get more tips from professionals about the game.

Impressions. Did not note anything impressive about Fan Village . . . said it was nice. Did learn more about LPGA from video.

Suggestions. Stated they were confused about what the Fan Village was but had no suggestions for improvement.

GROUP 9—TWO WOMEN EARLY THIRTIES, FIRST TIME TO AN LPGA EVENT

Learn about Fan Village. Knew nothing about Fan Village before arriving here.

Impressions. Thought it was nice—a good advertisement for the LPGA. Nothing was outstanding, but not weak either. Staff very friendly but merchandise was pricey, felt they were not pushing product but rather "working" the product. No interest in Kodak display.

Suggestions. Have greeter and explain purpose of Fan Village. Note "why is Fan Village here?" Concern that it is just another booth. Other booths all seemed to be here for another piece of the action. Need to label prices better on merchandise. Videos—good for daughter, liked the instructional aspects. Need brochures to take with you about the programs. Laptop—no time for it, no interest here. Overall—enjoyed time in Fan Village, but could be better.

GROUP 10—TWO WOMEN, MOTHER EARLY SIXTIES AND DAUGHTER LATE THIRTIES

Learn about Fan Village. Local, first time to this event, but had attended other LPGA events; knew about it from local paper.

Impressions. Expectations about Fan Village—met expectations. Did learn and see things about LPGA but did not learn anything new. Did not use web site or the Kodak display.

Suggestions. No real suggestions stated at first, after probing would suggest a bigger site or tent area. Interactive displays would be nice for golfers, but we are golf fans not necessarily players. More talk with pros would be great. Merchandise, especially sweatshirts, too expensive and clothing too pricey. Often buy merchandise, but not here, will shop around.

GROUP 11—GROUP OF THREE, TWO WOMEN AND ONE MAN IN THIRTIES/ FORTIES

Learn about Fan Village. First time to LPGA event, but follow seniors, saw Fan Village wanted to learn more.

Impressions. Expectation—met but expected more free stuff, autographs were great. Laptop OK, tried it, but hard to get it going; presentation on web site was nice. Purchased a photograph, but did not really know what it was at first; it was pricey.

Suggestions. Describe LPGA better to nongolfers. More information about current players. More information about tournaments. Not enough coverage of event . . . suggest more media events here. Like these events, as a man can relate to their game better and it is not overwhelming; like fact that one can get close to the players.

GROUP 12—SINGLE MAN, LATE TWENTIES

Learn about Fan Village. Came because got free ticket, first time visitor, like following women players. Men do want to see event, saw Fan Village and was curious.

Impressions. Expectations—was nice, learned more about LPGA.

Suggestions. Had no real suggestions about Fan Village.

GROUP 13—YOUNG FAMILY, MOTHER IN THIRTIES WITH TWO DAUGHTERS UNDER AGE 12 AND 10

Learn about Fan Village. First time to event, came to get autographs and see women play, saw sign for autographs.

Impressions. Daughters like that they got free autographed pictures. Like videos. Like the way the Fan Village is set up, like it the way it is. Would tell friends that it was fun and neat.

Suggestions. Would like to practice playing golf. Just fun . . . just got here and seems like there is lots to do.

again during tournament unless there was a specific reason . . . such as more autograph sessions. Location . . . needs to be closer to action, needs to be up front closer to the main action area and needs better signage. Rating on 1 to 6 scale with 6 being best . . . would give it a 4 or 5.

GROUP 19—TWO MEN, LATE FORTIES EARLY FIFITES, FOLLOW LPGA TOUR

Learn about Fan Village. Like to follow women golfers. Been to LPGA events before.

Impressions. Videos were nice and screen was large and easy to see. Would like to learn more about women's tour. Would like more golf questions answered . . . why are women allowed to wear shorts and men are not?? Autographs—good idea, cannot get this close to men. Area well set up.

Suggestions. Reverse role of players . . . make them even more accessible. Publicity on women's golf and Fan Village needs to be drummed up. Public needs to know more about this. Miniclinics would be real good, more might come down to this, Bell Atlantic gives miniles- sons at their golf fair booths. Rating on 1 to 6 scale . . . probably a 5 or so.

GROUP 20—YOUNG FAMILY, MOTHER IN LATE THIRTIES, DAUGHTER 13, AND SON 8

Learn about Fan Village. Learned about it in the newspaper.

Impressions. Computer—finally figured it out, did not know how it worked, it was hard to use, needs to be more user friendly. Video looked good, but did not stop to watch it. History of LPGA was good, kids did like computer but just not easy to use. Merchandise . . . looked at it and will save for later, like to shop around.

Suggestions. More instructional areas like swing analysis. Get advice from pros. Many of the people who come down here follow the LPGA and many are volunteers. Would like to see better coverage and press on this event and Fan Village. Like to see more rounds of LPGA on TV. Rating on 1 to 6 scale . . . rate about a 5. Fan Village is a good source of information, but kids did not want to stay long enough. Kids like to do things, not enough doing here. Need more pros in there.

GROUP 21—YOUNG FAMILY, MOTHER IN THIRTIES, DAUGHTER 13, AND SON 10

Learn about Fan Village. First-time LPGA event visitors. Saw Fan Village Tent and had no prior knowledge about it.

Impressions.   Nice to get the chance to see it. Like to enter to win free stuff. Learn more about LPGA and its history. Would like to do more things in there, need more fun things to do.

Suggestions.   Put in a putting area. Put in more fun things for kids. More kids come on weekends and want things to do while here. Would like more things to collect.

Interviews of Merchandise Purveyors Adjacent to Fan Village

Six of the twelve managers of the merchandise/promotional tents were approached and brief feedback was sought on the concept of the Fan Village. In addition, the tournament merchandise personnel and staff from *Women in Golf* were interviewed. Results were best described as mixed. Some felt the concept and idea was sound and good; however, the biggest complaint was the location and general lack of foot traffic. Other comments included that there were few sale opportunities. Two indicated that they would never return due to how they were treated and their location. However, others were happy to be inside the event even though the location was not ideal. Several felt that if the LPGA continued to work on the concept and got a better location, better signage, and had more events occurring in the tent positive things would be gained by all. Some felt that additional draws would be needed here . . . food and seating area(s) were suggested. Observations of foot traffic at the site indicated that the credit card company/bank was very aggressive in its promotional efforts, perhaps to the detriment of the other vendors. Others were new to the event and had no real expectations. Those who were pleased were simply happy to be inside the tournament area. Tournament merchandise tent personnel liked the concept, but do not want it near their tent. There is the perception that it creates too much unnecessary competition for them. However, they felt their sales were not hurt and generally support the concept and would like the LPGA to continue to promote the concept at other tournaments. They felt that purchase opportunities and merchandise were different enough that it had not hurt their sales, but were nonetheless quite strong about keeping it away from their prime location. They also commented on the different purchasing patterns throughout the course of the event, which should be of value to the LPGA.

The Ouray Case

Suzanne Lainson

Introduction

In Bob Smith's[1] mind, Ouray was the perfect home. He had moved to the small Colorado town a few years ago and was very happy—so happy, in fact, he was sure that others would want to visit the community as well. It was just a matter of finding a way to lure them there.

Ouray, Colorado, is located in the San Juan Mountains in southwestern Colorado. It has 700 permanent residents and enjoys a steady stream of tourists in the summer who take side trips from nearby larger towns such as Montrose (forty minutes away) and Durango (two hours away). To attract more winter tourists, the town worked out a promotional deal where skiers could ski in Telluride (one hour away) for half price when they stayed in Ouray. The town's largest source of income comes from a one-million-gallon hot springs pool, generating a $350,000 yearly profit.

In the fall of 1993, Smith gathered a group of businesspeople together to discuss the town's future. He was particularly interested in the possibility of constructing a world-class ice rink in town. Not only might this attract tourists but he thought such a rink could also bring the town international visibility. Ouray's high altitude (7,760 feet) would make it an ideal training location for elite skaters. About the same time, Gary Wild and Bill Whitt, who owned the Ouray Victorian Inn, were pursuing their own plans to make Ouray a destination spot for tourists. They had been investigating the possibility of developing a one-of-a-kind ice-climbing park in a nearby canyon. Although Smith's and Wild and Whitt's plans were not mutually exclusive, each might lead the town's tourism in different directions.

---

[1]Not his real name.

Rink Feasibility Study

Bob Smith's group agreed to contribute enough money for the University of Colorado Business Research Division to do an ice rink feasibility study. Part of that study involved obtaining financial figures from a variety of sources: rink construction companies; an Ice Skating Institute of America national survey of ice rinks; and CU's own survey of eleven rinks in Colorado and nearby states (see Exhibit 14.1). In its presentation and in the study, the Colorado team provided background on rink users and the economics of rink operation, described in the next section of excerpts from the feasibility study.

Exhibit 14.1   Regional rink survey results

	Average	Low	High
# of rinks at facility	1.67	1	3
Monday hours of operation	16.73	11	20
Tuesday hours of operation	16.8	12	20
Wednesday hours of operation	17.03	12.5	21
Thursday hours of operation	16.95	13	20
Friday hours of operation	17.28	12	20
Saturday hours of operation	17.65	14.5	20.25
Sunday hours of operation	16.15	10.5	19
Total weekly hours of operation	118.58	91.5	139.75
Weeks operated per year	44	22	52
Population of area served	422,500	10,000	2,000,000
# of public rinks in survey	9		
# of private rinks in survey	2		
# of rinks providing rental skates	11		
# of rinks providing seating	11		
Seating capacity	2,084	360	4,708
# of rinks providing snack bar	9		
# of rinks providing locker rooms	11		
# of rinks providing off-ice training	5		
# of rinks providing conference room	4		
# of rinks offering public skating	11		
# of public sessions per week	10	5	21
Length of public session (in hours)	1.79	1.25	2.5
Charge per skater for public session	$2.70	$1.90	$6.00
# of skaters on ice for public session	93	20	300
# of rinks offering contract ice	9		

Exhibit 14.1 Continued

	Average	Low	High
# of contract sessions per week	47	8	120
Length of contract session (in hours)	0.72	0.5	1
Charge per skater for contract ice	$4.90	$2.00	$7.50
# of skaters on ice for contract session	19	8	26
# of rinks offering precision	6		
# of precision sessions per week	2.83	1	6
Length of precision session (in hours)	1.17	0.75	2
Charge per ice rental for precision	$87.80	$60.00	$110.00
# of skaters on ice for precision	27	5	55
# of rinks offering hockey	11		
# of hockey sessions per week	28	12	40
Length of hockey session (in hours)	1.21	0.83	1.5
Charge per ice rental for hockey	$68.70	$60.00	$96.00
# of skaters on ice for hockey session	25	20	40
# of rinks offering club skating session	8		
# of sessions per week	4	1	14
Length of club session (in hours)	1.17	1	1.5
Charge per ice rental for club session	$88.00	$60.00	$135.00
# of skaters on ice for club session	58	20	150
# of rinks offering ice for parties	10		
# of hours per week for parties	2.54	1	5
Charge per hour for party	$92.10	$35.00	$125.00
Number of rinks offering lessons	9		
Hours per week of group lessons	6.38	4	10
Hours per week of private lessons	48.57	15	102
Hours per week of learn-to-skate	5.44	3	10.5
# of skaters per group lesson	11	8	20
# of skaters in learn-to-skate	121	10	500
# of rinks receiving private funds	4		
# of rinks receiving corporate funds	1		
# of rinks receiving public funds	8		
# of rinks receiving subsidies	6		
# of rinks receiving gvnmt subsidies	6		
# of rinks receiving corp. subsidies	0		
# of rinks receiving private subsidies	0		
Age of building (in years)	23.4	8	56
Sq footage of building	52,017	25,000	150,000
Sq footage of ice rink	36,486	15,000	162,000

Exhibit 14.1 Continued

	Average	Low	High
# of full-time staff	6	3	15
# of part-time staff	15	2	52
# of occasional staff	7	2	15
# of rinks with coaches on staff	10		
# of coaches on staff	8	1	25
Payroll costs	$158,927.20	$80,000.00	$280,000.00
Gross revenue	$487,095.00	$100,000.00	$1,300,000.00
% of business from tourism	13%	0%	60%
April through September costs			
Water per month per rink	$416.41	$102.30	$1,100.00
Energy per month per rink	$3,920.70	$500.00	$7,108.00
October through March costs			
Water per month per rink	$550.79	$125.00	$1,500.00
Energy per month per rink	$5,297.73	$3,029.33	$7,500.00

Excerpts from Feasibility Study

THE SKATING POPULATION

Recreational Skaters. Unlike many other sports, skating (both ice skating and hockey) has a relatively limited recreational appeal. To be even a moderately skilled beginner takes more time and resources than most people are willing to invest. Since rental equipment is often inadequate for skates to progress beyond basic gliding, the sport almost immediately demands an investment. Knowing that the dropout rate is high, most rinks offer learn-to-skate programs to continually generate a new group of skaters who might graduate into private and semiprivate lessons with coaches and contract for ice on a regular basis.

Hockey Skaters. Hockey has always been extremely popular in a few areas of the country and virtually nonexistent in others. In some areas, where hockey has been around for some time, the pace has been slowing. For example, enthusiasm for hockey in Minnesota, long a national stronghold for the sport, is cooling down. According to an article in the *Minneapolis Star Tribune* (March 13, 1993): "The sport has grown costly. No longer is it just pucks and ponds, but $85-a-hour rink time, $200 skates, and $150 shoulder pads—at least $500 to outfit each of the 75,000 kids who play youth hockey in Minnesota. Add summer camps and road trips, and parents can spend $3,000 to $5,000 a year. . . ." However, in warmer areas such as Southern California, where not only are professional hockey franchises increasing awareness of the sport but also in-line skating and roller hockey are introducing more people to the basics, more and more people of all ages are joining teams.

The Catch-22 with hockey is that people don't play hockey unless there are teams to join, and teams don't play if there aren't enough rinks, and rinks don't survive unless there are enough skaters. It is easier, therefore, to support a hockey program if there are other rinks within commuting distance.

In Colorado, there are a number of different hockey programs. Most rinks offer lessons and beginning-level teams. Colorado Springs has long been a state hockey stronghold. At one time, the only teams playing in the state hockey high school competitions were Colorado Springs schools. Colorado Springs is also host to a national youth hockey tournament that grows bigger every year, attracting teams as far away as Alaska and Europe. Colorado also offers elite club teams, often based in Denver or Colorado Springs, which draw top players who sometimes have to commute in order to participate.

Competitive Figure Skaters.   The number of serious ice skaters in the United States is relatively small. The United States Figure Skating Association, the official governing body for figure skating, holds a series of elimination competitions culminating in the United States Figure Skating Championships, which determine the world and Olympic teams. The competition breakdown is as follows: nine regionals, open to eligible skaters of a variety of levels who have met USFSA qualifications (i.e., skaters who are USFSA members; have passed the appropriate USFSA skating tests; are members of a skating club in that region; have met age requirements—only applicable at some levels); three sectionals, open to the top four finishers in each category from the three regions within each section; and nationals, open to the top four finishers in each category from the three sectionals.

The total number of skaters at all levels participating in the nine regional United States Figure Skating Association competitions is approximately 3,000. This is the population of skaters who can be counted on to skate several hours a day, every day. Of this group, only about 200 are competing at the senior level, the pool of skaters drawn upon for the United States National Team.

The professional coaches association, Professional Skaters Guild of America, has a membership of 2,000 coaches (perhaps 60% of active ice skating coaches currently teaching in the United States).

How Skaters Choose Rinks
Proximity.   Beginning skaters (both figure and hockey) usually start skating at a nearby rink that offers lessons. Most of them will

continue to use those facilities until they reach a skill level that might warrant relocation. Figure skaters may go to other rinks in search of better coaching; hockey players may go to other rinks to play on superior teams.

Facilities and Location. Of the various ice skating disciplines, only traditional speedskating puts primary emphasis on training facilities. This is due to the fact that there are very few Olympic-sized speedskating ovals in North America. (Short-track speedskating, on the other hand, can be done in most rinks.)

Hockey players are most concerned with the availability of practice ice and having enough teams in the area to make up a league. Young players hoping to land college scholarships or a career in the pros may choose to move to a region of the country with strong youth leagues and prep programs.

Figure skaters focus primarily on coaching. A rink is only as good as the reputation of the coach. Pueblo, Colorado, for example, has one of the best rinks in the state but few figure skaters use it. In fact, many of the better skaters from Pueblo commute to Colorado Springs to use the rink at the Broadmoor World Arena even though it's not as good a facility. They come to train with well-known coaches.

High-Altitude Training and the United States Olympic Committee. Each year the USOC develops more and more sophisticated training programs in conjunction with its sports science division. Because the USOC is located in Colorado Springs, it offers athletes the opportunity to train at moderately high altitude (5,980 feet), but high-altitude training has not been a primary focus of its research because Olympic-caliber athletes are based all over the country. The USOC has been especially involved in developing programs to improve the jumping skills and stamina of figure skaters. However, since success in the sport is based on coordination and artistic skill, skaters seek out successful coaches rather than rigorous training programs.

Although the USOC is located in Colorado Springs, the official Olympic training center for winter Olympic sports is Lake Placid, New York. However, it is not the home of the United States Figure Skating team, nor is it the only site of skating camps and training programs. Skaters do not train together as a team. There is no team coach. They train as individual competitors at rinks around the country or around the world. Approximately twice a year, the United States Figure Skating Association holds week-long training camps for top skaters and their coaches. They have been held most often in Colorado Springs at the Broadmoor World Arena, a private rink within walking distance of the USFSA. There is, however, no official connection between the two.

The Broadmoor World Arena was scheduled to be torn down in the spring of 1994. Private investors were hoping to build another rink and convention center nearby. Even if that rink was not built, Colorado Springs offered three other full-size rinks (a city-owned rink, one at Colorado College, and one at the Air Force Academy.) Although the rink proponents were hoping the USFSA and the USOC would use the facility for sporting events, those organizations, while supportive of the project, had not offered any financial backing or promises of future contracts. The money was expected to come from the Broadmoor Hotel, a Canadian rink management company, and the El Pomar Foundation. The land had been donated by Gates Land Development. There had been considerable coverage in the local paper about whether the city and county would fund roadwork and other improvements for the site.

Training Programs. Several rinks around the country have attempted to become major ice skating training centers, with varying success. Rinks in Indianapolis, Indiana, Lake Arrowhead, California, and Wilmington, Delaware, have all billed themselves as state-of-the-art programs. Indianapolis has never achieved a major international reputation because it has not produced any national or international champions. Wilmington was stronger a few years ago when most of the top dance and pairs teams trained there, but more recently the Broadmoor has had a stronger dance program. The Lake Arrowhead rink (Ice Castle) was the most visible of the three because it had a stronger contingent of skaters. The Broadmoor had long attracted international skaters, although it lost some of its prestige when Carlo Fassi left (coach of four Olympic gold medalists). In 1993 the U.S. National Men's Champion and the U.S. National Dance team trained there.

Coaches. The key to attracting top figure skaters is to have a top coach. However, most of them already have positions at other rinks and are not likely to relocate without substantial inducement. When Carlo Fassi left the Broadmoor a few years ago (to take a better-paying position in Italy), the Broadmoor had trouble finding a top coach to replace him. Both Carol Heiss Jenkins (herself a former Olympic gold medalist) and Christi Karsgaard (Kristi Yamaguchi's coach) turned the offer down.

A rink may have to pay a top coach $70,000 a year or more, over and above whatever he or she might earn by giving lessons. Occasionally coaches are forced to relocate for one reason or another and will consider offers. Alex McGowan, Debi Thomas's coach, for example, had to find a place for her to train when their California rink closed. He brought her to Boulder for the year before the 1988 Olympics, where she went to school and used the University of Colorado rink. Another example is Natalya Dubova, the best ice dancing coach in the world, who is teaching at Lake Placid. After Russia collapsed, she and Maia Usova and Aleksandr Zhulin, the current world champions, relocated.

SOURCES OF INCOME

Hockey. Most full-sized rinks can sell out their ice during hockey season if there are enough hockey leagues in the area. Since hockey is subdivided into many different age groups and skill levels and each needs a separate time to practice, the demand for ice can be high. In areas where hockey is popular, teams will rent ice any time it's available—even at 3 A.M. However, hockey is not the most profitable use of the ice because it is usually rented out at a set rate, no matter how many skaters are using it.

Contract Ice. At major training rinks contract ice can be profitable because competitive skaters usually pay top prices to rent the ice, sometimes as much as $7 to $8 a session. Most rinks sell ice directly to the individual skaters, but some sell blocks of ice time to local skating clubs, which then handle ice time for their members. Contract ice is more expensive than public ice because fewer skaters are allowed on at one time. Generally, sessions are run according to skill level. For example, national- and international-level skaters will probably not share the ice with more than ten to fifteen of their peers. Although some rinks run freestyle sessions that may have as many as forty skaters training at one time, something along the lines of twenty skaters per session is probably a reasonable upper limit. Contract ice is broken down into different kinds of skating: freestyle, patch (i.e., figure eight practice—skaters rent a "patch" of ice), dance, and pairs. Not all rinks offer all types of skating, but top rinks do.

Public Skating. Income from public skating can vary widely. Some rinks in high population areas such as Los Angeles can routinely attract 300 skaters per session. But most rinks will have considerably less, sometimes as few as 5 to 10 skaters. Determining when to offer public skating can be a big issue. Should the rink offer public sessions during times when other skaters aren't available (such as during the school day) or should the rink run them when it can attract the most skaters (such as after school and on weekends)? Often the funding of the rink determines how much ice will be set aside for public skating. Community rinks are generally expected (and even mandated) to offer more public ice time than private rinks, even when the ice could be rented out at higher rates for other purposes.

Tourism. A few rinks around the country are set up to attract tourists (Rockefeller Center always seems to be a must-see in New York City.) Often these are outdoor rinks at ski resorts. They are run as seasonal activities and require little maintenance or investment. However, the number of tourists who come to the area in order to skate (or to watch skating) is small. For example, the director of Aspen Central Reservations reports that 5% of the callers staying in Aspen ask for alternatives to skiing.

Camps, Competitions, and Summer School.   Some rinks that do not have large regular-season programs are able to augment their income by offering special summer programs. Both Aspen and Vail run a variety of hockey and figure skating camps and competitions throughout the summer. These usually do well for a number of reasons:

1. Families can combine sports training with vacations. Many families look forward each year to spending a week in a resort area while one or more of the children participate in a special sports activity;
2. Some rinks around the country close for the summer, so skaters training at them may choose to look elsewhere for ice during that time; and,
3. Top coaches are often willing to act as visiting professionals and may even bring some of their own students along, who would then rent ice time from the sponsoring rink. Sometimes coaches come because their home rinks have closed for the season; sometimes they come to earn extra money; and sometimes they come for a change of scenery.

Shows.   Most rinks hold at least one show a year as a way for local skaters to show off what they have learned. Although the shows are often used as fundraisers, the amount of effort involved can outweigh their monetary value. The most profitable shows are run as professionally as possible, with elaborate costumes and lighting and guest stars who sometimes charge as much as $5,000 a performance. Rinks hoping to stage shows like these must invest in seating, refreshment counters, and extra electrical capacity. Sun Valley, Idaho, is the only rink (other than some which are located in amusement parks such as Busch Gardens and Sea World) that features weekly ice shows as part of its program. Show tickets cost $23 for adults and $19 for children.

Sponsorship.   Most rinks do not receive sponsorship funds. However, a sophisticated marketing effort might attract some corporate sponsorship. The most likely sponsors would be local businesses wishing to support community efforts and teams. National and international companies are more likely to sponsor arenas in large cities (for example, around the country there are multipurpose arenas sponsored by Target, Delta, and Coors). Rinks trying to sell sponsorships have to be aware of USOC and USFSA restrictions. Since both of those organizations also pursue companies, individual rinks are not allowed to cut deals that interfere with Olympic sponsorships. Increasingly, the USOC bars individual sports from approaching potential sponsors in an effort to preserve the exclusivity of the sponsorships it sells for $40 million. Recently, for example, the USOC prevented the USFSA from selling a sponsorship to Sears because it conflicted with Home Depot's Olympic sponsorship.

One way for individual rinks to get around the USFSA restrictions is to find patrons to sponsor individual skaters or for corporations to donate money for a scholarship fund. The rinks can then display sponsorship logos at the facilities. (Skaters cannot wear corporate logos on their costumes, but it might be possible for them to display them on equipment bags and warm-up suits.)

As far as receiving money from the USFSA or USOC is concerned, that is not likely. The USFSA does not sponsor rinks and the USOC has budgeted the majority of its available funds for its three official training centers: San Diego, Lake Placid, and Colorado Springs. Typically, the way the USOC becomes involved in a local project is for a community to build a state-of-the-art facility with its own money and then provide attractive financial incentives for the USOC or a governing body to use it. This means, however, that the facility is not available for local use.

As a result of its research, the University of Colorado team provided a base scenario to demonstrate the cost of funding and operating an ice rink in Ouray. It also showed how the numbers might change if certain variables (such as usage patterns) were changed. Usage patterns were based primarily on what was being done at a rink in Aspen. The Aspen rink is a public rink subsidized by the city, drawing upon a population base of 15,000 within a forty-mile radius. Although Aspen is a more affluent area than Ouray, there are similarities: it is a Western Colorado mountain town, attracts tourists, and serves a region with a comparable number of residents.

The base scenario assumed that the Ouray rink construction would be funded through bonds and city subsidies (see Exhibit 14.2). Land for the rink would be purchased and the rink, 85 feet by 200 feet, would be cement block construction. Three full-time and several part-time employees would be used. The rink would be run 11.5 months a year and draw upon a population area of 11,000, which included two nearby towns within a thirty-five-mile radius. An estimated 5% of the tourist population base (194,000) would use the rink once, and 5% of the local residents would skate two times every month. The scenario estimated that a local hockey club (yet to be established) would contract ice for twenty-two hours a week, and it assumed that Ouray could set up summer hockey and skating schools to generate revenue. The hot

Exhibit 14.2 Financial scenarios

1. Base case. Required yearly subsidy: $208,315.

2. Constructing a larger rink for more usage flexibility (the only scenario using a larger rink). Required yearly subsidy: $227,690.

3. Land donated rather than purchased (a savings of approximately $880.000). Required yearly subsidy: $194,550.

4. Increasing paid hockey sessions from 22 a week to 32 a week. Required yearly subsidy: $185,380.

5. Land and site improvements donated (a savings of approximately $1,200,000). Required yearly subsidy: $175,397.

6. Hiring a famous coach and running a competitive figure skating program. Required yearly subsidy: $151,143.

7. Increasing public skating from 5% of local population skating twice a month to 10% of the population skating twice a month. Required yearly subsidy: $136,655.

8. Increasing public skating from 5% of local population skating twice a month to 10% of the population skating twice a month, and increasing paid hockey sessions from 22 a week to 32 a week. Required yearly subsidy: $114,798.

9. Having all initial investment costs donated (a savings of approximately $2,750,000). Required yearly subsidy: $78,122.

10. Increasing paid hockey sessions from 22 to 32 a week and having all initial investment costs donated. Required yearly subsidy: $53,099.

11. Running a competitive figure skating program and having all initial investment costs donated. Required yearly subsidy: $15,148.

12. Increasing public skating from 5% of local population skating twice a month to 10% of the population skating twice a month and having all initial investment costs donated. Required yearly subsidy: $0 (positive net present value of over $20,000).

13. Increasing public skating from 5% of local population skating twice a month to 10% of the population skating twice a month, and increasing paid hockey sessions from 22 a week to 32 a week and having all initial investment costs donated. Required yearly subsidy: $0 (positive net present value of over $450,000).

springs generates a profit of $350,000 and therefore this amount was considered to be the maximum yearly city subsidy available for the rink.

After hearing the report, Bob Smith continued to be excited about the concept of an ice rink. Some of the other townspeople were not as convinced. Although there were ways to cut corners so that a rink would not be a drain on the town's economy, would it accomplish the goal of bringing in more tourists?

Ironically, the night before the feasibility study presentation, figure skater Nancy Kerrigan was attacked at the 1994 United States Figure Skating Championships. No one realized at the time the extent to which that event would generate worldwide interest in the sport.

Ice-Climbing Park

At approximately the same time Bob Smith was pushing for the ice rink, Gary Wild and Bill Whitt were thinking about ice climbing. Whitt was an ice climber himself and introduced Wild to the sport. Climbers had been coming to the area for about twenty years. Each winter a deep narrow gorge (which began in town and ran for 1-1/4 miles to a hydroelectric dam) provided ice falls for them to climb. The area was particularly attractive to them because they could drive right up to the falls on well-maintained roads. More typically, climbers had to hike two to six miles into wilderness locations to find falls to climb. However, rather than being encouraged to come to Ouray, they were increasingly being met by "No Trespassing" signs erected by property owners.

The early 1990s saw a dramatic increase in both rock climbing and ice climbing. As more people took up rock climbing, more also took up ice climbing. Ice climbing presented new challenges and an alternative to increasingly crowded rock climbing spots. An estimated 500,000 Americans were serious rock climbers, and 5,000 were ice climbers. (Research on sports participation conducted in 1992 suggested that 4.3 million Americans had rock or mountain climbed at least once that year.) Although demographic information on climbers was limited, the numbers looked good. According to surveys done by *Rock & Ice* magazine, the average subscriber was thirty-two years old and had an income of $73,000. Eighty-two percent were college educated, 61% held professional or managerial jobs, and 27% participated in ice climbing. However, ice climbing was not considered much of a spectator sport. Although climbing had developed into a competitive sport in Europe, it had yet to become a form of entertainment in America. Ice climbing was still a niche sport, though it had a passionate group of practitioners.

The primary stumbling block to opening up Ouray to ice climbers in recent years had been liability concerns. The utility company that owned the hydroelectric plant did not want the climbers there. However, the utility company declared bankruptcy in 1992 and was purchased by a new owner who was willing to work with the climbers. Wild, who was a retired attorney, consulted the Access Fund, a nonprofit organization started in 1991 to keep climbing areas open for public use. He was told about the Colorado Recreational Users Statute, whereby a landowner is exempt from liability as long as climbers are not charged for access. In other words, if the new utility owner provided the county with a recreational access easement for $1 a year, the county would insure him from potential claims. Wild and Whitt also discovered that a water line could be run from an abandoned reservoir along the gorge rim. For very little cost, additional falls could be created to greatly expand the climbing area to make it one of the largest ice climbing areas anywhere in the world.

Looking at Options

The citizens of Ouray had several possibilities to consider. They could choose to spend very little money and see if an ice-climbing wall would bring in tourists. They could build a modest rink, which could serve the recreational needs of the community and possibly the region. They could build a world-class rink and hope an aggressive campaign would attract tourists and top-level athletes. They had to consider expenses and income for various scenarios, the mix of tourists the two projects might attract, what kind of publicity each project might generate for the town, and the extent to which one or both projects might offer Ouray a competitive advantage over other tourist destinations (within Colorado, within North America, and even against European winter destinations).

In addition, each sport offered a different culture, which had to be taken into consideration:

- Skating had wide fan interest, although fans were more likely to watch on television than to travel to an event. Recreational skaters spent relatively little on the sport; serious skaters spent a great deal. If sponsors could be found, they would be among companies wanting to reach the typical skating fan (i.e., largely female and middle class).
- Rink users might also be hockey players. Hockey players could be counted on to rent ice and buy equipment on a regular basis. They were most likely to travel for camps and competitions and often made such trips a family affair. If sponsors could be found, they would be among companies wanting to reach hockey equipment users and among companies wanting to support local teams and events.
- Ice climbing is an equipment intensive sport, so money must be spent in purchases or rentals. Because it is an outdoor sport, participants are prepared to travel to exotic locations and perhaps stay for several days or a week. If sponsors could be found, they would be among companies wanting to reach climbing enthusiasts and extreme sports fans.

15

Xerox and the Asian Winter Games

David K. Stotlar

Introduction

Xiang Wong attempted his favorite shot, a well-disguised drop shot to his opponent's backhand. His opponent, caught unaware, reacted too slowly . . . the shuttlecock dropped softly to the ground . . . 13–11! Xiang held a slight edge but knew his strategy would need to be sound the rest of the match if he were to emerge victorious. His mind kept drifting off, though, to the sponsorship proposal that he had recently received from the Asian Winter Games organizing committee. Xerox's sales in China, and his career, could be enhanced by a successful investment. A poor decision, however, could open the door to exploitation by ambitious colleagues.

Xiang Wong is the head of marketing for Xerox (China) Limited, a subsidiary of Xerox Corporation (also known as The Document Company–Xerox). All major marketing initiatives must be cleared through the director of international marketing at corporate headquarters. He had just been presented with a sponsorship proposal from the Asian Winter Games organizing committee. His task is to make a decision regarding the purchase of a sponsorship package (or individual components). A position statement and rationale in support of his recommendation must accompany this decision.

Background on Corporate Sponsorship

Corporate spending on sponsorship increased dramatically during the 1980s and 1990s, culminating with $13.5 billion (U.S.) spent worldwide in 1996. In the United States, 1997 spending on sponsorship was projected to rise to $5.9 billion from over 4,800 companies, up 9% from the $5.4 billion spent in 1996 and a 300% increase over the last ten years. Worldwide spending on sponsorship was projected to climb to $15.3 billion, 13% over 1996. Central and South America spent $800 million, Europe added $4 billion, and Pacific Rim businesses contributed $2.7 billion. Recently, sponsorship spending seems to be growing at double-digit rates in regions other than North America. North America clearly represents a more mature market where as the international sport sponsorship is still experiencing significant increases and growth. The Pacific Rim also appears to be the fastest-growing area, with Europe approaching maturity.

Sponsorship has its roots in philanthropy, the support of worthy endeavors by wealthy individuals or corporations in an effort to contribute to society. In the past, sport organizations attempted to obtain money from corporations using a charitable approach. In addition, "good citizenship" and "interest in the community" have been cited as reasons for corporations to engage in sponsorship activities. Sport-related businesses, like most corporations, have a desire to be seen as community citizens with a responsibility to contribute to the well-being of the communities where they do business.

The sponsorship of sports in years past was occasionally a function of a company executive's desire to mix socially with elite athletes and possibly provide some client entertainment activities. According to the managing director of a major sport management firm, in the early 1980s, the CEO was king, but that era is over. With changes in corporate culture and closer attention from shareholders, this rationale deteriorated substantially in the late 1980s. Thus, marketing strategies and tactics based on a CEO's fascination with celebrities or on whimsical notions of an organization's social responsibility yielded to effective business objectives as the primary criterion.

IBM's manager of their Olympic sponsorship program said, "It's not philanthropic; it's not corporate contribution money. The goal is to help gain market share." VISA stated its objective for involvement with the Olympic Games as "increase market share and sales volume." Data from the 1994 Winter Olympic Games indicated that VISA's sponsorship involvement was quite profitable. Sixty-eight percent of people surveyed were able to recognize VISA as an Olympic sponsor. Furthermore, the measure of consumer preference prior to the Games was 15%, compared to 30% during the Games and 8% after. In the $250-billion-per-year credit card industry, a 3% increase in user preference provides a substantial value. Similarly, during the 1992 Summer Olympics, the use of VISA cards in the marketplace rose 17%. Data collected during 1992–1996 showed VISA's market share rose from 45% to 49.4%, which indicated that its estimated $40-million, four-year costs associated with worldwide sponsorship of the Olympics should have been recovered.

Research on corporate criteria utilized in the measurement of sponsorship effectiveness has supported the emphasis on business objectives for sponsorship. These studies have found that market-driven objectives are highly ranked criteria in the sponsorship selection process. The relationship between sport organizers and sponsors has evolved, accentuating the measurement of return on investment (ROI). In the 1990s, calculated value assessment has replaced other factors as the primary strategy employed by both event owners and sponsors. Throughout this evolution, sport sponsorship has become entrenched as a viable business strategy.

Company Overview

The Document Company–Xerox, founded in 1958, is headquartered in Stamford, Connecticut (http://www.xerox.com; used with permission). Xerox develops, markets, and supports a wide range of hardware and software products, services, and technologies that enable users to create, manage, reproduce, and distribute every kind of document in both digital and hard-copy forms. The company works in association with other major companies and manufacturers of information and communications systems to deliver complete document solutions for any size of enterprise. The Document Company has subsidiaries in Europe and the Pacific Rim serving a worldwide network of dealers and distributors. Xerox sells its publishing systems, copiers, printers, scanners, fax machines, and document management software, along with related products and services, in more than 130 countries. Xerox's 1996 revenue was approximately $25 billion.

Xerox Corporation offers the widest array of document-processing products and consulting services in the industry. Xerox products and services are all designed to help customers master the flow of information from paper to electronic form and back again. The Xerox customer is anyone who uses documents: Fortune 500 corporations and small companies; public agencies and universities; and businesses run from the home. Xerox leads the field in digital imaging and what is called distributed electronic publishing. Xerox technology enables the home office to copy, print, scan, and fax documents using a single $700 device. That same technology also allows almost any enterprise to transmit complicated multipage documents across networks for copying or printing, down the hall or halfway around the world.

Xerox started the office copying revolution with the introduction of its 914 copier in 1959. Currently, Xerox stands poised for the continued expansion of the global document-processing market, already enormous at $200 billion a year and growing 10% a year. In 1996, 20% of company revenues were in businesses that grew more than 20%: personal copying and printing (29%); document outsourcing (50%); production publishing (24%); and color copying and printing (45%).

The company adopted "The Document Company–Xerox" as their corporate signature in 1994 to better reflect what has always been the real business of Xerox: document management. The company also adopted as its logo a stylized "X" to depict the pixels of digital imaging, the foundation of the second office revolution.

Global Scope and Emerging Markets

The Xerox name is synonymous with quality all around the globe. Not just in the United States, but from London to Vienna to Tokyo, and from Prague to Moscow to Beijing to New Delhi to Buenos Aires, Xerox services customers' requirements for document-processing services. Including Fuji Xerox (which is not consolidated in company accounting statements), about two-thirds of the company's $25 billion in revenues are generated outside of the United States. The company has three decades of global experience in addressing customer requirements in both developed and emerging markets and a significant market position in many of the developing markets in Latin America, Eastern Europe, Russia and the Commonwealth of Independent States, Africa, India, the Pacific Rim, and China. Revenues in most of these markets are growing by double digits. The emerging markets offer exciting future opportunities.

In China, for example, the document-services market is growing rapidly, reflecting the strong economy and China's ambitious goals, using modern technology as a springboard. Home to one-quarter of the people in the world, China has the fastest economic growth rate of any major country. The use of personal computers has increased rapidly in China and the expected demand for printers and copiers is growing at 20% per year. With fifteen years of experience selling document-processing products in China, Xerox's objective is to be a key player in the modernization of the business economy. Currently, Xerox manufactures, markets, and services office, desktop, and engineering copiers and a broad line of fax machines for this market. Manufacturing operations, all joint ventures with local partners, are in Shanghai, Suzhou, and Wuhan. In early 1996, Xerox and Fuji Xerox opened a facility near Shenzhen to produce desktop printers. Because of the rapid growth in 1995, Xerox (China) Limited was established to oversee operations in China and capitalize on the increasing demand for all document-processing products and services.

Sport Sponsorship: Background and Objectives

For more than thirty years, Xerox has participated in marketing activities with the International Olympic Committee and various Olympic Games organizing committees. Xerox is one of ten official worldwide sponsors of the Olympic Games as the exclusive provider of document services, products, and solutions. This relationship has offered Xerox an opportunity to showcase their company and technology to over 3.5 billion people.

To assist local Xerox retailers and sales representatives, corporate headquarters developed and provided a series of materials to coincide with national advertising campaigns. Specifically, Xerox's corporate Olympic advertising campaign was used to communicate its capabilities and document solutions. Xerox's presence on network television with Olympic-themed commercials was hard to miss. They developed and aired two documentary-style television commercials, one depicted how Xerox, by viewing the Olympic Games as an enterprise, re-engineered document processing to efficiently manage the one billion documents created during the Games.

Collateral print ads were also initiated in conjunction with *Sports Illustrated*'s (also a worldwide Olympic sponsor) special Summer Olympics issue. This included several full-page ads highlighting Xerox's sponsorship and document solutions. In addition, daily and weekly ads were placed during the Games in national newspapers. To carry their Olympic theme across all major media, existing radio spots were tagged with special Olympic sponsorship messages.

Marketing Tactics

To leverage the national campaign into local markets, sales representatives were provided with media kits containing preprinted advertisements, prerecorded commercial spots, and suggested activities that would connect potential customers with Xerox. Specific recommendations were as follows:

1. Host an appearance by an Olympic athlete, perhaps in collaboration with other area sales agents.
2. Develop an Olympic-themed sales incentive program for customers and staff.
3. Sponsor local TV and radio sports updates.
4. Develop Olympic-themed events in the local community, such as providing results documentation for high school and college events.
5. Prepare Olympic-themed premiums for distribution at local business and social events.

6. Add the Xerox Olympic Sponsorship logo to all direct mail, advertising, proposals, and collateral material (as specified by 36 USC 380, all uses of Olympic logos must be preapproved).

Finally, in an effort to enhance sales, Xerox developed the "Gold Lease Plus" program with special incentives to purchasers during 1996.

International Business Practices

General Market Conditions

From 1979 to 1995, the Chinese gross domestic product (GDP) grew at an annual rate of approximately 9%. However, in the years since 1995 that growth rate increased to 12% per annum. This ranks the Chinese economy as one of the fastest-growing economies in the world and seventh in GDP ($695.2 billion USD). Stated government goals are to double GDP during the period from 2000 to 2010. Foreign trade has had a substantial impact on the economy, with a fifteen-year history of 15% annual growth. This growth can be attributed in part to the relaxation of governmental regulations addressing trade.

Trade Regulations

Since World War II, much of international trade has been governed by the General Agreement on Tariffs and Trade (GATT). Through this accord, member nations agree to certain practices involving international commerce, but few of the member countries actually follow its by-laws. The People's Republic of China has been among the countries that have established and enforced trade agreements and tariffs to protect their products and restrict competition. However, since the 1994 publication of the "Outline of State Industrial Policy," China has relaxed many of its restrictive trading policies and has also prepared a *Guide for International Investment* encouraging international trade. From the viewpoint of the U.S. government, these moves helped China obtain a "most favored nation" trading status. This status has accelerated trade between the two nations.

International Marketing Structure

The structure of international marketing, no matter where it is conducted, contains more similarities than differences in contrast to that of domestic enterprises. However, they share the main concepts of selling directly to consumers or selling through agents. For Xerox, both sales channels are available. The traditional marketing activities employed by Xerox currently consist of direct mail, print media adver-

tising, electronic media buys, and special promotions. Current alloca-
tion of marketing dollars to these channels are 20% direct mail, 50%
print media advertising, 25% electronic media (TV, radio) buys, and
5% special promotions.

An increased amount of data is needed to make marketing decisions
in international settings because of the cultural differences that exist.
Many marketing decisions are made in U.S. corporations based on
knowledge of sport in our societal context. U.S. managers making decisions in foreign countries simply do not have such knowledge. To offset
this problem, most organizations will enlist the assistance of national
experts from the target nation. These experts can also be helpful in
communicating value differences between cultures. International managers must learn to respect the value systems of others, not merely
tolerate them.

As a geographic and social region, Asia is extremely diverse. Social
and political conditions affecting sport and business vary considerably
from predominantly Muslim nations, such as Malaysia, to the commu-
nist ideology in the People's Republic of China. In China, for example,
government-owned business can compete with privately held companies. Government-owned businesses and newly created quasipublic corporations may be granted exclusive manufacturing and distribution
rights in some sectors. Another complication is government subsidies
to local corporations. Either of these practices can severely restrict the
ability of U.S. companies to compete successfully in that market. In
addition, some Asian nations are newly industrialized (Singapore,
South Korea, Taiwan) and can provide active, growing markets for both
consumption and manufacturing, whereas other nations are still in the
early stages of economic development. Entry into the markets of Asia
demand considerable study and analysis, but the rewards can be im-
mense.

The U.S. government is one of the best sources for information on
foreign markets. A variety of government offices in the Department of
State have reams of information about foreign economies available at
little or no cost. The U.S. Agency for International Development, whose
main purpose is improving trade with developing countries, is also a
good source of information. Most foreign governments also attempt to
attract U.S. business and have personnel at their embassies to accommodate those interests. Other sources for international marketing contacts are international trade associations, economic development
councils at the state or local level, and international trade shows.

International Marketing Personnel

The selection of well-trained and experienced personnel is essential in
international marketing. Trying to enter global markets without the
expertise of someone experienced in international trade is a common

error made by many American companies. Arranging financing, marketing products, or negotiating contracts with foreign customers without assistance from experienced international management personnel often leads to disaster. Personnel managing foreign markets or heading up foreign units are trained in a variety of different ways. Some corporations conduct in-house training sessions using the expertise and experience of their existing staff. Some corporations handle the training through their foreign consultants. Both of these methods have proven to be equally successful. Regardless of the method employed, it is imperative that personnel be educated for cultural sensitivity prior to their involvement in international affairs. Research has indicated that adaptability to foreign cultures is equal in importance to marketing skills developed in a domestic position.

Adapting to Cultural Diversity

Although business personnel have a common bond with executives in other nations through their education and experience, cultural variations in appropriate business etiquette can sabotage chances for success. The successful market manager needs to have a clear understanding of the "do's and don'ts" of foreign culture. Before traveling and dealing with international executives, business executives should review the special characteristics of the host nation. What follows are some national and international customs in business relations.

TOUCHING

In much of North America, touching is acceptable between friends, but overt touching of casual acquaintances in a business setting is not tolerated. The local custom in many Latin countries allows for hugs following an introduction. However, in China, personal touching is restricted only for well-established relations and is not typically accepted in business transactions.

RELATIONSHIPS BETWEEN MALES AND FEMALES

Women have for many years played increasing roles in the conduct of business in the United States. Many women serve as CEOs of major corporations and marketing firms. In China, as in other parts of the world, women may not be accepted in business meetings. Because we believe in equality of the sexes in the United States does not mean that everyone in the world does. U.S. firms must make a decision whether to do business with countries that have different beliefs about the role of women in business relations and follow a strategy that will produce the best business results.

DRINKING

The easiest rule for drinking is to follow the lead of the host. If the host orders a drink, one is welcome to partake. But guests should be cautious about bringing alcoholic gifts for the host.

GIFTS

Exchanging gifts is a custom that is more prevalent in other countries than it is in the United States. In fact, in the 1970s the U.S. government passed the Foreign Corrupt Practices Act to curtail bribes and kickbacks. The line is very vague as to what constitutes a payoff and what is a generous gift. Most business executives will face difficulty in this area and should try to learn ahead of time from a confidant or fellow executive about the local custom and tradition. A good practice is to carry small company pins or souvenirs and to graciously accept similar extensions from a host.

BUSINESS ETIQUETTE

Every country has its unique protocol for conducting business, extending even to when to wear business attire and when to wear casual clothing. Rules about when and where to talk business can vary: in some countries, work is work and play is play; in other countries, the best deals are put together on the golf course. Business people also need to be perceptive about special interrelationships. In China, the most important person sits to the right of the host by custom.

Sponsorship Proposal: Asian Winter Games

The Asian Winter Games are held every three years. The first and second Asian Winter Games were held in Japan. China considers it a great honor to have been selected by the Asian Olympic Committee to host the Third Asian Winter Games. These Games will include forty-five events in nine categories and will constitute the largest event in scale and number of participants in the history of sports in Asia. See Table 15.1 for a complete schedule of events. This event will also be the largest comprehensive sporting event to be held in China before the end of the century, offering an excellent marketing opportunity for Xerox. Because sponsors are often judged by the quality of the event, the Asian Winter Games Organizing Committee has sought and secured sanctioning from the Asian Olympic Committee (OCA), with skiing events sanctioned by the International Ski Federation (FIS). Together, these organizations will produce an excellent event, which will enhance the reputation of Xerox as one of its sponsors.

Approximately 1,000 top athletes from fourteen countries and re-

Table 15.1 Schedule of events

Venue	Sunday, Feb. 4	Monday, Feb. 5	Tuesday, Feb. 6	Wednesday, Feb. 7
Feichi Ice Hockey Rink	09:00 Men's 12:30 Men's 18:00 Opening ceremonies	10:00 Men's 14:00 Men's 19:00 Men's	14:00 Women's 19:00 Women's	10:00 Men's 14:00 Men's 19:00 Men's
Figure Skating & Short-Track Speedskating Rink		16:00 Men's & women's 1500 m & 500 m	16:00 Men's & women's 1000 m, 3000 m, & relays	
Speedskating Rink		10:00 Women's 3000 m Men's 5000 m	10:00 Women's 500 m Men's 500 m	10:00 Women's 1500 m Men's 1500 m
Yabuli Alpine Courses		10:00 Men's Super G	10:00 Women's Super G	10:00 Men's Giant Slalom
Yabuli Cross Country Courses			10:00 Men's 15 km free 13:00 Women's 10 km free	
Yabuli Biathlon Courses		10:00 Men's 20 km 13:00 Women's 15 km		
Yabuli Freestyle Ski Jumps				10:00 Men's aerials
Yabuli 90-Meter Ski Jump		10:00 Men's individual jumping		10:00 Men's team jumping

Venue	Thursday, Feb. 8	Friday, Feb. 9	Saturday, Feb. 10	Sunday, Feb. 11
Feichi Ice Hockey Rink	10:00 Men's 14:00 Men's 19:00 Men's	14:00 Women's 19:00 Women's	10:00 Men's 14:00 Men's 19:00 Men's	09:00 Women's 12:30 Women's 18:00 Closing ceremony
Figure Skating & Short-Track Speedskating Rink	14:00 Men's & pairs short program; ice dancing compulsory	14:00 Original dance; women's short program; men's free	14:00 Women's & pairs free; ice dancing free	14:00 Exhibition
Speedskating Rink	10:00 Women's 1000 m Men's 1000 m	10:00 Men's 10000 m		
Yabuli Alpine Courses	10:00 Women's giant slalom			
Yabuli Cross Country Courses			10:00 Men's relay 13:00 Women's relay	09:00 Men's 10 km classical 10:30 Women's 5 km classical
Yabuli Biathlon Courses	10:00 Men's 10 km 13:00 Women's 7.5 km	10:00 Men's relay 13:00 Women's relay		
Yabuli Freestyle Ski Jumps		10:00 Women's aerials		
Yabuli 90-Meter Ski Jump				

gions throughout Asia will partake in the Games. More specifically, the nations scheduled to participate include

Japan	China	South Korea
India	Taiwan	Mongolia
Philippines	Uzbekistan	North Korea
Kazahkstan	Macao	Turkmenistan
Afghanistan	Iran	

Collectively, forty-three OCA member countries will send official representatives to observe or participate in the Games. During the eight days (February 4–11) of the Asian Winter Games, the venues in and around Harbin, Heilongjiang Province, China will come to life to showcase Xerox products and document solutions.

Media and Live Audiences

Over *one billion* (1,000,000,000) people throughout Asia and the rest of the world will watch, read about, or hear coverage of the Third Asian Winter Games.

MEDIA AUDIENCES

Television Coverage in China. When China is a medal contender, the people of China will be watching!

- Eight straight days, 120 minutes minimum each day of prime time broadcast coverage on China Central Television (CCTV), China's main domestic network (1.2 billion viewers as estimated by the Advertising Company of the Third Asian Winter Games).
- Additional live and taped coverage is planned to be broadcast later.
- The following stations will also have video crews covering the Games:
  Shanghai Television Station
  Shanghai Eastern Television Station
  Guangdong Television Station
  Tianjin Television Station
  Heilongjang Television Station
  Regional Television Coverage
- Over fifty countries will receive telecasts and highlights of the Games via international satellite transmissions.

Newspaper Coverage
- China's major newspapers will cover the Games daily, reaching an estimated 500 million people per day.
- Articles and photos of Asian Winter Games events will run in newspapers throughout the Asian region.

Live Audiences

- Live audiences at the Asian Winter Games will comprise citizens from forty-three Asian Olympic Council member countries, including official representatives, government officials, athletes, guests, and reporters,
- Guests, sports enthusiasts, and tourists from many other countries as well as all parts of China,
- Total event entrance tickets: 230,000.

Venues

There are four main venues in and around Harbin, China, that will host the events of the Asian Winter Games. These four venues, as well as Harbin International Airport, will see heavy consumer traffic during the period of the Games. Billboard advertising is offered at each of these locations.

FEICHI ICE RINK

- Feichi Ice Rink will host the opening and closing ceremonies for the Games, as well as men's and women's ice hockey competition.
- Exposure to 138,600 spectators.

FIGURE SKATING RINK

- The Heilongjiang Provincial Figure Skating Rink will host ten skating events, including men's, women's, and pairs short programs and free skating; ice dancing; and an exhibition program.
- The venue will also host ten short track speedskating events, including: women's 500 m, 1000 m, 1500 m, 3000 m, and 3000 m relay; and men's 500 m, 1500 m, 3000 m, and 5000 m relay.
- Exposure to 73,400 spectators.

SPEEDSKATING RINK

- The Heilongjiang Provincial Speed Skating Rink will host nine speed skating events, including: women's 500 m, 1000 m, 1500 m, 3000 m, and men's 500 m, 1000 m, 1500 m, 5000 m, 10000 m.
- Exposure to 18,000 spectators.

YABULI SKI AREA

- The Yabuli Ski Area, located 195 kilometers east of Harbin, will host twenty skiing events, including: men's and women's Super G, giant slalom, and freestyle aerials; men's 10 km, 15 km, and relay cross country; women's 5 km, 10 km, and relay cross country; men's 10 km, 20 km, and relay biathlon; women's 7.5 km, 15 km, and relay biathlon; and men's team and individual 90 km ski jump demonstrations.
- Exposure to 35,000 spectators.

HARBIN INTERNATIONAL AIRPORT

- During the Games, the Harbin International Airport will have direct air links to Japan, South Korea, the Commonwealth of Independent States, and Hong Kong as well as all major cities in China. Advertisers will have visibility with air travelers to and from Harbin, one of the ten largest cities in China, before, during, and after the Games.
- Exposure to international and domestic travelers.

Sponsorship Opportunities

There are three main packaged sponsorship opportunities: Gold, Silver, and Bronze. Each package offers a selection of billboard advertisements, merchandising rights, official sponsor recognition, and opportunities for additional exposure to Asian consumers. Gold Sponsors' products will have exclusivity in their particular product category. Individual billboard and other advertisement opportunities are offered separately or in addition to Gold, Silver, and Bronze packages (see Figures 15.1–15.4). Any official advertising equal to or greater than U.S. $100,000 qualifies an advertiser for all benefits of a Bronze Sponsorship.

Venues	Billboard (#) Size	Venues	Billboard (#) Size
Feichi Ice Rink		Figure Skating Rink	
Front of rostrum	12 m × 1 m	Front of rostrum	12 m × 1 m
Scoreboard	6 m × 4 m	Scoreboard	4 m × 6 m
Rink Boards	(3) 6 m × 1 m	Rink boards	(3) 6 m × 1 m
Yabuli Ski Area		Speedskating Rink	
Two of the following starting gates:		Rink boards	(8) 5 m × 1 m
Women's giant slalom	10 m × 0.9 m		
Men's giant slalom	10 m × 0.9 m	Harbin International Airport	
Women's Super G	10 m × 0.9 m	Billboards	(5) 10 m × 6 m
Men's Super G	6 m × 1.2 m		
Alpine finish line–Side			
Banner in front of			
audience in			
freestyle jump			
deceleration zone	10 m × 1 m		

INSTALLATION OF ADVERTISEMENTS

- All costs and expenses relating to the preparation and installation of the advertisements at the Venues shall be borne by the Sponsor. All advertising materials should be submitted by the Sponsor at least one (1) month before the commencement of the Games.

Figure 15.1 Gold sponsorship investment (U.S. $500,000)

MERCHANDISING RIGHTS

All Gold, Silver, and Bronze Sponsors are entitled to the following rights:

- During the competition, Sponsor's products are allowed to enter and be sold in all venues and in athletes' residences.
- The Sponsor has the right to use the name, emblem, and mascot of the Third Asian Winter Games in association with all products and promotional items, gifts, pins, etc.
- sponsor's products may be sold in the over 100 appointed shops and 500 appointed counters nationwide with the Developing General company of the Asian Winter Games as its general agent, on a commission basis.
- The Sponsor will have an opportunity to utilize exhibition halls and exhibition platforms for a tax-free, discounted fee. The Asian Winter Games Organizing Committee will expedite all necessary customs procedures for exhibition products.
- Where possible, Sponsor's products will be used in all official guest houses, restaurants, press conferences, banquets, and activities, when gifts are to be presented.

OFFICIAL SPONSOR RECOGNITION

Gold, Silver, and Bronze Sponsors will receive the following additional special recognition at the Third Asian Winter Games:

Public Visibility and Acknowledgments

- Sponsor's advertisements at Harbin International Airport will enjoy broad international public visibility during and after the Third Asian Winter Games. Harbin (population 3.5 million) is one of the ten largest cities in China.
- At press conferences and other official occasions, Asian Winter Games spokespersons will mention Sponsor's name, deeds, and recognize their participation whenever possible.

Acknowledgment of Sponsor in Printed Materials. Sponsor and/or products will receive lasting affiliation through the following Asian Winter Games printed materials:

Special Publications
- *The Third Asian Winter Games Contributors and Sponsors Commemorative Album*—a publication distributed to all guests and sponsors of the Games.
- *The Asia Winter Sports Report*—Asian Winter Games Edition—distribution of 300,000 domestically and abroad.
- *Asian Winter Games Special Report*—oversized format pictorial album distributed in China and abroad.
- *Asian Winter Games Promotional Posters*—twelve pictorial promotional posters of each event, the Asian Winter Games emblem, and the mascot. 50,000 copies of each poster will be distributed internationally.

Programs and Guidebooks
The following publications will be sold or distributed to spectators, visitors, honored guests, athletes, coaches, officials, and reporters who attend the Games:

Figure 15.1 Continued

- *Official Asian Winter Games Event Program*—over 100,000 copies.
- *Opening Ceremonies Program*—100,000 copies.
- *Closing Ceremonies Program*—over 100,000 copies.
- *Guide to the Asian Winter Venues and Athletes Village*—over 100,000 copies.
- *Guide to the Asian Winter Games Shopping and Tourism*— over 100,000 copies.
- *Guide to Transportation and Medical Services*— over 100,000 copies.

Asian Olympic Committee Recognition and Hospitality
- A ceremony to acknowledge the Sponsor will be held by the Chairman or Vice Chairman of the Asian Winter Games Organizing Committee and will be reported by the news media.
- The Sponsor's name will be inscribed on a prize cup or souvenir presented to the Sponsor.
- The Organizing Committee's gratitude will be expressed to the Sponsor in a commemorative album.
- A certificate of Honor will be presented to the Sponsor.
- One representative of Sponsor's organization will be invited to visit the Games, and his/her board and lodging will be arranged and paid by the Asian Winter Games Organizing Committee.
- Gold sponsors will receive 20 complete sets of tickets to the Asian Winter Games events and have priority in purchasing additional event tickets.

Figure 15.1 Continued

Venues	Billboard (#) Size	Venues	Billboard (#) Size
Feichi Ice Rink		Figure Skating Rink	
Scoreboard	6 m × 4 m	Scoreboard	4 m × 6 m
Rink boards	(2) 6 m × 1 m	Rink boards	(2) 6 m × 1 m
Yabuli Ski Area		Speedskating Rink	
Two of the following starting gates:		Rink boards	(3) 6 m × 1 m
Women's giant slalom	10 m × 0.9 m		
Men's giant slalom	10 m × 0.9 m	Harbin International Airport	
Women's Super G	10 m × 0.9 m	Billboards	(5) 10 m × 6 m
Men's Super G	10 m × 0.9 m		
Banner along side of landing area at freestyle ski jump	10 m × 1.2 m		

INSTALLATION OF ADVERTISEMENTS
- All costs and expenses relating to the preparation and installation of the advertisements at the Venues shall be borne by the Sponsor. All advertising materials should be submitted by the Sponsor at least one (1) month before the commencement of the Games.

MERCHANDISING RIGHTS
All Gold, Silver, and Bronze Sponsors are entitled to the following rights:

Figure 15.2 Silver sponsor investment (U.S. $200,000)

- During the competition, Sponsor's products are allowed to enter and be sold in all venues and in athletes' residences.
- The Sponsor has the right to use the name, emblem, and mascot of the Third Asian Winter Games in association with all products and promotional items, gifts, pins, etc.
- Sponsor's products may be sold in the over 100 appointed shops and 500 appointed counters nationwide with the Developing General company of the Asian Winter Games as its general agent, on a commission basis.
- The Sponsor will have an opportunity to utilize exhibition halls and exhibition platforms for a tax-free, discounted fee. The Asian Winter Games Organizing Committee will expedite all necessary customs procedures for exhibition products.
- Where possible, Sponsor's products will be used in all official guest houses, restaurants, press conferences, banquets, and activities, when gifts are to be presented.

OFFICIAL SPONSOR RECOGNITION
Gold, Silver, and Bronze Sponsors will receive the following additional special recognition at the Third Asian Winter Games:

Public Visibility and Acknowledgments
- Sponsor's advertisements at Harbin International Airport will enjoy broad international public visibility during and after the Third Asian Winter Games. Harbin (population 3.5 million) is one of the ten largest cities in China.
- At press conferences and other official occasions, Asian Winter Games spokespersons will mention Sponsor's name, deeds, and recognize their participation whenever possible.

Acknowledgment of Sponsor in Printed Materials. Sponsor and/or products will receive lasting affiliation through the following Asian Winter Games printed materials:

Special Publications
- *The Third Asian Winter Games Contributors and Sponsors Commemorative Album*—a publication distributed to all guests and sponsors of the Games.
- *The Asia Winter Sports Report*—Asian Winter Games Edition—distribution of 300,000 domestically abroad.
- *Asian Winter Games Special Report*—oversized format pictorial album distributed in China and abroad.
- *Asian Winter Games Promotional Posters*—twelve pictorial promotional posters of each event, the Asian Winter Games emblem, and the mascot. 50,000 copies of each poster will be distributed internationally.

Programs and Guidebooks
The following publications will be sold or distributed to spectators, visitors, honored guests, athletes, coaches officials, and reporters who attend the Games:
- *Official Asian Winter Games Event Program*—over 100,000 copies.
- *Opening Ceremonies Program*—over 100,000 copies.
- *Closing Ceremonies Program*—over 100,000 copies.

Figure 15.2 Continued

- *Guide to the Asian Winter Venues and Athletes Village*—over 100,000 copies.
- *Guide to Asian Winter Games Shopping and Tourism*—over 100,000 copies.
- *Guide to Transportation and Medical Services*—over 100,000 copies.

Asian Olympic Committee Recognition and Hospitality

- A ceremony to acknowledge the Sponsor will be held by the Chairman or Vice Chairman of the Asian Winter Games Organizing Committee and will be reported by the news media.
- The Sponsor's name will be inscribed on a prize cup or souvenir presented to the Sponsor.
- The Organizing Committee's gratitude will be expressed to the Sponsor in a commemorative album.
- A certificate of Honor will be presented to the Sponsor.
- One representative of Sponsor's organization will be invited to visit the Games, and his/her board and lodging will be arranged and paid by the Asian Winter Games Organizing Committee.
- Silver sponsors will receive 10 complete sets of tickets to the Asian Winter Games events and have priority in purchasing additional event tickets.

Figure 15.2 Continued

Venues	Billboard (#) Size	Venues	Billboard (#) Size
Feichi Ice Rink		Figure Skating Rink	
Rink boards	(2) 6 m × 1 m	Rink boards	(2) 6 m × 1 m
Yabuli Ski Area		Speedskating Rink	
Banner at side of starting line for one of the following:		Rink boards	(3) 5 m × 1 m
Women's giant slalom	6 m × 1.2 m	Harbin International Airport	
Men's giant slalom	6 m × 1.2 m	Billboards	(4) 10 m × 6 m
Women's Super G	6 m × 1.2 m		
Men's Super G			

INSTALLATION OF ADVERTISEMENTS

- All costs and expenses related to the preparation and installation of the advertisements at the Venues shall be borne by the Sponsor. All advertising materials should be submitted by the Sponsor at least one (1) month before the commencement of the Games.

MERCHANDISING RIGHTS

All Gold, Silver, and Bronze Sponsors are entitled to the following rights:

- During the competition, Sponsor's products are allowed to enter and be sold in all venues and in athletes' residences.
- The Sponsor has the right to use the name, emblem, and mascot to the Third Asian Winter Games in association with all products and promotional items, gifts, pins, etc.

Figure 15.3 Bronze sponsorship investment (U.S. $100,000)

- Sponsor's products may be sold in the over 100 appointed shops and 500 appointed counters nationwide with the Developing General company of the Asian Winter Games as its general agent, on a commission basis.
- The Sponsor will have an opportunity to utilize exhibition halls and exhibition platforms for a tax-free, discounted fee. The Asian Winter Games Organizing Committee will expedite all necessary customs procedures for exhibition products.
- Where possible, Sponsor's products will be used in all official guest houses, restaurants, press conferences, banquets, and activities, when gifts are to be presented.

OFFICIAL SPONSOR RECOGNITION

Gold, Silver, and Bronze Sponsors will receive the following additional special recognition at the Third Asian Winter Games:

Public Visibility and Acknowledgements

- Sponsor's advertisements at Harbin International Airport will enjoy broad international public visibility during and after the Third Asian Winter Games. Harbin (population 3.5 million) is one of the ten largest cities in China.
- At press conferences and other official occasions, Asian Winter Games spokespersons will mention Sponsor's name, deeds, and recognize their participation whenever possible.

Acknowledgment of Sponsor in Printed Materials

Sponsor and/or products will receive lasting affiliation through the following Asian Winter Games printed materials:

Special Publications
- *The Third Asian Winter Games Contributors and Sponsors Commemorative Album*—a publication distributed to all guests and sponsors of the Games.
- *The Asia Winter Sports Report* - Asian Winter Games Edition—distribution of 300,000 domestically and abroad.
- *Asian Winter Games Special Report*—oversized format pictorial album distributed in China and abroad.
- *Asian Winter Games Promotional Posters*—twelve pictorial promotional posters of each event, the Asian Winter Games emblem and the mascot. 50,000 copies of each poster will be distributed internationally.

Programs and Guidebooks
The following publications will be sold or distributed to spectators, visitors, honored guests, athletes, coaches officials and reporters who attend the Games:
- *Official Asian Winter Games Event Program*—over 100,000 copies.
- *Opening Ceremonies Program*—over 100,000 copies.
- *Closing Ceremonies Program*—over 100,000 copies.
- *Guide to the Asian Winter Venues and Athletes Village*—over 100,000 copies.
- *Guide to Asian Winter Games Shopping and Tourism*—over 100,000 copies.
- *Guide to Transportation and Medical Services*—over 100,000 copies.

Figure 15.3 Continued

ASIAN OLYMPIC COMMITTEE RECOGNITION AND HOSPITALITY

- A ceremony to acknowledge the Sponsor will be held by the Chairman or Vice Chairman of the Asian Winter Games Organizing Committee and will be reported by the news media.
- The Sponsor's name will be inscribed on a prize cup or souvenir presented to the Sponsor.
- The Organizing Committee's gratitude will be expressed to the Sponsor in a commemorative album.
- A Certificate of Honor will be presented to the Sponsor.
- One representative of Sponsor's organization will be invited to visit the Games, and his/her board and lodging will be arranged and paid by the Asian Winter Games Organizing Committee.
- Bronze sponsors will receive 5 complete sets of tickets to the Asian Winter Games events and have priority in purchasing additional event tickets.

Figure 15.3 Continued

The following billboard advertisements are available for sale separately or in addition to the Gold, Silver, and Bronze packages.

Feichi Ice Rink (Opening and closing ceremonies)

Position	Size	# Available	Unit Price (U.S.$)
Inside arena	6 m × 1 m	6	15,000
Inside arena	6 m × 1 m	18	13,000
Inside arena	6 m × 1 m	6	11,000
Opposite the scoreboard	30 m × 8 m	1	30,000
Base of the flame	6 m × 1 m	6	110,000
Rink boards	6 m × 1 m	6	18,000

Figure Skating Rink

Position	Size	# Available	Unit Price (U.S.$)
Inside arena	6 m × 1 m	6	11,000
Inside arena	6 m × 1 m	18	9,000
Inside arena	6 m × 1 m	6	7,000
Opposite the scoreboard	18 m × 6 m	1	15,000
Rink boards	6 m × 1 m	6	20,000

Speed skating rink

Position	Size	# Available	Unit Price (U.S.$)
Inside arena	5 m × 1 m	50	7,500
Above & below scoreboard	18 m × 1 m	2	110,000
Finish line	20 m × 1 m	1	60,000
Two sides of scoreboard	6 m × 4 m	2	30,000
Banners in center of rink	10 m × 1 m	4	15,000

Yabuli Ski Area

Position	Size	# Available	Unit Price (U.S.$)
Award rostrum backdrop (20 award ceremonies)	10 m × 5 m	1	300,000
Finish line of alpine events	25 m × 6 m	1	200,000
Cross country/biathlon Start/finish line	10 m × 1 m	1	200,000
Clock & leader board for Alpine events		1	110,000

Figure 15.4 Billboard Advertisment Pricing

Supporting posts for Gondola and lifts	10 m × 2 m (cir)	All	90,000
Banner at side of alpine finish lines	6 m × 1.2 m	2	25,000
90 m ski jump start	4 m × 1 m	4	25,000
Take-off point of 90 m ski jump	4 m × 2 m	1	60,000
Take-off point of freestyle ski jump	2 m × 1.4 m	6	70,000

INSTALLATION OF ADVERTISEMENTS
- All costs and expenses relating to the preparation and installation of the advertisements at the Venues shall be borne by the Advertiser. All advertising materials should be submitted by the Advertiser at least one (1) month before the commencement of the Games.

SPECIAL ADVERTISEMENT OPPORTUNITIES

Sports Lottery Tickets
- Official "Scratch & Win" Lottery Tickets will be sold all over the country to help raise money for the Asian Winter Games.
- Lottery tickets were tremendously popular nationwide in 1990 when they were issued for the 11th Asian Games held in Beijing.
- 20 Million lottery tickets will be printed and distributed throughout China with advertiser's name, logo, etc.
- Investment: U.S. $400,000.

Official Program
- Advertisements will appear in this complete listing of events, venues, activities, etc.
- 200,000 copies will be printed.
- Investment: U.S. $100,000.

Athletes' Number Bibs
- Advertiser's Name and Logo will appear on all athletes' bibs competing on a certain day.
- Investment: U.S. $300,000 per day.

Event Staff Clothing
- Advertiser's Name and Logo will appear on Event Staff's clothing.
- Investment: U.S. $40,000.

Special Vehicles
- Advertiser's Name and Logo will appear on all Asian Winter Games Special vehicles, including: VIP Vehicles, designated taxis, specially routed buses, Event Vehicles, etc.
- Investment: U.S. $200,000.

A LA CARTE ADVERTISEMENTS
A la Carte Advertising equal to or greater than U.S. $100,000 qualifies an Advertiser for all benefits of a Bronze Sponsorship.

Figure 15.4 Continued

In addition to those benefits in the packages, all Gold, Silver, and Bronze Sponsors are entitled to other numerous benefits. Sponsors may engage or employ key athletes, sports stars, or personalities associated with the Games to appeal at public or private functions organized by sponsors. In addition, sponsors have the right to erect courtesy tents and hospitality stations in and around all Asian Winter Games venues so long as they do not interfere with the events being held at the venues. The Asian Winter Games Organizing Committee will assist sponsors in setting up these stations. Sponsors also enjoy rights pertaining to related advertising campaigns through the use of the name, emblem, and mascot of the Asian Winter Games in their own advertisements and advertising campaigns. In addition, all sponsors will have the right to use Asian Winter Games video footage for current or future advertising. With regard to commercial television coverage of the Games, sponsors will have right of first refusal for available television spots offered by Chinese broadcasters. An additional advertising fee will be charged for available fifteen-second and thirty-second spots. Standard fee rates for the specific television station will apply.

Review of the Case Study Problem

Xiang Wong, head of marketing for Xerox (China) Limited was asked to prepare a report for the director of international marketing at corporate headquarters presenting a rationale for his decision regarding the purchase of sponsorship opportunities presented for the Asian Winter Games.

Xiang Wong was suddenly jolted back to reality, 14–13 . . . the next point would be decisive. So many choices, so little time. Xiang could go for the gold ($500,000) or pursue a less risky strategy of purchasing just a sponsorship component. Or were there other, better ways to expend these financial resources? Would such a purchase in the long run open doors to future business with the Chinese government? What cultural variables might impact sponsorship implementation? Xiang Wong slowly brought his racket back to serve, a strategy selected, he struck the shuttlecock . . . .

The Creation and Maintenance of Brand Equity—The Case of University of Massachusetts Basketball

Jay Gladden and Glenn M. Wong

Introduction

Chandra Goldberg gazed out at the empty Mullins Center and continued to ponder a dilemma that had been nagging her for months. As the director of marketing for the University of Massachusetts (UMASS), Chandra was responsible for generating nearly $4 million annually from ticket sales, concessions revenues, sponsorships, and fundraising efforts (see Table 16.1 for a summary of the UMass Athletic Department budget). Without this money, the Athletic Department would almost certainly be forced to operate at a deficit due to their $15 million overall budget. Although UMass basketball had been successful in recent years, Chandra feared new developments could alter the team's performance and thus ticket sales. Would the UMass brand name carry the team through rough times?

UMass Basketball—The Present

Central to this revenue generation was the men's basketball team. The team was a Final Four participant during the 1995–96 season and the Athletic Department had basked in the positive marketplace outcomes resulting from such success on the court. The bottom line was an $881,410 surplus from the basketball program (see Table 16.2 for the UMass basketball budget). Ticket sales, donations to the UMass

281

Table 16.1 University of Massachusetts Athletic Department budget, fiscal year 1996

Category/Item	Amount ($)
Revenues	
Allocations from the University	
State salaries and fringe benefits	3,348,511
General operating funds	534,532
Scholarship aid	724,691
Tuition grants (waivers)	1,515,802
Total University Allocations	6,123,536
Operating revenues	4,545,169
New nonoperating revenues: ticket sales, concessions, guarantees, and NCAA events	2,838,519
Contributions and revenue from fundraising events	1,233,166
Licensing revenue	71,500
NCAA scholarship distribution	137,381
Endowment interest scholarship aid	1,800
Total Revenues	14,951,071
Expenses	
Athletic trust fund operating expenses	4,544,883
University state-funded salaries and benefits	3,348,511
University general operating funds—salaries	522,052
Intercollegiate scholarship aid	3,173,523
Expenses involved in conducting events where tickets are sold	2,331,010
UMass Athletic Fund, intercollegiate program support, scholarships, and Court Club (top boosters) function expenses	810,611
Addition to department account balances	220,481
Total Expenses	14,951,071

Source: UMass Athletic Department 1995–96 Annual Report.

Athletic Fund (the athletic fundraising organization), corporate involvement, and licensing revenues were at all-time highs. However, Goldberg knew that it was not possible to make Final Four appearances every year. Furthermore, for a number of reasons, Goldberg knew that the UMass Athletic Department would have a hard time maintaining the current levels of positive marketplace outcomes.

The 1996–97 campaign had been quite difficult. First, Marcus Camby, the team's star and its first true "all-American" since Julius Erving in the early 1970s, announced his intention to forego his final year of eligibility and enter the National Basketball Association (NBA). UMass basketball fans had been vocal about wanting Marcus to stay in school for one final basketball campaign. For example, a local farmer used his barn on a busy thoroughfare near campus in an effort to persuade Marcus to stay in Amherst. The large painted roof read "Please stay, Marcus." However, Camby was ready to play in the NBA,

Table 16.2 UMass men's basketball income statement, 1995–96 season

Category/Item	Amount ($)
Income	
Ticket revenue	1,544,172
Less:	
Guarantees paid	65,000
Game expenses/officials	149,490
Net ticket revenue	1,329,682
Guarantees received	173,000
TV revenue	99,500
Atlantic 10/NCAA revenues	220,000
Radio	50,000
Signage	50,000
Total Revenues	1,922,182
Expenses	
Scholarship aid	207,934
Salary costs	
State coaching salaries	251,799
State secretary + ½ receptionist	30,842
General operating fund administrative	25,400
General operating fund salaries	30,000
General operating fund fringe benefits	18,788
Total salary costs	356,829
Operating expenses	
Dues	200
Midnight Madness	7,000
Equipment/uniforms	10,000
Lodging	78,500
Meals	79,675
Office supplies	1,000
Recruiting/scouting	85,000
Transportation	132,000
Mullins rental fee for practice	42,000
Total operating expenses	457,261
Administration overhead @ 4.10%	18,748
Total Expenses	1,040,772
Net Surplus	881,410

Source: UMass Athletic Department 1995–96 Annual Report.

and he was selected second overall in the annual draft, making him an instant millionaire.

Yet, it soon became evident that Camby accepted money and gifts prior to becoming a professional. In June of 1996, the *Hartford Courant* reported Camby accepted money and jewelry from two sports agents. Under the rules and regulations of the National Collegiate Athletic Association (NCAA), college athletes were forbidden from accepting money and gifts of any kind. Depending on the severity of the charges and the degree to which the UMass Athletic Department knew about the charges, UMass was faced with the possibility of being penalized by the NCAA.

The UMass Athletic Department was dealt another blow when later that week John Calipari, the team's charismatic head coach, announced that he was leaving UMass to become the head coach of the New Jersey Nets of the National Basketball Association. This was a crushing blow. Since his hiring in 1988, Calipari had resurrected the UMass program, culminating in the team's 1995–96 campaign of thirty-five wins and two losses. Not only had Calipari created one of the few New England basketball powers but he had also been an outstanding emissary for the university and a marketing maven for the basketball program. The number of applications from prospective students had increased, particularly from out-of-state students who paid a much higher tuition than in-state students.

However, Calipari's departure in the wake of the Camby scandal led many to question the moral makeup of UMass basketball. Most notably, public questions about Calipari's involvement surfaced. According to *Boston Globe* columnist Dan Shaughnessy, "(Calipari) knew what was going on. And (Calipari) certainly knew when to get out."[1] The media was suggesting that Calipari knew of the agents' dealings with Camby and did nothing. Further, there were suggestions that Calipari's departure for the Nets was partially spurred by his desire to distance himself from the scandal.

The doubt and concern was passed on to Calipari's replacement, James "Bruiser" Flint. A thirty-one-year-old former assistant to Calipari, Flint was left to weather the scandal and attempt to maintain the new-found tradition of UMass basketball. However, this was not going to be easy. Whereas Calipari was hired to coach a program that had not been successful in years, Flint was hired to coach a program that was considered to be one of the best in the country.

The 1996–97 schedule was filled with tough opponents (see Table 16.3). Further, UMass had lost three of its five starters from the 1995–96 campaign. In addition to Camby, Dana Dingle and Donta Bright had exhausted their eligibility. However, the remaining starters, guards Edgar Padilla and Carmelo Travieso, were proven players, each playing a key role in the Minutemen's 1995–96 success. In fact, the UMass publicity efforts prior to the beginning of the season termed the two guards "the best backcourt in the country." Such efforts reaped dividends: the two guards were pictured on the covers of two of the most popular preseason basketball magazines, *Sporting News* and *Street & Smith's*.

However, once the 1996–97 season began, it was evident that UMass

---

[1]Excerpted from the *Boston Globe,* December 20, 1997, p. C8.

Table 16.3 1996–97 UMass basketball schedule

Date	Opponent	Outcome
11/25/96	Chaminade (at Maui Classic)	W, 59–48
11/26/96	Virginia (at Maui Classic)	L, 68–75
11/27/96	California (at Maui Classic)	L, 55–59
12/4/96	Georgetown (at Great Eight tournament in Chicago)	L, 53–58
12/7/96	**Wyoming**	W, 90–72
12/10/96	**#19 Fresno State**	L, 81–102
12/12/96	**Drexel**	W, 69–48
12/14/96	at #2 Wake Forest	L, 47–71
12/20/96	#12 North Carolina at East Rutherford, N.J.	L, 69–83
12/22/96	at UNC Wilmington	W, 47–46
12/27/96	Connecticut at Hartford	L, 61–64
1/2/97	**Davidson**	W, 77–64
1/5/97	**St. Joseph's**	L, 68–72
1/8/97	at La Salle	W, 56–50
1/12/97	**Virginia Tech**	L, 47–63
1/14/97	at St. Bonaventure	W, 63–59
1/18/97	#19 Boston College at Fleet Center in Boston	W, 90–78
1/21/97	**Rhode Island**	W, 64–60
1/25/97	at Temple	W, 78–66
1/30/97	at George Washington	W, 68–63
2/1/97	**#20 Xavier**	L, 84–87 (OT)
2/3/97	at Fordham	W, 75–54
2/6/97	**Duquesne**	W, 73–71
2/8/97	at Rhode Island	W, 64–61
2/11/97	**St. Bonaventure**	W, 74–68
2/15/97	#15 Maryland at Worcester, MA	W, 78–61
2/20/97	**Fordham**	W, 75–58
2/23/97	at Dayton	L, 67–69
2/25/97	at #23 St. Joseph's	L, 63–78
3/1/97	**Temple**	W, 59–53
3/5/97	LaSalle (Atlantic 10 Tournament in Philadelphia)	W, 64–49
3/6/97	George Washington (Atlantic 10 Tournament)	L, 49–58
3/14/97	Louisville (NCAA Tournament at Pittsburgh)	

Bold typeface denotes a home game at the Mullins Center. The ranking of nationally ranked opponents is listed where applicable.

was not going to repeat its successes of the previous season. Playing an early schedule laden with nationally ranked opponents, UMass lost nine out of its first fifteen games. Attendance at home contests began to wane. For some games in the middle of the season, the 9,493 seat arena seemed only two-thirds full, even though the paid attendance was announced as a sellout. This did not go unnoticed, causing a local controversy in the press. UMass rallied toward the end of the season, winning ten of their last fourteen. As a result, they received a berth to the NCAA postseason tournament, where they lost their first-round game to the University of Louisville.

Also during the 1996–97 campaign, the NCAA rendered its decision on the Camby investigation. The good news was that the UMass Athletic Department (including the men's basketball coaches) was cleared of any institutional wrongdoing in the affair. The NCAA found that the UMass Athletic Department did not know about Camby's acceptance of gifts, nor should it have known. Yet, this did not stop the NCAA from stripping UMass of its Final Four appearance because it had used an ineligible player. Thus, the team's only appearance in the prestigious Final Four of men's basketball no longer counted. In addition, the Athletic Department was forced to return the $151,000 it received for participating in the NCAA tournament that year.

Goldberg was faced with this scenario as she began to formulate the marketing strategy for the University of Massachusetts Athletic Department. The performance of the current revenue streams needed to be maintained. This included complete renewal of 9,493 season tickets, not to mention the donations to the UMass Athletic Fund that came with many of the season ticket purchases. Although this year's team returned three starters, it had lost Padilla and Travieso, the leaders of the 1996–97 team. Bruiser Flint was entering his second year as head coach of the Minutemen. Although the team had finished strong during the 1996–97 season, "Bruiser Ball" would begin the 1997–98 with at least two inexperienced starters.

Thus Goldberg knew that success was not guaranteed. Accordingly, she began formulating a strategic vision for UMass basketball that would take it into the twenty-first century.

Brand Equity in Sport

Brand equity represents the sport consumer's associations (both positive and negative) with a sports team's name, logos, and images. Ultimately, there are four components to brand equity:[2]

---

[2]Four components of brand equity are derived from David A. Aaker's model for understanding brand equity as presented in *Managing Brand Equity* (1991).

- **Perceived quality**—consumer judgments of a product's excellence relative to its intended purpose. In the case of sport, this refers to the sport consumer's perception of the quality of a team relative to its competition. This competition would include other teams in the conference/league as well as other sport entertainment options in the geographic market.
- **Brand awareness**—the ease with which a consumer can recall a brand and its name. In the sport context, brand awareness represents the familiarity of sport consumers with a particular athletic team.
- **Brand associations**—tangible and intangible associations that a consumer has with a brand in addition to the perception of quality. In the sport context, brand equity represents the experiential and symbolic attributes offered through affiliation with a particular team. These associations together form an identity for a particular sports team.
- **Brand loyalty**—the ability to attract and retain customers. In sport, this can be seen by tracking season ticket figures, viewership of games on television, and listenership of games on the radio. Loyalty is critical because it provides a steady source of revenue. For example, sports teams generate significant revenues prior to their season through the sales of season tickets. Yet, such loyalty must be cultivated and nurtured. High-quality service and special recognition efforts are often used to develop loyalty.

The Importance of Brand Equity to Sport Managers

All too often in the past managers of sport organizations have relied upon success in athletic contests as the sole means of realizing positive outcomes in the marketplace. However, the sport product (in this case, the team) is inconsistent. It may perform well one day and poorly the next. Sport managers have only limited control over this performance. Furthermore, the recruitment of high-caliber athletes does not always guarantee success. In addition, the sport product satisfies numerous intangible needs. For example, attending a sporting event allows a person to socialize with others and affiliate with a group while watching an aesthetically pleasing competition. Examining sport within the context of brand equity allows the sport manager to account for such intangible needs through such components as brand associations. Because of these factors, a more holistic means for marketing a sports team is needed. Winning is very important; however, the sport marketer must be prepared to capitalize on success when it occurs and to prevent a radical downturn in the absence of short-term success. In order to do this, the sports team must be seen as a brand to be managed, and the sport marketer must exhaust all means to manage that brand.

Understanding Brand Equity in Team Sport

The development of brand equity in team sport can be seen as a cyclical process as illustrated in Figure 16.1.[3] First, a variety of antecedent conditions leads to the creation of brand equity, consisting of four components—perceived quality, brand awareness, brand associations, and brand loyalty. Once brand equity is created, it results in marketplace outcomes, which can be both positive and negative. From these outcomes, the perception of the sports team is then modified. This perception then impacts the antecedents of brand equity, creating a circular process where brand equity is continually changing. To better understand the system, a discussion of the antecedents and consequences is useful.

Antecedents of Brand Equity

There are twelve antecedents, or factors, that can lead to the creation of brand equity. They can be grouped into three distinct categories: team-related, organization-related, and market-related. Team-related antecedents represent all attributes of the sport product directly related to performance (success, head coach, star player). Organization-related antecedents represent all attributes of the sport product directly related to the organization (tradition, conference/schedule, product delivery, logo design, and stadium/arena). Finally, market-related antecedents represent all attributes of the sport product directly related to the market in which the particular team exists (local/regional media coverage, competitive forces, geographic location, and team support/following).

SUCCESS

Success in competition is the most powerful creator of brand equity. Ultimately, there is no substitute for winning athletic contests. Success can produce all of the desired consequences: ticket sales, television appearances, merchandise sales, additional marketing revenues, corporate support, and atmosphere. In addition, success is not always defined by the ratio of wins to losses or the frequency with which a team makes the playoffs. Instead, success may be defined based on the expectations of a set of sport consumers. For example, Northwestern's Rose Bowl appearance following the 1995 football season was extremely special

---

[3]The description of the Conceptual Framework for Assessing Brand Equity in Team Sport was drawn from *Evaluating Brand Equity in the Team Sport Setting,* an unpublished doctoral dissertation by James M. Gladden (1997).

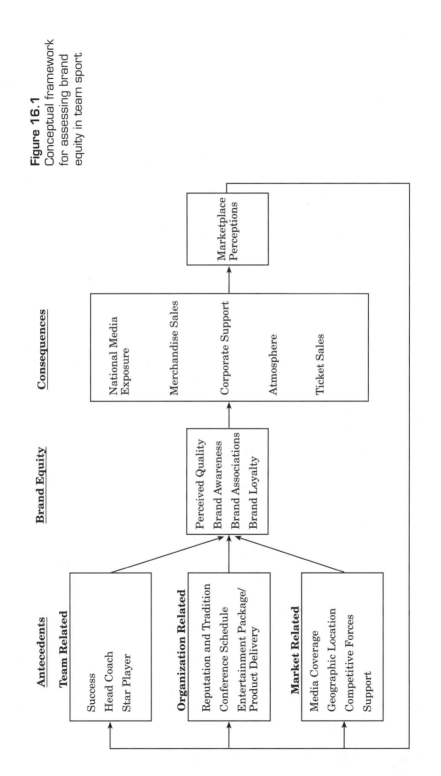

Figure 16.1
Conceptual framework for assessing brand equity in team sport

because sport consumers had come to expect losing seasons from North-western football.

HEAD COACH

A coach with a proven track record generates publicity and expectations of success. Different coaches adopt different styles. Some are fiery and aggressive, while others are mild-mannered and polite. As such, the image of the coach often personifies the image of the team. Further-more, this image can create awareness and a perception of quality. The successful tenures of Dean Smith as men's basketball coach at the University of North Carolina and Pat Summitt as women's basketball coach at the University of Tennessee help their respective programs to garner instant credibility, regardless of the players.

STAR PLAYERS

Star players can also enhance the brand equity of a team. Players that gather remarkable statistics or win national awards generate tremendous media exposure. The presence of a star player may also impact the long-term development of brand equity for a given team. For example, the impact of Michael Jordan on the Chicago Bulls will continue long after his retirement.

TRADITION

Teams can develop traditions of success, fan support, or style of play. In each of these cases, brand equity can be enhanced or reduced. For example, a tradition of success, like that of the University of Notre Dame football team, leads to expectations that Notre Dame will annu-ally compete for the national championship. Fulfillment of this tradition further fuels brand equity, while a below-average season can subtract from brand equity. In college sport, tradition may also incorporate three other components: the university's reputation for academic excellence, the athletic department's reputation for ethical conduct, and the reputa-tion of the entire athletic program.

CONFERENCE AND SCHEDULE

A team's affiliation with a conference or league is important because it determines scheduling and creates rivalries. For example, marketing directors in the Southeastern Conference (SEC) are regularly assisted by favorable scheduling of women's basketball games. At any given time there might be five or six SEC teams ranked in the Top 25 nation-wide. Such quality leads to highly competitive games that receive exten-sive attention from media outlets.

ENTERTAINMENT PACKAGE/PRODUCT DELIVERY

The attraction to sport is at least partially attributable to the entertain-ment value that it offers. Apart from performance, the entertainment value of the experience for the spectator can be influenced by the sport marketer. Promotions, special product giveaways, marching bands, and other traditional activities such as cheers and songs all enhance the overall experience of attending. As such, they enhance the associations of the sport consumer with the team's brand.

LOGO DESIGN

Only in recent years has the importance of the impact of a team's logo design been recognized. The San Jose Sharks crafted an identity for their team before it ever played a game through a logo that was developed in conjunction with their fans. Colleges and universities are also beginning to redesign their logos in an attempt to enhance brand equity. For example, in 1997 the University of Pittsburgh changed their school colors and announced that they would no longer refer to themselves as "Pitt."

STADIUM

The building in which a sport team plays may significantly impact the creation of brand equity. The tradition of the stadium and its design play an important role in the creation of brand equity. Certain stadiums, such as Pauley Pavilion where the UCLA men's basketball team plays, possess long and storied histories. In addition, new stadiums and arenas are increasingly designed with the comfort of the attendee in mind. For example, Clemson University is adding luxury suites to its football stadium, where catered food and beverage will be offered along with theater-style seats. In both cases, the stadium can help enhance brand equity.

LOCAL/REGIONAL MEDIA COVERAGE

All media coverage (television, radio, and print), other than that at the national level, can add to or subtract from a team's brand equity. While positive media attention can enhance a team's brand equity, negative media attention can decrease it. In addition, independent, cable, or pay television agreements, as well as local radio networks, contribute to the creation of brand equity. "Radio networks" or the stable of radio stations that broadcast a team's games help increase the exposure and affiliation with a particular team.

GEOGRAPHIC LOCATION

Certain areas of the country are renowned for certain sports. For example, volleyball is extremely popular in the western United States, particularly in California. Similarly, men's college basketball is strongest in Illinois, Indiana, Kentucky, and North Carolina. Because of these geographical differences, the ease with which brand equity is established may be somewhat dependent on the region where a team is located.

COMPETITIVE FORCES

Competition is important to the creation of brand equity, particularly for teams located in major metropolitan markets. Anything that can compete for the consumer's entertainment dollar (both sport and non-sport related) could be considered a competitive force. With respect to sport, this includes both the major college and professional teams that compete in a market. Colleges and universities in smaller markets where they do not have to compete for the entertainment dollar find brand equity easier to achieve.

TEAM SUPPORT/FOLLOWING

Critical to a team's maintenance of brand equity is the established base of support of sport consumers who attend and help subsidize athletic competitions. Essentially, these are the sport consumers who are brand loyal. Included among these consumers are the groups that strongly identify with the individual teams. These supporters can be further subdivided into casual, focused, and vested fans.

Consequences of Brand Equity

After the antecedents create brand equity, marketplace consequences result. These consequences, of which there are six, can be either positive or negative, depending on whether the antecedents effected a positive or negative change in brand equity.

NATIONAL MEDIA EXPOSURE

Live national television coverage, televised news stories during live broadcasts and pregame programs, and national coverage in newspapers, magazines, and on the radio all constitute national media exposure. National media exposure often can be seen as legitimizing a team. The producers and directors of athletic contests will not schedule a game or cover a story that will not appeal to a national audience. Therefore, a team must posses brand equity before it receives national attention.

MERCHANDISE SALES

Sales of apparel and other items containing a sports team's name or logo signify an attempt by a sport consumer to identify with a particular team. People purchase team-logoed merchandise because it represents an image important to the purchaser. If brand equity did not exist, this would not occur. By wearing the caps, buttons, T-shirts, and sweatshirts of their favorite team, people realize identities. The sales of team-logoed merchandise provides a good management of the strength of intangible associations.

CORPORATE SUPPORT

Since the mid-1980s, corporate support, mainly in the form of advertising fees, has become increasingly important to the operations of a sport organization. Corporations ally with teams possessing equity in order to transfer the pride in the team to their products. Good examples of such alliances are the colleges and universities that shoe and apparel manufacturers choose to sponsor. North Carolina, Ohio State, Florida State, and Michigan are all universities with proven track records for success and visibility. Nike sees these teams as worthwhile advertising vehicles. In contrast, how many times do you see Nike logos on Iowa State or Oregon State uniforms?

ATMOSPHERE

The excitement and level of entertainment provided by attending an event can be enhanced by brand equity. In general, the atmosphere is more electric and energized where there is more brand equity. For example, if a team wins more than it loses under a charismatic coach while playing before a throng of frenzied fans, then the atmosphere surrounding the game is likely to benefit. Enhancing atmosphere is important because the sport consumer takes nothing away from an athletic event other than memories of the experience. By improving the atmosphere, the experience and the brand associations are enhanced.

TICKET SALES

The creation of brand equity can also lead to improved ticket sales. Furthermore, when brand equity drives ticket sales to the extent that arenas and stadiums sell their complete allotment of tickets, teams are then able to require payments for the rights to purchase season tickets. Crucial to this tactic, however, is the maintenance of brand equity to the extent that the demand for seats outstrips the supply. Ticket sales are also important to the enhancement of the entertainment package. With more fans in attendance, people will be more likely to enjoy the experience of attending.

ADDITIONAL REVENUES

Revenues besides those generated through ticket sales, media agreements, and merchandise sales may also benefit or suffer depending on the creation of brand equity. If a team is able to develop high levels of brand equity, its ability to create revenue-generating marketing extensions will increase. At the college level, additional revenues would include such things as donations from supporters and sales at a university-operated merchandise store. Such additional marketing revenues provide important capital that is often used to support other parts of an athletic program.

The University of Massachusetts at Amherst

Unlike many other state schools, which are located in the center or capital of their respective states, the University of Massachusetts (UMass) is located in a small western-Massachusetts town called Amherst. Amherst is twenty miles from Springfield, the nearest metropolitan area. Springfield's sport-related offerings are limited to the Basketball Hall of Fame (Dr. James Naismith invented the sport of basketball at Springfield College) and the Springfield Falcons, a minor-league hockey team. However, Amherst is only a moderate drive from Hartford, Connecticut (one hour), Boston (two hours), and New York City (three hours). Additionally, UMass is within fifteen minutes of four other area colleges. Smith College, an all-women's college, is in Northampton, a larger, more trendy town seven miles southwest of Amherst. Another women's college, Mt. Holyoke, is eleven miles south of Amherst in the bedroom community of South Hadley. Hampshire College and Amherst College also are in Amherst. Compared to its four private school neighbors, UMass is much larger. In addition, Smith, Mt. Holyoke, and Amherst are regularly ranked among the top liberal arts schools in the country.

In existence for well over 100 years, the University of Massachusetts has always struggled to find its identity. Part of this struggle is exemplified in the different names by which the university has been known. UMass opened in 1867 as Massachusetts Agricultural College; in 1931, the name was changed to Massachusetts State College; and in 1947 the name changed again, this time for good, to the University of Massachusetts at Amherst. While UMass has approximately 25,000 undergraduate and graduate students today, it was only recently that the university became so large. As late as 1961, it had only 10,000 students. However, in the late 1960s and early 1970s the campus grew by nearly 2,000 students per year. With this growth came high-rise dormitories and a high-rise library that completely altered the face of the UMass campus. At the same time, UMass became known as "zoo mass" due to accounts of the many wild parties thrown on campus. Over the past twenty-plus years, the university has exerted greater control over the nightlife of its student body. However, the stigma of "party school" still stays with UMass in comparison to its more cerebral liberal arts neighbors.

Today, UMass is the largest public research campus in New England, offering ninety-two bachelor's degree programs, seventy-two master's degree programs, and fifty-one doctoral programs. The university's polymer science and engineering department is the top-ranked program in the country. In addition, UMass has numerous nationally recognized programs including computer science, education, and sport management. Notable UMass faculty include Pulitzer Prize winners Madeline Blais (journalism) and James Tate (English), novelist John Edgar Wideman, and economists Sam Bowles and William Shepherd. Notable alumni of UMass include actor Bill Cosby, singer Natalie Cole, Nobel Prize winner Russell Hulse, and Jack Welch, CEO of General Electric.

UMass Athletics

Men's basketball is not the only athletic program that is successful at UMass. Ten of the twenty-nine sports sponsored by the Athletic Department earned part of their regular season or conference championships during the 1996–97 academic year. UMass teams that competed in postseason play during 1996–97 included men's water polo (which went to the Final Four), women's softball (which went to the College World Series), and women's crew (which finished second in the country).

However, UMass competes in football at the Division I-AA level, which is one level below the premier play of Division I football. Based on geographic location and the competitive nature of its entire athletic program, UMass could align with the highly visible Big East Conference or Atlantic Coast Conference. However, both of these conferences require its members to play Division I-A football. Thus, such alliances with premier collegiate athletic conferences are impossible. As a result, the University of Massachusetts competes in the Atlantic 10 Conference, which crowns champions in twenty-one sports every season. The Atlantic 10, like many other conferences, has recently undergone significant expansion. (Table 16.4 provides a listing of the Atlantic 10 Conference members.) In addition to UMass, Rhode Island, Temple, St. Joseph's, and Xavier competed in the 1997 NCAA men's basketball tournament. In 1997, the Atlantic 10 had a football champion for the first time. The ice hockey team participates in the Hockey East Conference, one of three premier collegiate ice hockey conferences in the country.

Table 16.4 Atlantic 10 conference members

East Division	West Division
Fordham	Dayton
UMass	Duquesne
Rhode Island	George Washington
St. Bonaventure	La Salle
St. Joseph's	Virginia Tech
Temple	Xavier

An Historical Look at UMass Basketball[4]

Competition in intercollegiate basketball first became part of the athletic program at Massachusetts Agricultural College in 1901–02, when the team won five games and lost three. From that point on, there were only several pockets of noticeable success. In fact prior to the 1991–92 season, UMass had only appeared in the NCAA tournament one other time, after the 1961–62 season. The only other noticeable era of prominence for UMass basketball was during the reign of head coach Jack Leaman, who coached UMass from 1966 until 1979. In winning better than 60% of his games during those thirteen years, UMass developed a regional reputation as a basketball power. During its first ten years under Leaman, UMass won or shared the Yankee Conference title in eight of those years (Dobrow, 1996). However, winning the title did not guarantee a berth in the NCAA tournament. Instead, UMass appeared in the National Invitation Tournament (NIT) three times. While today the NIT is a tournament for teams not selected for the NCAA tournament, it was more prestigious during Leaman's era. In fact, some teams that were selected to play in the NCAA tournament chose to play instead in the NIT at Madison Square Garden in New York City.

Perhaps the peak of the Leaman era were the two seasons when Julius Erving played forward for the Minutemen. Erving was not a highly-sought-after recruit, playing his high school basketball for Roosevelt High in New York. However, after he grew nearly four inches during his freshman year, Erving became a sensation on the basketball floor. During his sophomore and junior seasons (1969–70 and 1970–71) Erving electrified the Curry Hicks Cage, the 4,200 seat stadium where UMass played its games. The future NBA hall-of-famer played to sellout crowds both years. In fact, students showed up four hours before games in cold winter weather to assure themselves a seat. However, despite the presence of Erving and the successful seasons under Leaman, UMass failed to gain much national notoriety. Part of this was due to the overall lack of notoriety for college basketball in general (its popularity began in 1979). The boom in sports programming was also yet to occur. For example, ESPN was not created until 1978. *The Boston Globe* rarely sent reporters two hours west to cover UMass games.

Following the Leaman years, UMass basketball hit rock bottom. During Leaman's final season (1978–79) UMass won only five of its twenty-seven games in the recently formed Eastern Eight Conference. From 1979 to 1988, the Minutemen suffered through ten consecutive

---

[4]The historical summary of UMass basketball incorporates accounts provided by Marty Dobrow (1996) in *Going Bigtime* and John Calipari and Dick Weiss (1996) in *Refuse to Lose*. In addition, supporting information was obtained from the UMass Athletic Department in their *1995–96 Annual Report* and *1996–97 Men's Basketball Media Guide*.

losing seasons and three head coaches. Following the 1987–88 season, UMass completed a ten-year stretch that was better than only eight of the 267 Division I men's basketball teams in America. The 1980-81 Minutemen won only three of twenty-eight games. The once-loud Curry Hicks Cage was empty for UMass games as no one, not even fans of the team in the 1970s, had the patience to watch such a dismal performance.

In 1988, the University of Massachusetts committed to improving the performance of its men's basketball team. It formed a search committee to find a new head coach, a coach that could turn around the fortunes of UMass basketball. An integral member of that search committee was a former UMass player, who also happened to be a nationally recognized head coach at the University of Kentucky, Rick Pitino. The committee and Pitino convinced twenty-nine-year-old John Calipari to take the head coaching position at the University of Massachusetts. He was paid $63,000 and received no guarantees of million-dollar shoe contracts. Although the initial $63,000 salary now represents Calipari's weekly earnings (from a $3 million contract), it represented the standard pay for a men's basketball coach in the Atlantic 10. The press conference to announce Calipari as UMass' fourth coach in the last ten years received little attention. This was because no one could predict what would happen in Amherst over the next eight years.

Although John Calipari was only an average basketball player, he had always been charismatic. Calipari's salesmanship was evident early, as he was elected president of his senior class at Moon Township High School. A marketing degree while playing basketball at Clarion State honed Calipari's ability to sell himself and whatever he was involved with. When Calipari interviewed for the UMass job, he brought written materials to leave behind with the committee and had already viewed film of UMass in preparation for the interview. Such preparation and sales ability enabled John Calipari to completely rebuild the UMass basketball program. However, in 1988 he had a long way to go.

First of all, the team played in the Curry Hicks Cage, a fifty-eight-year-old, 4,300-seat arena that became both hot and loud when it was sold out. When Calipari arrived at UMass to begin his new job, he found himself sharing office space in the Boyden Building with the women's basketball program. During games, the team sat on old folding chairs borrowed from the Biology Department. Only 1,100 people watched John Calipari coach his first game, a 84–61 triumph over Southern Connecticut. In addition, Calipari did not have high school All-Americans on his roster. With his inherited players, Calipari guided the Minutemen to a record of ten wins and eighteen losses during the 1988–89 season. To make matters worse, three of his players were arrested for burglary in the middle of the season. Through it all, Calipari remained an enthusiastic promoter. He spearheaded the first

UMass basketball banquet. Approximately thirty people attended the event, held at the Depot Restaurant in nearby Northampton (only ten of the people in attendance were not somehow closely involved with the UMass basketball team). Calipari's emotional demeanor on the sidelines, however, was enough to instill hope. For the 1989–90 home opener, 3,666 watched UMass lose to American International College, a team that competed in Division II of the NCAA, one rung below Division I. Although UMass improved to seventeen wins and fourteen losses that season, it was not enough to secure an invitation to postseason play.

At the same time, Calipari was working with the UMass administration and Athletic Department to improve the basketball program at UMass. A budget increase was obtained that allowed Calipari and his coaching staff to recruit high school players from a broader geographic area. Calipari knew that he had to increase the area from which UMass recruited. In particular, Calipari saw the recruitment of in-state players as essential to improving media coverage, particularly in the Boston area. Such efforts began to reap dividends, as good players began to attend UMass. Calipari also worked hard to increase the awareness and fan base for UMass basketball. Prior to the 1989–90 season he held practices open to the public all over western Massachusetts. Along these lines, Calipari was very concerned with the image of his team. Upon taking the position, he looked at game films and developed an intense dislike for the team's uniforms, which said "Massachusetts" on the chest. People had always referred to the University of Massachusetts as "UMass," so Calipari shortened the lettering and redesigned the team logo. The redesign was specific to basketball, so neither the Athletic Department nor the University immediately adopted the logo change.

The 1990–91 season was a breakthrough year for Calipari and the Minutemen. The team improved to twenty and thirteen and appeared in postseason play (albeit the now second-rate NIT) for the first time in nearly twenty years. Calipari's promotional efforts had reaped dividends. Near-capacity crowds watched UMass throughout the 90–91 season. In fact, the team averaged 95% capacity for its home games. With the increased attendance came an increased entertainment factor. Games had become fun to attend, and people were becoming very interested in UMass basketball. Also in 1991, ground was broken on the new Mullins Center, a state-of-the-art basketball/hockey arena that would seat nearly 9,500 people for basketball games. It would house the men's basketball program (in addition to the women's basketball program and men's ice hockey team), but most important, it was a place that UMass could use in recruiting nationally acclaimed high school basketball players.

The momentum continued and Calipari kept being aggressive. He knew that media exposure was crucial to UMass becoming well recognized. In radio contract negotiations, Calipari insisted that a Boston radio station be included in the UMass Basketball Network, the network of radio stations that broadcasted UMass games. Although this was not a profitable move, Calipari knew that it was crucial to recruiting that UMass obtain exposure in the Boston market. Calipari also sought national television coverage. Prior to the 1991–92 season, he convinced ESPN to broadcast a UMass game, thus giving it much-needed exposure. But ESPN only agreed to do so if UMass would play at 12 midnight on a Saturday night. Calipari turned it into a wonderful campus-wide event. Capitalizing on the popularity of the event, prior to the 1992–93 season UMass held its first "Midnight Madness," a 12-A.M. scrimmage on the first official day of practice.

The 1991–92 season marked UMass' return to the NCAA tournament for the first time since 1962. It was the first of six consecutive appearances by UMass in the prestigious postseason tournament. In addition, the team posted thirty wins against only five losses and began to draw national attention. With this attention, UMass was able to continually increase the caliber of player it was able to recruit. When Lou Roe announced he planned to attend UMass in 1992, it marked the first time UMass successfully recruited a player ranked among the top forty players nationwide. Then, in 1993, Marcus Camby announced his intention to attend UMass. In addition, Calipari announced they had signed a high school player from the Boston area, Carmelo Travieso.

Meanwhile, Calipari continued to relentlessly promote UMass basketball. He regularly honored the season ticket holders and students by calling them the "best fans in college basketball." In addition, he instilled a motto that would become known nationwide—"Refuse to lose." First used in 1993 to motivate the team, Calipari eventually had applied for a trademark with the federal government and placed the slogan on the team's warm-up suits. It came to embody the spirit of UMass basketball. In addition, Calipari never missed an opportunity to express his gratitude for fan support. He regularly visited the student dorms in an effort to maintain enthusiasm. When students waited outside of the Curry Hicks Cage for game tickets, Calipari ordered pizza for them to enjoy while they waited. In an effort to help the greater university, Calipari donated money to the library, which created the "John and Ellen Calipari Library Instruction Room," named for Calipari and his wife.

The Fruits of Success

From 1993 to 1996, the Minutemen certainly refused to lose, compiling an amazing ninety-two and fourteen record over three seasons, culminating in the momentous 1995–96 campaign. On the shoulders of the basketball program, UMass and its Athletic Department reaped many benefits. The Mullins Center, which opened in 1993, regularly sold out its 9,493 seats (see Table 16.5 for a reporting of men's basketball attendance from 1989 to 1996). Such success helped recruiting even more. Calipari's 1995–96 recruiting class yielded several acclaimed high school players. Included in this mix were two players from the Boston area, Mike Babul and Monty Mack.

The demand for tickets at the Mullins Center was such that the UMass Athletic Department began requiring people to make donations of at least $100 in order to be eligible to purchase season tickets. While this greatly enhanced the revenue generated by the UMass Athletic Fund (UMAF), it angered some fans loyal to the program prior to its ascension. Many of these fans were forced to accept downgrades in their seat locations. In some cases, loyal fans actually were denied season tickets because they had not generated enough priority points, the donation-driven seat assignment index.

The UMAF was created in 1992 to oversee donations to the fundraising arm of the Athletic Department. By 1996, the UMass Athletic Fund raised more than $1.25 million from over 3,000 different donors. However, it is estimated that two-thirds of all donations were linked to the priority points system established to allot tickets based on donations to the Athletic Department. Table 16.6 presents the development of the UMAF from 1992 to 1996. In addition, auxiliary fundraising events had been successfully implemented. Following the 1995–96 season, 1,200 people paid $50 apiece to attend the team's awards banquet, which was also televised locally. Calipari had started generating auxiliary revenues through T-shirt sales, and upon his departure he had contracts for weekly television and radio shows, highly successful summer basketball camps, and a lucrative shoe contract. Furthermore, the success of the UMass team resulted in significant national television

Table 16.5 Attendance at UMass basketball games, 1989–1996

Year	Average Attendance
1989–90	3,715
1990–91	4,019
1991–92	4,351
1992–93	7,079*
1993–94	9,493
1995–96	9,493

*The 1992–93 season was split between the Curry Hicks Cage (capacity 4,351) and the Mullins Center (capacity 9,493).
Source: UMass Athletic Department 1995–96 Annual Report.

Table 16.6 UMass athletic fund performance, 1992–1996

Year	# of Donors	$ Raised
1992	1,331	256,258
1993	1,763	374,794
1994	2,265	672,508
1995	2,697	1,012,143
1996	3,072	1,262,953

Source: UMass Athletic Department 1995–96 Annual Report.

exposure. The Minutemen appeared on ESPN eleven times during the 1995–96 season and ten times during the 1996–97 season. This was certainly a far cry from Calipari's begging for coverage prior to the 1991–92 season.

In addition to individual donors, corporations were also interested in being involved with UMass athletics. Twenty sponsors had signed agreements with UMass athletics amounting to more than $1.3 million. In addition, prior to the 1996–97 season, Nike became the official supplier of shoes and apparel for several UMass athletic teams, an agreement that involved hundreds of pieces of clothing and footwear for the UMass athletic teams. Along with these corporate sponsorship agreements came in-game promotions tied to promoting selected sponsors. USAir, for example, sponsored a long-distance shootout at half time where a randomly selected fan attempted to win a free airline ticket to somewhere in the United States. The rise in popularity afforded UMass the ability to increase the professionalism of its basketball program. The team now enjoyed first-class treatment—office furniture, videotape equipment, travel accommodations. The Athletic Department began publishing an annual report on the revenues generated by UMass athletics, much of this from basketball.

UMass-logoed merchandise was in demand nationwide. Prior to Calipari's arrival the Athletic Department did not have a licensing program, but now UMass was one of the top-selling collegiate logos nationwide. UMass merchandise could be found on people as far away as Zimbabwe. The UMass name was now recognizable throughout the world. Such recognition appears to have benefited the University of Massachusetts as a whole. Concurrent with the rise of UMass basketball, prospective student interest in UMass also rose. Over the last five years the number of applications to UMass had increased 29%. In addition, and perhaps more importantly, applications from out-of-state students, who pay much higher tuition than students from Massachusetts, had increased 50%. In an age of declining enrollments and financial crises at many colleges and universities nationwide, such increases were of great comfort to UMass.

The Present

Unfortunately, though, Chandra Goldberg knew that it would be very difficult for the men's basketball team to maintain its incredible success rate. Although the prospects for the 1997–98 season were positive, Goldberg knew how inconsistent the sport product could be. The program was still trying to put the Marcus Camby scandal behind it. However, that seemed impossible. Only recently, the *Boston Globe* had run an article suggesting Camby had received approximately $40,000 in gifts and cash from a different agent while a student at UMass. This left open the possibility that more investigation might be necessary. Camby had further tarnished his image during the summer of 1997 when he was arrested for possession of marijuana in his hometown, nearby Hartford, Connecticut.

In addition, given the recent success, the Athletic Department was now planning a number of capital improvements. In order to make these improvements possible, existing revenue streams must not only be increased but new ones must be found. Goldberg was hoping for some help in generating revenues from women's basketball, football, and men's ice hockey, as these were the other sports for which UMass sold tickets. (Table 16.7 presents the growth of ticket sales for those three teams over the past five years.) Men's basketball had no more seats to sell. Approximately 4,000 tickets for every game were allotted to students. Because they paid an "activity fee" as part of their fees for attending the university, these tickets were free. As a result, the only ways to increase revenues through basketball ticket sales was to in-

Table 16.7 UMass men's ice hockey and football average attendance, 1989–1996

Year	Men's Ice Hockey	Football
1989–90	N/A	6,744
1990–91	N/A	6,209
1991–92	N/A	8,214
1992–93	N/A	6,940
1993–94	2,504	8,304
1994–95	3,454	10,138
1995–96	3,499	7,901

Source: UMass Athletic Department 1995–96 Annual Report.

crease ticket prices or to increase the required donation to the UMAF. As Goldberg looked at the 1997–98 home schedule, she knew it was an unattractive schedule (see Table 16.8 for the 1997–98 UMass men's basketball schedule). Again, UMass was playing most of its marquis games at neutral sites. For example, the Minutemen were scheduled to play the University of Connecticut at the Hartford Civic Center and

Table 16.8 1997–98 University of Massachusetts men's basketball schedule

Date	Opponent	TV
11/7/97	**Converse All-Stars (Exhibition)**	
11/15	**Marathon Oil (Exhibition)**	
11/22	at Fresno State	ESPN
11/26–29	Great Alaska Shootout at Anchorage, Alaska	
12/2	**College of Charleston**	
12/6	**Marshall**	
12/10	at Kansas	ESPN
12/14	Boston College at the Fleet Center in Boston	ESPN2
12/20	Colorado at Las Vegas	ESPN2
12/23	Connecticut at the Hartford Civic Center	ESPN
12/27	Cincinnati at Gund Arena in Cleveland	ESPN2
1/3/98	at St. Joseph's	
1/6	at Fordham	
1/10	**George Washington**	
1/15	UNC Charlotte at Providence Civic Center	ESPN
1/17	**Fordham**	
1/19	**St. Bonaventure**	
1/22	at Davidson	
1/24	at Virginia Tech	
1/29	at Rhode Island	ESPN
2/1	**Dayton**	
2/3	**Temple**	ESPN2
2/8	at Xavier	ABC
2/10	at Duquesne	
2/14	**La Salle**	
2/18	**Rhode Island**	
2/21	**St. Joseph's**	ESPN
2/24	at St. Bonaventure	
3/1	at Temple	
3/4–7	Atlantic 10 Tournament at Philadelphia	

Bold typeface denotes a home game at the Mullins Center.

the University of Cincinnati in Cleveland. By playing marquis games at larger, neutral site arenas, UMass received an appearance fee and a share of the ticket sales. Through these games, the basketball team generated more revenue than it did from a typical home game in Amherst.

But the 1997–98 season did hold promise. Three starters were returning from the 1996–97 team—center Lari Ketner (projected to be an NBA first-round pick), forward Tyrone Weeks, and guard Charlton Clarke. Although none of the three was predicted to be an All-American, all three had the potential to be all-conference selections. The problem rested on the inexperience of the other two starters. Yet to be identified, Goldberg knew that both would be relatively inexperienced and unheard of freshmen or sophomores. Poor performance from these newcomers could greatly detract from the success realized by the 1997–98 Minutemen.

Further, Coach James "Bruiser" Flint appeared to lack the promotional skills of his predecessor. Goldberg longed for the days that she struggled to monitor the speaking engagements and promotional efforts started by John Calipari. Flint was very personable one-on-one, but he lacked Calipari's ability to instantly energize a large crowd. However, Goldberg knew Flint was young and energetic and, most importantly, had the utmost concern for the student-athletes who played for him.

Ultimately, Goldberg knew some sort of long-term strategic vision was needed. Numerous questions needed to be answered. Most important, what was the long-term vision for the identity of UMass basketball? Within the vision, what activities could be undertaken to enhance the brand equity of UMass basketball both immediately and over the long term? As she boarded the elevator for the ride to the lower level and the parking lot, Goldberg was unsure where to begin.

17

Miami University—The Redskins Name Controversy

Thomas C. Boyd and David W. Rosenthal

Introduction

In September 1996 the Miami University board of trustees met to deliberate over whether the University's nickname should be changed. Since 1928 the university had been known as the "Redskins." However, several factors had recently converged to necessitate careful consideration of a change. It was the board's responsibility to decide whether to keep the Redskin nickname or change it.

The decision was important because of the depth of emotion on both sides of the issue. The supporters of the Redskin name defended its use vehemently. This group represented many alumni and long-time friends of the school, who were also some of the university's largest contributors. As word of the pending decision spread, visible evidence of support for retaining the Redskin name appeared around the campus. Bumper stickers, T-shirts, and letters to the editor espoused phrases such as "Redskin 'til I die." Supporters of the name were angered over the board of trustees' apparent willingness to even consider pressure from outside groups who, they believed, had little understanding of the traditions or significance of the Redskin name.

Those who supported changing the nickname thought that the term *Redskin* was derogatory and inappropriate for use by a university. Further, they believed that the term was racist and did not show proper respect for Native Americans. Those within the university community who supported a change also believed that the image of the university was hurt by the use of "Redskin" because it projected an image of the school as "out of touch," and insensitive to minorities. This latter concern was important because the school had been trying to increase its minority enrollment.

The current controversy followed an attempted compromise in 1993 by the then University President, Paul Risser. At that time the university community was engaged in a long and sometimes contentious debate over whether to drop the Redskin nickname. In December 1993, President Risser proposed a compromise: to allow the continued use of the Redskins name while setting the stage for gradual change. The compromise was that all teams and publications currently using the nickname could continue its official use. All other organizations and publications of the university not currently using the nickname would adopt "Miami Tribe" as the nickname of athletic teams. Following the board of trustees meeting at which the compromise measure was approved, Joseph Marcum, board chairman, said the decision allowed for change without causing deeper division between both sides. He said, "I think the term will eventually phase out, but instead of a jolt, it will be more of an evolutionary process." The Native-American Miami Tribe of Oklahoma supported the compromise.

The compromise measure itself was controversial. The board of trustees voted to accept President Paul Risser's recommendation by 4–3 with one abstention, one absent. Sister Jean Patrice Harrington said, regarding the vote, "I think that it was the only decision that could possibly be made at this time without bringing about further division within the academic community and all the constituencies with whom Miami works."

Harold Paul, trustee from Strongsville, Ohio, voted against the proposal, and said that he thought Risser's plan would satisfy no one. "I just felt we needed to make a decision. If the connotation Redskins is offensive and those people who are offended protest, then I feel that we have to seriously consider making a change."

In the years following the compromise decision little changed. Although the university did what it could to promote the use of "Miami Tribe," few adopted the new name and "Redskins" continued in common usage. The Indian tribe had formally supported the use of the name and its logo since 1972 and had renewed its support in 1991 (Exhibit 17.1). Then, in July 1996 the Miami tribe withdrew its support for the use of Redskin, reopening the controversy. The action by the Miami tribe constituted a significant change in position (Exhibit 17.2).

Background

Miami University was founded in 1809 and was the seventh-oldest state-assisted university in the United States. Frequently referred to as a "public ivy," Miami was known primarily for its excellent undergraduate teaching. Its emphasis on liberal education for all undergraduates was intended to encourage problem solving and critical thinking, preparing students for the ever-changing work environment. Miami's

Exhibit 17.1 1972 Resolution of Miami tribe supporting use of "Redskins" by Miami University Proclamation

WHEREAS: We, the elected leaders of the 1,500 member tribe of Miami Indians are meeting this day in solemn council in the state of Oklahoma on the lands bequeathed to the Miamis by treaty with the government of the United States for "as long as the wind shall blow." and:

WHEREAS: In the territory of what is now Ohio, Indiana, Illinois, and Michigan our ancestors once lived in peace among the forests and long waters under the hand of the Great Spirit, and:

WHEREAS: At Oxford, Ohio where there once stood a village of the Miamis, there stands today a University bearing the name Miami and bestowing upon its young athletes the name Miami Redskins, and;

WHEREAS: It is our counsel that the name Redskins is a revered and honored name in the eyes and hearts of the people of Miami University, and that it signifies to them as to us the qualities of courage, self-discipline, respect, kindness, honesty, and love exemplified by generations of young athletes,

THEREFORE Know all peoples, that we of Miami blood are proud to have the name Miami Redskin carried with honor by the athletic representation of Miami University on the playing fields of Mid-America and in the arena of the world in International Olympic competition.

We, the Miami Redskins of Indian blood, and our namesake, the Miami University Redskins, have a mutual and cherished heritage. May it be blessed by Moneto as long as the wind shall blow.

main campus, in Oxford, Ohio, had an enrollment of about 16,000 students.

Miami had recently received a significant amount of favorable publicity related to a number of national rankings. In 1995, *U.S. News and World Report* ranked Miami as the eighth best undergraduate teaching institution in the United States. It was also named a best buy in the *Fiske Guide to Colleges* in 1996, one of only twenty public institutions listed. As a result, in 1996, 11,600 prospective freshmen applied for admission to the school.

Miami University was named for the Native-American Miami tribe that had once inhabited the rolling hills of the Ohio Valley where the school is located. Over the years, the University and tribal elders maintained a close and cordial relationship, in which university officials consistently stressed the school's desire to honor the Miami tribe and its history. The university logo was a realistic Indian head in front of the university's block M (Figure 17.1).

Although seldom considered a national power in a major sport, Miami athletics had an interesting history. Known as the "Cradle of Coaches," Miami had been the one-time home to many top college and professional football coaches. John Pont, Woody Hayes, Bo Schembechler, Ara Parsegian, and Weeb Ewbank were among those who had coached and/

Exhibit 17.2 1996 resolution of Miami tribe withdrawing support for the use of Redskins by Miami University Resolution

Whereas: The Miami Tribe of Oklahoma is a federally recognized Indian Tribe organized under the Oklahoma Indian Welfare Act of 1936, with a Constitution and By-Laws approved by the U.S. Secretary of the Interior on February, 22, 1996, and

Whereas: In the territory of what is now Ohio, Indiana, Illinois, and Michigan our ancestors once lived in peace among the forests and long waters under the hand of the Great Spirit; and

Whereas: At Oxford, Ohio, where there once stood a village of the Miamis, there stands today a University bearing the name Miami; and

Whereas: In 1972, the Miami Tribe of Oklahoma acceded to the request of Miami University to bestow upon its young student athletes the nickname Miami Redskins; and

Whereas: The bonds of friendship and shared heritage between Miami University and the Miami Tribe of Oklahoma have grown stronger over the last twenty-five years; and

Whereas: Miami University and the Miami Tribe of Oklahoma have worked together harmoniously to make sure that the nickname Miami Redskins be used to signify the qualities of courage, self-discipline, respect, kindness, honesty, and love by generations of young student athletes; and

Whereas: We realize that society changes, and that what was intended to be a tribute to both Miami University, and to the Miami Tribe of Oklahoma, is no longer perceived as positive by some members of the Miami Tribe of Oklahoma, Miami University, and society at large; and

THEREFORE, BE IT RESOLVED, that the Miami Tribe of Oklahoma can no longer support the use of the nickname Redskins and suggest that the Board of Trustees of Miami University discontinue the use of Redskins or other Indian related names, in connection with its athletic teams, effective with the end of the 1996–97 academic school year.

BE IT FURTHER RESOLVED, that the Miami Tribe of Oklahoma does not associate the athletic team nickname of Redskins with Miami's logo, exemplified by the artist's portrait of an Indian Chief. The Miami Tribe therefore urges Miami University to continue use of the respectful and dignified portrayal of the Indian Chief as its logo and as a reminder to all of the shared heritage of Miami University and the Miami Tribe of Oklahoma; and

BE IT FURTHER RESOLVED, that the Miami Tribe of Oklahoma stands ready to assist the University and to offer its counsel, as the University begins the debate on an appropriate nickname for its athletic teams; and

THEREFORE, know all peoples that we of Miami blood are proud of our relationship with our namesake, Miami University, and of our mutual and cherished heritage and that we hope to continue to strengthen this relationship for our mutual benefits. May this relationship be blessed by the Creator as long as the winds shall blow.

Figure 17.1   The Miami University logo in September 1996

or played at Miami. The school currently had a reputation as a "giant killer" that commonly created major upsets in NCAA Division 1A. For example, in 1995 the school upset Arizona (a fourth seed) in the first round of the NCAA basketball tournament and then took Virginia to overtime in the second round. Also that year, Miami's football team was the only team to defeat eventual Big Ten champion Northwestern in the regular season. Recently, however, attendance at Miami home football games had dropped to levels that potentially put its Division 1A status in question.

Despite a number of recent successes, Miami traditionally had trouble competing with larger schools in the region for fans. Miami teams were always in the shadow of Notre Dame, Ohio State, and Michigan, and played in the less-competitive Mid-American Conference. Thus, drawing media and fan support outside the university community was difficult. Even at the school, Miami athletic officials were constantly concerned with how to increase attendance at football and basketball games. Another factor that affected attendance was the relative isolation of the campus, which was about a one-hour drive from Cincinnati or Dayton and almost two hours from Indianapolis. The bucolic setting, usually a factor seen as an asset, was a liability when competing for fans on a fall afternoon.

At the time of the board's decision, Miami was working hard to increase interest in and support of its athletic programs. It was the consensus of the athletic administration that it needed to inject some life into the game experience for fans and improve Miami's image both regionally and nationally. Also at this time the school's admissions office was working hard to improve minority enrollments, currently at about 3% of the student body. Minority recruiting was made harder by the image of the school as a place for upper-middle-class whites and also by the rural location.

The Miami Tribe

The Miami tribe had its beginnings with people living on the shores of the Great Lakes, the woodlands of southern Indiana, and southwestern Ohio. At one time the tribe controlled a large inland empire. The Miamis were part of the Algonquin race. Their golden age was in the sixteenth century. During the seventeenth century, other Indian tribes began to challenge them and moved onto parts of their land. One tribe was the fierce Shawnees, who established settlements in southwestern Ohio prior to the beginning of white settlement. Eventually, the Miamis were confined to an area along the Mississinewa River, a tributary to the Wabash in Indiana.

The word *Indian* came from the same root as *Hindoo,* the native name of the Indus meaning *water.* The Persians interpreted the word as *Hindu,* the Greeks made it *Indos,* and the Romans, *Indus,* and it passed into the European languages. Columbus, thinking he had arrived not in a new world but in India, called the natives *Indios,* which evolved into *Indians.*

The word *Miami* referred to a group of Indians who were a part of the Illinois division of the Algonquin family. In the group were more than eighty tribes with their own names, and these all eventually associated themselves with six bands. Most who became Miamis called themselves "Twightwees," meaning "cry of the crane"; others being known as "Oumamik," "people of the peninsula." According to one version of the story, these bands became so intermingled that the French converted their names to one—"Miami"—and by the 1740s, these bands accepted a chief of all the Miamis. The word meant "all friends" and was of European origin, not a native word. The United States federal government uprooted the tribe twice in the 1800s, eventually in 1846 moving them to northeastern Oklahoma. In 1996 about 1500 individuals with some Miami ancestry survived, the last full-blooded Miami having died about sixty years before.

Miami University Historical Context

1809	Miami University was chartered by the Ohio Legislature and named in honor of the Miami tribe, which gave up rights to most of its Ohio homeland in the 1795 *Treaty of Greenville.*
Prior to 1928	Miami's intercollegiate athletic teams were called "The Miami Boys," "The Big Reds," or "The Red and Whites." The university's colors of red and white had nothing to do with Indian heritage. Competing campus literary societies founded in 1825 adopted the colors, one picking red and the other white.
1928	Miami Publicity Director R.J. McGinnis coined the term *Redskins* for athletic teams; the Varsity M Club became *Tribe Miami.*
1931	*Redskin* first appeared in the school yearbook in reference to athletic teams.
1940s	Student snack bar became the Redskin Reservation, also known as "The Res."
1950s	Students dressed as Indians began to appear with the marching band.
1960s	The marching band's Indian mascot gave way to Hiawabop, a student usually dressed as a Plains Indian in a war bonnet and painted face.
Late 1960s	A visit to the Miami campus by Miami Chief Forest Olds resulted in a formal relationship between the Miami Tribe of Oklahoma and the university.
1972	Miami President Phillip Shriver appointed a task force to examine the use of Indian symbols; the Miami tribe passed a resolution of support for a relationship with the university (Exhibit 17.1).
Mid-1980s	Hiawabop was retired in favor of Chief Miami, whose regalia were provided by the tribe; students who appeared in the role were required to learn authentic Indian dances. During this time, a liason between the tribe and the University was established.
1984	Tom-O-Hawk, a student dressed as a comical red bird, began entertaining at athletic events.
1988	The Business Committee of the Miami Tribe of Oklahoma released a resolution reaffirming their 1972 resolution.
Spring 1993	Newly appointed President Paul Risser announced a process to study the use of the term Redskins; University Senate passed a resolution recommending the nickname be discontinued.
Nov. 1993	President Rissler listened to nearly 70 individuals at a Redskin Forum on the campus. About 200 attended the meeting.

Dec. 1993	President Risser made the recommendation that all Miami University teams and publications currently using the nickname Redskins should continue to do so and that all other university-sponsored publications and organizations were to adopt the nickname Miami Tribe.
Dec. 3, 1993	The Miami Tribe of Oklahoma released a letter stating in part: "The Miami Tribe supports the recommendations as set forth by President Paul Risser . . . We would be pleased with the use of the term 'Miami Tribe'."
Dec. 10–11	The board of trustees approved President Risser's decision to allow groups currently using Redskins to continue to do so and for all other groups to use Miami Tribe.
July 1996	The Miami Tribe of Oklahoma adopted a resolution saying it could no longer support Redskins as Miami University's athletic nickname. (Exhibit 17.2)

Related Issues

Historically, Miami University's official position on the use of "Redskin" had been that the name honored the Miami tribe, for which the school was named, and that the nickname was used with the approval of tribal elders. Further, the nickname was symbolic of a long relationship of mutual respect between the university and the tribe. A standing commission to study the relationship between the tribe and the university, headed by the university vice-president for student affairs exemplified the importance and consideration accorded to this relationship. In the past, when the issue arose, the school consistently took the position that as long as the Miami tribe supported the use of "Redskin" the university should not change its nickname.

In July 1996 the Miami tribe changed its position on the use of "Redskins" and withdrew its support of the nickname. Opponents alleged, and it was widely believed, that university officials with a personal political agenda had coerced the tribe, a charge the university vehemently denied and for which no evidence was ever produced. The tribe stated its decision was based on the changing priorities and attitudes of society.

In recent years a number of universities and teams had updated their nicknames and/or symbols, recognizing how old names could be offensive to certain parties or cultures. These changes removed ethnic references, sex biases, and images perceived to glorify war or killing. In contrast, a number of groups had chosen not to change their names or symbols. In 1991, Eastern Michigan University had changed its name from "Hurons" to "Eagles". The school had experienced a drop in gift money in the short term but had quickly returned to normal. (A summary of nickname and/or symbol status is presented in Tables 17.1 and 17.2.)

The social environment in which the board of trustees was to make its decision was unsettled. Many people believed that no matter the intent, nicknames, that could be perceived to reflect derogatory attitudes about sex, race, culture, or any group characteristic were unacceptable. In addition, students complained increasingly that team mascots and nicknames were not representative of the student body. However, the changes brought about by groups who opposed the use of certain names had resulted in a backlash by those who believed that tradition and honor were being sacrificed to a sense of political correctness that had gone too far.

The Redskin name and images had played an important role in student life at the university for over sixty years. For almost all alumni

Table 17.1 Schools and organizations that have changed nicknames or logos

Organization	Old Name/Logo	New Name/Logo	Reason
Alabama-Birmingham	Blazers-Nordic	Blazers-Dragon	Remove ethnic/gender reference
Arkansas State	Indians-Indian figure	Indians-ASU with headdress	Remove Indian figure
Lehigh University	Engineers	Mountain Hawks	Gender neutral
Stanford University	Indians	Cardinal	Remove Indian reference
Marquette University	Warriors	Golden Eagles	Remove Warlike/Gender reference
Eastern Michigan	Hurons-Indian tribe	Eagles	Remove Indian reference
St. Johns	Redmen	Red Storm	Remove Indian reference
SUNY Stony Brook	Patriots	SeaWolves	Remove Warlike/Gender reference
Tennessee-Chattanooga	Moccasins (Indian)	Mocs (Mockingbird)	Remove Indian reference, use state bird
U. of Mississippi	Rebels-Confederate flag	Rebels/No flag allowed	Remove Civil War/racial/political reference
Bradley University	Braves-Indian	Bobcats	Remove Indian reference
Rutgers	Scarlet Knights-male knight	Scarlet Knights-gender neutral	Remove gender reference

Table 17.2 Schools and organizations that have not changed nicknames or logos

Organization	Nickname	Logo
University of Nevada-Las Vegas	Hey Reb	Cartoon Rebel
U. of Massachusetts-Amherst	Minutemen	Minuteman
Florida State University	Seminoles	Indian Head
Washington (Football)	Redskins	Indian Head
Cleveland (Baseball)	Indians	Chief Wahoo
Kansas City (Football)	Chiefs	Arrowhead
Atlanta (Baseball)	Braves	Tomahawk

and current students, the nickname, mascot, and images symbolized university life, pride, excellence, and tradition. The Redskin mascot was linked to student life in many ways.

> At the start of every home football game, the Redskin mascot entered the football stadium on a horse at full gallop. The mascot wore authentic regalia designed by chiefs of the Miami tribe.
>
> The Redskin symbol, Chief Miami, performed traditional dances at many athletic events.
>
> A group of avid student fans came to athletic events wearing red and white face paint and feathers in their hair; they were called the "featherheads."
>
> The Indian-head logo appeared on the football stadium, on center court of the basketball arena, at the center of the ice arena, and at most other sports venues.
>
> University apparel, particularly athletic apparel, made heavy use of the Indian-head logo.
>
> The student union was call the "Res" (short for reservation) by students and faculty.
>
> The union housed a lounge with historic displays of Miami Indians, honoring the links between the university and the tribe.
>
> A portrait of a Miami Indian by the famous artist John Ruthven proudly adorned the homes or offices of many alumni and faculty. The Miami tribe had been consulted in the commissioning of this "official portrait." (Miami's Indian-head logo was a stylized version of this portrait.)

A number of prominent alumni, among them board of trustees member William Gunlock had come out in vehement opposition to any change. Some had also threatened to withhold donations and gifts if a change were made. According to Chris Wyrick, head of athletic fundraising, many of the people most likely to oppose the change were the biggest givers to athletics. Others opposed to the change included many current students, student-athletes, coaches, faculty, staff, and fans. Many expressed the belief that a change was simply bowing to pressures brought to bear by a small, vocal minority who were pushing a political agenda and who cared nothing for the school's traditions. "Alternative" merchandise and apparel had already appeared around campus. Bumper stickers and T-shirts bearing the motto "Redskin 'til I die!" or "Always a Redskin" were common. A letter from Lloyd O'Hara (Miami class of 1939), received by the board of trustees in early September, seemed to reflect the sentiment of those who opposed the change (excerpted):

> First of all, may I suggest there is no real problem. You and I and a vast number of Miami alumni well know that the term "Redskins" as applied to Miami's athletes is one of reverence, honor, and fighting spirit—one which is entirely complimentary and in no way demeaning.
>
> I dare say that had this "problem" appeared on the agenda of Miami's board of trustees during the sixteen years that I served as a member thereof, our Board would have given about five or ten minutes to the subject and then voted to retain the very meaningful and appropriate Redskin appellation. We would then have moved on to *important* Board business. . . .
>
> I thought it was near ludicrous when former President Paul Risser devoted the better part of a day to a public discussion of the Redskin "problem" and then recommended to your body that the Redskin name could continue in use for presently existing athletic teams, but forbidden to newly created teams. That's really some way to "ride the fence" on the "problem."
>
> . . . Miami's unique heritage is one of the University's big assets. It is one of the factors that sets Miami apart from its counterparts and entitles Miami to a place on everybody's list of outstanding educational institutions in the country. Other parts of Miami's heritage which come to mind are her outstanding academic program going back to the days of the McGuffey Readers; her beautiful campus situated in a typical college town; her retention of consistent architectural design in campus buildings; her production of outstanding leaders in government, academia, business and industry; the Cradle of Coaches; the Mother of Fraternities; her successes in inter-collegiate athletics established by her athletic teams known throughout the land as the "Miami Redskins"; and last but not least, her outstanding alumni relations program which has developed a strong and loyal body.
>
> . . . If you were to poll Miami's alumni body, I feel certain they would vote overwhelmingly to retain the Redskin name . . . . The name is right— there is nothing wrong or demeaning about it . . . .

The negligible change brought about by the compromise position adopted by the board of trustees in 1993 was evidence of the prevailing sentiment. Few groups adopted the new nickname and common usage was still overwhelmingly in favor of "Redskins."

The cost of a name change was estimated to be about $100,000 for the Athletic Department to change uniforms and markings at venues. However, this did not consider the cost of developing new logos and trademarks or the lost revenues from donors who chose to withhold gifts in protest of change. Miami currently had approximately 120,000 living alumni. In 1996 the university had received approximately $15.5 million in gifts. During the year roughly 68,000 alumni received solicitations for gift money from the university, and roughly one-third had responded with a gift. Miami's annual budget was approximately $250 million, with roughly $8.4 million expended on athletics. Annual gifts specifically earmarked for athletics totaled approximately $1 million and originated with some 1,700 individuals.

Another important consideration was the value of brand equity to be given up by a change. At the time, Miami received over $100,000 per year in royalty proceeds from sales of apparel and other merchandise (Exhibits 17.3 and 17.4). In addition, sales of merchandise at the Miami University Bookstore totaled nearly $1 million during the past year, of which the school received nearly a 50% percent markup (Exhibit 17.5).

Exhibit 17.3 Royalties from merchandise sales

Year	Sales ($)	Royalty ($)	Commission (%)
1987–88	120,615	7,840	0.065
1988–89	436,831	28,394	0.065
1989–90	691,262	44,932	0.065
1990–91	1,185,292	77,044	0.065
1991–92	1,031,708	67,061	0.065
1992–93	1,083,615	70,435	0.065
1993–94	1,408,800	91,572	0.065
1994–95	1,622,114	115,548	0.07
1995–96	1,558,800	109,116	0.07
1996–97*	987,357	69,115	0.07

*Partial year figures.

Exhibit 17.4 Royalties from merchandise sales—Quarterly results

Year	Q1	Q2	Q3	Q4	Total
1994–95	$33,208	$35,831	$19,053	$25,456	$113,548
1995–96	$38,457	$33,160	$20,605	$16,894	$109,116
1996–97	$32,317	$36,798	N/A	N/A	$ 69,115

Exhibit 17.5   Miami University bookstore (all campuses) apparel and souvenir sales ($ 000)

Fiscal Year	Apparel*	Souvenirs**	Total
1993	650	236	886
1994	582	261	843
1995	648	278	926
1996	659	293	952
1997	660	302	962

*Apparel markup: 45%.
**Souvenir markup: 50%.

Conclusion

"I know that this is an important issue to many members of the Miami University community. The board will give thoughtful consideration at its September meeting," said Sister Jean Patrice Harrington, chairwoman of the board of trustees.

Miami University—The Creation and Transfer of Brand Equity

Thomas C. Boyd and David W. Rosenthal

Introduction

It was the last week of July 1997 and Richard Little, Miami University director of communications, had a big task ahead. In the past year the university's board of trustees had decided, amidst great controversy, to drop the nickname "Redskins" from the school's athletic teams. In April they had approved "RedHawks" as the new nickname, and just this week a committee had chosen the design of the new university logo. Now, with less than a month before the fall semester started, Richard had to decide what recommendation to make to the president about how and when to unveil the new logo. The late date meant that if they announced the logo at the start of the school year they would not have time to perform any research on the new logo, nor could they have merchandise in place with vendors and retailers. If they waited until the winter, they faced the prospect of a fall sports season with no clear identity and a renewal of the divisive controversy that had raged over the past several years.

Background

On September 25, 1996, the Miami University board of trustees voted to drop the Redskin nickname for its athletic teams. The decision was difficult and came amidst impassioned arguments on both sides of the issue. In July, the Miami tribal council had asked the university to drop the Redskin nickname but endorsed the continued use of the university's logo of an Indian head and a block *M*. The university senate also overwhelmingly supported the change, citing the need for an institute of higher learning to avoid the use of names or labels that were offensive to people of any ethnic or racial background. Those opposing a change were primarily alumni, current students, and long-time fans who cherished the Redskin name as one that honored a great tradition. The trustees then charged university President James Garland with the task of making a recommendation for a new name for the school's athletic teams. Garland appointed a committee to consider the issue, chaired by Dr. Phillip Shriver, the widely respected former university president.

Between the time of the trustees' decision to drop Redskin and the selection of a new name a number of events took place. Many parties engaged in actions intended to make public their feelings about the decision. It was in such an environment that the committee began its deliberations. On September 25, 1996, the day of the trustee's decision to drop Redskin, the *Dayton Daily News* published a profile of people on both sides of the issue. On the anti-Redskin side was Guy Jones, executive director of the Miami Valley Council for Native Americans. He cited the exploitative use of Indian names by American companies and organizations and explained that such use was demeaning to Native Americans. The article also cited several prominent alumni of Miami who did not want a change and emphasized the respect signified by the use of the term *Redskin*. During the first week of October 1996 the Miami Student Aid Association (MSAA), the group responsible for athletic fundraising, received a number of resignations in protest over the name change. In an internal memo from Chris Wyrick, MSAA director, to the athletic director, Wyrick identified six key alumni donors who had threatened to withhold pledges and future gifts. Those six alone accounted for $75,000 in annual giving with an identified potential for special gifts of over $1 million. Also during that week, in a call-in program soliciting suggestions for a new name sponsored by the *Dayton Daily News,* over half the callers wanted the university to keep "Redskins."

The committee first met on October 21, 1996. At that time it publicly solicited suggestions from the public and performed research on the suggestions. The process, as described by Committee Chair Phillip R. Shriver to President Garland, was as follows:

1. After soliciting suggestions from the public, the committee deliberated on the various attributes of the 3,000-plus suggestions that resulted in nearly 700 unduplicated ideas. Among criteria for the name were that it be related to Miami's unique heritage as a major university named for an Indian tribe without being politically offensive. Also, it had to win broad acceptance among Miami's various constituencies and be gender neutral. Finally, the name must facili-

tate marketing and graphic design—with potential for increased revenues from merchandising for the Athletic Department.

Meanwhile, State Representative Bob Corbin requested a resolution be drafted in the Ohio House that would allow the board of trustees to reconsider their decision to drop "Redskins" without requiring them to reinstate it. The resolution was to be modeled on one passed by the Illinois General Assembly regarding The University of Illinois and its mascot, Chief Illiniwek.

On November 25, 1996, Tamra R. West wrote a letter to the editor of the *Dayton Daily News* expressing support for the name change. She wrote, "Indians find the slang term 'Redskins' offensive and insensitive. Rest assured, if Miami University had called its teams the black, brown or yellow skins, it would have ceased to be tolerated long ago . . . . The suggestion that the Miami Valley Council for Native Americans 'might spend their time better by contributing to today's society' rather than 'tear down an honorable tradition' is repugnant. Today's society is built directly on a shameful foundation of American Indian blood, broken dreams and lost traditions . . . . I for one, appreciate the Miami University trustees for their honorable, courageous and sensitive decision to discontinue using the offensive slang term 'Redskins'."

At about the same time a bumper sticker became very popular on the Miami campus and in surrounding communities. It said simply, "Redskin Forever," and expressed the feelings of people opposed to the change.

2. Keeping its guiding criteria in mind, the committee narrowed its list to eighteen names by December 2, 1996.

3. The committee voted on the eighteen names, resulting in a list of five names: Thunderhawks, WarHawks, The Miami(s), RedHawks, and Arrows.

4. The five finalists were turned over to Richard Little, Miami University director of communications. Mr. Little's staff and an outside consultant then performed analysis and testing on the five names. Tests included:

   • A linguistic analysis focusing on usage and how all parties might use the words, rhymes, synonyms, cliches, or related quotes in an effort to apply ridicule or abuse to university teams,

   • A trademark search to identify current uses of the names or existing trademarks,

   • An analysis by an outside consultant with extensive experience in analyzing the marketing advantages and public relations risks of names and logos,

   • Soliciting advice from executives who were testing nicknames for the new women's NBA league,

- Six focus groups—two of alumni, two of students, and one each of faculty and staff,
- A meeting with representatives of the Miami tribe to discuss the alternatives.

5. On January 24, 1997, the committee met to hear results of the testing process. They then forwarded three choices to President Garland. The committee strongly recommended Thunderhawks and Red-Hawks. They unanimously found both acceptable, with about equal numbers favoring one over the other. As a third and less strongly supported choice, the committee also forwarded The Miami(s).

In addition to the names, the committee recommended that the existing logo be elevated to the status of university logo and remain available to all who desired to use it. The committee also explained its rejection of suggestions such as "Chiefs" and other Indian-related names. It was its opinion that those names would not put the original controversy to rest and would therefore be counterproductive.

On February 4, 1997, thirteen plaintiffs, including Miami alumni and an American Indian, filed suit in the Butler County Common Pleas Court to block the university from dropping "Redskins." Among the claims filed in the suit were: breach of trust on the part of the board of trustees in marring the Redskins name, deprivation of due process, conflict of interest by certain board members and university officials, civil conspiracy to deprive plaintiffs of right to officially remain "Miami Redskins," defamation, and violation of the First Amendment principle of separation of church and state. The suit accused the board of secretly discussing the name change even though the change had been the subject of much public dialogue, a campus forum, and news reports. When asked about the lawsuit, university spokesman Richard Little said, "It's ridiculous, it's hardly worth me commenting on, to be honest with you."

President Garland was scheduled to recommend a new nickname to the board of trustees on February 7. University spokesman Little, responding to questions about the lawsuit, said that the university had no plan whatsoever to delay the scheduled vote on a new mascot. After a judge refused to issue a temporary restraining order against the university on February 5, it appeared that a new name was imminent. On February 7, 1997, President Garland recommended "RedHawks" to the board of trustees. There were a number of reasons cited for his decision, including that it received the most first-place votes from the committee, the hawk had great potential as a mascot, its potential for use with the Indian head logo, and its potential graphic appeal. The trustees decided to table the issue for further consideration, an action taken amidst considerable interest and controversy.

About the Red Hawk

In a letter to Dr. Shriver about the president's recommendation, Richard Little explained some of the rationale for choosing the name "Red-Hawks." To paraphrase:

> The name "RedHawk" is derived from the red-tailed hawk. It is indige-nous to the Miami Valley, where the school is located, is a dominant predator in the area, and has a red tail and white breast, the school's colors. In focus groups it was described as powerful, fierce, fearless, unrelenting, and brave. The hawk was also perceived by focus groups to be related to Native-American heritage, and its feathers and talons traditionally have been part of ceremonial regalia. The "Red Hawk" ap-pears on the medicine wheel that has an honored place in Indian history. There was a famous Lakota Sioux chief RedHawk and a minor chief of the Shawnees of that name.
>
> Those who nominated "RedHawks" cited the fact that the name is symbolic to Native Americans and has special meaning to the Miami tribe. The bird has always been in the skies where the Miami tribe was located and has, like the tribe, survived the most adverse circumstances.
>
> On a more practical level, supporters of "RedHawk" cited its originality, the fact that it contains the same number of letters as Redskin and rolls off the tongue in much the same way, and it can be easily shortened to a familiar term.

During the period between the tabling of a vote by the board of trustees on the RedHawk recommendation and the next board meeting, public discourse continued. On February 27 a letter to the editor of the Hamilton (Ohio) *Journal News* said, ". . . a board of trustees who demonstrated a total lack of leadership and courage to stand up to the plague of political correctness." And ". . . If we are so misguided in ending our honorable recognition of a once mighty native tribe with 'Redskin,' we might as well be equally misguided and say farewell to the equally honored name of Miami." On March 8, John D. Leucke, a Miami alumnus, wrote in the *Cincinnati Enquirer* about the Miami tribe's withdrawal of their support for the Redskin name. ". . . by conforming to society's distorted views and trampling its own proud tradition, the tribe has lost more than a piece of its relationship with the alumni, faculty and students. The Miami tribe is failing to preserve the historically proud beliefs once firmly upheld by its own people."

On April 18, 1997, the board of trustees voted unanimously to adopt "RedHawks" as the new nickname for the university's athletic teams. Board President and Cleveland Cavaliers general manager Wayne Embry, a former basketball star at Miami and supporter of the name change, said, "I don't think it was a politically correct move, I think it was a humanely correct move." On April 29, 1997, Miami alumnus

Richard H. Rogers wrote a letter to President Garland indicating his disgust and sadness at the board's decision. "This issue is not behind you. It has just begun," he wrote. He further charged that, "1. This was an 'inside job' by a few campus dissidents. . . . 2. Your public statements, which if accurate, tell me that you are not aware of the tradition and deep pride with which alumni hold the word 'Redskins'. . . . 3. There was no poll of alumni or students, 90% of whom would have supported 'Redskins.' 4. Miami is subjecting its student athletes, as well as alumni, to derision, nationwide. The new name adopted makes no sense. It is the name of a pistol . . . ." On May 20, 1997, the plaintiffs in the lawsuit against Miami gave up their suit and grudgingly accepted the new nickname "for the sake of harmony." "Rather than tear the school apart over this issue, the plaintiffs have decided to throw their support behind the university," said Robert Croskery, their lawyer. "They are now supporting the school with their contributions, and encourage others to do the same."

Now the difficult task of implementing the RedHawk name remained. Richard Little formed a new committee composed of athletic staff, student athletes, professors, a representative of the board of the Miami University Student Aid Association, and university staff involved in merchandising. The university hired a consulting firm with extensive experience in designing new logos and trademarks for college and professional teams. The consultant worked with the committee to develop a whole family of logos based on a primary logo design. The flexibility of the design concept meant that secondary designs could be created from related marks designated by the committee or from elements (i.e., either the pictures, parts of pictures, or print) of the primary mark. For example, text could be borrowed from the primary logo and combined with the old Indian head to create a new mark.

After carefully considering the key traits to be conveyed by the new logo, the committee spent three months working to narrow down different artists' concepts to arrive at a new primary logo. On June 13, the consulting firm and members of the logo selection committee presented five preliminary concepts to the board of trustees. They all portrayed a red hawk in some form with the words "Miami University RedHawks." Although the committee planned to keep the original Indian head logo as a secondary mark for athletic teams, there was no evidence of the old Indian head in any of the five new marks. Board member William Gunlock expressed displeasure and surprise that the Indian head was not the basis for the new logo. The consultant explained that the new logos would be more marketable and appealing to certain target markets, such as children and students. After much debate the board agreed to let the committee continue its work in developing a new logo for Miami athletics based on one of the concepts presented.

On June 30, the logo development committee met and selected a final concept for development. On July 1, William Gunlock resigned from the board of trustees to express his distress over the direction of the logo development. He stated, "I just can't take it anymore, I think it's disgraceful. You don't [upset] all your alumni and friends and then go ask them for money." Gunlock estimated that he had given the university about $600,000 over the years and announced that he would not give any more that year. In particular, he was upset that the final primary logo concepts did not include the Indian head, although the committee agreed that the old logo—and still official university logo— would remain as a secondary trademark and would still be available for use by athletic teams.

Announcing and Implementing the New Logo

On July 28, 1997, the logo selection committee met for the last time to finalize its recommendation for a family of logos and symbols based on the RedHawk mascot. Although there would be a little additional tinkering, the primary mark was chosen and ready for final approval from the president and athletic administration. (See Figure 18.1.)

Richard Little faced a decision about how and when to announce the new logo and how to coordinate the announcement with other key events in the athletic and academic year. He also had to decide whether there should be any market research performed on the final concept before adoption. In particular, there was little information about how the new logos would be received by the primary target markets for the athletic program: students, alumni, faculty and staff, children, and regional families. Nothing had been formalized regarding a rollout of the new logo. Further, no announcement date had been set. "I think the earliest we can announce anything will be at our first home basketball game in January," he said. "We may announce in the fall, I'm not sure yet." Among the possible actions being considered were to work with the licensing representative for an exclusive contract in the Dayton and Cincinnati areas for a period to immediately precede general market availability of apparel and souvenirs.

Richard was concerned about several issues related to the new logo announcement. Of primary concern was how to minimize controversy and anger over the loss of the old nickname. Obviously, the announcement would have to be carefully planned to put the controversy behind the school. Also, Richard did not want to do a formal announcement until merchandise was in place. He wanted to be sure to capitalize on the novelty of the new logo family. However, if he waited to make the announcement he had to worry about the vacuum created by having no logo available. What would people buy, if anything? Would they buy

Figure 18.1   Miami University Family of New Marks and Logos

apparel and souvenirs with text only? Would people start calling the old logo "Chief RedHawk"?

Conclusion

Richard told a committee member in late July, "We must establish what it [RedHawk] is," but the question was how and when. "I plan to get advice from the consultant who designed the logo and from our licensing agent," he continued. "I'll also ask [the athletic director, the athletics administrator for marketing, and our head of purchasing] to help me plan a recommendation to the president."

Race for the Cure

T. Bettina Cornwell and Donald P. Roy

Introduction

As Ann exited the meeting with Greenway, her head was spinning. It had not occurred to her that a grocery chain would demand category exclusivity in sponsoring the Race for the Cure. She had always thought in terms of "the more the better." Hindsight being 20/20, it did make perfect business sense from the perspective of the potential sponsor to want to be the only one in the grocery category. Unfortunately, Greenway's demand for exclusivity put a hard choice before her and the Race for the Cure organizing committee. How could she suggest granting exclusivity to Greenway after their boycotting behavior? If they did take the Greenway offer for sponsorship, how could she face Mr. Henderson, who, along with his stores, had supported her event from the very beginning? These and other questions weighed heavily on her mind as she drove to the race committee meeting.

History

In 1982 The Susan G. Komen Breast Cancer Foundation was founded by Nancy Brinker in memory of her sister, who died at age 36 after a three-year struggle with breast cancer. The national organization began with a network of volunteers who decided that breast health was a very important issue, with over 182,000 women being diagnosed with this disease each year and 46,000 of those women dying. They looked for an event that would raise much needed funds for research, while joining people together to increase awareness about the need for early detection, self-examination, and screening for women who could not afford it or who had no insurance. Because regular exercise is vital to everyone's health and had been proven to be directly related to improved chances of survival of breast cancer, a 5K walk/run called "Race for the Cure" was initiated. Since its inception, the Komen Foundation through

329

Race for the Cure has become the largest private funding source dedicated solely to breast cancer, raising more than $40 million. Important to the race sponsorship concept is that the majority of funds generated by the race stays in the local community. Even more important than the money generated by the races is that the awareness about breast cancer has increased, making this cause a very public priority.

The Emergence of Sponsorship-Linked Marketing

Corporate event sponsorship has become a popular form of communication for many organizations. According to the International Events Group, a sponsorship monitoring organization, sponsorship spending in North America was approximately $5.4 billion in 1996, which represents a 15% increase over 1995. Sponsorship spending has experienced double-digit growth every year since 1985, when spending totaled $850 million. During that same period, traditional advertising spending grew at rates between 4 and 9%. Sporting events are the most popular event type: approximately two-thirds of all sponsorships are sports related. Pop music and entertainment tours are the second-most popular type of sponsorship, and they account for only 10% of sponsorship expenditures.

Cause Sponsorships: A Hybrid

It is important to point out that cause sponsorship is different from cause marketing. The term *cause marketing* is oftentimes used to describe programs where corporate donations to a designated cause are tied to the consumer's purchase of that company's products. Donations are often based on a percentage of the sale.

Cause sponsorships are a special form of event sponsorship because they combine a worthy cause with an event. For example, Race for the Cure is a running event that is the vehicle used to raise money for a cause, the Susan G. Komen Foundation (and associated local charities). Using an event as a means of calling attention to a cause benefits the entity seeking to gain publicity and or monetary support. Also, it benefits the sponsor because it calls attention to the sponsor's participation in a worthy cause. Using event sponsorships to build a company's image of "good neighbor" can be more effective than donating money to a cause because the event is usually promoted in print and broadcast media.

Corporate support of important causes is more important than ever. As societies become more knowledgeable about the activities of corporations they are beginning to demand that firms do more than pay lip service to promoting certain values. Consumers expect commitments from corporations that are in keeping with their own value system. Cause sponsorships are a means of demonstrating such support. A survey reported in *Marketing Week* (Vol. 19, No. 9, 57–60) on this topic showed that 60% of adults and 67% of young people said that they would definitely be more interested in buying a company's products if it is associated with a charity. The same study found that only 21% of companies realized that a link to a charity plays a role in a young person's decision process.

Beginning the Memphis Race

In 1990, a thirty-five-year-old housewife, Ann Smith-Hall, with no history of breast cancer and no known risks, was diagnosed with the disease. Ann knew no one to talk to about this disease in the Memphis area and found no support groups or information to educate herself and her family. Following her mastectomy, she was told to get her life in order because it was improbable she would live past one year. With a husband of fourteen years and two young sons, ages 6 and 9, she was suddenly faced with chemotherapy, radiation, and planning her own funeral. Always a stubborn person, she fought and fought, prayed and prayed, and after one year she was bald and bloated from drugs but still alive! One day in the doctor's office she saw an article about the Komen Foundation and the Race for the Cure events held in various cities. She wrote to them, asking for permission to organize a race in her community. It took one year for a decision to be made, partially because she was an individual seeking to start a local race and most cities have an organization, like Junior League, to begin a race. She constantly hounded the Komen office with correspondence until they finally gave her permission to organize a race to be held in 1993. At her own expense, she traveled to Dallas, home of the national headquarters, for an intense, four-day training session by the Komen Foundation. While there, she had the opportunity to meet with chairpeople from other cities and hear their ideas on how to begin a race from scratch. Upon returning to Memphis, she quickly called many of her friends whom she knew to be good workers in PTA and various other organizations in which she was active. They began meeting on Saturday mornings in church basements, homes, and any other place that could accommodate the growing group. Finally, they "were ready" to make this public but they desperately needed that first sponsor to back the event.

In Dallas, Ann had learned that it would cost about $25,000 to put on the first-year event and that the Komen Foundation carefully studied your financial reports, wanting you to keep expenses very low. Given this challenge, the Memphis committee brainstormed about local individuals and corporations it could possibly ask for funding. It also realized how difficult this would be since it had no experience in planning and organizing a race. Therefore, several members of the committee began attending local races to get ideas but saw that most were billed as athletic events and not events for a cause. Also, they were told that an all-women 5K would never work in Memphis because there were just not enough women runners to compete. Discouraged but not dissuaded, they hired two members of the local track club to advise them on aspects of running a race, choosing a course, and timing the event. Even these two consultants told them not to expect more than 200 people.

With all this information, Ann, as chairperson of the committee, decided it was time to call on a prospective sponsor. But who could this be? Since she had no business experience, her husband advised her on sales calls and how to make them. One day, while reading the newspaper following a second surgery and still in bandages, she read about a family-owned supermarket's efforts to be more environmentally friendly by encouraging consumers to use canvas shopping bags rather than paper or plastic "throwaway" bags. She thought that this was a very community-minded campaign. Then the idea came to her that mostly women shop at grocery stores and this one was locally owned and operated, so she dialed the number. Not really knowing who to ask for, she asked for Mr. Henderson of Henderson's Grocery Store. Believe it or not, he came to the phone and listened to her for a moment before telling her he would be glad to meet with her and he would bring along his marketing person. The meeting was set for the following week at one of the ten grocery stores Mr. Henderson owned. Armed with what little information she had and still in bandages, she had a story to tell. Mr. Henderson was brought to tears, as was his marketing director, and they promised her right then they would give her $1,000 and furnish all the fruit and cookies for after the race!

Now, she had a place to start. She could tell every other businesses that Henderson's grocery stores was sponsoring the race. After discussing the issue with her committee, several of them thought, "Why not go to the big national grocery store chain, Greenway?" They had twenty-three stores in the area. After all, women are the primary shoppers in Greenway stores as well, and they should be interested in the health of their customers too, just like Henderson's. Calling the office of the national chain, Ann quickly realized, was very different from calling the local one. Again and again, she was put on hold or told the marketing director was unavailable. Undaunted by this, she called continually for weeks without receiving a return call. Finally, one morning the marketing director returned her call, asking her what she wanted from him. She began by telling him that money was a top need and help with advertising would be another. He told her that corporate policy required that all potential sponsorship proposals be in writing. She prepared and sent a proposal that described the value of the sponsorship to the company as a potential sponsor but did not hear from the marketing director for weeks. When she called the Greenway office, she was told that the marketing manager was busy. After two months of trying to land Greenway as a sponsor of the event, Ann announced to her committee that Greenway's was evidently not interested. She also told them that she had now been turned down by several businesses. However, none had treated her as rudely as Greenway's. Most at least asked for breast cancer information and were delighted to put posters up in their headquarters and in retail locations. The committee decided to boycott Greenway's as their own little way of rebellion. They did not demand it, of course, but most members decided not to shop at Greenway's again.

In October 1993, over 1,753 women lined up to run or walk in the first Race for the Cure in the Memphis area! The $35,000 profit was given back to the community for cancer research, screening, and education. Everyone who worked on the race was a volunteer, with the exception of the two people hired to do the timing, and their fee was $2,000. The two race consultants said after the race, with tears in their eyes, that they had never seen anything like it before and they would be honored to work at this event every year.

Success Builds on Success

Immediately after the successful race of 1993, the Memphis race committee began work on the 1994 event. It hoped to perfect the few things they felt could work better and to add new ideas that they had discovered during the year. The incorporation of men into the race was one challenge to be managed. Memphis was perhaps too conservative to have the "breast-buddy" participants found in some cities, but still there needed to be a recognized role for the men and significant others that supported women through their fight with breast cancer. Again, working from the home of the chairperson, the committee took over her dining room, garage, and sunroom and sometimes the kitchen. They met regularly to make sponsorship proposal packets to send out, and they put together a demonstration video to show to groups that might be interested in participating in the event in any way. Nothing seemed impossible to this team.

Beginning in 1994, the committee once again called on local businesses to sponsor the race. They were feeling especially confident now that it had proven itself. Henderson's was thrilled to be involved again and sponsored the group at the same level it had in 1993. Mr. Henderson did not attend the race due to an out-of-town wedding, but his marketing director walked with a friend and was deeply touched by the celebration of the day. To avoid the old saying, "Don't cut off your nose to spite your face," the race chairperson had once again tried to contact Greenway's for potential sponsorship but got no response. The boycott of Greenway's among the race committee continued.

In October 1994, over 3,029 women walked or ran in the second annual Race for the Cure! More than $81,000 was raised through sponsorships, entries, and donations, with all proceeds once again going back to the community. The volunteer committee was ecstatic! The chairperson was asked by the Komen Foundation to give a speech at a national convention in January of 1995 on the phenomenal success of the Memphis event. In the audience were all other race chairpeople, many national celebrities interested in the cause of breast cancer, and representatives from Congress, the LPGA, and other national organizations who had adopted the Komen Foundation as their charity.

Planning the 1995 event was much easier because the committee had two successful races behind it and people realized this was a big event. Also, recent studies of cause sponsorships found that when price and quality were equal, cause marketing could sway consumers to switch retailers, and Ann did not miss the opportunity to communicate this fact to potential sponsors. On the volunteer side, each person who attended an organizing meeting brought someone else, and the sponsors were thrilled with the thousands who wore their corporate logos proudly on the T-shirts. Again, the Memphis Race for the Cure was an unprecedented success (see Table 19.1) and the amount of money going to local charities had gained considerable recognition in the large Memphis medical community (see Table 19.2).

Table 19.1 Memphis Race for the Cure growth statistics

Year	Net Revenue ($)	Number of Participants
1993	35,000	1,753
1994	81,000	3,029
1995	200,000	6,000
1996 (projected)	500,000	13,000

Table 19.2 Local grants funded by Race for the Cure*

American Cancer Society—to augment current budget to expand breast cancer prevention and detection through free physical examinations, screening, and testing for early detection.

Baptist Cancer Institute—to be used for educational materials and equipment and to establish a resource center for breast cancer patients.

Carpe Diem of the Mid-South—to continue support retreats for breast cancer patients.

Germantown Library Commission—to provide books on all aspects of breast cancer from diagnosis, treatment, surgery, and recovery, to humor and support.

Memphis Cancer Center Foundation—to provide educational materials for use in Flying Colors, a free resource center open to the entire community.

Mroz-Baier Breast Health Clinic—to provide one-day seminars for regional primary care physicians, radiologists, and residents emphasizing that early diagnosis of breast cancer offers the best chance for cure.

Regional Medical Center—to fund "Faithful Partners," a new program establishing a collaborative effort with churches to provide breast cancer education to a select and needy population.

St. Joseph Hospital—to fund transportation of elderly women for free mammography screening and educational materials.

West Clinic—for educational materials to be used in Wings, an on-site center.

Women's Health Center—Baptist Memorial Hospital—to provide free mammography screening for medically underserved women in our community plus any necessary follow-up screening.

YWCA of Greater Memphis—to fund Encore Plus, a comprehensive breast health program of YWCA in the USA. This program provides screening, outreach, education, and follow-up for populations at Shelby County Correction facilities, churches, and senior-citizen and YWCA centers.

*Seventy-five percent of Race proceeds remain in Memphis to fund breast cancer education and screening. Twenty-five percent of Race proceeds are contributed to national research grants and educational programs through the Susan G. Komen Foundation.

Sponsor Continuity or Change

In early 1996, preparations for the for the fourth race were underway. Henderson's, as events had shown, was an excellent partner, and the race committee decided they really did not need Greenway's to have a successful race and moreover that it was Greenway's loss. Their sponsor solicitation was primarily directed to increasing the sponsorship level of previous participants and encouraging new sponsors to become involved. It was no less than ironic when Greenway's called the chairperson in late spring, wanting to set up a meeting to talk about the Race for the Cure. Once again, Ann had the best interests of the race in mind and so went to the meeting. All the executives were present, including the one that had been so rude. He seemed a little sheepish when his boss wanted to know why they were not involved with the race. Without going into detail and in a businesslike manner (she had learned a great deal in the past few years), Ann told of the development of the Memphis area Race for the Cure and its sponsorship. The Greenway executives told her *they* would like to make a written proposal *to the race.* The Greenway executive committee felt as though they could certainly be a good partner for the community. Ann was told that the proposal would be delivered to her in four days. She did not leave without telling them that Henderson's continued to be one of their sponsors, as they had been since the beginning.

The proposal was delivered on time and was very professional. The Greenway proposal included promotional aspects that had not been included in the Henderson sponsorship, such as advertising space in regional magazines and constant reminders of the upcoming race on the music station in their stores. The cash donation offered in the proposal was $10,000. Although the cash donation was in keeping with the top sponsorship level now typical for Race for the Cure (see Table 19.3) the overall offering far exceeded that typical of sponsors. Greenway's proposal was offering over $120,000 in in-kind donations. With the added publicity of the Greenway proposal, Ann was sure that the net revenues for 1996 would exceed projections and allow additional funding of mammography screening for medically underserved women. This was a project of personal concern to her because early detection of breast cancer was proven to save lives.

Ann felt it was only right to go to Mr. Henderson and tell him about the Greenway offer, so she set up a breakfast meeting with him and his marketing director. A very gracious offer was made by Mr. Henderson during the meeting. He said, "Regardless of the competition between the two store chains, I would be happy to come together for this cause." Ann left the meeting thinking what a great thing this could be for the community if the big national chain and the locally owned chain were able to share sponsorship in support of the women of the Memphis area and their fight against breast cancer!

Ann was excited to tell her entire committee about this proposal at the upcoming meeting that evening. But first, she had to call Greenway's. When she did, they wanted to meet to talk in person instead of discussing details over the phone. This suggestion was well received, especially after all those times when Ann couldn't get a meeting with the Greenway marketing director. One more meeting with Greenway today and Ann would secure the funding for mammography screening for literally hundreds of women. What a wonderful year this fourth annual Race for the Cure would have with these two big sponsors joining forces for a mutual cause!

The meeting was short and simple. The Greenway executives wanted to point out something that Ann, in her excitement, had missed in their proposal. There in the fine print of their proposal was the stipulation

Table 19.3 Sponsorship levels and related sponsorship benefits

Platinum Sponsor $10,000–$14,999
- Logo-sponsor level on entry forms
- Logo on Race posters
- Logo on Race T-shirts
- Mentions in Race press releases
- Opportunity to display banner on Race Day
- Booth space at Race Day Expo
- 20 complimentary Race entries
- Complimentary tickets to Race-related events
- Company name listed in newspaper thank-you ads
- Educational seminar about breast cancer arranged for your employees
- Framed Race poster

Gold Sponsor $7,500–$9,999
- Logo-sponsor level on entry forms
- Logo on Race posters
- Logo on Race T-shirts
- Mentions in Race press releases
- Opportunity to display banner on Race Day
- Booth space at Race Day Expo
- 14 complimentary Race entries
- Complimentary tickets to Race-related events
- Company name listed in newspaper thank-you ads

Silver Sponsor $5,000–$7,499
- Logo-sponsor level on entry forms
- Logo on Race posters
- Logo on Race T-shirts
- Mentions in Race press releases
- Opportunity to display banner on Race Day
- Booth space at Race Day Expo
- 10 complimentary Race entries
- Complimentary tickets to Race-related events
- Company name listed in newspaper thank-you ads

Bronze Sponsor $2,500–$4,999
- Logo-sponsor level on entry forms
- Logo on Race posters
- Logo on Race T-shirts
- Mentions in Race press releases
- Opportunity to display banner on Race Day
- Booth space at Race Day Expo
- 8 complimentary Race entries
- Complimentary tickets to Race-related events
- Company name listed in newspaper thank-you ads

Crystal Sponsor $1,000–$2,499
- Logo-sponsor level on entry forms
- Booth space at Race Day Expo
- 4 complimentary Race entries
- Complimentary tickets to Race-related events
- Company name listed in newspaper thank-you ads

that Greenway would have category exclusivity in their sponsorship of the Memphis Area Race for the Cure. This meant that if Greenway Foodstores signed on as a sponsor, it expected to be the only grocery chain sponsoring the race. Ann understood this idea in a way—it seemed to be a trend in the sponsoring of events that sponsors didn't want consumers to be confused about what company was the sponsor —still, she left the meeting a bit dazed. As she drove to the race committee meeting she admired the dogwoods and azaleas in full bloom; it was late spring. A decision had to be made quickly.

SPORT MARKETING THEORY

Review of Sport Marketing for Case Analysis

Introduction

This chapter provides a brief review of basic marketing terms and concepts as related to the field of sport marketing. Understanding these terms and concepts will enhance your ability to analyze and write-up sport marketing cases.

Mullin, Hardy, and Sutton (1993) define sport marketing as follows:

> Sport marketing consists of all activities designed to meet the needs and wants of sport consumers through exchange processes. Sport marketing has developed two major thrusts: the marketing of sport products and services directly to consumers of sport, and marketing of other consumer and industrial products or services through the use of sport promotions.

The four most important areas of focus in marketing are known as the four Ps (also called the marketing mix): Product, Price, Promotion, and Place (see Chapter 2). When thinking about what combination of the four Ps will create the most successful marketing plan, we start by asking basic questions about the customer base.

- Who is most likely to buy my product or service?
- What does the customer want to buy?
- Where does the customer want to buy it?
- How much will the customer pay?
- How and when will the customer collect information about products and services like ours?

The answers to these questions will define your customer base and provide you with a marketing mix. The right marketing mix will allow you to market your product and help your organization reach its goals. Over the next four sections, we will discuss each of the four Ps as they relate to sport marketing.

Product

A sport product can be tangible, such as athletic footwear or a tennis racquet. It can also be as intangible as trying to satisfy a want or need in a consumer through entertainment or by providing an environment for socializing. Different people are looking for different things from a sport product, and purchases are often based on emotion and esoteric features rather than on easily identifiable and comparable attributes like price. For instance, even something that seems straightforward like a tennis racquet can be fraught with underlying meaning to the consumer. One person may buy a racquet based solely on its function and features while another may see the racquet as a way to recapture lost youth, and yet a third person because she identifies with a role model who endorses the racquet.

Product Life Cycle

Traditional products follow a sales pattern that progresses from the introduction of the product to a growth phase and finally to a phase of declining sales. This pattern is known as the product life cycle. A graphical representation of the product life cycle is shown in Figure 20.1.

The introduction phase of the product life cycle is marked by a slow growth of sales typically showing high costs, low demand, and low profits. The second phase is the growth phase. The growth stage is where one sees a fast increase in sales and profits. Next, the maturity

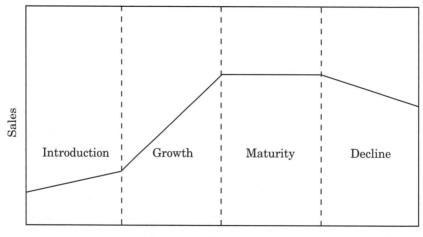

Figure 20.1 Product life cycle

phase is marked by a slowdown of demand; costs of sales increase and profits decline. Finally, the decline phase is marked by a further reduction of sales and profits. For example, roller blades and snowboards are currently in their growth stage, experiencing rapidly increasing sales and profits for manufacturers and retailers. In contrast, skis have entered their mature phase, enjoying stable or slightly declining demand.

Unique Nature of Sport Product

A whole body of theory has been developed in the field of marketing to help guide the efforts of practitioners. The unique nature of the sport product, however, provides some interesting challenges and opportunities for the sport marketer. The following list describes some of the unique aspects of the sport product (Mullin et al, 1993).

1. The sport product is unpredictable and inconsistent. No two athletic contests are identical, and therefore the experience of spectating at each event is different. A whole host of variables, such as weather, injuries to players, momentum, crowd involvement, team records, and time of year, combine to make the excitement level and outcome of each contest unpredictable and the fan's experience inconsistent. This core-product inconsistency forces sport managers to focus their efforts on marketing controllable product extensions—special promotions, ambiance, pregame tailgate parties, concessions, fan companionship, half-time shows, cheerleaders, and so forth.

2. The sport product evokes a strong emotional attachment from sport consumers. No other industry has such personal identification by the consumer for the product. Fans form strong emotional bonds with sport organizations, often identifying themselves as part of the team. Spectators, as well as participants, make sport a critical component of their lifestyles. Sport marketers benefit from this emotional bond because it translates into fierce product loyalty. On the downside, however, strikes, lockouts, trading of popular players, and team relocations can evoke an equally powerful backlash by fans.

3. The sport product is simultaneously produced and consumed. Fans who attend a sporting event become part of the pageantry and festivities. Without the yelling and cheering of the fans, the game would be less exciting for all attending. Therefore, the consumers of sport simultaneously serve as part of the production function. A pumped-up crowd can lift an average game to a new level, while fans sitting on their hands can dull a competitive match. The same dynamic operates in participant sport where the consumer, based on his performance and attitude, also produces the product.

4. It is a perishable product that must be presold. There are no inventories for sporting events. No one will buy a ticket for yesterday's soccer match. In fact, the value of a ticket falls close to zero by half-time. Likewise, yesterday's ski lift ticket has no residual value. The implication for sport marketers is that the sport product must be pre-sold. Time and money must be allocated to ensure the selling of season tickets (spectators) or annual memberships (participants).

5. *Teams both compete and cooperate.* Professional sport and collegiate teams, for example, compete on the playing field but cooperate in the boardroom. Fan interest depends on vigorous competition between the various teams in a league. Each team depends, to a large extent, on interest in the sport as a whole to ignite fan interest in attending games, buying merchandise, or watching the sport on television. However, profit maximization for the combined teams in a league (conference) requires cooperation in marketing the product. Hence, sport leagues work in tandem to sell broadcasting rights and merchandise and share in the resulting proceeds.

6. *Enjoyment of the sport product is affected by social facilitation.* It is estimated that less than 2% of people attending college or professional sports events attend by themselves. Therefore, the purchase decision is influenced by more than one person. Some tickets are used by businesses to reward clients or employees. Families attend sporting events together as a way of connecting to one another. Some fans see the event as an excuse to drink beer and carouse with their buddies. The product (the event), while consumed by all these groups in a similar way, is actually a different experience for each group.

Price

Traditionally, there are three methods for determining the best price for a product. These are:

Cost-Based Pricing

For cost-based valuation, you first determine the cost of manufacturing the product or providing the service. This is often done using break-even analysis (see Chapter 3). Then you determine how much profit is desired. You add this amount (called the *markup* or *margin*) to the cost to determine the final price.

$$Cost + Markup = Selling\ price$$

Value-Based Pricing

Another method used to determine price is the value-based method. Marketers try to determine an amount of value-in-use of their product compared to a similar product. For instance, producers of a tennis ball that lasts two times longer than the leading brand may decide to price their tennis balls at double the leading brand's price, thinking that customers will pay more for a more durable product.

Competition-Based Pricing

This method focuses on the other products in the market that offer similar benefits. The customer won't pay more for a similar item unless there are distinct differences. The competition-based method also looks at other products competing for the same consumer dollar. For instance, a person could spend her leisure money attending a soccer game or seeing a movie. The price and perceived utility of watching a movie will therefore influence the price of a ticket to a soccer game.

Price Sensitivity (Elasticity)

Whichever method is used for pricing a product, marketers must be aware of the sensitivity of their product to changes in price. Price sensitivity, or the extent to which demand is affected by changes in price, is called *elasticity*. If a small change in price creates a relatively large change in demand, the product is said to be elastic. If a large change in price creates a relatively small change in demand, the product is inelastic. Soccer is usually considered a sport with elastic demand. Raising the price of a soccer game will result in a larger percentage decline in attendance at that game. Sports with inelastic demand, like football or boxing, would experience a lower percentage increase in ticket sales if ticket prices were lowered. Elasticity is discussed in greater detail in Chapter 3.

Price/Value Relationship

Another variable to consider when looking at the price of a product is the relationship between price and value. As with most products, the price for sports products is associated with value. It can be disastrous to lower a price by such an amount that the consumer then perceives he is receiving a cheap product. It is important in sport not to take actions that hurt the product's image. If an exercise club lowers membership price well below market value, membership may decline because people will not want to be associated with the cheapest club in town. As a result, marketing managers use nonprice promotions such as free giveaways or two-for-one memberships to lower the perceived price of the product without inadvertently damaging the product's image.

Finally, when pricing some sport products, it is interesting to note that the core product being sold (a baseball game, for example) is not always the item that generates the most revenue. For instance, nonoperating revenue from sales of food, parking, merchandise, and memorabilia all add greatly to the overall money generated from sporting events. It is estimated that only 33% of the cost of attending a major league baseball game is paid for admission to the game. The remaining 67% is spent on items such as food, parking, souvenirs, and merchandise.

Promotion

In sport marketing, promotion is defined as the use of tools to communicate to the customer about the product: what it is, where one can purchase it, how it compares to the competition, and so forth. Promotion includes advertising (paid TV, radio, etc.), face-to-face selling, publicity (free exposure), sales promotions (give-aways, two-for-one sales) and promotional licensing (sponsorships). Sport, unlike other industries, has been able to rely heavily on the media for free publicity and exposure. The broadcast media spends approximately 20% of news time devoted to sport coverage and nearly every newspaper has a separate section devoted to sports.

However, free publicity is usually not adequate to properly position a sport product. Paid advertisement must bridge the gap between what is being said about the sport and the image or message management wants to convey. Deciding on the most effective way to spend advertising money is not easy. The average person receives more than 5,000 selling messages every day. Advertising costs, especially in television, continue to rise. The combination of advertising saturation and high costs accentuates the need to focus your promotional dollars correctly to reach the intended consumer.

Market Segmentation

In order to try to get the most out of advertising dollars, it is useful to try to determine who is currently buying your product and who might be willing to buy it. Each sport attracts a distinct type of consumer. People who watch bowling on television have a different customer profile than those who play polo. Determining what types of people are attracted to which products is called *segmentation*. Market segmentation is the act of creating specific groups of customers or potential customers based on similar characteristics like age or income. In sport, there are five bases for market segmentation:

1. *Demographic*: Income, age, gender, profession, education, place of residence, home ownership, social class (lower, upper, or middle), family size, marital status;
2. *Psychographic*: Interests, hobbies, opinions, desires, lifestyles, how the target audience spends leisure time and disposable income;
3. *Product usage rate*: How often a group uses/buys the product; heavy users, medium users, and light users;
4. *Product benefits*: Consumers' opinions of the most important benefits of the product or service; and,
5. *Relationship strength*: The relative strength of the emotional bonds between the consumer and the sport product.

Target Market

Once you have segmented your market, you determine which segments are most likely to purchase your product. You now have a group upon which you can effectively focus your advertising efforts. This process is referred to as *target marketing,* and the group you choose to focus on is the *target market.*

Knowing your target market and effectively focusing your promotional efforts to those consumers is even more important given the 80-20 rule of marketing. The 80-20 rule states that 80% of the market consumption comes from only 20% of the customers. This is especially true in spectator sports, where repeat fans (full and partial plan holders) are the lifeblood of a sports organization.

Marketers have to decide where to concentrate the limited time and money budgeted for advertising. How much effort should be made to attract new customers and how much to satisfy the customers you already have? Focusing money and attention on someone who comes to one game a year while neglecting the satisfaction of the season ticket holder is a questionable strategy given the 80-20 rule. Not all customers are equally important.

Promotional Licensing

One effective promotional tool used by the sport industry is promotional licensing, which includes sponsorships and tie-ins (joint ventures). Promotional licensing is the purchase by a business of the right to associate with a product or event in order to gain from the affiliation. An example of this would be Coca-Cola purchasing the right to be an "official sponsor" of the Olympics. Coca-Cola hopes that people will feel positive about drinking Coke because Coke is associated with a positive, exciting, patriotic event — the Olympics. The better people feel about drinking Coke, the more Coke people will drink.

Event Underwriting

Another type of promotion in sport marketing is the use of companies to underwrite sporting events. Because of the persuasiveness of the goodwill associated with sport, businesses are willing to create an association with a team by underwriting the cost of an event or promotion. In exchange for financing an event, the business gets exposure in a setting where people are relaxed and open-minded. The business gains from the positive affiliation between its product and the sport, and the team benefits by reducing the cost of the sporting event and its promotions.

Product Extensions

Promotion for the sport marketer has many advantages over promotion of other products like cars or adhesive bandages. As we have seen, sport promotion is facilitated by free exposure from the media, promotional licensing, and underwriting. However, one major disadvantage in promoting many sports products such as professional sports teams is that sport marketers generally have little control over their product. One would not expect the general manager to consult the marketing department about a potential trade of a popular player. As a result, marketers must focus on product extensions to promote their product. Product extensions include special promotions (like half-time entertainment) and giveaways (such as Cap Day at baseball games) to attract and retain customers but may also include facility cleanliness and customer service.

Place (Distribution)

The fourth category included in the marketing mix is place, often referred to as distribution. Place, within the sport industry, includes the sports facility, retail distribution of sporting goods, the ticket distribution system, and broadcast networks (TV, radio).

In general, place decisions have the most long-term effect on the marketing effort. It is difficult to change the sport facility: imagine the expense of making major changes to the location, layout, and/or physical attributes of a stadium such as parking. The distribution of the sport product is different (with the exception of traditional sporting goods) in that there is no physical movement of the product. The location of the facility will greatly determine who attends the game. Generally, 90% of fans attending a sports event will live less than one hour from the stadium (Leve, 1980). Similarly, for sports facilities (health clubs) and retail outlets (sporting goods stores), most customers live within twenty minutes of their destination.

Channels of Distribution

Another aspect of the "place" concept in marketing relates to channels of distribution. Channels describe the groups involved in delivering a product from the manufacturer to the consumer. The number and types of groups involved in delivery vary depending on the product. Different groups in the channel system include:

- manufacturers
- wholesalers
- brokers
- retailers
- consumers

In an industry such as skiing, the typical supply channel goes directly from manufacturer to consumer. The skier generally purchases his ticket at the ski resort and uses his ticket for skiing on that day. This is known as *direct distribution*. A more complicated channel system might involve the distribution path of a running shoe. The manufacturer makes the product then sends it to a wholesaler who sells it to a retailer before the shoe finally reaches the consumer. As you might expect, this is called *indirect distribution*.

Distribution Intensity

Another marketing concept relating to "place" is called *distribution intensity*. Distribution intensity looks at how available the product is across different types of buying outlets. In sport marketing, there are three different levels of distribution intensity:

1. *Exclusive:* Available in one outlet; expensive, upscale (sky boxes)
2. *Selective:* Limited distribution; moderately priced (lower level seats)
3. *Intensive:* Available in large number of outlets; inexpensive (regular seats)

A new line of expensive sport apparel designed by Snobé of Paris and sold exclusively at her fashion boutiques on Rodeo Drive and Fifth Avenue would be an example of exclusive distribution. Alternatively, cheap running shorts sold at K-mart and Wal-Mart by the line Cheaper-by-the-Dozen would use an intensive distribution.

Some of the biggest changes in the sport industry relating to distribution are occurring because of the increased popularity of the Internet.

Fans can now (or soon will be able to) purchase tickets for games, buy merchandise, and check scores and batting averages all from their home computers. The broad use of the Internet will most likely reduce the use of indirect methods of ticket distribution such as ticket agencies, grocery stores, and banks.

Another area in which technology is having an impact on sport is in the wide variety of TV coverage. Football games were once limited to Sunday afternoon and you had only one game to watch during a specific time. Now we have cable TV and the satellite dish, which offer a broad range of choices of professional and college football games. Additionally, with the advent of DirectTV, fans can choose which game to watch from stations all over the United States. If you want sports news, you no longer have to wait for the sports segment on your local or national news; you can tune into ESPN, ESPN2, or CNNSI for twenty-four-hour sports news, or regional sports networks like SportSouth or SportsChannel, or log on to ESPN SportsZone on the Internet.

Summary

Sport marketing is a challenging area of study and application. The product itself is unpredictable, inconsistent, and subjective. The price structure is affected as much by the value of the core product (e.g., ski lift ticket) as by the product extensions being offered (food, equipment, and lessons). Promoting sports is unlike promoting any other product due to the free publicity from the news media and the desire of businesses to associate with the product. Sports facilities offer unique challenges because of the huge costs involved in changing them and the changes in distribution caused by new technology.

The job of a sport marketer is to pick the best combination of the marketing mix (product, price, promotion, and place) to maximize the potential for exchange between the organization and its customers. In order to be successful, a marketer must have two types of skills. She must be quantitatively adept to use formulas like break-even analysis to compute the financial repercussions of various strategies. At the same time, her qualitative skills must be strong. Her powers of persuasion and group skills are needed to manage the marketing mix in a company whose structure may be rigid and resistant to change.

References

Leve, M. *"Making Marketing Research Hustle: The Essential Sweat of Attendance Building and Fund Raising."* Paper presented at Athletic Business Conference, Las Vegas, December 8, 1987.

Mullin, B., S. Hardy, and W. A. Sutton. *Sport Marketing*. Champaign, IL: Human Kinetics, 1993.

Addendum

Additional sources of information are available to the sport marketer:

Athletic Business Magazine
1846 Hoffman St.
Madison, WI 53704
608-249-0186; fax: 608-249-1153
www.athleticbusiness.com

Athletic Management
438 W. State St.
Ithaca, NY 14850
607-272-0265; fax: 607-272-2015

Club Business International
263 Summer St.
Boston, MA 02210
617-951-0055; fax: 617-951-0056
www.ihrsa.org

IEG Sponsorship Report
640 N. La Salle, Suite 600
Chicago, IL 60610-3777
312-944-1727; fax: 312-944-1897
www.sponsorship.com

Marketing News
American Marketing Association
250 S. Wacker Dr., Suite 200
Chicago, IL 60606-5819
312-648-0536; fax: 312-993-7540
www.ama.org

Sport Marketing Quarterly
1137 Van Voorhis Rd., Suite 32
Morgantown, WV 26505
304-599-3482; fax: 304-599-3482
www.fitinfotech.com

Team Marketing Report
660 W. Grand Ave, Suite 100E
Chicago, IL 60610
312-829-7060; fax: 312-733-4071
www.teammarketing.com